Queer Traversals

Queer Traversals

Psychoanalytic Queer and Trans Theories

Chris Coffman

BLOOMSBURY ACADEMIC
LONDON • NEW YORK • OXFORD • NEW DELHI • SYDNEY

BLOOMSBURY ACADEMIC
Bloomsbury Publishing Plc
50 Bedford Square, London, WC1B 3DP, UK
1385 Broadway, New York, NY 10018, USA
29 Earlsfort Terrace, Dublin 2, Ireland

BLOOMSBURY, BLOOMSBURY ACADEMIC and the Diana logo are
trademarks of Bloomsbury Publishing Plc

First published in Great Britain 2022
This paperback edition published 2023

Copyright © Chris Coffman, 2022

Chris Coffman has asserted her right under the Copyright, Designs and
Patents Act, 1988, to be identified as Author of this work.

For legal purposes the Acknowledgments on pp. vi–vii constitute an
extension of this copyright page.

Cover design: Eleanor Rose
Cover image © VBaleha/ iStock

All rights reserved. No part of this publication may be reproduced or transmitted
in any form or by any means, electronic or mechanical, including photocopying,
recording, or any information storage or retrieval system, without prior
permission in writing from the publishers.

Bloomsbury Publishing Plc does not have any control over, or responsibility for, any
third-party websites referred to or in this book. All internet addresses given in
this book were correct at the time of going to press. The author and publisher
regret any inconvenience caused if addresses have changed or sites have
ceased to exist, but can accept no responsibility for any such changes.

A catalogue record for this book is available from the British Library.

A catalog record for this book is available from the Library of Congress.

ISBN: HB: 978-1-3502-0000-5
       PB: 978-1-3502-0004-3
       ePDF: 978-1-3502-0001-2
       eBook: 978-1-3502-0002-9

Typeset by Integra Software Services Pvt. Ltd.

To find out more about our authors and books visit www.bloomsbury.com
and sign up for our newsletters.

Contents

Acknowledgments   vi

Introduction: Queer Traversals: Beyond the Fantasy of (Hetero)sexual Difference   1

1   Queering Žižek   25
2   *No Future*? Traversing the Fantasy of (Hetero)sexual Difference   55
3   Žižek's Antagonism and the Futures of Trans-Affirmative Lacanian Psychoanalysis   97
4   Cavanagh and Gherovici: Toward a Transfeminist Theory of Embodiment   119
5   Traversing the Atlantic, Traversing (Hetero)sexual Difference   151
6   Traversing North America, Traversing (Hetero)sexual Difference   167

Coda: Traversing the Fantasy of Authoritarian Patriarchy   213

References   226
Index   238

Acknowledgments

Although the seeds of what eventually became *Queer Traversals* were planted over twenty years ago, I completed it over the last ten years with support from numerous organizations and individuals.

In 2018–19, I benefited from a sabbatical leave funded by the University of Alaska Fairbanks and from a March–June 2019 appointment as the Fulbright-Freud Visiting Scholar of Psychoanalysis at the Sigmund Freud Museum in Vienna, Austria. Daniela Finzi at the Freud Museum and Susanne Hamscha at Fulbright Austria facilitated a very productive visit to Vienna; Sandra Sparber provided valuable help locating texts; and other colleagues there—especially Marlen Bidwell-Steiner, Esther Hutfless, and Daniela Kammerer—asked excellent questions that helped me refine my arguments in Chapters 2, 3, and 4. Thanks as well to the Gender Studies Program at the University of Vienna for co-hosting my Fulbright course on Queer Theories and lecture on Transfeminist Theories of Embodiment; especially helpful were Dorith Weber in facilitating teaching arrangements and Katrin Lasthofer in coordinating my talk.

In the years preceding the Fulbright, Deborah Cohler and William Spurlin offered invaluable affirmation for this book's direction; Sheila Cavanagh—who accepted an early version of Chapter 3 for the *Transpsychoanalytics* issue of *TSQ*—provided much-needed praise and validation for my arguments. Christopher Peterson gave generous feedback on an early version of an article that eventually became part of Chapter 2. Judith Roof held my feet to the fire with regard to Lacanian sexuation. Social media posts by Kami Chisholm and Sara Eliza Johnson brought my attention to materials I discuss in the third and fourth chapters. Conversations with Lee Callahan, Karen Grossweiner, and Elizabeth Richmond-Garza about *Hedwig and the Angry Inch* oriented my reading of the film in Chapter 5. I am grateful to Cathy Irwin for encouraging me to submit to *Transpsychoanalytics* as well as for her friendship over many years. Another friend, Alla Ivanchikova, proved an insightful test audience for my Fulbright talk as well as a valuable interlocutor about theory.

I am grateful to Joshua Jennifer Espinoza for permission to cite from "Things Haunt." Some materials that are now part of *Queer Traversals* originally appeared elsewhere. Early versions of Chapter 1 and Chapter 3 appeared in *Postmodern*

Culture 23(1) in 2012 and *TSQ: Transgender Studies Quarterly* 4(3–4) in 2017, respectively; the latter is republished by permission of the copyright holder, Duke University Press. Chapter 2 is a revision of articles initially published in *Angelaki* 18(4) and *Culture, Theory, and Critique* 54(1) in 2013. The Modern Language Association of America's Psychology, Psychoanalysis, and Literature Forum and Sexuality Studies Forum included portions of *Queer Traversals* on roundtables for the Annual Convention. The Comparative Gender Studies Committee of the International Comparative Literature Association selected several parts of this book for panels at American Comparative Literature Association conferences; special thanks to William Spurlin and Liedeke Plate for their leadership of that committee. I also benefited from travel funding from United Academics AAUP/AFT Local 4996, the UAF College of Liberal Arts, the UAF English Department, and the UAF Women, Gender, and Sexuality Studies Program. UAF's Interlibrary Loan department has provided extensive assistance in securing items referenced in *Queer Traversals*; I am especially grateful for Brad Krick's help.

Special thanks are due to CLA Dean Ellen López for encouraging me to move forward with this book, as well as to Maureen Hogan and Shayle Hutchison for their friendship and support in Fairbanks amid many challenges. But the most thanks are due to my mother, Anne W. Coffman, for her calm and thoughtful presence in my life for the last fifty years.

Introduction

Queer Traversals: Beyond the Fantasy of (Hetero)sexual Difference

On June 10, 2019—Whit Monday—the Vatican's Congregation for Catholic Education issued thirty-one pages of guidance meant to help educators stave off the supposed threat of the "society without sexual differences" they believe to be heralded by increased acceptance of transgender people.[1] This document—titled "'MALE AND FEMALE HE CREATED THEM': TOWARDS A PATH OF DIALOGUE ON THE QUESTION OF GENDER THEORY IN EDUCATION"—acknowledges the distinction between sex and gender but goes on to critique the "*separation of sex from gender*" at work in concepts such as sexual orientation, "which are no longer defined by the sexual difference between male and female" and so have taken on "other forms"—that is, queer forms (Congregation for Catholic Education 2019: 5–8).

The Vatican's document is startling because it was issued during the reign of a pope known for his expressions of compassion toward LGBTQ people, yet still participates in several reactionary discourses about gender running counter to his progressive stance. For example, the Vatican's document questionably assumes that what it describes as the "sociological" concept of gender is radically voluntarist: a claim trenchantly challenged by queer theory, which the Vatican erroneously characterizes as promoting "the complete emancipation of the individual from any *a priori* given sexual definition" (Congregation for Catholic Education 2019: 7–8). A similar fallacy is at work in the document's critique of the idea that "the concept of gender" is increasingly "seen as dependent upon the subjective mindset of each person, who can choose a gender not corresponding to his or her biological sex" (Congregation for Catholic Education 2019: 8). Finally, projection animates the Vatican's simultaneous critique of the contemporary "ideology of gender" and reiteration of the scientifically unsound claim that a putatively natural and anatomically grounded complementarity between male and female necessarily organizes sexuality around the imperative to reproduce (Congregation for Catholic Education 2019: 5).[2] This claim, too, is ideological and advances a view of sexuality that much Christian imagery undercuts (Zupančič 2017: 12–15).[3]

That the Vatican's guidance reproduces the heteronormative rhetoric of "reproductive futurism" exploded in Lacanian queer theorist Lee Edelman's *No Future* (2004) comes as no surprise (Edelman 2004: 28). More striking are the document's loud echoes with the discourse of another Lacanian, Catherine Millot, whose notorious *Horsexe* (1983) argues that gender transition constitutes a psychotic attempt to bypass the Real and abolish sexual difference. Writing in 1983, Millot complains about the possibility that "the law… will clearly differentiate *sex* (organ) and *gender* (identity)"; she fears that "[t]he individual right to choose one's sexual identity is not far off" and might be extended to those seeking "surgery" as well as those who "choose to retain their original sex" (Millot 1990: 13).[4]

Even more noteworthy is the emergence of these echoes at the same time as one of Lacan's most celebrated explicators, Slavoj Žižek, has taken to exploiting transpeople as clickbait in the popular online press. On May 30, 2019, *Spectator Life* published Žižek's poorly researched and deeply misguided essay "Transgender Dogma Is Naïve and Incompatible with Freud," which analyzes several contemporary films, advertisements, and examples of transgender discourse to build a dubious case that transpeoples' claims are at odds with basic psychoanalytic principles (Žižek 2019b). The essay in *Spectator Life* followed three 2016 pieces in *The Philosophical Salon* that brought Žižek's understanding of Lacanian sexual difference to bear on transgender issues without acknowledging the path-breaking work of psychoanalytic trans theorists such as Shanna Carlson, Sheila Cavanagh, Patricia Gherovici, Oren Gozlan, and Gayle Salamon. These writers' deep engagements with Lacanian and post-Lacanian accounts of psychical sexual difference animate their affirmative accounts of trans embodiment and challenge transphobic Lacanian claims circulating in the wake of *Horsexe*.[5]

There are significant differences between orthodox Lacanians' conceptualization of sexual difference and the Vatican's understanding of it as reproductively oriented complementarity. Lacan famously asks in *Seminar XX* (1972–3) whether it is "possible that language may have other effects than to lead people by the nose to reproduce yet again (*encore*)," rejecting anatomical and reproductive accounts of sexual difference (Lacan 1998: 46). Citing his argument that "there's no such thing as a sexual relation," contemporary Lacanians claim not that the sexes complement one another but that sexual difference functions as an intractable antinomy that operates psychically, forcing a choice between masculine and feminine subjective positions (Lacan 1998: 126). Unlike the Vatican, Lacanians do not use these claims to repudiate queer sexualities, which they figure (along with heterosexualities) as among the many different ways the "sexual relation" may fail (Lacan 1998: 126). Strict Lacanians such as Millot and Žižek do, however, continue to use Lacan's account of sexual difference to pathologize transgender despite the potentially radical implications of his statement, immediately following his repudiation of "sexual relation," that "[i]t's only speaking bodies… that come up with the idea of the world as such" (Lacan 1998: 126).

This gap between Lacan's words and his interpreters' unnecessarily constrictive rhetoric about sexual difference exposes the ideology *Queer Traversals* seeks to overcome. As different as orthodox Lacanians' discourse is from the Vatican's, two commonalities stand out: the assumption that the difference between masculine and feminine is foundational, and the reiteration of that presupposition through a projective rhetoric characterizing their critics as ideological while refusing to consider that their own positions may be so as well. James Penney's anti-homophobic critique of queer theory in *After Queer Theory* (2014) falls into this trap by pointing to the Lacanian distinction "between a *psychical*" sex, "a *biological* sex," and social "*gender*" while overlooking the psychoanalytic concept of embodiment and failing to question Lacan's theorization of sexual difference in 1970s terms distinguishing only between masculinity and femininity (Penney 2014: 147).

These writings' defensiveness masks the way sexual difference—which I will henceforth call (hetero)sexual difference—functions as a fundamental fantasy structuring orthodox strains of Lacanian psychoanalysis and broad swaths of contemporary culture. Whereas Penney reasserts the orthodox Lacanian notion that the intractable antinomy of "sexual difference stubbornly remains the same," *Queer Traversals* contends that it is a fantasy that can be traversed and thereby altered (Penney 2014: 147). Moreover, building on Judith Roof's distinction in *What Gender Is, What Gender Does* (2016) between gender performance and Lacanian sexuation, I argue that this fundamental fantasy is distinct from yet also sets into motion "the world of normative gender," which Ann Pellegrini and Avgi Saketopoulou aptly describe as "itself a fantasized construction" (Pellegrini and Saketopoulou 2019).[6]

Queer Traversals argues, on the one hand, that orthodox interpretations of Lacan are manifestations of a broader problem: the sway that ideological fantasies such as (hetero)sexual difference continue to hold over so many people and cultures. At the same time, *Queer Traversals* contends that revised forms of Lacanian psychoanalysis remain useful for teasing out and addressing societal and cultural dynamics' psychical underpinnings. At its core, psychoanalysis offers a theory and practice of profound individual and cultural transformation. When adapted for queer- and trans-affirmative purposes, Lacan's theory of traversing the fantasy makes change possible within seemingly intractable cultural formations.

This argument for queer adaptations of Lacanian psychoanalysis may seem utilitarian, devoid of the playful defiance often characterizing queer reading. Ben Nichols' *Same Old: Queer Theory, Literature and the Politics of Sameness* (2020) emphasizes queers' long-standing association with aestheticism, whose critique of utilitarianism contests "the assumption that we must at all costs avoid the useless," among other things (Nichols 2020: 37). Nichols rightfully observes that aestheticists and theorists are sometimes homophobically charged with avoiding material reality by engaging in "art for art's sake" and "theory for theory's sake," respectively, and that recent work in queer theory innovates by reclaiming the ostensibly useless.

However, there is also a long-standing history of pragmatic approaches to queer theory. Janet Halley and Andrew Parker note in *After Sex?* (2011) that queer theorists Gayle Rubin (in a 1997 interview) and Carla Freccero (in *After Sex?*) take a "pragmatic attitude to theory" (Halley and Parker 2011: 7). The editors of the 2005 "What's Queer about Queer Studies Now?" issue of *Social Text* similarly interrogate "the *utility* of queer as an engaged mode of critical inquiry" for understanding "historical emergencies… of both national and global consequence" (Eng, Halberstam, and Muñoz 2005: 2). They thereby set the stage for the "pragmatic" and intersectional re-imagining of Lacan that *Queer Traversals* envisions.

Similarly, in *What's the Use?* (2019), Sara Ahmed provides an extended argument for queering "use." Ahmed argues that "[w]e might respond to the problem of instrumentalism not by rejecting the idea of useful knowledge but by calling for knowledge that is useful to others, with this 'to' being an opening, an invitation, a connection" (Ahmed 2019: 222). Her "project of queering use does not aim to create distance from use but to inhabit use all the more" by imagining queer-affirmative modes of "reuse" (Ahmed 2019: 222, 198). She offers "[d]esire lines"—unofficial pathways created by off-trail hikers—as a metaphor for "queer use," noting that they "are created only by use and can be thought of as the promise of queer use: trails that remind us where we have been, trails that tell us where to go to find each other" (Ahmed 2019: 228). Observing that "the more" such "a path is traveled upon the clearer it becomes," Ahmed stresses the value for marginalized populations of queering the way pathways are used (Ahmed 2019: 120).

A premise of *Queer Traversals* is that even queer responses that misconstrue core elements of Lacan's thinking constitute "desire lines" revealing a need for continued engagement. Although I will engage primarily with queer- and trans-affirmative thinkers I believe to have the clearest grasp of his thought—Shanna Carlson, Sheila Cavanagh, Tim Dean, Lee Edelman, Patricia Gherovici, Oren Gozlan, James Penney, Mari Ruti, and Gayle Salamon—I nonetheless view misguided queer responses to Lacan as indicating a need for the new pathways this book develops.

Queer Traversals makes several queer uses of Lacanian psychoanalysis. First, I cast a light on and challenge orthodox interpretations of Lacan that create barriers to queer- and trans-affirmative rearticulations of his work. Ahmed observes that "things can be slowed down or stopped by being made harder to use" (Ahmed 2019: 12). Writings by orthodox Lacanians such as Joan Copjec and Žižek have had the salutary effect of exposing problems with some queer responses to Lacan—most notably, with Judith Butler's interpretation of the Real—yet also create the appearance that his thinking is hostile to queer theorizing when it could be interpreted elsewise. *Queer Traversals* aims to expose the ways orthodox Lacanian claims make Lacan's writings seem unsuitable for "queer use" and to make less usable those doctrines about the putative intractability of (hetero)sexual difference promulgated by orthodox Lacanians. As Ahmed puts it, "the point can be to stop something from working as it usually works" (Ahmed 2019: 53).

Second, Ahmed's argument for understanding "queer use as reuse"—for the value of redirecting objects or ideas "for a purpose that is 'very different' from that which was 'originally intended'"—illuminates another of *Queer Traversals*' implications (Ahmed 2019: 198–9). Ahmed observes that "[u]se does *not* necessarily correspond to an intended function" and that "[t]he failure of things to work creates an incentive to make new things" (Ahmed 2019: 24–5). Although Lacanian psychoanalysis has not always worked for queer and trans theory, *Queer Traversals* seizes the opportunity "to make new things" (Ahmed 2019: 25). Because "things can be strengthened or kept alive by easing their use," *Queer Traversals* seeks to amplify and sustain progressive readings of Lacan (Ahmed 2019: 12). Ahmed points out that "use is not only about conservation" and that "deviation is always possible, even when connections have become strong. Other paths can be created by being used" (Ahmed 2019: 42). My argument promotes the development of such "paths" by following the "fainter trail" of "what is left behind when you leave the official routes" of orthodox Lacanianism, and attempts to draw more attention to those paths' potentialities to create more livable lifeworlds for queer and transpeople (Ahmed 2019: 42, 20). I find novel ways of pushing Lacanian thinking away from well-trod anti-queer and anti-trans patterns by challenging the fantasy of (hetero)sexual difference.

Before I go any further, I should clarify my use of the words "sex," "gender," and "sexual difference." Freccero explains that in queer theory, "sex" tends to function as a "catchall word" indicating "gender, desire, sexuality, and perhaps anatomy" (Freccero 2011: 22). Because *Queer Traversals* works at the intersection of North American and French approaches to these concepts, I employ divergent vocabularies whose incommensurability is heightened by problems of translation. North American queer theory's crossovers with continental European psychoanalysis and poststructuralism vex the English distinction between bodily "sex" and cultural "gender," which North American trans theory and activism also challenge.

Two key Lacanian terms—"sexual difference" and "sexuation"—enter English as translations of the French phrases "la différence sexuelle" and "l'identité sexuée," whereas gender—a concept introduced by English-language feminisms grounded in sociological accounts of gender roles—does not have a French equivalent. However, as Penney points out, French feminist thinking has long distinguished between "a *sexe biologique* and a *sexe social* or *culturel*" (Penney 2014: 148).[7] Moreover, the French word "genre"—frequently mistranslated as "gender"—invokes the concept of literary genre and also, grammatically, marks what English speakers would call anatomical sex.[8]

Unlike social, linguistic, and biological designations, Lacanian terms such as "sexual difference" and "sexuation" refer to psychical structures emerging from within the dialectic of desire. As Ellie Ragland explains, "Lacan coined the term *sexuation* to describe a subject's choice of sex as masculine or feminine in assuming an active or passive position vis-à-vis his or her object of desire"—to describe "the way a subject is split by language (or not)" through Oedipalization (Ragland 2004: 65–7). Moreover, as Carlson clarifies, "the formulas of sexuation" articulated in Lacan's *Seminar XX* "provide the 'logical matrix' (Salecl 2) of the deadlock of sexual difference" in the Real that forces the subject to choose between masculine and feminine positions within desire's dialectic (Carlson 2010: 52). She asserts that these two stances cannot be reduced to "gender," insofar as they "signal two different logics, two different modes of ex-sistence in the symbolic, two different approaches to the Other, two different stances with respect to desire, and (at least) two different types of jouissance" (Carlson 2010: 64). As Roof notes, these divergent positions reflect "how individuals unconsciously situate themselves in relation to ascriptions of power and possibility" (Roof 2016: 244). Within these two "psychic identifications," the "masculine identifies primarily with the symbolic order of language and social conventions, while the feminine identifies with the real of affect, loss, and trauma" (Ragland 2004: 179). This results not in a binary opposition between the masculine and feminine but rather in an antagonistic clash between incommensurate positions.

Despite Lacan's stress on psychical positioning, his thesis that "sexuality is structured—that is, imposed from the outside"—is somewhat "compatible with sociological feminisms," as Ragland notes (Ragland 2004: 74). Even though his thinking diverges from sociologists' arguments about gender "role behavior," he demonstrates that "[o]ne 'learns' one's sexual identifications—one's sexuation— from the symbolic order" as a correlative of "imaginary identifications, not biological anatomy" (Ragland 2004: 74). Ragland explains that "Lacan recast the Freudian cause of human *behavior and motivation* away from anatomy and biology to the subjective sexual identifications he called differential structures of desire. Each structure of desire establishes a pattern connecting it to jouissance depending on the way lack… is filled in reference to the Father's Name… and the object (*a*) that marks the primordial subject as real" (Ragland 2004: 98). Yet as she also observes, Lacan's anti-essentialism creates overlaps between his theories and sociologists' accounts of gender. These two lines of thinking are not equivalent, however, for Lacanians and gender theorists diverge in understanding the *mechanisms* leading to gender diversity. But if we stress their theories' intersections rather than their divergences, we can see the complex interplay between the psychical and the social at work in the contemporary proliferation of genders.

It is also worth noting that Lacan formulated these concepts in the 1950s through the 1970s, when one typically spoke of "men" and "women" but not of other genders. Although Lacanians have a long history of opposing "historicist" and "rhetoricalist" readings of Lacan, I see no reason to lock his theory of sexuation into the language that was available to him at that time (Copjec 1994; Dean 2000a). Lacan insists upon the opposite, stating in *Seminar XX* that "[m]en, women, and children are but signifiers" (Lacan 1998: 33). Rather than reading Lacan more literally than he read the texts of psychoanalysis' founder in his return to Freud, I propose that queer and trans theorists are especially well equipped to expand our vocabularies for gender, sexual difference, and sexuation. Lacan's rereading of Freud attended to his text's "letter" but was also transformative, detaching his predecessor's insights from anatomical difference and considering instead their ramifications for the signifier. If Freud is what Michel Foucault calls an "initiator" of a "discursive practice" that subsequent theorists revised and transformed, Lacan—who initiated structuralist and poststructuralist psychoanalysis—must be read similarly: not as a thinker whose vocabulary locks the formulae of sexuation into place for all time but as a theorist whose most radical insights reveal possibilities for their reformulation (Foucault 1977: 132).

Queer Traversals therefore contends that because—as Ragland puts it—"[s]exual difference is not innate" but symbolic—because sexuation "does not" determine "one's biological sex but the position one occupies in reference to the masculine *all* of knowledge, or the feminine *not all* of knowledge"—this theory may be rearticulated in contemporary vocabulary for queer and trans theory (Ragland 2004: 125, 179). The Lacanian subject is free to choose between the masculine and feminine positions without regard to anatomical differences. Moreover, these psychical differences set into motion numerous possibilities for social gender. In her cross-reading of Lacan with systems theory, Roof points out that one of the functions of the "castration complex"—even when strictly defined—is to propel "a perpetual process of sorting differences into difference as the symbolic condition for desire" (Roof 2016: 60). Roof's interpretation of Lacan's account of "subjective sexuation" acknowledges that subjects may adopt "multiple postures and attitudes in relation to difference," which may include a variety of transsubjectivities (Roof 2016: 60).

Moreover, *Queer Traversals* contends that these anti-essentialist but still orthodox accounts of sexuation can be revised to go beyond the claim that all subjects must assume a masculine or feminine position with regard to the phallus. To do so, Chapter 4 draws on psychoanalytic visual artist Bracha Ettinger to argue that traversing the fantasy of (hetero)sexual difference could lead to subjectivities that, without risking psychosis, either refuse or operate alongside the phallus. The latter possibility recalls the varied relationalities Eve Kosofsky Sedgwick associates with the "beside," whose vicissitudes range from "desiring, identifying, representing, repelling, paralleling, differentiating, rivaling, leaning, twisting," and "mimicking" to "withdrawing, attracting, aggressing," and "warping" (Sedgwick 2003: 8). By validating diverse modes of relation, *Queer Traversals* argues that "sexual difference" and "sexuation"—"la différence sexuelle" and "l'identité sexuée"—extend well beyond the masculine and feminine positions Lacan imagined in the 1970s. Moreover, *Queer Traversals*' attention to the many ways of being "beside" foregrounds a multiplicity that is amenable to theorizing gender's and sexuality's intersection with other formations—such as race, ethnicity, and nationality—without the a priori claims to sexual difference's primacy that hamper so much Lacanian thinking.

Multiplicity has long been a prominent concern of queer theory, and *Queer Traversals* employs "queer" in the word's broadest possible sense. Emphasizing sexuality, *After Sex?* develops the implications of what Sharon Marcus describes as "the multiple ways that sexual practice, sexual fantasy, and sexual identity fail to line up consistently": a claim wholly compatible with Lacanian psychoanalysis (Marcus 2005: 196). For Halley and Parker, Marcus' statement also indexes queerness's potential to offer a capacious account of sexual diversity extending beyond contemporary LGBQ identities and the concept of sexuality. As they point out with regard to essays by Joseph Litvak and Elizabeth Freeman, psychoanalysis makes everything—not just bodily pleasure—queer (Halley and Parker 2011: 5–6).

Although *After Sex?* exemplifies queer theory's long-standing tendency to stress sexuality even when pointing beyond it, since Butler's 1990 *Gender Trouble* the word "queer" has also signaled the subversion of gender norms. The word "genderqueer" gained currency in the 1990s in the wake of *Gender Trouble* as a politicized way of describing approaches to gender that are now more frequently described as "nonbinary." *Queer Traversals* challenges Butler's 1990s readings of Lacan and refuses her critique of Lacan's purported normativity, which overlooks Lacan's trenchant critique of normalizing North American ego psychology.[9] I nonetheless follow her example by using feminist theory to analyze queer sexualities *and* genders simultaneously. For sexualities, "queer" presents a challenge to heterosexual dominance. For genders, "queer" contests the presumption that everybody's gender embodiment matches what was assigned at birth. As the Vatican's opposition to all forms of transgender illuminates, those who transition from one side of the gender binary to the other join non-binary people in powerfully challenging assertions that people should remain locked into initially assigned genders.

Vocabulary for these new genders is currently in flux; terminological preferences vary culturally and geographically. Although the University of California Press published Jack Halberstam's *Trans** in 2018, "transgender" and the unmarked "trans" are beginning to supplant formulations using the asterisk. Accordingly, *Queer Traversals* uses "transgender" as an umbrella term for anybody whose gender differs from that assigned at birth; I also use words such as "trans" and "transpeople" in the broad sense in which I employ "transgender." I will avoid the term "transsexual," despite its continued presence in trans-affirmative Lacanian literature, for two reasons. First, it has historically been used to pathologize transpeople. Second, it draws an overly simplistic distinction between those transpeople who surgically or hormonally alter their bodies and those who do not. Moreover, I employ two other terms for gender, "non-binary" and "genderqueer," that have been less extensively explored in the Lacanian literature. These words refer to individuals whose gender identities fall outside of or between the socially constructed gender binary of "man" and "woman." Although these two categories are similar and I will discuss them in tandem with one another, "non-binary" tends to function neutrally, whereas "genderqueer" often marks an explicitly political program of disrupting—queering—the binary.

I will use the term "cisgender" only sparingly because the distinction between it and transgender is suspect. First, not all persons at odds with their embodiment or socially assigned gender act on those sensations or affiliate with any gender category. Second, as Finn Enke argues, the word "cisgender" facilitates questionable "investments in a gender stability that undermines feminist, trans, queer, and related movements" (Enke 2012: 61). For Enke, the "cis/trans binary" is problematic because it simplistically "name[s] cis as trans's absence" while overlooking "gender variance and diversity among everyone" (Enke 2012: 76).

Enke's argument is compatible with Lacan's thesis that subjectivity is inevitably split and does not negate the fact that at present, some people identify as cisgender and others do not—often for important personal and political reasons. Although Gherovici defends the term "cisgender" for facilitating "the depathologization of gender variance and sexual non-conformity," she overlooks the way the distinction between cisgender and transgender conceals the "structural failure" Lacanians view as rendering all forms of gendered and "sexual identity... precarious" even as trans-affirmative psychoanalysis seeks to depathologize and affirm transsubjectivities' validity (Gherovici 2019a). I will therefore use the word "cisgender" sparingly, and only in reference to others' use of it.

Queer Traversals ultimately envisions an expansive revision of Lacanian psychoanalysis that explicitly affirms all modes of embodiment and views them as intersecting with other axes of identity such as race, ethnicity, and nationality. To do so, I use a revised version of Lacanian psychoanalysis to argue that (hetero)sexual difference—the ideology holding that a putatively foundational antagonism between masculine and feminine structures desire—is not transhistorical, as orthodox Lacanians claim, but rather a historically contingent fantasy that psychoanalytic theorists need to go beyond to better register the implications of diverse sexualities and modes of embodiment. This fantasy is so deeply entrenched in the psyche that it functions as what Butler—in an otherwise misguided critique of Žižek—rightfully calls an untouchable "'law' prior to all ideological formations" enabling (hetero)sexual difference to go unacknowledged and unquestioned (Butler 1993: 196).

Distinct from daydreams and other conscious fantasies, what Lacanians call the fundamental fantasy—which sustains desiring subjectivity and orients the subject—is an unconscious formation supported by the imaginary, symbolic, and Real.[10] The *point de capiton* ties the "symbolic"—the realm of language and signification—to the two other orders. The imaginary order is that of the specular image, the visual. It is not opposed to reality but rather plays a part in its constitution. While specularity is a crucial component of fantasy, the latter places the former in a "signifying structure," and so cannot be reduced to the imaginary (Lacan 2006a: 532). Lacan claims in *Seminar III* (1955-6) that being a subject (rather than a psychotic) within signification requires that one accept the "name of the father" as the "primordial signifier" grounding the symbolic (Lacan 1993: 96, 150). Feminist and queer theorists such as Butler have thus long viewed the Lacanian doctrine of sexual difference as unacceptably patriarchal and heteronormative.[11] Even though Bruce Fink clarifies that any name—not just that of the Father—could serve this function, many contemporary Lacanians insist that the law governing the symbolic must be that of the father and that sexual difference always motivates desire (Fink 1995: 56).[12] Challenging such orthodoxies, *Queer Traversals* argues that traversing the fundamental fantasy—which Lacan first describes in *Seminar XI* (1964)—could reformulate language, signification, and desire by changing the three orders' configuration.[13]

Crucially, traversing the fantasy engages the imaginary, symbolic, and Real—the psyche's deepest source of resistance. The Real is not the symbolic's outside but rather the site of its failures, as Copjec observes (Copjec 1994: 201-36).[14] Traversing the fundamental fantasy asks the unhappy subject to engage the Real and temporarily embrace "subjective destitution": a state of dispossession Ruti describes as entailing loss of the fantasies structuring subjectivity yet motivating unconscious investments in constricting life patterns (Ruti 2008a: 498; Žižek 1996: 166). This experience sets a process of profound change into motion, entailing the "radical transformation of the very universal structuring 'principle' of the existing symbolic order" as well as its imaginary and Real coordinates (Žižek 2000b: 220). This overhaul of the symbolic creates, in turn, the conditions through which a new fundamental fantasy—and therefore a new form of subjectivity—can emerge, clearing the ground for a future that could be lived otherwise (Ruti 2008a: 498).

However, traversing the fundamental fantasy can be profoundly threatening because it entails the loss of fantasies that structure and constrain the subject (Ruti 2008a: 498). The potential for this experience to be devastating explains the intense defensiveness that emerges whenever the claim that (hetero)sexual difference is a foundational truth of human existence is challenged. Whereas the Vatican and orthodox Lacanians such as Copjec and Žižek present two very different versions of such a reaction, *Queer Traversals* explores ways traversing the fantasy of (hetero)sexual difference could instead open up possibilities for new configurations of language, signification, and desire. Going beyond or even outright rejecting (hetero)sexual difference creates an opening for theorizing sexualities other than heterosexuality and embodiments other than "man" and "woman." Doing so also dethrones (hetero)sexual difference's privileged position within Lacanian discourse, placing it on the same level as intersecting formations such as race, ethnicity, and nationality.

Others who offer valuable queer- or trans-affirmative Lacanian arguments nonetheless overlook (hetero)sexual difference's status as a fundamental fantasy structuring contemporary discourse. Penney's *After Queer Theory*, for example, offers a Lacanian critique of poststructural queer theory that, affirming homo- and bisexualities, centers Marxist concerns shared with Žižek. However, Penney does not offer alternatives to claims to the phallic signifier's putative primacy or sexual difference's supposed intractability in the Real. Instead, he situates male homosexuality with respect to the phallus in an orthodox Lacanian account of sexuation (Penney 2014: 145–74). By contrast, Dean's *Beyond Sexuality* (2000) conceives of sexual difference and the phallus as "secondary" rather than primary (Dean 267). Salamon's *Assuming A Body* (2010) and subsequent writings approach sexual difference as a dynamic "relation" rather than an intractable antinomy, and Ruti's *The Ethics of Opting Out* (2017) sidesteps long-standing controversies over Lacan's vocabulary (Salamon 2016: 317). Whereas in *Sex, or the Unbearable* (2014) Edelman and Lauren Berlant acknowledge that "the negativity of relation" can make "transformation possible" but claim that concepts such as reparation are of limited use, Ruti emphasizes Lacan's usefulness for understanding queer affect and relationality (Edelman in Berlant and Edelman 2014: 29).

Queer Traversals goes farther than these thinkers by arguing that (hetero) sexual difference is a fundamental fantasy available for traversals that can reconfigure the Real, marginalizing (hetero)sexual difference or even rendering it obsolete. Disproving orthodox Lacanians' assumption that sexual difference is foundational, such traversals challenge claims that transgender is pathological and that race and ethnicity are second-order phenomena less significant to subjective formation than sexuation.[15] Jan Campbell's *Arguing with the Phallus* (2000) begins this work by stressing the phallus's historical contingency and exploring psychoanalysis's implications for feminist and postcolonial theory. However, Campbell does not imagine how traversing the fantasy of (hetero) sexual difference might dethrone phallic privilege in ways that further existing intersectional approaches to psychical difference.

Moreover, these thinkers do not consider ways traversing the fantasy of (hetero)sexual difference might create possibilities for theorizing diverse sexualities *and* embodiments. *Beyond Sexuality* does the former, arguing that for Lacan, "the unconscious has no knowledge of sexual difference" and that therefore "as far as the unconscious is concerned heterosexuality does not exist" (Dean 2000a: 86).[16] However, Dean does not challenge the pathologizing approach to transgender, exemplified by Millot's *Horsexe*, dominating all but the most recent Lacanian theory. *Queer Traversals*, by contrast, lays the groundwork for both queer- *and* trans-affirmative uses of Lacan.

Gherovici offers one approach to trans-affirmative psychoanalysis. She notes that for Lacan, "[i]n the unconscious there is no representation or symbol of the opposition masculine-feminine" affording "a normal, finished sexual positioning"; this failure of symbolization makes "sexual identity ... precarious" (Gherovici 2019a). The resulting subject is propped up by "fantasies" that "veil the structural failure" on which sexuation turns (Gherovici 2019a). Whereas Gherovici and other transpsychoanalytic thinkers such as Carlson (2010, 2014), and Gozlan (2015) work within an orthodox Lacanian account of sexuation to challenge transphobic interpretations such as Millot's and offer trans-affirmative accounts of embodiment, *Queer Traversals* contends that (hetero)sexual difference itself operates as a fundamental fantasy whose traversal opens up new—and potentially intersectional—ways of queer and trans theorizing.

Although other queer theorists have utilized Lacan's account of traversing the fantasy, none have argued that (hetero)sexual difference itself is a fundamental fantasy. Edelman's influential *No Future*, for example, puts Lacan into queer theory's service by offering a Lacanian argument against reproductive futurism— the ideology that seeks to guarantee the future in the name of the child. Edelman forcefully argues that reproductive futurism is a heterosexist fundamental fantasy queers should traverse by embracing the drive in the Real. In so doing, he hints at—but does not explicitly theorize—the argument at *Queer Traversals'* heart: that (hetero)sexual difference, too, is a fantasy that can be traversed.

Like Edelman, Frances Restuccia hints in *Amorous Acts* (2006) at the possibility of (hetero)sexual difference's traversal. Building on an early version of a chapter from *No Future*, she argues that queer theorists Leo Bersani, Butler, Dean, Edelman, and David Halperin strive to traverse the fantasy. Although Restuccia states that queer theory enacts a "social traversing of heterosexist fantasy," she focuses on traversing "the fundamental fantasy of heterosexual reproduction" (Restuccia 2006: 144). She asks, "[i]f we were to put 'the social' on the couch... could the result of its experiencing queer/Lacanian Love, Love in the Real... be to demystify or wipe out the fundamental fantasy of heterosexual reproduction on which the social is currently predicated, ... collapsing the historically heterosexist Symbolic regime?" (Restuccia 2006: 144). This formulation makes the destruction of a heterosexist symbolic a consequence of relinquishing a reproductive aim Restuccia places at the social's heart. Yet *Amorous Acts* backgrounds fantasy until the book's closing pages, instead stressing Lacan's ideas about ethics and love. Moreover, Restuccia's archive consists of canonical masterpieces of modernist literature and art film: novels by Forster, Greene, Lawrence, and Woolf; films by Jacquot, Kieslowski, Malle, and von Trier. Structurally, Restuccia's insights into queer theory's traversals of the fantasy collapse the reproductive ideologies motivating these works. Although *Amorous Acts* advances the argument that traversing the fantasy could topple heterosexist society, Restuccia does not extend this reasoning to the ideology of (hetero)sexual difference.

Hart's *Between the Body and the Flesh* (1998) inflects the idea of traversing the fantasy quite differently from Edelman and Restuccia. Hart is interested not in challenges to reproductive futurism but in ways lesbian sadomasochism's engagement of the Real provides women with ways to traverse oppressive fantasies governing patriarchal societies and strict lesbian-feminist cultures. She is particularly interested in sadomasochism's capacity to move women beyond cultural barriers against speaking about prohibited and traumatic topics such as incest. Doing so allows them to traverse the fundamental fantasy and go beyond the limits imposed by the symbolic order's exclusion of the impossible Real (Hart 1998: 203). At one point, Hart notes that one of Anna Freud's case studies features a girl whose fantasy defies the "teleology of sexual difference": a break in psychoanalysis's story that "is sutured only by the arbitrary intervention of a social prohibition against the fantasy" imposed by the analyst (Hart 1998: 30). Although this observation suggests that (hetero)sexual difference is a fundamental fantasy available for traversal, Hart does not develop this insight.

In *After Queer Theory*, Penney argues that queer theory itself needs to traverse the "liberal fantasies" governing its neoliberal and anti-neoliberal strains (Penney 2014: 67). After distinguishing the United States' neoliberal politics of gay rights activism from poststructural queer theories focused on subverting norms, he contends that "[t]hese seemingly contrary and politically irreconcilable structures" are both "transferential" appeals "to an idealized symbolic authority" (Penney 2014: 67). For Penney, traversing the "fantasy" entails admitting "that the idealized queer big Other… is increasingly the middle-class or upper-middle-class, elite-educated, savvy consumer, almost always located in the global North, or else the 'securitized' enclaves of the megalopolises of what we used to call the third world" (Penney 2014: 68). This formulation rightfully calls attention to material privileges many queer theorists share with the gaystream, challenging us to better address ethnically diverse and economically marginalized populations. However, Penney does not adequately theorize transgender, despite the economic hardships transpeople often face. His few references to transgender concern either Serge André's arguments about "homosexuality" or Mario Mieli's queer psychoanalytic Marxism (Penney 2014: 155–68).

Penney ultimately does not relinquish the Lacanian fantasy of (hetero) sexual difference's primacy that *Queer Traversals* challenges. This fantasy is neither transcultural nor transhistorical, but contingent and available for traversal. Whereas Penney uses orthodox Lacanian tenets to ground a critique of neoliberal queer politics, Edelman, Restuccia, and Hart all hint at—but do not explicitly argue for—the possibility of (hetero)sexual difference's traversal. They focus on other concerns, such as reproduction (Edelman and Restuccia) or lesbian sadomasochism (Hart).

By contrast, the first four chapters of *Queer Traversals* provide the theoretical basis for the claim that (hetero)sexual difference is a fundamental fantasy available for traversal, and explore its implications for queer and transgender theories. The fifth and sixth chapters consider several works of queer literature and film from the 1980s to the present, examining potential routes to and consequences of traversing that fantasy. Reading narratives of queer migration and border negotiation, these chapters illustrate intersectional possibilities lying beyond (hetero)sexual difference and demonstrate that its traversal allows queer subjects to remake themselves. These chapters also show that although those traversing the fantasy risk relinquishing familiar patterns, practices such as queer performance, activism, and care can provide grounding and reorientation after fantasy's traversal, fostering—though not guaranteeing—progressive outcomes.

Whereas Edelman's, Hart's, Penney's, Restuccia's, and Ruti's work on the fundamental fantasy focuses on queer sexualities, *Queer Traversals* contends that traversing the fantasy of (hetero)sexual difference will benefit our understanding of both sexuality and gender. Whereas queer readings of Lacan can be traced back to the 1990s, trans-affirmative rereadings have largely emerged in the last decade.[17] This is not surprising, given orthodox Lacanians' ongoing resistance to such work and queer theorists' initial subsumption of gender to sexuality in the late 1980s and 1990s.[18] Because of these histories, Lacanian psychoanalysis has only just begun to think through what it might mean to live as a gender other than that assigned at birth, whether within or outside the gender binary.

Trans "embodiment" does not refer to the "physical body" but rather to a person's psychical mapping of it, as Salamon explains (Salamon 2010: 59). Gherovici notes that "[w]hen someone realigns an inner sense of sexual identity with the flesh they inhabit, the possibility of embodying a different gender from the one assigned at birth implies that the materiality of the body is not immediately given" (Gherovici 2019a). The varied "changes" individual "[t]ransgender people" and "other gender dissidents" make to their "social presentation, gender roles, legal documents," and "bodies" support the "search for a more livable embodiment" than the one assigned at birth (Gherovici 2019a). Grace Lavery further argues that for "trans women and femmes," gender "realness" (as distinct from the Lacanian Real) is experienced "as a kind of embodiment" (Lavery 2020: 721). Whereas Salamon stresses embodiment's imaginary and symbolic components, invoking the Real only to critique Jay Prosser's conflation of it with the material body in *Second Skins* (1998), subsequent revisions of Lacan have emphasized the need to engage and reconfigure all three orders to successfully anchor trans embodiments. Challenging Millot's claim that transpeople psychotically seek to evade the symbolic and overtake the Real, Cavanagh (2017), Gherovici (2010, 2017), Gozlan (2015), and others rework Lacan to theorize transition as a process that successfully reconfigures the relationship between the imaginary, symbolic, and Real.

Queer Traversals, too, uses Lacan to theorize queer genders *and* sexualities, understood to encompass binary *and* non-binary subjectivities. Though the term "genderqueer" emerged within North American queer communities in the 1990s, it and the more recent designation "non-binary" have not been adequately theorized.

This oversight continues in trans-affirmative psychoanalysis prioritizing those who cross sides of the gender binary. By theorizing sexualities *and* genders, and by examining strategies for traversing the fantasy of (hetero)sexual difference, *Queer Traversals* opens up space for theorizing within and beyond binaries. Embracing the Sedgwickian "beside," *Queer Traversals* reformulates Lacanian accounts of difference to think sexuality, gender, ethnicity, and nationality intersectionally (Sedgwick 2003: 8). Expanding the scope of existing Lacanian queer and transgender theory, *Queer Traversals* argues that fantasy's traversal makes it possible to reconstitute or even go beyond the three orders to make room for an expanding range of desires, embodiments, and subjectivities.

Lacan's account of fantasy's traversal offers a theory of transformation that aims for a better future. Especially in the clinic, psychoanalysis's purpose is to change life for the better. Ruti has thus repeatedly and compellingly argued that Lacanian psychoanalysis is not nearly as negative or anti-social as Edelman claims. Though I agree that his relentless negativity obscures the Lacanian *sinthôme*'s generativity, I do not embrace Ruti's account of the subject, especially her claim that moments of subjective "dissolution" paradoxically "make us feel... well... immediately real" and "may... be the closest we ever get to feeling fully present to ourselves" (Ruti 2008b: 122). Her hesitant diction—her ellipses, her concession that subjective dispossession is not total self-presence but merely "the closest we ever get to" it—simultaneously props up and self-reflexively distances Lacan's critique of imaginary and symbolic illusion. I am nonetheless struck by Ruti's repeated emphasis on feeling's immediacy as a guarantor of reality. This recalls Michael Snediker's case in *Queer Optimism* (2009) for the importance of attending to affective immanence, yet Ruti importantly reclaims the self-shattering he rejects.

Queer Traversals similarly holds out hope that traversing the fantasy can be generative rather than destructive, yet is more interested than Ruti in this theory's political implications: especially in the way the changes wrought by fantasy's traversal may be for better or worse. The recent worldwide resurgence of xenophobic right-wing nationalism shows as much. The expulsion of Central European University from Hungary because of its degree in gender studies and increasingly vocal manifestations of homophobia in Poland and Russia demonstrate that massive structural transformations such as the fall of the Iron Curtain do not guarantee a better future—especially for women, queers, and transpeople.

Xenophobia has recently re-emerged because moments of upheaval and uncertainty risk being co-opted by ideologies offering the illusion of symbolic closure. Building on Žižek's analysis of the overthrow of Nicolae Ceaușescu by rebels flying a version of the Romanian flag leaving a gaping "hole" where a "communist symbol" had once been, Yannis Stavrakakis argues that traversing the fantasy makes visible an ordinarily hidden "hole in the big Other" that risks "reoccupation" by a seemingly "new" form of "traditional politics" eager to cover over the lack revealed by political disruption (Stavrakakis 1999: 135). He proposes that in the face of such developments, "critical intellectuals" should instead "occupy all the time the space of this hole" to maintain its visibility and keep the democratic field radically open (Stavrakakis 1999: 135).

As Stavrakakis suggests, traversing the fantasy clears ground for a complex and negotiable future.[19] Recent work on queer temporality reveals the risks and potentialities of such transformations. Commenting on Freccero's self-positioning as "a future dead person writing myself out of my time while time is running out," Edelman observes that her formulation recalls "Barthes's observation that in writing we're always already dead. And together these insights reinforce what it means to be subjects of a drive, to be 'written' by what we do not control or recognize or even desire" (Freccero in Dinshaw et al. 2007: 184; Edelman in Dinshaw et al. 2007: 189). Although I join Ruti in stressing the drive's generativity over and against Edelman's apocalyptic negativity, I concur with his emphasis on the temporal complexities at play in the drive's unpredictable psychical inscriptions, which split the subject and queer temporality. He observes that "[w]e're never at one with our queerness; neither its time nor its subject is ours. But to try to think that tension ... to try to move, as Carla suggests, into the space where 'we' are not: that is a project whose time never comes and therefore is always now" (Edelman in Dinshaw et al. 2007: 189). Despite Edelman's claims, this insight does not release us from the obligation to tap the drive's productive capacities for the "good": a responsibility Ruti explores in *The Ethics of Opting Out* (Ruti 2017: 189). However, his attention to the queer temporalities mobilized through psychoanalysis's splitting of the subject has enabled others to theorize their potential generativity.

Over and against Edelman's negativity, Freeman argues in *Time Binds* (2010) for an expanded version of what Sedgwick calls "reparative criticism": for a recognition "that because we can't know in advance, but only retrospectively even then, what is queer and what is not, we gather and combine eclectically, dragging a bunch of cultural debris around us and stacking it in idiosyncratic piles '*not necessarily like any preexisting whole*,' though composed of what preexists" (Freeman 2010: xiii). Freeman also observes that "[f]or queer scholars and activists, this cultural debris includes our incomplete, partial, or otherwise failed transformations of the social field" (Freeman 2010: xiii). The work of queer artists and writers is thus that of "mining the present for signs of undetonated energy from past revolutions" and creatively redeploying it in new contexts (Freeman 2010: xvi).

Freeman offers an innovative approach to queer historiography that valuably corrects Edelman's negativity and refusal of politics. Crucially, she finds a wide range of queer temporalities in those "moments when an established temporal order gets interrupted and new encounters consequently take place" (Freeman 2010: xxii). Less concerned than Freeman with historiographical method, *Queer Traversals* argues that traversing the fantasy enables new orders to emerge. Stavrakakis describes fantasy's traversal as creating an opening: a "brief moment, after the collapse of an order and before the articulation of another one," enabling something new to materialize (Stavrakakis 1999: 135). This short period of uncertainty could be restabilized by one of the forms of "traditional politics" he decries (Stavrakakis 1999: 135). Alternatively, if the "hole in the big Other" is held open, it could mobilize the sort of recombinatory generativity Freeman describes (Stavrakakis 1999: 135).

Although these temporalities' potential queerness does not make them inherently revolutionary, *Queer Traversals* stresses the productive rather than destructive force of the ground-clearing gesture opening space for their emergence. By examining works of queer literature and film that traverse the fantasy of (hetero)sexual difference, *Queer Traversals*' fifth and sixth chapters illuminate strategies such as queer performance, activism, and care that—despite the uncertainties accompanying fantasy's traversal—encourage outcomes that are for the better. Searching the queer cultural archive from the 1980s to the present for examples of "failed transformations of the social field" that could be reprised in the present to create "new encounters," these chapters illustrate multiple routes for fantasy's traversal and suggest several ways of tapping its progressive possibilities (Freeman 2010: xii–xiii).

Queer Traversals is comprised of an introduction, six chapters, and a Coda. The Introduction and the first four chapters argue that despite orthodox Lacanians' protestations to the contrary, Lacan's writings make it possible to conceive of (hetero)sexual difference as a fundamental fantasy available for traversal. Reading Lacan's texts as closely as he reads Freud's; using concepts from queer and trans theory to transform and revitalize his ideas just as he uses Saussurian linguistics to reanimate Freud: taken together, these chapters contend that Lacanian theorists should traverse the fantasy of (hetero)sexual difference to make room for a more diverse range of sexualities and embodiments.

The final two chapters offer readings of films and literary texts exploring several different outcomes of fantasy's traversal. Films such as *In & Out* (Frank

Oz, 1997) point beyond the fantasy in ways that challenge cultural prohibitions against homosexuality but that otherwise continue to prop up sexism and normative institutions such as marriage, as I argue in Chapter 1. By contrast, as I show in Chapters 5 and 6, Monika Treut's film *The Virgin Machine* (1988), John Cameron Mitchell's film *Hedwig and the Angry Inch* (2001), and Andrea Lawlor's novel *Paul Takes the Form of a Mortal Girl* (2017) track their protagonists' successful escapes from constrictive fantasies structuring their desires. Similarly, queer Chicana writer Gloria Anzaldúa's multi-genre *Borderlands/La Frontera* (1987) and *Light in the Dark/Luz en lo Oscuro* (2015) work at literal and metaphorical borders to promise of a "new *mestiza* consciousness" in which "duality is transcended" (Anzaldúa 1987: 77, 80). These works all illustrate several different possibilities for intersectional lifeworlds opened by traversing the fantasy of (hetero)sexual difference.

Whereas this Introduction has demonstrated that Dean, Restuccia, and Hart all hint at—but ultimately do not argue for—the possibility that (hetero)sexual difference is a historically contingent fantasy available for traversal, Chapter 1—"Queering Žižek"—reads Žižek's work against itself to advance that thesis. By examining his reading of Lacan, I expose and critique orthodox Lacanians' continued investment in a heterosexist and transphobic account of sexual difference. Attending to Žižek's politicized recasting of Lacan's argument that one can traverse—and thereby alter—the fundamental fantasy structuring subjectivity, this chapter argues that despite Žižek's protestations to the contrary, sexual difference is not inalterable. Rather, (hetero)sexual difference is the fundamental fantasy Lacanian psychoanalytic theory needs to traverse to fully register the many possible configurations of desiring subjectivities.

Chapter 2, "*No Future*? Traversing the Fantasy of (Hetero)sexual Difference," engages Edelman's *No Future* to ask what follows after one has traversed the fantasy of (hetero)sexual difference. Edelman adapts Lacan's theory of the *sinthôme*—the individual mode of *jouissance* tapping into the Real and the drive—to critique the homophobic ideology of reproductive futurism that seeks to guarantee the future in the name of the child. He argues that queer theory should forego any engagement with a politics of the future and that queers should instead embrace the position of the reviled *sinthom*osexual, whose embrace of *jouissance* in the Real undoes the symbolic order and undercuts reprofuturity. Arguing that Edelman's *sinthom*osexual challenges but ultimately does not abolish Lacanian sexual difference, this chapter offers an interpretation of Lacan's theory of the *sinthôme* that sustains several accounts of a future beyond reproductive futurism—options far more promising for queer theory than Edelman's refusal of all politics and signification.

Chapter 3, "Žižek's Antagonism and the Futures of Trans-Affirmative Lacanian Psychoanalysis," argues that despite Žižek's protestations to the contrary, transitioning people can successfully traverse the fantasy of (hetero)sexual difference and anchor viable subjectivities. Building on the work of Carlson, Gherovici, and Salamon, this chapter argues that despite itself, Žižek's work offers a way of traversing the fantasy of (hetero)sexual difference structuring Lacanian accounts of gender. By going beyond the assumption that the antinomy animating subjectivity must always and only be named sexual difference, this chapter creates an opening for thinking sex, gender, and sexual difference otherwise.

Chapter 4, "Cavanagh and Gherovici: Toward a Transfeminist Theory of Embodiment," draws on visual artist Bracha Ettinger's feminist reinflection of the *sinthôme* to argue for a psychoanalytic transfeminism that traverses the fantasy of (hetero)sexual difference and clears ground for an expansive theory of transgender embodiment. Building on Cavanagh, Gherovici, and Gozlan—whose work has been vitally important in understanding transpeoples' desire to transition as healthy and life-affirming rather than psychotic—this chapter reinflects trans-affirmative work on the *sinthôme* to theorize forms of embodiment unique to non-binary and genderqueer people. Supported by structures of sexual difference that need not be anchored by the phallus, these subjective experiences of embodiment extend beyond the gender binary and the body's material contours.

Chapter 5, "Traversing the Atlantic, Traversing (Hetero)sexual Difference," reads queer and trans traversals of fantasies in two fictional narratives featuring immigrants to the United States: Treut's *The Virgin Machine* and Mitchell's *Hedwig and the Angry Inch*. Both of these narratives traverse the fantasies of (hetero)sexual difference and romantic love while also engaging the fantasies motivating their protagonists' migrations. Whereas *The Virgin Machine* refuses to present migration as utopian and rejects the fantasy of a rootless queer nation, *Hedwig* repudiates its protagonist's fantasy that leaving the Eastern Bloc would be inherently freeing. In so doing, these films challenge simplistic ideas about gender, sexuality, and nationality.

Chapter 6, "Traversing North America, Traversing (Hetero)sexual Difference," analyzes three queer texts navigating oppositions that often structure our understanding of North America: Anzaldúa's *Borderlands/La Frontera* and *Light in the Dark/Luz en lo Oscuro*; and Lawlor's *Paul Takes the Form of a Mortal Girl*.

The first section places *Queer Traversals*' re-envisioning of Lacan in dialogue with Anzaldúa's embodied, intersectional, feminist, and queer experimental writing to argue that her analysis heralds traversals of the fantasy of (hetero) sexual difference and of linguistic, ethnic, and national divisions. The second section concerns *Paul*, which returns to the 1990s and features a shape-shifting protagonist whose peregrinations across the United States complicate urban and rural understandings of queerness. Demonstrating the inadequacy of existing gender and sexual identities, Lawlor's novel repudiates the idea that romantic fantasy should structure desire, and rejects all available queer subject positions. By the end of Chapters 5 and 6, readers are left contemplating a future in which desire's and gender's trajectories open onto various things "beautiful and new" yet unrevealed.

The Coda, "Traversing the Fantasy of Authoritarian Patriarchy," returns to *Queer Traversals*' opening: to the resurgence of authoritarian patriarchy—and the recent backlash against several decades' worth of queer and trans activism—in the twenty-first century's second decade. While gesturing to the global rise of authoritarianism, the Coda analyzes the politics of gender, sexuality, race, ethnicity, and nation in the United States under President Trump before and during the Covid-19 pandemic. If (hetero)sexual difference is indeed a fantasy available for traversal, these developments point to the challenges involved in moving from individual to broader societal transformation.

Notes

1. https://www.newwaysministry.org/wp-content/uploads/2019/06/Male-and-Female-Document-June-10-2019.pdf?fbclid=IwAR2srbdxtNrPdGbvQKWuVsaf3h6ZL0GYGDaqsICRGW9sdT4-toAv4R9Zk0k.
2. See Fausto-Sterling (2000) and Kessler (1998) for discussion of the intersexed persons whose existence demonstrates the fictitiousness of the claim that there are only two "sexes."
3. As Alenka Zupančič observes, Christianity is saturated with images of polymorphous perversity undercutting this ideology, from instances "of canonized saints eating the excrements of another person" to other "objects related to different partial drives" such as "Saint Agatha's cut-off breast and Saint Lucy's gouged-out eyes" (Zupančič 2017: 13). For Zupančič, this imagery shows that the "norm" conceals "the *ontological negativity* of sexuation and sexuality as such" (Zupančič 2017: 16).

4   See Chiesa (2016), Dean (2000a), Gherovici (2010), Millot (1990), Morel (2000), and Shepherdson (2000) for further examples of work using Lacan's conceptualization of sexual difference to pathologize transgender. See Cavanagh (2015), Cavanagh (2016), Cavanagh (2018), Gherovici (2012), Gherovici (2014), Gherovici (2017), Gherovici (2019a), Gherovici (2019b), and Gozlan (2015) for trans-affirmative reinflections of Lacan challenging Millot.
5   See, for example, Sheila Cavanagh (2017), Patricia Gherovici (2010, 2017), Oren Gozlan (2015), and Gayle Salamon (2010).
6   Roof offers a helpful intervention into the confused state of English-language discourse about the distinct concepts of gender and sexual difference but regrettably lapses into a hostile dismissal of non-binary subjectivities that are increasingly assumed by "[y]ounger 'queer' advocates of whatever ilk" (Roof 2016: 247).
7   See also Roof (2016: 243).
8   Pamela Caughie notes that in recent years "the French, for whom the word 'genre' (gender) refers not to sexuality but to linguistics, have begun to use 'transgenre' to translate the English 'transgender'" (Caughie 2013: 502). At the time of this writing, this welcome development has not yet arrived in Lacanian approaches to transgender.
9   See Roudinesco for discussion of Lacan's critique of ego psychology's normalizing practices (Roudinesco 1990: 270–6; Roudinesco 1997: 250–2).
10 For further explanation of the concept of the "fundamental fantasy," see Ruti (2008a) and Ruti (2010).
11 See, for instance, Butler (1990, 1993, and 2004). While it is easy to find support in *Seminar III* for her reading of the symbolic order as heteronormative—Lacan's discourse is at its most homophobic in that seminar, invoking phrases such as "sexual normalization"—he moves away from these concepts in his subsequent work, as Roudinesco demonstrates (Lacan 1993: 189; Roudinesco 1990: 270–6; Roudinesco 1997: 250–2). Moreover, he eventually revised his early account of signification, as Pluth (2007) shows. Žižek's reactions to Butler have further polarized this debate, as he relies heavily on Lacan's account of sexual difference in *Seminar XX* without discussing the implications of the psychoanalyst's move away from terms such as "the symbolic" in this phase of his work. For Žižek's responses to Butler, see Žižek (2000a), Žižek (2000b), Žižek (2000c), and Žižek (1999). For Butler's replies to Žižek, see Butler (1993), Butler (2000a), Butler (2000b), and Butler (2000c).
12 For examples of contemporary Lacanians' insistence on sexual difference's foundational role, see Copjec (1994 and 2010); and Žižek (2000a, 2000b, 2000c, and 1999). These two theorists have sustained a dispute with Butler over the status of sexual difference. Butler sees sexual difference as symbolic and available for

resignification, whereas Copjec and Žižek view it as Real and intractable. As I argue in Chapter 1, traversing the fantasy of (hetero)sexual difference would obviate this disagreement by targeting both orders.

13 Lacan discusses fantasy's traversal most extensively in *Seminar XI* (Lacan 1977) and *Seminar XXIII* (Lacan 2016). For a detailed explication of this theory, see Chiesa (2007) and Ruti (2008a). Žižek (1989) develops his own politically inflected theory of traversing the fantasy. Chiesa (2007), Pluth (2007), Ruti (2008a), and Stavrakakis (1999) offer divergent accounts of what may follow an analysand's traversal of the fantasy—a concept that, as Chiesa observes, is not fully developed in Lacan's thought.

14 Traversing the fantasy is thus a far more viable strategy for change than Butler's argument for symbolic resignification.

15 See Seshadri-Crooks (2000) and Viego (2007) for Lacanian theories of race that assume sexual difference to be foundational.

16 See Penney (2014), pp. 145–74, for further critique of *Beyond Sexuality*.

17 See Elliot and Roen (1998) for an early trans-affirmative Lacanian perspective. Prosser's *Second Skins* (1998) engages Lacan without advancing a Lacanian argument.

18 For trans critiques of the latter, see Prosser (1998) and Stryker (2004).

19 See Stavrakakis (1999) for a lengthy argument that fantasy's traversal does not result in utopias and that utopian thinking is driven by fantasy.

1

Queering Žižek

Queer theorists have long had a vexed relationship to Slavoj Žižek, whose work has attracted considerable criticism from Judith Butler's *Bodies That Matter* (1993) to Jack Halberstam's *The Queer Art of Failure* (2011) and others' writings.[1] Despite these critiques, a revised version of Žižek's theoretical framework would be useful for queer theory because his politically oriented psychoanalysis offers strategies for altering existing social structures. Bringing Jacques Lacan's account of subjectivity and the social to bear on cultural and political concerns, Žižek asks how existing ideological formations are constituted and how they might be transformed. He adapts Lacan's theory of the interlocking imaginary, symbolic, and Real orders to account for the way fantasies and desiring subjectivities arise through engagement with existing social formations. Within the Lacanian triad, the Real is the deepest source of psychical resistance and therefore, for Žižek, the order in which intervention must happen for change to succeed. He proposes a politicized twist on Lacan's argument that the goal of analysis is for the analysand to traverse and thereby go beyond the fantasies animating subjectivity. Whereas the point of traversing the fantasy in the clinic is to open up alternative ways of structuring individual experience, for Žižek its objective is to reconfigure the symbolic by intervening in the Real and prompting social change.

The argument that traversing the fantasy can rearticulate the Real can be reframed as useful to queer theory's goal of fundamentally transforming the social, despite Žižek's hostility to poststructural queer theory. Queer people stand among those Žižek has "not deemed useful enough to be preserved or retained"—albeit not, as Butler claims, as the unsymbolizable Real (Ahmed 2019: 20). I nonetheless contend that his work remains useful for queer theory, in Sara Ahmed's sense of "queer use as reuse... for a purpose that is 'very different' from that which was 'originally intended'" (Ahmed 2019: 198–9). Arguing for uses of Lacan that Žižek would likely refuse, this chapter rearticulates the latter's ideas in queer-positive terms, clearing one of psychoanalysis' "fainter trails" that adapts Lacan's thinking for queer and trans-affirmative ends (Ahmed 2019: 20).

Žižek's insistence that sexual difference is Real and thus intractable has been a stumbling block for queer theorists interested in developing an account of subjectivity that apprehends desire's workings across the full range of genders and sexualities. This position has animated a longstanding dispute with Butler. Whereas she interprets Lacanian sexual difference as a binary opposition located in the symbolic and therefore available for resignification, Žižek insists that it is instead an antagonism in the Real, and therefore immovable.[2] Žižek also notes that its inevitable failure produces myriad sexual possibilities, including queer ones. Although James Penney rightfully asserts that Žižek "decisively 'won'" the debate with Butler, this chapter pushes past it by turning Žižek against himself in the service of—rather than in opposition to—the aims of queer theory he and Penney critique (Penney 2014: 47).

Žižek's interpretations of sexual difference's intractability are problematic. Notwithstanding the potentially queer effects of its failure, its underpinnings are defined heterosexually, according to the logic I describe in the Introduction as (hetero)sexual difference. Joan Copjec similarly promulgates this account of (hetero)sexual difference in *Read My Desire* (1994), which—as Adrian Johnston notes—questionably argues that Kant's "antinomies" anticipate Lacan's theory of sexuation despite not making any "explicit references to... sexuality or gender identity" (Johnston 2008: 28). Nonetheless, in *Sex and the Failed Absolute*, Žižek repeats and expands upon Copjec's argument (Žižek 2019a: 107–18). However, their interpretation of sexual difference as an antinomy resulting in "the deadlock of sexed being" mobilizes a circular logic conflating sex with gender and conceiving of desire in heterosexual terms, even if—as Copjec and Žižek claim—sexual difference's failures animate sexual diversity (Johnston 2008: 28).

It is important to understand that Žižek reiterates this ideology within a body of writing that has a different aim than that of other Lacanian work, for he does not seek to explicate the "true" meaning of Lacan's texts. Instead, he grafts the psychoanalyst's ideas into new philosophical and political contexts to alter existing social formations. This chapter, too, is not a return to a "true" or "pure" Lacan but rather a queer reworking of Žižek. By exploiting ways Žižek's argument for sexual difference's intransigence undoes itself, I turn his political version of Lacan's theory of traversing the fantasy against itself to argue that it is possible to go beyond (hetero)sexual difference. Despite Žižek's protestations to the contrary, (hetero)sexual difference is a fantasy Lacanian psychoanalytic theory needs to traverse to fully register the many possible configurations of desiring subjectivities. Doing so also opens up possibilities for understanding other axes of identity—such as gender, race, ethnicity, and nationality—as operating "beside" or even independently of (hetero)sexual difference in subjective formation (Sedgwick 2003: 8).

(Hetero)sexual Difference and the Real

I emphasize the need to traverse the fantasy of (hetero)sexual difference because such a move dislodges the *point de capiton* quilting the imaginary, symbolic, and Real. In Lacanian theory, these three orders are inextricable. Though the imaginary can be roughly described as the realm of the specular image and the symbolic as that of the signifier, they are bound up in one another. Lacan explains that within "the symbolic matrix in which the *I* is precipitated in a primordial form," imaginary identification "situates" yet alienates the ego through the subject's *mis*recognition of his or her mirror image (Lacan 2006e: 76). The symbolic—the realm of the signifier, the big Other, and the law—is linked to the Real, a concept that has been the site of frequent conceptual misprisions in debates over sexual difference. As Charles Shepherdson and Bruce Fink observe, the Real has two distinct but related meanings for Lacan, one "presymbolic" and the other "postsymbolic" (Shepherdson 2008: 27). Shepherdson explains that the process of "symbolic retroaction"—Freudian *Nachträglichkeit*—produces the former as a mythological effect of the latter (Shepherdson 2008: 37, 47). Whereas the presymbolic Real is a "hypothesis" formulated in the symbolic's terms, the postsymbolic Real "is characterized by impasses and impossibilities due to the relations among the elements of the symbolic order itself" (Fink 1995: 27). My own use of the term "Real" references its postsymbolic sense. This Real is not radically unreachable by the symbolic but rather, as Copjec points out, the site at which the failures of symbolic mandates are inscribed (Copjec 1994: 201–36).

Žižek's own inflection of Lacan turns on the three orders' inextricability but also on the possibility of transforming their coordinates by altering the *point de capiton*. As Mari Ruti explains, for Lacan the fundamental fantasy—the unconscious fantasy structuring experience—drives psychical life and "perpetuate[s] unconscious patterns of behavior" constricting the subject (Ruti 2008a: 498). Psychoanalysis's objective is to traverse this fantasy and attenuate its grip on the psyche. Grafting this theory into the realm of politics, Žižek argues that by targeting the quilting point, traversing the fantasy seeks not to undo the subject's surface-level "*symbolic identification*," but to gain "distance towards"—and ultimately go beyond—the underlying, "*fundamental fantasy that serves as the ultimate support of the subject's being*" (Žižek 1999: 266).

This involves an intervention in the Real that prompts a radical divestiture in the terms governing the symbolic order and that clears ground for them to be supplanted by a new paradigm. I will explain the technical workings of this process further as my argument proceeds.

At this point, I will note that traversing the fantasy offers a more trenchant challenge to the symbolic's coordinates than Butler's argument (first put forth in *Gender Trouble* [Butler 1990] and refined in *Bodies That Matter* [Butler 1993]) that it is possible to change the symbolic order by resignifying its phallogocentric terms.[3] As Žižek, Penney, and others observe, a central problem with Butler's strategy—and reading of Lacan—is that it engages only the symbolic and imaginary but not the Real.[4] By contrast, traversing the fantasy unsettles the symbolic, imaginary, *and* Real by dislodging the *point de capiton*.

Like Žižek, Butler is concerned with the interplay between psychical and social resistance, and with the way—as they and Ernesto Laclau put it in the introduction to *Contingency, Hegemony, Universality*—"new social movements often rely on identity-claims, but 'identity' itself is never fully constituted; in fact, since identification is not reducible to identity, it is important to consider the incommensurability or gap between them" (Butler, Laclau, and Žižek 2000: 1). My argument for queering Žižek carries forward this joint project of *undercutting* categories of identity that *Contingency* shares with queer theory, which initially emerged as a challenge to identity-based formations of "gay and lesbian studies." While uneven in its grasp of the particulars of Lacan's thought, queer theory aligns with his work in this persistent *refusal* of stable identity. If Butler, Laclau, and Žižek agree that social movements cannot remain "democratic" without engaging "the negativity at the heart of identity," however, they disagree significantly about that negativity's form and consequences (Butler, Laclau, and Žižek 2000: 2).

Butler often presents negativity as the result of the imaginary undercutting of symbolic law. She focuses on those two orders in critiquing Lacanian arguments that the psyche is capable of resistance, and rightfully notes that symbolic mandates' failure does not ensure their transformation. However, she assumes that "Lacan restricts the notion of social power to the symbolic domain and delegates resistance to the imaginary" (Butler 1997: 98). Arguing that the *imaginary* "thwarts the efficacy of the symbolic law, but cannot turn back upon the law, demanding or effecting its reformulation," she concludes that "psychic resistance thwarts the law in its effects, but cannot redirect the law or its effects" (Butler 1997: 98). She thereby downplays the potential for transformation via the Real, which is quilted to the other two orders and is the deepest source of resistance.[5]

When Butler addresses the negativity at play in Laclau's and Žižek's accounts of the Real, she emphasizes that order's role as "the limit-point of all subject-formation"—as "the point where self-representation founders and fails" (Butler 2000c: 29–30).[6] Reading the Real in Žižek as "that which resists symbolization" (Butler 1993: 21) and as the "limit-point of sociality" (Butler 2000a: 152), she asks,

> why are we compelled to give a technical name to this limit, "the Real", and to make the further claim that the subject is constituted by its foreclosure? The use of the technical nomenclature opens up more problems than it solves. On the one hand, we are to accept that "the Real" means nothing other than the constitutive limit of the subject; yet on the other hand, why is it that any effort to refer to the constitutive limit of the subject in ways that do not use that nomenclature are considered a failure to understand its proper operation? Are we using the categories to understand the phenomena, or marshaling the phenomena to shore up categories "in the name of the Father", if you will?
> (Butler 2000a: 152)

While Butler is right to question the tautological logic through which Žižek and other Lacanians prop up the law of the Father and its corollary, (hetero) sexual difference, through appeals to the Real, the questions of terminology at stake in their disagreement are more significant than she suggests. In the above passage, she misinterprets and misuses Lacan's concept of "foreclosure," as I argue in *Insane Passions* (Coffman 2006: 18–22). In *Seminar III*, Lacan uses the term "foreclosure" to refer to a psychotic's rejection of the primal signifier anchoring the symbolic and grounding "normal" subjectivity. In *Bodies That Matter*, Butler correctly notes that foreclosure happens to *signifiers*: she writes that "what is foreclosed is a signifier, namely, that which has been symbolized" (Butler 1993: 204). However, she goes on to generalize that mechanism as foundational to all forms of subjectivity rather than as specific to psychosis: she writes that foreclosure "takes place within the symbolic order as a policing of the borders of intelligibility" (Butler 1993: 204). This claim misses *Seminar III*'s presentation of foreclosure as the governing mechanism of *psychosis*—not necessarily of *all* forms of subjectivity. Upon this error Butler builds a case that the symbolic order *itself* is capable of effecting foreclosures that consign queer bodies to the unsymbolizable Real (Coffman 2006: 18–22).[7] In the above passage from *Contingency*, this difficulty leads Butler erroneously to conceptualize the Real as *itself* foreclosed.

Similar misprisions inform Butler's claim that Žižek renders those who do not conform to hegemonic definitions of gender the unlivable, "permanent outside" of the social and figures "a whole domain of social life that does not fully conform to prevalent gender norms as psychotic and unlivable" (Butler 1994: 37). She justifiably questions the presuppositions through which Lacan's *Seminar III* defines the symbolic as the realm of paternal law in which the subject is constituted by taking the Name of the Father as a metaphor for his own being, subjecting himself to phallic signification and the law of castration. This account implies that to "foreclose" the Name of the Father, rejecting phallic primacy and sidestepping (hetero)sexual difference, is to court psychosis characterized by the delusional return in the Real of inversions of normative genders and sexualities. Butler's critique of this theory fuels her argument that Žižek, in *The Sublime Object of Ideology* (1989), rigidifies sexual difference as the "rock of the real" consigning queers to the social's "permanent outside" (Butler 1993: 197; Butler 1994: 37).

Although Butler's concerns about Žižek's account of sexual difference are well justified, problems arise in her construal of the Real as the realm of psychosis. First, by equating the Real with "abject" queer bodies, she attempts to symbolize the unsymbolizable. As Tim Dean points out, "[t]he theory that attributes to the real specific social and sexual positions is Butler's own, since Lacan characterizes the real as asubstantial, unsexed, and ungendered" (Dean 2000a: 210). Second, Butler misreads Lacan's account of psychotic "foreclosure"; her conflation of the Real with psychosis results from this error (Coffman 2006: 18–22). Though in psychosis, the Real is the realm in which the foreclosed signifier returns, the Real is not equivalent to psychosis. To the contrary: for Lacan, even "normal" subjectivity is anchored by interlocking the imaginary, symbolic, and Real. As Malcolm Bowie notes, the principal difference between the psychotic and the "normal" subject is that for the former, the relationship between the three orders becomes incoherent as the result of a "mispositioning of Subject and Other" in which the "imaginary becomes real… by passing through the symbolic dimension without being submitted to its exactions and obliquities" (Bowie 1991: 109). In this account, the queer appears as psychotic only if the Name of the Father remains the anchor of the symbolic order and the signifier the psychotic forecloses.

Yet to state—as Lacanians such as Žižek often do—that the Real is the site at which the symbolic *fails* is not the same as to say that the Real is constituted through *foreclosure* in the technical sense. Moreover, to argue that foreclosed signifiers return in the Real or that the symbolic fails there is not to say that the Real is reducible to those phenomena. As Penney notes, Butler's critique reflects "a misapprehension of the relation between the symbolic and the real," the latter of which "manifests the symbolic law's own externality to itself, its self-difference" (Penney 2014: 60). Because "[t]he real imposes as the symbolic order's destiny the ceaseless repetition of its failure to totalize itself in such a way that it might impose a normative matrix for both sexual identity and kinship relations," it does not necessarily shut down theorizations of diverse sexualities; instead, it actively facilitates "the subversion of normativity," sexual or otherwise (Penney 2014: 60).

Butler also overlooks the Real's potential for facilitating transformative resistance, even though she is right to argue that it is problematic to insist—as Žižek often does—that the Name of the Father must always be the primal signifier. Moreover, she is well justified in criticizing the circular claim that sexual difference is permanently inscribed in the Real because of paternal law's presumed inalterability. These assertions have pernicious consequences for theorizations of same-gender desire and transgender subjectivities. But as I will go on to show, the central problem Žižek's work poses for queer theory is that he resists the possibility that the Name of the Father might be supplanted by another master signifier and that sexual difference, too, might be ideologically contingent—not that he situates negativity in the Real or that the Real is radically unchangeable.

Whereas Butler sees few prospects for a politics of the Real, Žižek offers an account of the Real as the site of both resistance to and possible rearticulation of the terms of the symbolic. For him, traversing the fantasy is crucial to such a transformation. However, despite the potential his work holds for queer theory, Žižek (and similarly minded Lacanians such as Copjec) insists that sexual difference is transhistorical and unchangeable because it is Real.[8] This brings us to a key difference in the significance the term "contingency" takes on in *Contingency*. Whether explicitly (in Laclau's case) or implicitly (in Žižek's), Laclau and Žižek distinguish between contingencies and universalities, whereas Butler considers that everything—including sexual difference—is historically contingent and subject to change. Thus over and against Butler, who assumes that sexual difference is an effect of social structures, Žižek argues that a fundamental antinomy in the Real provides a negative backdrop for a diverse field of contingent empirical possibilities. Criticizing Butler for interpreting sexual difference as a contingent opposition between two positive terms subject to displacement through symbolic resignification, he asserts that sexual difference and the Real are transhistorical and unchangeable. He further claims that it is unfair to charge Lacan and Lacanians with heterosexism because the masculine and feminine positions can be occupied by persons of any gender.[9]

The assertion that these aspects of Lacanian theory obviate critiques of the ideology of (hetero)sexual difference is insufficient, however, for the false naturalization of sexual difference poses significant problems for theorizations of gender and desire.

Such interpretations of Lacanian theory can only conceive of desire as heterogendered—as a matter of an antinomy between masculine and feminine—and so fail to capture the multiplicity of possibilities for genderings and erotic investments. At their worst, they become philosophical pretexts for demonizing queer sexualities and transgender embodiments. For instance, in *Violence: Six Sideways Reflections*, Žižek invokes Alain Badiou to argue that masturbation, homosexuality, and transgender are solipsistic phenomena demonstrating the dangers of the postmodern age's lack of a "Master-Signifier" (Žižek 2008: 34). Even though Žižek does not openly equate this "Master-Signifier" with the Name of the Father, his description smacks of the kind of patriarchal authoritarianism embodied in a "decisive gesture which can never be fully grounded in reasons": the gesture of "a Master" (Žižek 2008: 35). He praises Badiou's use of "gender studies with its obsessive rejection of binary logic" and support for "multiple sexual practices" as an example of the way postmodernism "tolerates no decision, no instance of the Two, no evaluation, in the strong Nietzschean sense of the term" (Žižek 2008: 35).

Progressive Lacanians such as Tim Dean have pushed beyond such readings by observing that in Lacan's account of desire in *Seminar III*, the *objet a*—object-cause of desire—"conceptually precedes gender" and is only subsequently inscribed by a symbolic whose terms and effects are inconsistent (Dean 2000a: 194–7). Dean further notes that "symbolic *castration* is simply a metaphor, based on the resonance of the imaginary phallus," and that there are other ways of "describing the subjective division imposed on us by symbolic existence—*alienation* is one of them" (Dean 2000a: 84–5). Ruti similarly emphasizes that castration and lack are existential. These formulations helpfully stress that the symbolic phallus is only provisional—only a signifier propped up by the imaginary—and so is contingent rather than necessary.

However, work still needs to be done to separate what Dean calls Lacanian theory's "scaffolding"—the claim to the phallic signifier's primacy that has rightly caused feminist and queer suspicion—from the structural elements of Lacan's account of desire that open up possibilities for queer theorizing (Dean 2000a: 47).[10] For instance, Laclau notes that the "'Phallus,' as the signifier of desire, has largely been replaced in Lacan's later teaching by the '*objet petit a*'" (Laclau 2000: 72). However, during this period what Lacan calls "something symbolic of the function of the lack, of the appearance of the phallic ghost" haunts the analogy through which he uses the distortions of a tattoo on an erect penis to explain the shifting gaze's effects. Lacan mentions this tattoo as an example of "*[t]he objet a in the field of the visible*" in anamorphic painting (Lacan 1977: 87–8, 105). While Lacan's invocation of phallic spectrality reveals its status as a second-order symbolic inscription, *Seminar XI* demonstrates his discourse's residual phallogocentrism.

Žižek's and others' insistence that sexual difference is the fundamental antagonism prompting varied symbolic inscriptions is even more pernicious than Lacan's lingering phallogocentrism, however. Such arguments fallaciously assume that (hetero)sexual difference is a motivating fantasy for all people across place and time, upholding a discourse supporting such a fantasy's hegemony by presenting an antagonism between masculine and feminine as the only possibility, however diverse its effects may be. As Butler observes, positing sexual difference as structurally transcendent is theological. The claim to sexual difference's putative universality rests on the assertion of belief rather than on evidence and argumentation (Butler 1997: 120–31; Butler 2004: 46). Such claims create problems for theorizing same-gender desire as anything other than a permutation of (hetero)sexual difference. Moreover, this reasoning leads to an account of the body that elides the existence of intersex persons and pathologizes transgender embodiments.[11] While intersex and transgender subjectivities are distinct from lesbian and gay male subjectivities—and while all identities, those included, are undercut by the gap between identity and identification—the inability of much Lacanian discourse to theorize them adequately is a consequence of the hegemony of the fantasy of (hetero)sexual difference.

The tenuous nature of the ideology of (hetero)sexual difference suggests that it operates within certain Lacanian circles as a fundamental fantasy. I view the most important task of psychoanalytically informed queer theory as that of traversing this fantasy, given its potentially oppressive consequences for queer and trans persons. While Frances Restuccia has similarly suggested that queer theorists such as Leo Bersani, Butler, Dean, Lee Edelman, and David Halperin challenge the fundamental fantasy that she—following Edelman—describes as "reproductive heterosexual normality," existing work in queer theory has yet to dislodge the ideological kernel keeping that fantasy in place (Restuccia 2002: 94).[12] That kernel is the doctrine of sexual difference.

Despite Žižek's claims to the contrary, his politicization of Lacan's theory of fantasy's traversal offers a means of rearticulating the Real and grafting Lacanian theory into contexts other than those governed by (hetero)sexual difference. Doing so makes it possible to rework Lacanian theory to revise and expand psychoanalytic accounts of gender and sexuality. Moreover, doing so makes it possible to theorize other aspects of identity—such as gender, race, ethnicity, and nationality—as primary rather than secondary influences that can operate alongside or supplant sexual difference's importance in subjective formation.

Earlier queer Lacanian work does not argue that (hetero)sexual difference is a fundamental fantasy available for traversal. Instead, scholars such as Lynda Hart, George Haggerty, and Valerie Rohy invoke the Real to analyze queer representation. In *Impossible Women* (2000), for example, Rohy uses Lacan and Žižek to argue that lesbianism works analogously to the Real by functioning as "the limit of symbolization, the 'rock' on which figurality founders" (Rohy 2000: 23). And for Haggerty in *Queer Gothic* (2006), Žižek demonstrates that "[i]f 'what was foreclosed from the Symbolic returns in the Real of the symptom,' then... woman returns as the symptom of man... [and] the predatory homosexual, foreclosed from the symbolic,... return[s] as the symptom of a culture so caught up in its own sexuality that it cannot see its sexual obsessions for what they are" (Haggerty 2006: 189). Similarly, for Hart in *Fatal Women* (1994), the Real is the site at which heterosexist societies render the lesbian unrepresentable. She asserts that "in the psychoanalytic symbolic," and in society more generally, "lesbians are only possible in/as the 'Real,' since they are foreclosed from the Symbolic order" (Hart 1994: 84; Hart 1998: 91).[13] In these formulations, the Real is construed at best as a means of elucidating homophobia's structural mechanisms and effects (Rohy, Haggerty).

Although in *Between the Body and the Flesh* (1998), Hart engages Lacan's theory of traversing the fundamental fantasy, she stresses that that fantasy's traversal could help lesbian sadomasochists transcend oppressive patriarchal and lesbian-feminist cultures. Although she suggests via Anna Freud that (hetero)sexual difference could be traversed, she does not explore that possibility's implications (Hart 1998: 30). By contrast, Edelman's *No Future* (2006) goes well beyond Hart, Haggerty, and Rohy by employing the Real not only to elucidate homophobia's mechanisms but also to undermine their force. Edelman contends that queers can collapse the social order by traversing the fantasy of "reproductive futurism" and embracing the role of the *sinthomo*sexual, who rejects symbolic politics' orientation toward a better future by embracing the drive's *jouissance* in the Real (Edelman 2004: 28). In so doing, he repudiates Butler's interpretation of Žižek and her optimistic argument that queers can resignify the symbolic. However, as I argue at greater length in Chapter 2,

Edelman's book overlooks the way not only reproductive futurism but also (hetero) sexual difference might be a fantasy Lacanian theory needs to traverse.

Moreover, Edelman's relentlessly nihilistic book overlooks Žižek's highly political orientation and the ambivalent mix of pessimism and optimism at play in his reworking of Lacan's theory of fantasy's traversal. Both Michael Snediker (2009) and Ruti (2008b, 2017) have criticized *No Future* for its excessively negative interpretation of Lacan. And though Ed Pluth (2007) makes a similar assertion about Žižek, I find more cause for optimism in his theories than in the use to which Edelman puts them in *No Future*.[14] The optimism in Žižek's work is not to be found in a naïve vision of a better future—an attitude Edelman rightfully skewers—but rather in what Snediker identifies in *Queer Optimism* (2009) as "immanence" (Snediker 2009: 3). Whereas for Snediker, optimism can be found in brief moments of "positive" affect, in Žižek's theory, this potential lies in the unpredictable, ground-clearing process of fantasy's traversal (Snediker 2009: 3). Žižek's commitment to politics animates his argument that by traversing the fantasy, an act in the Real *can* prompt symbolic changes by altering the *point de capiton*: an aspect of his theory Edelman ignores. In the close reading of Žižek that follows, I create an opening for a different mode of Žižekian queer politics: one focused on the possibility of altering the symbolic through intervention in the Real.

The Radical Contingency of (Hetero)sexual Difference

In *Sublime Object*, Žižek considers the potential the symbolic's failures in the Real create for social change by cross-reading what Lacan (in *Seminar XI*) calls the anamorphic "stain" through what he (in *Seminar III*) calls the *point de capiton*, which quilts the imaginary and symbolic with the Real. In *The Ticklish Subject* (1999), he concurs with Butler that imaginary resistance is a "false transgression that reasserts the symbolic status quo and even serves as a positive condition of its functioning" (Žižek 1999: 262). However, he distinguishes imaginary resistance, which manifests clinically in the transference, from the sociopolitical resistance available at the intersection of the symbolic and the Real (Žižek 1999: 262). Žižek claims that the latter can take place through an "actual symbolic rearticulation via the intervention of the Real of an act," through which a "new *point de capiton* emerges" to displace the socio-symbolic field and change its structuring principle (Žižek 1999: 262). In *Sublime Object*, he explains that the "tautological, performative operation" halts and fixes "free floating... ideological elements" into a "network of meaning" structured around lack as the *point de capiton* (Žižek 1989: 99, 87). Žižek's claim usefully opens up the possibility of the symbolic's wholesale transformation.

In *Sublime Object*, Žižek explicitly identifies the *point de capiton* with the Name of the Father and paternal law, but fails to recognize that his own theory makes them available for transformation. Instead, he remains faithful to the father and (hetero)sexual difference. In *Undoing Gender* (2004), Butler points out that Lacanians' insistence that "'It [sexual difference] is the law!' becomes the utterance that performatively attributes the very force to the law that the law itself is said to exercise" (Butler 2004: 46). She observes that the claim that "'It is the law' is... a sign of allegiance to the law, a sign of the desire for the law to be the indisputable law," and observes that this "theological impulse within the theory of psychoanalysis... seeks to put out of play any criticism of the symbolic father, the law of psychoanalysis itself" (Butler 2004: 46). These assertions constrain possibilities for gender and sexuality by continuing to subject them to paternal law.

Whereas Butler's critique of Lacanians' performative utterances fails to engage the Real and therefore to offer a viable strategy for transformation, Žižek's argument in *Ticklish Subject* for supplanting the *point de capiton* with a new master signifier holds out the possibility of radically abandoning paternal law: even though he refuses to acknowledge as much. If we understand Lacan's assertion of paternal law as a gesture that installs the Name of the Father and its corollaries not as timeless but as contingent, we open up new, potentially non-phallogocentric ways of thinking of the law grounding the symbolic. Kaja Silverman argues that in Lacan's *Seminar XI*, the Name of the Father appears as "one of the signifiers that impart a retroactive significance to the lack introduced by language, rather than as a timeless Law that will always preside over the operations of desire" (Silverman 1992: 112). Shanna Carlson similarly explains that Lacan's theory of linguistic castration distinguishes "between representations of castration and the structural fact of castration" (de la Torre 2018: 10).[15] Citing Tracy McNulty, Carlson clarifies that this distinction enables us to "extract the concept of the symbolic from the institutions, norms, and prohibitions that represent it," exposing "its structural dimension" (de la Torre 2018: 7). If we understand Lacan's assertions about paternal law and the phallus through Silverman and Carlson—as identifying contingent signifiers and representations filling the gap opened by "the structural fact" of castration—Žižek's argument that the symbolic can wholly be rearticulated through the "Real of an act" suggests that the Name of the Father could be supplanted by another signifier and the symbolic restructured according to a law that would not necessarily be paternal or beholden to the phallus (Žižek 1999: 262).

While Žižek's allowance for possible rearticulations of the *point de capiton* makes the prospect of supplanting the Name of the Father thinkable, other aspects of his work resist that very possibility. His logic in *Ticklish Subject* and *Contingency* is characterized by a contradictory movement that both reinscribes sexual difference as a foundational doctrine and raises the possibility of rearticulations of the symbolic that explicitly contest the priority of the Law of the Father. As Butler persuasively argues in *Bodies That Matter*, Lacan's argument in "The signification of the phallus" both opens up and precludes the phallus's transferability. Similarly, Žižek's reasoning in *Contingency* both opens up and precludes the possibility of revoking the phallic signifier's privilege. Thus any attempt to enlist his ideas for queer theory must first work through his resistance to contesting sexual difference's priority.

Even though he argues that it is possible to rearticulate the *point de capiton* and completely overhaul the symbolic, Žižek continues to insist on sexual difference's primacy, falsely elevating its status to what Butler calls an unchangeable, phallogocentric "'law' *prior* to all ideological formations" (Butler 1993: 196). In *Ticklish Subject*, for example, he insists on the intractability of (an always already failed) sexual difference over and against the more progressive readings his theory of "symbolic rearticulation" could enable (Žižek 1999: 262). Assuming heterosexuality to be paradigmatic, he asserts that what Lacan calls the "impossibility of the sexual relationship" lies "in the fact that the identity of each of the two sexes is hampered from within by the antagonistic relationship to the other sex which prevents its full actualization" (Žižek 1999: 272). This formulation of sexual difference as "the Real of an antagonism, not the Symbolic of a differential opposition" continues to privilege the antinomy of sexual difference, if only through its negation (Žižek 1999: 272). This formulation's heterosexism is evident in Žižek's framing of sexuality as an antagonism between "the two sexes" as well as in his mournful suggestion that the Law of the Father's decline "entails the malfunctioning of 'normal' sexuality and the rise of sexual indifference" (Žižek 1999: 272, 367).

However, in *Contingency*, Žižek positions the Real as site of failure in terms of sexual difference, and claims that

> for Lacan, sexual difference is not a firm set of symbolic oppositions and inclusions/exclusions (heterosexual normativity which relegates homosexuality and other "perversions" to some secondary role), but the name of a deadlock, of a trauma, of an open question, of something that resists every attempt at

its symbolization. Every translation of sexual difference into a set of symbolic opposition(s) is doomed to fail, and it is this very "impossibility" that opens up the terrain of the hegemonic struggle for what "sexual difference" will mean.
(Žižek 2000a: 110–11)

Because every attempt to symbolize the fundamental antagonism as an opposition between masculine and feminine inevitably fails, Žižek allows that positive manifestations of sexual difference could be sites of hegemonic struggle: which could include opposition to heterosexual dominance. In the above formulation, he sidesteps binary formulations of sexual difference—which he characterizes as merely "a deadlock, a trauma, ... an open question"—and allows for contestation over its positive meaning. What he still misses, however, is that his insistence upon calling this antagonism "sexual difference"—rather than merely "difference," for example—is misleading.

Similarly, in *Tarrying with the Negative* (1993d), Žižek draws on Lacan's sexuation diagrams to conceive of sexual difference as a Kantian antinomy. Rather than allowing "us to imagine in a consistent way the universe as a Whole," as does the binary logic of all-encompassing oppositions, viewing sexual difference as an antinomy presents us with the simultaneous and contradictory presence of two "mutually exclusive versions of the universe as a Whole" (Žižek 1993d: 83). For Žižek, the value of considering sexual difference in this fashion is that it allows us to view it not as "the polar opposition of two cosmic forces (yin/yang, etc.)" but as "a certain crack which prevents us from even consistently imagining the universe as a Whole" (Žižek 1993d: 83). In *The Indivisible Remainder* (1996), he further explains that

> What the Lacanian "formulas of sexuation" endeavor to formulate... is not yet another positive formulation of the sexual difference but the underlying impasse that generates the multitude of positive formulations as so many (failed) attempts to symbolize the traumatic real of the sexual difference. What all epochs have in common is not some universal positive feature, some transhistorical constant; what they all share, rather, is the same deadlock, the same antinomy.
> (Žižek 1996: 217)

The notion that empirical data are mere covers for a more fundamental fissure in the universe presents an alternative to the more common claim that it is organized through binary oppositions producing a false sense of totality. This approach accounts for much of the appeal of Žižek's thought. However, questions remain about the way he conceives of the fundamental antagonism he believes to provide a negative, structural backdrop for empirical reality.

Though in the above passage from *Indivisible Remainder* Žižek acknowledges the multiplicity of past and present genders, his references to "*the* sexual difference" are symptoms of a blockage in his own thinking about it (Žižek 1996: 217, emphasis added). The word "the" implies that the "fundamental antagonism" is mobilized by a singular split rather than by multiple fractures. His insistence on this point is peculiar given his openness elsewhere to considering forms of antagonism—nationalism and ethnic hatred, for example—that can be driven by more than two divergent points of view.[16] In *Contingency*, he presents both sexual difference and national difference as divisions that are falsely naturalized as causes for what he views as a more "fundamental antagonism" that cannot itself be symbolized (Žižek 2000a: 112–14).

At other points, Žižek even takes the antinomy of sexual difference as a model for other forms of fundamental antagonism he conceives as sites of ideological struggle and transformation. In *Contingency*, he uses ideological differences to exemplify the fundamental antagonism's effects, explaining that "the notion of antagonism involves a kind of metadifference: the two antagonistic poles differ in the very way in which they define or perceive the difference that separates them (for a Leftist, the gap that separates him from a Rightist is not the same as *this same gap* perceived from the Rightist's point of view)" (Žižek 2000b: 215). Jodi Dean similarly observes that for Žižek, antinomy underpins class struggle (Dean 2006a: 57–60).

Yet curiously, Žižek resists considering sexual difference as subject to the same kinds of transformations he would allow for similarly positioned political struggles. While he views the fundamental antagonisms underpinning other sorts of struggles as available for wholesale transformation, he does not question the presupposition of paternal law through which he inscribes the antagonism of sexual difference as fundamentally inalterable. Staging sexual difference as exempt from transformation contradicts his claims about the potential for radical overhauls of other political antagonisms. This formulation also questionably assumes that other divisions—such as those concerning race, ethnicity, nationality, or social class—are secondary to sexual difference in subjective formation.

Moreover, posing the fundamental antagonism as a matter of the inevitable failure of the masculine and the feminine to understand each other entails presenting the problem of sexual difference in heterosexual terms, even though masculinity and femininity are not ideals but sites of failure. This formulation continues to ignore Žižek's complicity in upholding the Name of the Father and the reign of paternal law by insisting on sexual difference's primacy. Though Žižek rightfully observes that theorists such as Butler mistake the negative space of antagonism for a positive terrain of social contestation by viewing sexual difference as a potential site of ideological struggle and transformation, he refuses to consider that a change in *point de capiton* could radically overhaul it.

Yet to the displacement of which master signifier *other* than the phallus—which Lacan famously designates "*the privileged signifier* of this mark in which the role [*part*] of Logos is wedded to the advent of desire"—could Žižek possibly be referring when he emphasizes the possibility of rearticulating the symbolic's structuring principle through a change in *point de capiton*? (Lacan 2006g: 581, emphasis added). Interestingly, the overall arguments of *Ticklish Subject* and Žižek's contributions to *Contingency* background castration such that the substitution of another *point de capiton* for the Name of the Father becomes thinkable, even if effectively thwarted by argumentative relapses. In his response to Butler in *Ticklish Subject*, Žižek drops the language he uses in *The Sublime Object* to describe the Real as an unsymbolizable "rock" or "kernel," and instead foregrounds the Real as the site of symbolic mandates' failure (Žižek 2000c: 309; Žižek 1996: 166). This suggests that, contra Butler, we need not read his emphasis on negativity's structuring role as affirming castration's timelessness, even though he reiterates that doctrine in other sections of the book. Instead, following Silverman, we might read Žižek's presupposition in *Sublime Object* of castration's role in structuring sexual difference as the result of installing the Name of the Father as master signifier (Silverman 1992: 112).

In *The Metastases of Enjoyment* (1994b), Žižek comes close to acknowledging sexual difference's tenuousness, but ultimately falls short. Drawing on Lacan's arguments in *Seminar XX*, Žižek writes that

> Apropos of the two asymmetrical antinomies of symbolization (the "masculine" side that involves the universality of phallic function grounded in an exception; the "feminine" side that involves a "non-all" field which, for that very reason, contains no exception to the phallic function) a question imposes itself with a kind of self-evidence: what constitutes the link that connects these two purely logical antinomies with the opposition of female and male, which, however symbolically mediated and culturally conditioned, remains an obvious biological fact? The answer to this question is: *there is no link*. What we experience as "sexuality" is precisely the effect of the contingent act of 'grafting' the fundamental deadlock of symbolization on to the biological opposition of male and female.
>
> (Žižek 1994b: 155)

He reiterates this viewpoint in *Sex and the Failed Absolute*, claiming it to be proven by the fact that "the majority of individuals perceive themselves as (heterosexual) men or women," and contending "that this basic couple is clearly somehow grounded in biology, in the way we humans reproduce" (Žižek 2019a: 131–2). He nonetheless admits that for Lacan, "sexuality is not just a fact of biology but also, primarily even, a fact of psychic and symbolic identification which is at a distance from biology" (Žižek 2019a: 132).

In *Metastases*, Žižek acknowledges that grafting makes the *link* between sexual difference and "biological" sex contingent, but does not press this observation far enough to recognize that grafting makes sexual difference *itself* contingent. This impasse in Žižek's reasoning comes from his continued reiteration of the false notion of binary sex, which facilitates the parallelism involved in "grafting" the antinomy of sexual difference (itself questionably formulated in terms of masculinity and femininity) onto an idea of "sex" misrecognized as natural rather than cultural. His unqualified assertion that "the opposition of female and male" is "an obvious biological fact" ignores a long history of feminist work concerned with intersex persons and other species. This work demonstrates that the binary distinction between "male" and "female" is a social construct maintained both discursively (through the dominance of the false idea that there are only two "sexes") and surgically (through procedures that align intersex children's genital appearance with dominant expectations for "males" and "females").[17] That Žižek has not assimilated this information is especially surprising given his sustained engagement with Butler, who raises this very problem and observes that American feminism draws a false distinction between "sex" as natural and "gender" as cultural even though the concept of "sex," too, is cultural.[18] The false naturalization of "sex" in Žižek's language continues in his assertion that the "parasitic 'grafting' of the symbolic deadlock on to animal coupling undermines the instinctual rhythm of animal coupling and confers on it an indelible brand of failure: 'there is no sexual relationship'; every relationship between the sexes can take place only against the background of a fundamental impossibility" (Žižek 1994b: 155).

As Lacanians are quick to point out, because sexual difference is merely structural, people of any gender can occupy the masculine and feminine positions. Lacan writes in "The Signification of the Phallus" that the "relation of the subject to the phallus is... established without regard to the anatomical difference between *the sexes*," understood as man and woman (282, emphasis added). Žižek and similarly minded Lacanians seize upon this language and formulate sexual difference as an antinomy driving the "relationship between the sexes" (Žižek 1994b: 154–5). Through this maneuver, Žižek's conception of "sex" as the "biological opposition of male and female" becomes particularly insidious once it is *aufgehoben* into a difference that is neither material nor phenomenal but rather a differential opposition between masculine and feminine (Žižek 1994b: 155). Žižek is right that this is not a "gender" difference, for it takes negative rather than positive form. Given its role as that which sets phenomenal reality into motion, we should think of Žižekian sexual difference as that which prompts positive manifestations of gender and sexuality, as Judith Roof argues in *What Gender Is, What Gender Does* (2016). Nonetheless, within Žižek's thought, sexual difference—however Real—is the dialecticized consequence of his false assumptions about binary "sex."

Laclau's intervention in Žižek's debate with Butler over the status of the Real offers another approach to this problem. Like Žižek, Laclau argues that Butler misses the way "the Real becomes a name for the very failure of the Symbolic in achieving its own fullness. The Real would be, in that sense, a retroactive effect of the failure of the symbolic" (Laclau 2000: 68). Laclau further clarifies, however, that the name of the Real thus becomes "both the name of an empty place and the attempt to fill it through that very naming of what, in De Man's words, is nameless, *innommable*. This means that the presence of that name within the system has the status of a suturing *topos*" (Laclau 2000: 68). Drawing on Fink's explanation of the distinction between the "presymbolic real" (R1) and the postsymbolic Real—the latter "characterized by impasses and impossibilities due to the relations among elements of the symbolic order itself (R2), that is, which is generated by the symbolic"—Laclau argues that the postsymbolic Real effects a "hegemonic operation" of suture that "involves both the presence of a Real which subverts signification and the representation of Real through tropological substitution" (Laclau 2000: 68). In my view, what Žižek calls "the contingent act of 'grafting' the fundamental deadlock of symbolization on to the biological opposition of male and female" can be seen as the kind of "suture" Laclau describes (Žižek 1994b: 155). The latter theorist's explanation is crucial to understanding the ideological character of Žižek's claim. The "grafting" he describes is, in Laclau's terms, a "hegemonic operation" using substitution to represent R2 as R1—that is, to suggest that R2 (the aporias produced by the symbolic order's failures) is somehow connected to R1 ("the biological opposition of male and female") (Žižek 1994b: 155).

Curiously, though, when Laclau concurs with Žižek that sexual difference "is linked not to particular sexual roles but to a real/impossible kernel which can enter the field of representation only through tropological displacements/incarnations," he does not point to this operation's suturing effects or role in consolidating hegemony (Laclau 2000: 72). Instead, he claims that

> [i]n terms of the theory of hegemony, this presents a strict homology with the notion of "antagonism" as a real kernel preventing the closure of the symbolic order... antagonisms are not objective relations but the point where the limit of all objectivity is shown. Something at least comparable is involved in Lacan's assertion that there is no such thing as a sexual relationship.
>
> (Laclau 2000: 71)

I have no quarrel with Žižek's and Laclau's insistence that a fundamental antagonism mobilizes the symbolic's failed attempts at coherence. However, they both fail to consider the ideological character of their characterization of desire as driven by "difference" that is consistently brought back—through what Laclau calls the "hegemonic operation" of suture—to a question of failures in what Žižek repeatedly terms the "relationship between the sexes" (Laclau 2000: 68; Žižek 1994b: 155). To choose different diction—to say, for example, that *desire* emerges from a fundamental antagonism, negativity, or trauma—would avoid suturing antagonism's effects to heterosexist conceptions of "sex." But to call this operation sexual difference introduces confusion by recalling a polarity invoking bodily materialities that appear within Žižek's discourse even as he tries to get past them.

Because Žižek fails to see the ideological character of suture's effects, the heterosexism at play in his appeals to sexual difference's supposed unchangeability remains a significant problem in his work. In his diction, relationships are "between the sexes," and this wording matters, because it sets up a parallelism between "female" and "male" and Kant's mathematical ("feminine," to Lacanians) and dynamic ("masculine") antinomies that Žižek uses to position (hetero)sexual difference as Real and beyond dispute (Žižek 1994b: 155). This creates the false impression that as an antinomy, sexual difference—rather than *other* kinds of difference—must be the motivating force behind all forms of desire and their manifestations in sexuality.[19] I use this diction to describe the consequences of Žižek's assumptions and to mark the difference between, on the one hand, Lacanian psychoanalysis's theorization of sexual difference as a negative antagonism motivating *desire*, and on the other hand, the resulting experience of *sexuality* described in positivist terms. The presence of these different vocabularies in the ongoing dialogue between Žižek and queer theorists has muddied the issues considerably. Lost in the resultant fractiousness is the way Žižek's suturing of the masculine and feminine antinomies to binary "sex" causes his account of desire to render many contemporary sexual practices and gender embodiments untheorizable, for they cannot be accounted for as consequences of sexual difference's failure.

First, his theory renders intersex and transgender subjectivities inconceivable by defining the "sexes" as exclusively "female" and "male" (Žižek 1994b: 155). Second, he inaccurately assumes that all sexual encounters are driven by the interplay between masculine and feminine, and renders invisible those sexual practices in which gender embodiment is secondary (some BDSM practices, for example). However, given what we now know about diverse genders and sexualities, whence the assumption that all experiences of desire and embodiment are motivated by sexual difference conceived in such narrow terms? And whence the resistance—manifest in the defensiveness characterizing orthodox Lacanian writing on sexual difference—to the suggestion that it is possible to think otherwise? Žižek's oversights call into question his theory's presumed universality. What might it mean to think of the fundamental antagonism *itself* as motivated by multiple differences rather than by the difference between masculine and feminine?

Moreover, a larger question lies behind Žižek's narrow reasoning about sexual difference: why does symbolization have to be about "sex" at all? Such an assumption is evident in his explication in *Metastases* of the difference between Foucauldian and Lacanian perspectives on "sex":

> It is here that Foucauldian "constructionists" and Lacan part company: for the "constructionists", sex is not a natural given but a *bricolage*, an artificial unification of heterogeneous discursive practices; whereas Lacan rejects this view without returning to naïve substantialism. For him, sexual difference is not a discursive, symbolic construction; instead, it emerges at the very point where symbolization fails: we are sexed beings because symbolization always comes up against its inherent impossibility. What is at stake here is not that "actual", "concrete" sexual beings can never fully fit the symbolic construction of "man" or "woman": the point is, rather, that this symbolic construction itself supplements a certain fundamental deadlock.
>
> (Žižek 1994b: 160)

Although it is quite plausible that sexual difference might be *one* of the differences that could emerge "at the very point where symbolization fails" and that it "supplements a certain fundamental deadlock," there is a logical problem with the assertion that "we are sexed beings *because* symbolization always comes up against its inherent impossibility" (Žižek 1994b: 160, emphasis added). Žižek offers no proof for this circular claim about causality. The same problem besets his rejoinder to Butler's argument that his insistence upon sexual difference's transcendental status creates problems for theorizing intersex subjectivities. Revising one of her formulations, he asserts that "sexual difference has a transcendental status *because* sexed bodies emerge that do not fit squarely within ideal gender dimorphism" (Žižek 2000c: 309). For this, too, he offers no proof of causality, and falls back upon the circular assertion that "sexual difference is that 'rock of impossibility' on which every 'formalization' of sexual difference founders" (Žižek 2000c: 309). Elided here is what is at stake in calling the fundamental antagonism sexual difference at all. Moreover, many of Žižek's writings graft the notion of the fundamental antagonism into political contexts that have nothing to do with sexual difference. If symbolization's failure could have consequences other than that of making us "sexed beings," then his claim that failures of symbolization are its *cause* is far too strong.

Nevertheless, to read the Real not as "the rock of castration," as Žižek does in *Sublime Object*, but as the space of excess produced through the failure of symbolization, as he does elsewhere, is to understand it as a site of possible rearticulation. As Jodi Dean argues, Žižek theorizes the means through which "one can intervene in, touch, and change the Real" by engaging the symbolic (Dean 2006a: 181). While Žižek's claim that sexual difference is "real"—that it is "that which, precisely, resists symbolization"—may appear to insist stubbornly on essentialist doctrine, he nonetheless acknowledges that the Real's contours can change (Žižek 2000b: 214). Startlingly, he concedes in *Contingency* that "Butler is, in a way, right" to insist that the Real is "internal/inherent to the symbolic" (Žižek 2000a: 120-1). However, he qualifies his concession by stipulating that the Real "is nothing but [the symbolic's] inherent limitation, the impossibility of the symbolic fully to 'become itself,'" and that therefore the Real "cannot be symbolized" (Žižek 2000a: 120-1). The insight that the Real is unsymbolizable yet circumscribed by the symbolic suggests that the Real can serve as a site of radical ideological struggle. If the Real is the site of the symbolic's failures, it is consistent throughout time only in its structural function—in its position as the realm in which the symbolic fails. To the extent that the symbolic's terms can change, the ideological material that fails in the Real can change as well: Žižek asserts that "There will always be some hegemonic empty signifier; it is only the content that shifts" (Žižek 2000a: 111). If what he calls the *point de capiton* changes, a different set of failures could be inscribed at and as the Real.

Elsewhere in *Contingency*, Žižek points out that to focus on the Lacanian Real is to open up a means of understanding the regime of the father as an imposture. He notes that "the very focus on the notion of the Real as impossible... reveals the ultimate contingency, fragility (and thus changeability) of every symbolic constellation that pretends to serve as the a priori horizon of the process of symbolization" (Žižek 2000b: 221). Noting that "Lacan's shift of focus towards the Real is strictly correlative to the devaluation of the paternal function (and of the central place of the Oedipus complex itself)," Žižek explicitly names paternal law as one "contingent" formation "susceptible to a radical overhaul" (Žižek 2000b: 221). Observing that Lacan's "constant effort from the 1960's onwards... is... to expose the *fraud* of paternal authority," Žižek asserts that the "'Name-of-the-Father' is for Lacan a *fake*, a *semblance* which conceals [the] structural inconsistency of the symbolic" (Žižek 2000b: 255; Žižek 2000c: 310). As a consequence, he asserts, "paternal authority is ultimately an imposture, one among the possible 'sinthoms' which allow us temporarily to stabilize and co-ordinate the inconsistent/nonexistent 'big Other'" (Žižek 2000b: 221). Žižek does not, however, reconcile this insight with his continued insistence on the relevance of the paradigm of sexual difference. In failing fully to dislodge the regime of the father and the logic of (hetero)sexual difference, Žižek fails to pursue his work's most radical implication for queer theory: the possibility that the Name of the Father could be supplanted and the terrain of ideological struggle remapped through a change in *point de capiton*.

The Real of the Act

Even though Žižek disavows the possibility of such a remapping, his work clears theoretical ground for it when he argues that by traversing the fantasy, we can completely overhaul the symbolic's terms (Žižek 1996: 166). He elaborates this idea by revising Louis Althusser. In so doing, he offers an account of the processes through which ideological contents pass themselves off as natural through reification in the "kernel" of the "Self," and holds out the possibility of radically altering those false naturalizations (Žižek 1996: 166). He argues that "the crucial dimension of the ideological *effet-sujet*" lies "not in my direct identification with the symbolic mandate... but in my experience of the kernel of my Self as something which pre-exists the process of interpellation, as subjectivity *prior* to interpellation" (Žižek 1996: 166). What Žižek, following Lacan, calls "traversing the fantasy" brings about "subjective destitution" by "induc[ing]… the subject to renounce the 'secret treasure' which forms the kernel of" subjectivity (Žižek 1996: 166). Traversing the fantasy is thus "[t]he anti-ideological gesture *par excellence*," the means by

> which I *renounce* the treasure in myself and fully admit my dependence on the externality of symbolic apparatuses—fully assume the fact that my very self-experience of a subject who was already here prior to the external process of interpellation is a retroactive misrecognition brought about by that very process of interpellation.
>
> (Žižek 1996: 166)

This process of gaining distance from the fantasy supporting subjectivity undoes its power as "the ultimate 'passionate attachment' that guarantees the consistency of… being" (Žižek 1999: 266).

What is sexual difference in Lacanian and Žižekian theory if not an ideology that passes itself off as natural, as the true "kernel" of the "Self," and that can only be dislodged by traversing the fantasy? Sexual difference is the fundamental fantasy structuring Lacanian and Žižekian theory, and that which it needs to traverse to be fully useful to queer theory. The vehement resistance manifested across all of Žižek's texts to queer theorists' assertions of sexual difference's contingency is an indication of how trenchantly this fantasy is lodged within his texts. Here, it is crucial to read Žižek's (and also Lacan's) texts with an eye to their manifestations of "resistance" in the psychoanalytic sense. Read in this fashion, Žižek's and other Lacanians' assertions of sexual difference's fundamental intractability are unpersuasive: all the more so because of their proponents' increasingly desperate insistence despite challenge. This resistance points to sexual difference's status not as an "outside" to ideology pertaining to all persons across place and time, but rather as an ideology that has falsely installed itself as natural and subsisting prior to interpellation.

To view the "subjective kernel" not as ideology's outside but as the most deeply seated space of its entrenchment is to re-open the questions of how it becomes lodged as such, and of how its terms can be rearticulated. Countering Butler, who is suspicious of the Lacanian Real and seeks transformation through acts of linguistic performativity that resignify the symbolic's terms,

Žižek asserts that only an act of the Real can radically reconfigure "the field which redefines the very conditions of a socially sustained performativity" (Žižek 1999: 264). He opposes the "Real of an act" to the psychotic's "false" *passage à l'acte*, which does not "confront the real kernel of the trauma (the social antagonism)" to prompt a traversal of "the fantasy towards the Real" (Žižek 2000a: 126-7). According to *Seminar III*, psychosis entails permanent *foreclosure*—repudiation—of a privileged signifier, causing language to be distorted and hallucinations to appear in the Real as if it were radically external to the symbolic. Psychotic foreclosure pre-empts the establishment of a *point de capiton*, and, consequently, renders impossible an "act" that would intervene in both the symbolic and Real. "[H]ysterical 'acting out,'" too, takes place in the imaginary and cannot effect change (Kay 2003: 155). From Hitler's initiation of the Holocaust to psychosis, hysteria, and obsession, any action that disavows or avoids—rather than directly confronts—the fundamental "social antagonism" is for Žižek a "false act" (Žižek 2000a: 124-6). By contrast, the "act" is a form of "*symbolic suicide*," of "withdrawing from symbolic reality, that enables us to begin anew from the 'zero point,' from that point of absolute freedom called by Hegel 'abstract negativity'" (Žižek 1992: 49). This gesture temporarily voids symbolic mandates, opening up the possibility of adopting different ones and assuming a new symbolic identity.

For Žižek, only such an act provides the resistance enabling symbolic rearticulation. For him "the act proper"—with its capacity to intervene in the Real—"is the only one which restructures the very symbolic co-ordinates of the agent's situation: it is an intervention in the course of which the agent's identity itself is radically changed" (Žižek qtd. in Kay 2003: 155). As Sarah Kay puts it, this kind of act allows us to "treat the symbolic by means of the real"—"to reboot in the real" and refresh "our relationship with the symbolic" (Kay 2003: 155). Such a "reboot" could change the *point de capiton*, supplanting the Name of the Father with another master signifier and opening ground for a regime unlimited by sexual difference.

Such a transformation involves not psychotic foreclosure of the Name of the Father but "traversal of the fantasy" structuring our experience. For Žižek,

> What the Lacanian notion of "act" aims at is not a mere displacement/ resignification of the symbolic coordinates that confer on the subject his or her identity, but the radical transformation of the very universal structuring "principle" of the existing symbolic order... the Lacanian act, in its dimension of "traversing the fundamental fantasy" aims radically to disturb the very

"passionate attachment" that forms, for Butler, the ultimately ineluctable background of the process of resignification.

(Žižek 2000b: 220)

He further explains that this "act disturbs the underlying fantasy" trapping us in restrictive patterns while disavowing the fundamental kernel of our being (Žižek 2000a: 124). The proper act

> does not only shift the limit that divides our identity into the acknowledged and the disavowed part more in the direction of the disavowed part, it does not only make us to accept as "possible" our innermost disavowed "impossible" fantasies: it transforms the very coordinates of the disavowed phantasmatic foundation of our being. An act does not merely redraw the contours of our public symbolic identity, it also transforms the spectral dimension that sustains this identity, the undead ghosts that haunt the living subject, the secret history of traumatic fantasies transmitted "between the lines," through the lacks and distortions of the explicit symbolic texture of his or her identity.

(Žižek 2000a: 124)

As Žižek argues in *Sublime Object*, this kind of change rearticulates the *point de capiton* quilting the symbolic and Real. He understands the symbolically transformative "act" as the installation of a new *point de capiton* through fantasy's traversal, and implies that this "act," while "*irreducible* to a 'speech act'" and distinct from Butler's performative resignification, produces that new *point de capiton* by engaging all three orders (Žižek 1999: 263, emphasis added).[20] Writing about the theory from which Žižek's account is derived, Pluth clarifies that while "Lacan's notion of an act is… not far removed from what Austin called a performative speech act," the former's theory importantly differs from the latter's in its consequences: "Lacan shares with Austin the idea that [speech] acts are transformative, and such acts are clearly 'signifying,' but Lacan's focus is not on acts that change the situation of the world or the set of facts within it. Instead he focuses on acts that change the structure of a subject" (Pluth 2007: 101). These acts are "transgressive" because "[i]t is not the case that someone is simply changed by an act: he or she is reinaugurated as a subject" through a change in *point de capiton* touching the symbolic and Real (Pluth 2007: 102).[21] Somewhat differently than Lacan, Žižek also addresses acts challenging the political terrain's fundamental structure. Restructuring this landscape through a change in *point de capiton* would be analogous to reinaugurating the subject as Pluth describes.

The Promises and Perils of Fantasy's Traversals in *In & Out*

However, Žižek offers neither a promise that change will be for the better nor a clear picture of the future that will emerge through fantasy's traversal. As Yannis Stavrakakis observes, not all traversals ultimately lead to progressive change—to the symbolic order's wholesale rearticulation. The "hole in the big Other" cleared through fantasy's traversal risks being filled by "traditional politics" instead of progressive change (Stavrakakis 1999: 135). Here we encounter the limit of Žižek's reading of Frank Oz's *In & Out* (1997), a film set in a predominantly white Indiana town that features two Lacanian "acts" with gay-positive consequences. Žižek points to the moment at which closeted schoolteacher Howard Brackett says "I'm gay" instead of "Yes!" at his wedding after having been outed several days earlier by a former student, Cameron Drake, during his acceptance speech at the Academy Awards ceremony (Žižek 2000a: 122). This "authentic act" takes place in language—in the symbolic—yet successfully intervenes in the Real (Žižek 2000a: 122). It rejects the symbolic apparatus—heterosexual marriage—that would have sustained Howard's public identity as a person presumed to be straight, and blasts away the "disavowed phantasmastic foundation" that had supported his own and others' fantasy that he was heterosexual (Žižek 2000a: 124). Howard's change is both internal, in that he accepts that he is gay, and external, in that he changes how he identifies publicly.

Žižek overlooks the film's second Lacanian act: the community's public show of solidarity with Howard. After Howard comes out, the principal fires him despite his record of acclaimed teaching; then, when Cameron appears at graduation to support Howard, large numbers of graduating students—and the entire Brackett family—declare themselves to be gay. This moment represents a turning point in the family's and town's attitude toward Howard's gayness. Whereas an early scene vocalizes his and his father's homophobic disavowals, at graduation his mother, father, and brother join townspeople in a transformative act of acceptance. Both of these Lacanian acts represent positive developments for the film's gay characters.

Nonetheless, *In & Out* fails to challenge patriarchy and the conservative institution of marriage: aspects of the film Žižek overlooks. The closing sequence teases the viewer with the possibility that Howard and the reporter whose kiss caused him to recognize his own desires might be heading to church for their own wedding. However, the film quickly cuts to their arrival as guests at the service in which Howard's mother and father renew their wedding vows, and ends with a celebration in which the community dances to the gay classic "Macho Man."

Although this scene reinforces the idea that the town has accepted Howard's sexuality, the film's closing emphasis on the restoration of (hetero)sexual difference within the context of the patriarchal Christian church—to which earlier scenes had appealed to guide Howard toward being honest about his sexuality—shows that challenges to homophobia do not always undo paternal law.

Moreover, *In & Out* grates for its misogynist portrayal of two women as vacuous: Emily Montgomery, Howard's fiancée, is a self-hating wreck who— herself a teacher—nonetheless expresses the desire to be educated by her future husband; Sonia, Cameron's girlfriend, is a whiny and entitled supermodel who cannot even operate a circular telephone dial. The film systematically upholds paternal law and even perpetuates misogyny despite its critique of hypocritical silences around homosexuality in educational and religious institutions. In so doing, *In & Out* furthers a conservative, white, middle American worldview whose limitations Žižek leaves unremarked.

As such, *In & Out* illustrates that it is impossible to predict the consequences of the "authentic act" (Žižek 2000a: 122). Given Žižek's attitude toward North American gender politics, it is unsurprising that his brief gloss of the film misses the way Howard's coming out undoes homophobia but not patriarchy or white supremacy. Yet in earlier texts, Žižek recognizes that there is no certainty about Lacanian acts' consequences. Elaborating on the act that would prompt fantasy's traversal, Žižek argues that the structure of the Kantian categorical imperative is "tautological," an "empty form" that "can deliver no guarantee against misjudging our duty" (Žižek 1996: 170). Coming up with "a minimal positive definition" of the act is a "game" involving guesses that "fill up the abyss of tautology that resonates in 'Do your duty!'" (Žižek 1996: 170). Žižek presents as the "best candidate" for such an uncertain act the case of a man who "dress[es] up as a woman and commit[s] suicide in public" (Žižek 1996: 170). This example's misogynistic and transphobic character is outrageous and inflammatory, suggesting that revolution be purchased at the price of the lives of those who challenge the prevailing gender system. By no means do I wish to endorse this example as a program for queer or trans theory. As Butler and Gayle Salamon compellingly argue, queer and trans theory should work to make gender diversity more rather than less livable.[22] Yet Žižek's example also points to an aspect of his thought that allows for his ideas to be appropriated and reworked for queer-theoretical ends. The relativism and ambiguity he attaches to acts—including the example he gives here, which he presents as "the best candidate" rather than a sure success—concedes that they take place within an inherently conflicted field of competing ideologies available for challenge and transformation (Žižek 1996: 170). In this context, Žižek's example of the man who commits suicide in drag represents a startling concession that the fundamental fantasy of (hetero) sexual difference is contingent, ideological, and subject to traversal.

A strength of Lacanian theory is its potential to offer a flexible account of the structure of desire and its consequences: of desire as motivated by lack, and as potentially productive of all manner of genderings. At its best, Žižek's politics of the Real offers queer theory not a release from the symbolic but the possibility of changing its coordinates. It is thus unfortunate that debate over his theories' more radical implications has been grounded by his insistence on presenting them in the language of sexual difference. This move limits his work's usefulness for queer and feminist theories by constricting accounts of desire and tacitly upholding the assumption that the symbolic must be anchored by the Name of the Father.

Even though orthodox Lacanian writings—including Žižek's—attempt to forestall challenges to the claim that sexual difference is unalterably lodged in the Real, the more radical strain within the his texts opens up the possibility of contesting them. By traversing the fantasy of (hetero)sexual difference, the entire ideological apparatus of what Gayle Rubin calls the "sex/gender system" could be overhauled through a change in *point de capiton* (Rubin 1976: 159).[23] Although Copjec and Žižek questionably argue that (hetero)sexual difference is a fundamental antinomy, the latter suggests that it is a fantasy available for traversal. If—as Žižek states—paternal law is an "imposture" and the Name of the Father could be supplanted by another master signifier, (hetero)sexual difference's phallogocentric structure could be radically overhauled (Žižek 2000b: 221). Doing so would not necessarily render (hetero)sexual difference entirely obsolete, but would allow us to understand it as having an incidental— rather than a determining—effect on the structuring of subjectivity and desire. Even if desire is subtended by a fundamental antinomy determining that "there is no sexual relationship," there is no good reason to insist on calling this antagonism sexual difference or on formulating it in terms of the masculine and feminine (Žižek 1999: 272). Numerous other differences would do just as well, whether they concern gender, sexuality, race, ethnicity, or nationality—or a combination thereof.

Thus, as a provocation to fantasy's traversal, I close this chapter with a sole injunction, directed at all who remain invested in insisting that the fundamental antinomy that mobilizes desire must ever and always be called sexual difference: Give it up!

Notes

1. See Halberstam (2011b) for criticism of Žižek's account of Occupy Wall Street.
2. See Butler's (1990, 1994, 1998, and 2004) challenge to Lacanian sexual difference, especially Žižek's view of it (2000a, 2000b, 2000c). See Copjec (1994, 2010) and Žižek (1999) for responses. Also see Butler, Laclau, and Žižek (2000) for further debate.
3. In *Gender Trouble*, Butler (1990) argues that linguistic performativity could subvert symbolic heterosexism. She refines this argument further in Chapters Two and Three of *Bodies That Matter* (1993), focusing on the way a phallogocentric symbolic's terms create possibilities for certain kinds of gender identifications while precluding others.
4. See Penney (2014) for further assessment of this debate's implications for queer theory.
5. See Tim Dean's *Beyond Sexuality* (2000a) and Lee Edelman's *No Future* (2004) for extended accounts of the limitations for queer theory of work focusing on the Imaginary without considering the Real.
6. See *Bodies That Matter* Butler (1993) and *Contingency, Hegemony, Universality* (Butler, Laclau, and Žižek 2000) for Butler's critiques of Laclau and Žižek.
7. In addition to *Bodies That Matter* Butler (1993), see Butler (1994) and Butler (1998) for texts employing the term "foreclosure" in this manner.
8. In addition to Žižek's texts I cite in this chapter, see Copjec (2010). Copjec's essay offers a useful—though general—defense of psychoanalytic approaches to sexuality but remains locked into a Lacanian model of sexual difference that conflates "sex" with "sexuality" and fails to ask what it might mean to theorize subjectivity from the perspectives of intersex and transgender people—an exercise that would expose aporias in her account of subjectivity.
9. Fink observes that in the clinic, "a great many biological females turn out to have masculine structure, and a great many biological males prove to have feminine structure" (Fink 1995: 108).
10. It is curious and unfortunate that despite Dean's challenge in Chapter One of *Beyond Sexuality* to the account of the symbolic as grounded through acceptance of the phallic signifier, Chapter Two reverts to a strict account of sexual difference as intractably Real. See especially Dean (2000a: 86).
11. For Lacanian arguments pathologizing transgender and arguing against gender reassignment, see Millot (1990); Shepherdson (2000); and Tim Dean (2000a). Gherovici (2010) disentangles more carefully than Millot those examples of transgender its author considers symptoms of an underlying disorder—and therefore not adequately addressed through gender reassignment—from those for which she considers gender reassignment an appropriate response. Nonetheless, her analysis

continues to rely upon problematic presuppositions about phallic primacy, staging challenges to sexual difference as signs of pathology rather than resistance to ideology. See Chapter 4 for discussion of Gherovici's recent turn to a more consistently supportive view of transgender as well as others' trans-affirmative rereadings of psychoanalysis.

12 Restuccia revises this thesis in her argument for a Lacanian conception of self-shattering "queer love," arguing that Tim Dean's *Beyond Sexuality*—which she views as making a similar argument about "desire"—"locates... Lacanian Love in a place beyond sexual difference" (Restuccia 2006: 130). While Dean challenges the privileging of the phallus in readings of Lacan and focuses on the *objet a* that emerges as desire's genderless object-cause in his later work, he retains the emphasis on sexual difference that remains so problematic in Lacanian discourse. See especially Chapter Two of *Beyond Sexuality* Dean (2000a) for examples of this problem.

13 For a critique of Hart, see Coffman (2006: 18–22).

14 Though Pluth similarly recognizes that Lacan enables restructuring of subjectivity through an "act" that traverses the fantasy—which Pluth identifies as offering "freedom" and that I am more concerned to identify as a form of "optimism"—I find such potential in Žižek's work as well.

15 De La Torre 2018 establishes through reference to her previously published article in *differences* 21(20) that she is Shanna Carlson.

16 See, for example, his critique in Žižek (2008) and *Žižek: The Reality of the Virtual* of North American multicultural discourse's emphasis on "tolerance."

17 See, for example, Kessler (1998) and Fausto-Sterling (2000).

18 See Butler (1990).

19 See Chapter 2 for a reading of *Seminar XI* that uncouples "sex" from "sexuality."

20 Butler's and Žižek's approaches to the symbolic are grounded in different theories of linguistic performativity: see Žižek (1992), Žižek (1989), and Butler (1993). Rather than focusing on their debate over language, I focus on their deployments of the Real, which must be engaged along with the symbolic to dislodge the *point de capiton*.

21 Though he shares Žižek's view of the way the Lacanian "act" can overhaul the subject by intervening at the juncture of the symbolic and Real, Pluth (Pluth 2007) rereads Lacan's late work on the *sinthôme* to critique Žižek's account of subjective structure following fantasy's traversal.

22 See especially Chapter Seven of Salamon (2010), which challenges reductionist uses of the symbolic.

23 For another argument for sexual difference's incidental rather than determining function, see Tim Dean (2000b).

2

No Future? Traversing the Fantasy of (Hetero)sexual Difference

Lee Edelman's polemical *No Future* (2004) comes closer than any other work of Lacanian queer theory to the revision of Slavoj Žižek I propose in Chapter 1: that (hetero)sexual difference is the "fantasy Lacanian psychoanalytic theory needs to traverse to fully register the many possible configurations of desiring subjectivities" and contemporary genders (26). *No Future* harnesses Žižek's theory to target not Lacanian sexual difference but one of its corollaries: the ideology of "reproductive futurism" that would secure the Future by protecting the presumably innocent Child (Edelman 2004: 28). Arguing that queers should assume the loathed position of the *sinthom*osexual by refusing this vision and embracing the drive's *jouissance* in the Real, Edelman offers a strategy for collapsing the configuration of the imaginary, symbolic, and Real orders on which the fantasy of "reproductive futurism" depends (Edelman 2004: 28).

However, consistent with his repudiation of futurity, Edelman does not consider what may come after fantasy's traversal. Nor does my first chapter address what might lie beyond fantasy—a matter that "remains unconcluded in Lacan's work" (Chiesa 2007: 189). In this chapter, too, I resist mapping out the contours of such a beyond, for such a gesture would be just as prescriptive and constraining as (hetero)sexual difference. However, in contrast to Edelman, who repudiates any engagement with futurity, *Queer Traversals* seeks to embrace those productive and unpredictable futures for the signifier that traversing the fantasy could engender. To do so, this chapter provides the theoretical basis for my final two chapters' readings of narratives that go beyond the fantasy of (hetero)sexual difference in ways that reflect varied relationships to gender, sexuality, race, ethnicity, and nationality.

The *Sinthom*osexual's Challenge to (Hetero)sexual Difference

Calling upon queers to go beyond the fantasy of "reproductive futurism," Edelman cites numerous examples of anti-gay and pro-gay platitudes appealing to the Child as an image of the Future (Edelman 2004: 28). He carefully distinguishes this figure from actual children and argues that queers should traverse "the collective fantasy that invests the social order with meaning by way of reproductive futurism" (Edelman 2004: 28). This is the argument—made notorious by his call for queers to "Fuck the social order and the Child in whose name we're collectively terrorized… fuck Laws both with capital ls and with small; fuck the whole network of Symbolic relations and the future that serves as its prop"—for which *No Future* is best known (Edelman 2004: 29).

Instead of arguing for the Child's future, Edelman asserts that queers should embrace the structural position of the reviled *sinthom*osexual—a neologism he forms by punning on the Lacanian *sinthôme*. The *sinthôme* refers to the unique form that *jouissance*—ecstatic pleasure going beyond symbolic inscriptions of desire to engage the Real and the drive—takes in each subject.[1] Edelman's coinage, "the *sinthom*osexual," designates the queer figure a homophobic symbolic associates with pure *jouissance*, and therefore with refusing reproductive futurism. He views "structurally determinative violence" against the *sinthom*osexual as inescapable, even though the identity of those filling the *sinthom*osexual's role may change (Edelman 2006: 822). He insists that the *sinthom*osexual is a structural place that may or may not be occupied by an actual queer, yet also demonstrates through analysis of right-wing discourse that homosexuality currently takes this position within a homophobic symbolic governed by reproductive futurism. Edelman advocates embracing the figure of the *sinthom*osexual—and thereby traversing the homophobic fantasy of reproductive futurism—rather than engaging in the imaginary and symbolic strategies motivating mainstream gay politics and Judith Butler's theories.

Though Edelman's largest wager is on the potential of the *sinthom*osexual's *jouissance* to undercut reproductive futurism, he intimates that fantasy's traversal could also undermine sexual difference, which he describes as "merely a *supposition*, merely a *positing*" that is part of reproductive futurism's edifice (Edelman 2004: 139). Presenting "negativity as society's constitutive antagonism," Edelman starts from the Žižekian premise that the symbolic and imaginary cover an antagonism in the Real (Edelman 2006: 822). Queer theorists' discussion of *No Future* has thus largely focused on its exemplification of what Robert Caserio, in a 2006 *PMLA* forum, calls the "anti-social thesis": the argument that queer sexuality is inherently opposed to society and community (Caserio 2006: 819). Scholars have emphasized Edelman's claim that traversing the fantasy of reproductive futurism would devastate the symbolic that Edelman equates with the social; they have paid little attention to his reading of Žižek or to alternative accounts of fantasy's traversal. This is unfortunate, as Edelman's overly pessimistic interpretation of Lacan and Žižek is largely responsible for *No Future*'s nihilism—for the way Edelman's refusal to posit an alternative to reproductive futurism is as vehement as his justifiable rage against it. While I sympathize with Edelman's aim of reworking Žižek for queer ends, I find in the latter an ambivalent combination of pessimism and optimism that—unlike *No Future*—does not exclude agitation for positive structural change. Žižek and others present traversing the fantasy not as a refusal of all forms of futurity but as a ground-clearing gesture that *is* directed toward a future.

Edelman's denial of all forms of futurity is a central point of contention in the *PMLA* forum, which positions *No Future* in relation to Leo Bersani's groundbreaking argument that gay sex informs an "anticommunitarian, self-shattering, and anti-identitarian" ethos (Halberstam 2006: 823). In a similar vein, Edelman insists that queer sexuality embodies an inescapable antagonism at the social's heart, and Jack Halberstam associates queer resistance with "bleak," "angry," and antisocial emotions engendered by multiple forms of oppression (Halberstam 2006: 824). Yet as Damon Young and Joshua J. Weiner observe, queer theory's "so-called anti-social thesis" is a false binary, "as if queer social negativity engendered no bonds and queer collectivities did not take shape precisely in relation to some negation or incommensurability" (Young and Weiner 2011: 224). Using the *PMLA* forum to challenge accounts opposing queerness to the social, Caserio emphasizes the role of late nineteenth- and early twentieth-century writers such as Edward Carpenter, J. A. Symonds, and Oscar Wilde in sublimating queer desire into a "[h]eroic... responsibility to society and community" (Caserio 2006: 820); José Esteban Muñoz positions queerness as a "collectivity" whose value lies in being "visible only on the horizon" pointing to the future (Muñoz 2006: 825); and Tim Dean argues that the subjective "shattering" promoted by the anti-social thesis actively *produces* new possibilities for the future (Dean 2006: 827).

James Penney's *After Queer Theory* (2014) insists on sexuality's apolitical nature yet challenges Edelman's repudiation of all forms of "politics"—especially those "based on a sense of hope for a better future" (Penney 2014: 180-7). Whereas Penney defends the realm of politics Edelman dismisses as merely symbolic, Ben Nichols' *Same Old* (2020) contests Edelman's critique of imaginary sameness, stressing its importance to "the successful reproduction of" gay male "social form" (Nichols 2020: 76–7). Emphasizing *No Future*'s use of Lacan's early work to argue that a homophobic symbolic accuses queers of sameness only to reject them for it, Nichols rightfully observes that "Edelman does not acknowledge that embracing the abjection that reproductive futurism ascribes to queers *also* reproduces the values of reproductive futurism" (Nichols 2020: 87). However, Nichols misses sameness's importance to Edelman's engagement of the late Lacan: the way the *sinthom*osexual's *jouissance* in the Real at "'circuit parties' that gesture toward the circuit of the drive" uses repetition to short circuit reproductive futurism's imaginary and symbolic representations (Edelman 2004: 75).

If anything, Edelman characterizes the drive as too bound up in negativity's sameness. In *The Ethics of Opting Out* (2017), Mari Ruti complicates his emphasis on the drive's negativity and joins Dean in reclaiming it for more generative theorizing (Ruti 2017). Teresa de Lauretis' *Freud's Drive* (2008), too, uses Freudian and Laplanchian psychoanalysis to present a comparable argument about the drive's potential productivity. These responses to *No Future* have illuminated broad questions about queerness' place in society—and indeed about the very constitution of the social—but with the exception of Dean, Ruti, and de Lauretis have not focused on assessing the theoretical underpinnings of Edelman's claim that queerness is anti-social and future-negating.[2]

As Edelman's call to "fuck the whole network of Symbolic relations" suggests, his assault on the Future embodied in the figure of the Child entails a broader attack on the symbolic (Edelman 2004: 29). He considers that mainstream gay and lesbian politics and the ideology of reproductive futurism rely upon illusory meanings and misrecognitions supported by the symbolic and imaginary (Edelman 2004: 7–9). Over and against Butler, who argues that resignifying a heterosexist symbolic can make queer lives more livable, Edelman advocates embracing the drive's queer possibilities in the Real (Butler 1990, 1993, 1994, 1998 and 2004).[3] Doing so would traverse the fantasy of reproductive futurism, shattering the symbolic and imaginary misprisions on which it depends.

Edelman's *sinthom*osexual taps into the drive's queerness and capacity to disrupt reproductive futurism. For Lacan, traversing the fantasy begins by embracing the *sinthôme*. Edelman proposes that queers should bring this strategy to bear on the fantasy that animates reproductive futurism by claiming the *sinthom*osexual's position, rejecting imaginary and symbolic misprisions locating meaning in the future and the figure of the Child. *No Future* offers numerous examples of *sinthom*osexuals: Ebenezer Scrooge in Charles Dickens' *A Christmas Carol*; the eponymous protagonist of George Eliot's *Silas Marner*; Leonard in Alfred Hitchcock's *North by Northwest*; the birds in Hitchcock's *The Birds*. Whereas the first three characters are either rehabilitated for reproductive futurism (Scrooge and Marner) or expelled (Leonard), Hitchcock's birds come closest to effecting fantasy's traversal. While not refuting outright those who would read these characters as actual homosexuals, and at times even offering evidence that would support such interpretations, Edelman places strongest emphasis upon the *sinthom*osexual's function as a *figure* produced by—but disruptive of—reproductive futurism.

No Future excites for its insistence on queers' ethical obligation to traverse the fantasy of reproductive futurism and, in so doing, unravel the logic of (hetero) sexual difference serving as its prop. Importantly, Edelman insists that such a challenge must intervene not only in the symbolic—as Butler would have it— but also in the Real. His book relies upon orthodox Lacanians' language about (hetero)sexual difference, yet labels it as contingent and deploys it with an irony questioning its terms.

Although Halberstam justifiably criticizes *No Future* for its archive of white gay male cultural examples, it is important to recognize that conceptually, the book performs both queer and feminist critique by questioning Lacanian sexual difference. In Edelman's framework, reproductive futurism's traversal is also (hetero)sexual difference's traversal—a ground-shifting possibility with as many implications for feminist as for queer theory. Despite the book's promise, however, Edelman's reworking of Lacan does not succeed in theorizing the possibility of traversing those fantasies, and instead leaves their symbolic edifices intact. This is problematic for several reasons: first, because *No Future*'s argument does not deliver on its promise to collapse heteropatriarchy, and second, because it leaves other axes of difference—such as race, ethnicity, and nationality—entirely unaddressed.

There are also dangers present in the overgeneralizations whereby Edelman appears unable to imagine scenarios that do not involve complicity—whether as normative subjects or as *sinthom*osexuals—in the fantasy of reproductive futurism. Though the 2006 *PMLA* forum opposes Edelman's and Halberstam's "anti-social" stances to Muñoz's and Dean's "utopian" theories, *No Future* instead strikes me—as it does Ruti—as a Möbius strip whose ostensibly "anti-social thesis" turns into the most radical form of the utopian thesis (Ruti 2008b: 116). In suggesting that queers embrace the position of the *sinthom*osexual and dispense with reproductive futurism, he holds out the utopian possibility of imploding *all* imaginary and symbolic misrecognitions, homophobic or otherwise, and of *persisting* in an utopian space of negativity defined by the absence of strictures. Although this move promises to dethrone (hetero)sexual difference from its position of primacy and enable psychoanalytic theories of difference that cross multiple categories of identity, Edelman's utopia is not as radical as his rejection of the imaginary and symbolic makes it seem: the *sinthom*osexual is only able to ignore the symbolic by accepting the space of *jouissance* the symbolic—and (hetero)sexual difference—circumscribe.

The *Sinthom*osexual's Failed Challenge to (Hetero)sexual Difference

No Future's challenge to (hetero)sexual difference is especially evident in the book's final two chapters, on *North By Northwest* (1959) and *The Birds* (1963). Chapter Three opens by analyzing a scene from *North By Northwest* in which Leonard refuses compassion and the entire edifice of reprofuturity it sustains. Attributing reproductive futurism to a symbolic structuring desire around (hetero)sexual difference, Edelman argues that Leonard occupies the position of the *sinthom*osexual by refusing that structure and embracing the drive's *jouissance*. Edelman asserts that "*Sinthom*osexuality... affirms a constant, eruptive jouissance that responds to the inarticulable Real, to the impossibility of sexual rapport or of ever being able to signify the relation between the sexes" (Edelman 2004: 74). The *sinthom*osexual "stands in the place of the" death drive (Edelman 2004: 74) and "opposes the fantasy that generates endless narratives of generation": that "of heterosexual love, and the reproductive Couple it elevates" as capable of "delivering us from the pull of the Real and the absence of sexual rapport" (Edelman 2004: 82).

Edelman further clarifies that the *sinthom*osexual challenges the symbolic order's patriarchal underpinnings when he observes that Leonard refuses Thornhill compassion on the face of Mt. Rushmore. Edelman asserts that "beneath the eyes of America's patriarchs, who stand in for symbolic law," Leonard's action allegorizes Lacan's claim that "to trample sacred laws under foot... itself excites some form of *jouissance*"—that is, that it entails the ecstasy of defying the patriarchal symbolic and its regime of (hetero)sexual difference (Edelman 2004: 85). Though Edelman's diction reveals his alignment with the orthodox Lacanian assumption that sexuality and sexual difference concern "the relation between the sexes," he elevates the *sinthom*osexual as the subversive element that undoes their illusions by embracing *jouissance* (Edelman 2004: 74).

However well Edelman makes the case for the *need* to traverse the fantasies of reproductive futurism and (hetero)sexual difference, *No Future* does not succeed in doing so. His logic in Chapter Three appears to critique, but ultimately parallels, *North By Northwest*'s allegorical restoration of (hetero) sexual difference. Edelman argues that in this film, "The relation of desire's dialectic, with its endless unfolding of futurity," stands in relation to "the *sintho*mosexual's death drive" as allegory stands with regard to irony in Paul de Man's "The Rhetoric of Temporality" (Edelman 2004: 91). If allegory and desire imagine a perpetually deferred future, irony and the death drive negate futurity and embrace the "now," reducing "time to 'one single moment' ... that allows 'neither memory nor prefigurative duration'" (Edelman 2004: 92). Carefully examining Hitchcock's editing, Edelman asserts that the film "resists, while carrying forward... the negativity condensed in irony's big bang" as Leonard is shot and Thornhill—to whom the *sintho*mosexual refused compassion—prevails in a narrative emphasizing his heterosexual coupling (Edelman 2004: 92). But if what *North By Northwest* predictably offers in Leonard is the failed promise of (hetero)sexual difference's traversal, Edelman more surprisingly disappoints by doing the same.

As *No Future* swerves away from Edelman's critique of allegory's implication in reproductive futurism into an argument that makes of Hitchcock's ending an allegory for orthodoxies about the inevitable misprisions attending (hetero) sexual difference, the *sintho*mosexual emerges as little more than a placeholder whose deviance enables the normative order's functioning. Edelman valorizes Leonard's refusal of compassion as the only alternative to the traps of (hetero) sexual difference and its order of false meaning, finding resistance in his defiance of the symbolic's illusory definition of humanity and insistence on embracing the *sintho*mosexual's dehumanizing stance. However, that character is expelled at the end of the scene on Mount Rushmore, the film then jumping to Thornhill's and Eve's departure on a train.

Commenting on Hitchcock's discontinuous editing of the transition from Mount Rushmore to the train, Edelman argues that the film's ending elevates that couple as an emblem of the future, yet simultaneously exposes (hetero) sexual difference's fictitiousness and inevitable failure. He writes that "Out of this gap thus opened in the 'reality' of the film, which responds to the ruptures of space and time (divided between events on the cliff and on the train) that close-ups and editing conceal, a voice that comes from somewhere else... delivers them into [the] future," and thereby "lifts us *all* into that future" (Edelman 2004: 96). Here Edelman points to a cinematic moment of subjective destitution after fantasy's traversal. Though this collapse of the fantasy could enable a new gap to emerge, the one opened within *North By Northwest* does not prompt (hetero)sexual difference's traversal. Instead, the film enacts its fantasmatic re-emergence. Edelman observes that "fantasy alone" drives the final scene on the train: "the fantasy, first and foremost, that this whole scene is *not* a fantasy but, rather, a return to what is plausibly mundane; the fantasy, then, that futurity, the temporality of desire, can effectively structure our reality by denying the pressure of the Real" (Edelman 2004: 96).

Though it comes as no surprise that *North By Northwest* offers no viable strategy for (hetero)sexual difference's traversal, Edelman's apparent capitulation to the orthodox Lacanian account of desire startles. Like Žižek and Copjec, Edelman makes much of the claim that (hetero)sexual difference is not symbolic but Real and of the argument that it is an antagonism rather than a binary opposition, arguing that *North By Northwest*'s narrative trajectory shows that the desiring subject is fated to suffer from "the fact of 'sexed reproduction'" (Edelman 2004: 97).[4] Copjec, Edelman intones, "rightly" proclaims (hetero)sexual difference "a real and not a symbolic difference," and Žižek insists that "sexual difference is the Real of an antagonism, not the Symbolic of a differential opposition" (Edelman 2004: 97). These are assertions with which I have no quibble, insofar as they demonstrate that a fundamental antinomy in the Real creates the rift upon which (hetero)sexual difference builds its shaky edifice of misrecognitions. But Edelman baffles by repeating the orthodox Lacanian argument that (hetero)sexual difference *itself* is intractable despite this highly unstable ground.

Although one way of describing the effect of the film's closing scene could be that it invites spectators to gain distance from the fantasies of (hetero)sexual difference and reproductive futurism—a key step in traversing the fantasy and supplanting it with another—Edelman's argument, like the film, does not press beyond this moment. Instead, he reneges on the promise of fantasy's traversal by recuperating the scene into a conventionally Lacanian framework and domesticating the gap opened within the film's "reality" as nothing more than an instance of (hetero)sexual difference's inevitable failure. Edelman writes that the film inscribes the "gap [between jouissance and the Other]" that

> is coextensive with the subject "*qua* living being" destined to suffer, as a consequence of *the fact of "sexed reproduction*," an irreparable loss of what nothing in the Symbolic is sufficient to restore: "the part of himself, lost forever,

that is constituted by the fact that *he is only a sexed living being,* and that he is no longer immortal"—no longer, in other words, whole, complete, or sufficient unto himself.

(Edelman 2004: 97, emphasis added)

For Edelman, this "primal or originary lack precludes the One of sexual relation, the reconstitution of unity anticipated by reproductive coupling across the divide of 'sexual difference'" (Edelman 2004: 97). This explanation adheres to an orthodox Lacanian understanding of (hetero)sexual difference.

Lacan's Radicalism, Lacanians' Orthodoxies

Edelman's account of (hetero)sexual difference's failure reproduces Lacan's own language in *Seminar XI*. He states that

Sexuality is established in the field of the subject by a way that is that of lack.

Two lacks overlap here. The first emerges from the central defect around which the dialectic of the advent of the subject to his own being in the relation to the Other turns—by the fact that the subject depends on the signifier and that the signifier is first of all in the field of the Other. This lack takes up the other lack, which is the real, earlier lack, to be situated at the advent of the living being, that is to say, at *sexed reproduction*. The real lack is what the living being loses, that part of himself *qua* living being, in reproducing himself through the way of sex.

(Lacan 1977: 204–5, emphasis added)

Both this passage and Edelman's reinflection of it stage sexuality as symbolizing the body by subjecting it to the signifier. The subject is not "immortal" but divided, and the resulting lack—rather than the quest for the perfect "sexual complement" promoted by Aristophanes—is taken up by signification in the Other, driving desire (Lacan 1977: 205).

Debates about this account of sexuality have been confounded by vestiges of biologistic discourse persisting in Lacan's and Edelman's language. For instance, Lacan's writings sometimes conflate the phallus with the penis. He states that the phallic "signifier is chosen as the most salient of what can be grasped in sexual intercourse [*copulation*] as real" and that "by virtue of its turgidity" the phallus "is the image of the vital flow as it is transmitted in generation" (Lacan 2006g: 581). This formulation offers the penis as an "image" of reproductive fluid, foregrounding its capacity to represent reproduction that can now also take place through other means. In so doing, Lacan's language confirms Butler's observation that "the phallus would be nothing without the penis" (Butler 1993: 84).

Nonetheless, by presenting the body as subject to representation, Lacan and Edelman ultimately challenge the idea that sexuality is essentially reproductive. As Lacan explains, the lack created through signification "takes up the other lack" entailed in "sexed reproduction," rendering the latter a ruse of representation (Lacan 1977: 205). Moreover, he notes that even though the "function of reproduction" exists on the "biological plane," it "is not represented as such in the psyche" (Lacan 1977: 204). Instead, sexuality is situated—and "by no means... in an exhaustive way"—by reproduction's symbolic "equivalents," "activity and passivity" (Lacan 1977: 204). Although this formulation is unnecessarily limiting, it does not suggest that sexuality is solely reproductive. Later, in *Seminar XX*, Lacan asks whether it is "possible that language may have other effects than to lead people by the nose to reproduce yet again (*encore*)" (Lacan 1998: 46). He then stresses the importance to desire of "another effect of language, which is writing (*l'écrit*)" (Lacan 1998: 46). By rejecting reproductive futurism, Lacan excises biologically grounded heteronormativity from desire.

Edelman, however, rests content to observe (hetero)sexual difference's failure and does not press forward to theorize Lacanian psychoanalysis' most radical possibilities. After Lacan insists that the "function of reproduction" is not "represented as such in the psyche," he concludes that "[i]n the psyche, there is nothing by which the subject may situate himself as a male or female being" (Lacan 1977: 204). That is to say that the psyche is asexual: not sexuated. Differing from everyday English-language use of the word "asexual" to designate individuals who do not experience sexual attraction, Lacan's understanding of psychical asexuality holds that the psyche inhabits neither masculine nor feminine positions within sexual difference. The psyche thus has neither "sex" nor "sexual orientation." Foregrounding Lacan's queer and trans potential, this idea—while neither naming nor discussing intersex and transsexed bodies' implications for subjectivity—clears ground for their theorization.[5] Moreover, in decoupling desire and sexuality from reproduction, Lacan acknowledges their heterosexual *and* non-heterosexual possibilities.

However, in going on to detail sexuality's vicissitudes when subject to the signifier, Lacan falls back on language his theory of the psyche otherwise would reject. Only three paragraphs after his statement about the psyche's asexuality, he writes that "the human being has always to learn from scratch from the Other what he has to do, *as man or as woman*" (Lacan 1977: 204, emphasis added). Though this claim squares with his account of the psyche by presenting the positions of "*man*" and "*woman*" as emerging from the Other—that is, from within signification—it remains problematic that Lacan offers only two options.

Despite his earlier insistence that the psyche knows no "sex," Lacan relies upon the binary language of "*man*" and "*woman*" that likely reflects the fact that he was writing in the 1970s, when these were the only words available to designate genders despite androgyny's growing popularity.

Similarly, Lacan explains in "The signification of the phallus" that sexual difference is a matter of positionality rather than biology, yet his diction reveals a residual investment in binary "sex." He writes that the "relation between the subject and the phallus... forms without regard to *the anatomical distinction between the sexes*" (Lacan 2006g: 576, emphasis added). While his point about the subject's relation to the phallic signifier would stand if revised to accommodate a broader range of anatomical differences including intersex and transsexed bodies, his reliance upon binary terms for a singular "anatomical distinction" remains problematic. This formulation of anatomical difference as binary opposition backhandedly animates the distinction between masculine and feminine positions that Lacan describes as "having" or "being" the phallus (Lacan 2006g: 582). Though Lacan's elaboration of the psyche's asexuality hypothetically enables theorizations of the intersex and transsexed bodies he leaves unmentioned, his failure to think through their implications persists in his exclusive use of the categories of "man" and "woman."

The possibility that sexual difference might be theorized more expansively has only recently begun to be explored by scholars such as Butler (1990, 1993, 2004), Sheila Cavanagh (2015, 2016, 2017, and 2018), Patricia Gherovici (2010, 2012, 2014, 2017, 2019a,b), and Gayle Salamon (2010, 2016), as I will discuss in Chapters 3 and 4. Such work—while powerful—has met with considerable resistance from orthodox Lacanians such as Copjec (1994, 2010) and Žižek (1989, 1999, 2000a, 2000b, 2000c), who argue that (hetero)sexual difference is Real and therefore intractable. Edelman's capitulation to this orthodox Lacanian position surprises given his commitment to queer theory.

The Real's shifting status within Lacan's *oeuvre* has further confounded this discussion. We might read his references to "sexed" bodies and reproduction as invocations of what Charles Shepherdson describes as the Real's first sense, as a "presymbolic" and prediscursive materiality, though not necessarily as evidence of essentialism in his account of the Real in its second, "postsymbolic" sense (Shepherdson 2008: 27). The latter Real emerges through the lack introduced by signification—through "the central defect around which the dialectic of the advent of the subject to his own being in the relation to the Other turns" (Lacan 1977: 204–5). In this sense, the Real is neither internal nor external to the symbolic. Instead, it is what Shepherdson, following Lacan, describes as "extimate" (Shepherdson 2008: 2). Produced as a mythical "excess, a remainder or surplus-effect" generated *by* "the symbolic order, but not reducible to it," the Real is excluded from yet paradoxically necessary to the symbolic (Shepherdson 2008: 38).

Like Žižek's, Shepherdson's account of the "postsymbolic" Real emphasizes Lacan's elevation of the phallus and Name-of-the-Father as signifiers quilting the three orders. Shepherdson further notes that "the phallus," which Lacan considers "the paradoxical signifier of signifiers," signifies "only through a substitution that dissimulates... a natural anatomical ground guaranteeing signification" (Shepherdson 2008: 25). However, Shepherdson misses the way this dissimulation renders the phallus and Name-of-the-Father contingent: and therefore potentially supplantable by other signifiers through a traversal of the fantasy that would, in turn, dethrone (hetero)sexual difference from its privileged place in Lacanian accounts of subjectivity. Seen from this perspective, sexual difference is far less intractable than orthodox Lacanians claim.

Edelman's Ambivalence

Edelman's *No Future*, too, appeals to sexual difference's status as Real while disavowing the way the Real is produced by the symbolic and determined by the signifier. Against Butler, whom Edelman charges with assuming that "'the unspeakable' intends, above all else, to speak," he deploys Copjec's insistence "that sex, as 'the structural incompleteness of language' is 'that which does not communicate itself, that which marks the subject as unknowable'" (Edelman 2004: 107). He explains that for her, "the meaning... of Lacan's notorious assertion that 'there is no sexual relation'" is that "sex, in opposing itself to sense, is also, by definition, opposed to relation, to communication" (Edelman 2004: 108). This formulation turns on a familiar conflation of "sex" and "sexuality," the latter emerging from sexual difference's failure and the former retroactively posited by that difference's circular terms.[6] This confusion recurs in Edelman's theorization of the *sinthom*osexual as the figure that "bear[s] the burden of embodying... a 'moralized sexual horror'" that "responds to something in sex that's inherently unspeakable: the Real of sexual difference, the lack that launches the living being into the empty arms of futurity" (Edelman 2004: 107–8). Edelman's formulation recalls Lacan's comments about "reproduction," but the former conflates the "presymbolic real"—to which the latter's references to reproduction refer—with the "postsymbolic real" emerging from symbolic lack (Lacan 1977: 204; Shepherdson 2008: 27).

It is the latter—postsymbolic—account of (hetero)sexual difference that queer theory needs to traverse, but *No Future* fails to press beyond it. Instead of critiquing Copjec's conflation of "sex" and "sexuality," Edelman reproduces her language and ideology of (hetero)sexual difference.

Yet if for Dean in *Beyond Sexuality*, sexual difference *must* be Real because it is neither imaginary nor symbolic, for Edelman it is "merely a *supposition*, merely a *positing*" (Dean 2000a: 86; Edelman 2004: 139). And though Edelman engages in this positing by reciting orthodox language about (hetero)sexual difference, his performance is purely rhetorical, and not a claim to a timeless truth, for *No Future*'s overarching argument is that queers are ethically compelled to traverse the fantasy of reprofuturity, "the world-making logic of heterosexual meaningfulness" (hetero)sexual difference sustains (Edelman 2004: 139). Though Edelman does not acknowledge it—and though he replicates this problem—what he calls the "ideology of reproductive necessity" involves a passing of the presymbolic (i.e., reproductive) sense of sexual difference into the term's postsymbolic sense (Edelman 2004: 121). Moreover, the most radical aspect of Edelman's diction—his labeling of "reproductive necessity" as an "ideology"—might cause one to question Lacan's assumption that all human beings seek immortality through reproduction and, in so doing, encounter their own lack (Edelman 2004: 121). But regrettably, Edelman falls back upon Lacan's language about reproduction instead of critiquing it. Though at this and other times Edelman's argument conflates the presymbolic and postsymbolic Reals, within the larger context of *No Future*, his appeals to sexual difference's Real status ironize its futility, pointing up its imbrication in desire's impossibility over and against the *sintho*mosexual's *jouissance* in the drive.

Nonetheless, Edelman's rhetoric fails to traverse the fantasy trapping subjects within this narrow set of options. Even the irony at work in his reference to "the *fact* of 'sexed reproduction'" fails to undermine (hetero)sexual difference's allegorical force, and is quickly overcome by a lengthy recitation of Lacanian orthodoxies concluding with a decidedly unironic recapitulation of the Master's allegory of the brother and sister who, seated across from one another on a train, will never be able to agree about whether they have arrived at "ladies" or "gentlemen" (Edelman 2004: 97, emphasis added). What may at first glance have appeared to be a subversive ironization of the orthodox Lacanian allegory of (hetero)sexual difference turns instead into a wholesale capitulation to its terms. And even though Edelman concludes Chapter Three with a call for queers to embrace Leonard's stance as the *sintho*mosexual who refuses (hetero)sexual difference and reproductive futurism, that character's fate—and Edelman's analysis of it—ultimately do not persuade of such a stance's efficacy. Though Leonard's act exposes the gap in the Other that Hitchcock's editing awkwardly patches over with the image of the Couple departing on a train to the future, neither *North By Northwest* nor Chapter Three of *No Future* makes it through the fantasies of (hetero)sexual difference and reproductive futurism.

This failure happens not only because *North By Northwest*'s narrative trajectory concludes with Leonard's expulsion and the restoration of the fantasy of the couple's future, but also—and more importantly—because Edelman's own conceptual framework neutralizes the *sinthom*osexual. Edelman exposes the limits of his theory's challenge to (hetero)sexual difference and reproductive futurism early on in Chapter Three, where he observes that the *sinthom*osexual's *jouissance* is produced and sustained by symbolic law. He asserts that, because *jouissance* constitutes the *objet a* around which desire circles in futility, "*sinthom*osexuality... brings into visibility the force of enjoyment that desire desires to put off. In doing so, the *sinthom*osexual reveals, unendurably to the subject of the law, *enjoyment's* infiltration of, its *structural implication in, the very law of desire that works to keep jouissance at bay*" (Edelman 2004: 86, emphasis added). Similarly, in Chapter Four, he claims that the *sinthom*osexual, like the Lacanian *sinthôme*, appears as "the inescapable Real of the drive," yet only "in abjection, *to support the emergence of Symbolic form... as a figure for what*" the symbolic's order of "meaning can never grasp" (Edelman 2004: 106–7, emphasis added). Though Edelman does not acknowledge it, these statements reveal the limits of the *sinthom*osexual's challenge to (hetero)sexual difference and reproductive futurism. Produced by the very law he challenges, the *sinthom*osexual offers an alternative to the symbolic order's regime of (hetero)sexual difference and perpetually unfulfilled desire, but no strategy for transforming its coordinates (Edelman 2004: 86).

Instead, Edelman's theory locks the *sinthom*osexual into his alternative to the symbolic in the same way Julia Kristeva's writings trap queer women in the pre-Oedipal realm of the homosexual-maternal (Kristeva 1980, 1977, 1982).[7] That Edelman does not avoid this trap symptomatizes the way his book's challenge to (hetero)sexual difference—despite its feminist potential—has not yet fully assimilated several decades of psychoanalytic feminism. As Ruti observes, *No Future* not only overlooks the similar—yet far less nihilistic—work of Hélène Cixous but is also remarkably unaware of resonances between Kristeva's *Revolution in Poetic Language* and Lacan's *Seminar XXIII* (Ruti 2008b: 116, 122). Ruti, in turn, obscures the problems Kristeva poses for queer theory—difficulties especially relevant to an assessment of Edelman's appeal to the Lacanian Real as a space of resistance to a homophobic symbolic. There are, of course, significant differences between the ways Kristeva and Edelman carve out alternatives to the symbolic: the former's pre-Oedipal is located in an imaginary bond to the mother existing prior to symbolic inscription, whereas the latter's *jouissance* is in the Real. Yet both theories pin the queer into a place allowing for same-gender erotics in a way that is not governed by the logic of (hetero)sexual difference but that offers no viable strategy for changing the symbolic's terms. If Edelman is right that in *North By Northwest*, Leonard's "jouissance that is unconstrained by fantasy or desire" goes "beyond transgression and so beyond the law," it nonetheless does not unsettle the law (Edelman 2004: 85). The *sintho*mosexual "opposes" *but does not traverse* the fantasy sustaining the symbolic order of (hetero)sexual difference (Edelman 2004: 82). Ultimately it matters very little whether the queer embraces the *sintho*mosexual's position or capitulates to the terms of the symbolic, for either way, both desire's impossibility and its underbelly, the drive's *jouissance*, remain locked within (hetero)sexual difference, leaving no possibility for structural change.

Hitchcock's Challenge to (Hetero)sexual Difference

Edelman's analysis of *The Birds* in Chapter Four goes one step further toward fantasy's traversal by explicitly acknowledging (hetero)sexual difference's rhetorical contingency, demonstrating that the film tracks its and reproductive futurism's challenge by the birds' descent upon Bodega Bay. In a reading of the scene in which Cathy thanks Melanie for bringing her family lovebirds, Edelman calls attention to the former's questioning of their "sex": "Is there a man and a woman?," she asks; "I can't tell which is which!" (Edelman 2004: 137). Edelman does not remark upon Cathy's excited exclamation that these lovebirds are "just what I wanted!," but her enthusiasm strikes me as evidence of the film's challenge to (hetero)sexual difference. Taking both figuratively and literally Melanie's response, "I suppose" (Edelman 2004: 137), Edelman asks: "what if the structuring principle, the world-making logic of heterosexual meaningfulness were merely a *supposition*, merely a *positing*, as de Man would say, and not, therefore, imbued with the referential necessity of a 'meaning'?" (Edelman 2004: 139). He goes on to argue that Cathy's question casts

> doubt on the subjectifying principle that collocates meaning itself with the structures of sexual difference.... No birdbrain, Cathy must understand that the

lovebirds, in their sameness, their apparent interchangeability, resist, or suggest a resistance to, this heterosexual dispensation by suggesting the unintelligibility *inherent* in sexual difference itself.

(Edelman 2004: 139, emphasis added)

Edelman aligns this scene with a passage from Proust's *Sodom and Gomorrah* in which Charlus and Jupien are compared to male and female birds, with Jupien marked as female. Edelman observes that for them, "'male' and 'female' are positional attributes deprived of any self-evidence for the reader from the start" (Edelman 2004: 139). Though these "positional attributes" are so naturalized that Cathy's question would seem "simply cuckoo" if asked about a man and a woman, Edelman insists upon (hetero)sexual difference's illusory nature for *all* couplings—and insists that those who wonder "Is there a man and a woman?" of same-gender pairs evade (hetero)sexual difference's "unintelligibility" by imposing its meaningless order on same- and opposite-gender couples alike (Edelman 2004: 139). However, as in Chapter Three, Edelman's awareness of (hetero)sexual difference's and reproductive futurism's fictitiousness does not dislodge their pull. Indeed, as he states in a claim betraying the ideology creating systematic problems in his argument, their "unintelligibility" is "inherent in sexual difference itself" (Edelman 2004: 139).

Nonetheless, Edelman's argument for the disruptive role of the birds' descent upon Bodega Bay does come one step further toward fantasy's traversal. For him, the birds serve as figures for the *sinthom*osexual by disrupting reproductive futurism and the fantasy of (hetero)sexual difference on which it is founded. He reads the attacking birds as "refus[ing] the promise of meaning condensed in the seed that is the Child" and as "giv[ing] the bird to the fantasy of reproduction as the seedbed of futurity" (Edelman 2004: 132–3). The birds "gesture... toward the death drive that lives within reproductive futurism" (Edelman 2004: 132) and

> expose the misconception on which its reality rests: the misconception that conception itself can assure the endurance, by enacting the truth, of the Symbolic order of meaning and preserve, in the form of the future, the prospect of someday redeeming the primal loss that makes sexual rapport impossible and precludes the signifying system from ever arriving at any closure.
>
> (Edelman 2004: 134)

Ultimately, the birds function as "reified obstacles to the dominant fantasy of (hetero)sexual rapport.... They come... to trace a connection, as directly as the crow flies, between 'disorder in the family' and the rupture, the radical loss of familiarity, unleashed by jouissance" (Edelman 2004: 147–9). It is clear at this point in *No Future* that Edelman is no true believer in (hetero)sexual difference's fantasies of reproductive futurism, and that he embraces their undoing by the *sinthom*osexual's death drive.

However, this is a strategy for (hetero)sexual difference's collapse but not necessarily for its traversal. It is unclear that the embrace of *jouissance* that Edelman's final chapter upholds as a herald of the heteronormative symbolic's destruction promises any change whatsoever, given his book's thoroughgoing demonstration that the *sinthom*osexual is already a prominent feature of reproductive futurism and (hetero)sexual difference. As he acknowledges in Chapter Three, the *sinthom*osexual is produced *by* the symbolic, and props up its illusions by challenging them. Edelman thus ends *No Future* by forecasting a vicious cycle in which the symbolic will continue to produce and flog the *sinthom*osexual for figuring the impossibility of (hetero)sexual difference and reproductive futurism. He concludes that

> The political regime of futurism, unable to escape what it abjects, negates it as the negation of meaning, of the Child, and of the future that the Child portends. Attempting to evade the insistent Real always surging in its blood, it lovingly rocks the cradle of life to the drumbeat of the endless blows it aims at *sinthom*osexuals. Somewhere, someone else will be savagely beaten and left to die—sacrificed to a future whose beat goes on, like a pulse or a heart—and another corpse will be left like a mangled scarecrow to frighten the birds who are gathering now, who are beating their wings, and who, like the drive, keep on coming.
>
> (Edelman 2004: 153–4)

Despite Edelman's vehement repudiation of futurity, this scene depicts a future: a bleak one whose centripetal movement sacrifices the occasional *sinthom*osexual to allow the symbolic to continue to function. Conceptually, this is as far as Edelman's reworking of Lacan enables his argument to go.

Nonetheless, through this montage of Matthew Shepard's murder and the narrative trajectory of Hitchcock's *The Birds*, the closing paragraph of *No Future* hints at the possibility of breaking this circuit. Edelman's final sentence implies that, despite the inevitable murder of the next Matthew Shepard, *sinthom*osexuals could eventually gain sufficient numbers to cause the demise of the "the world-making logic of heterosexual meaningfulness" and its prop, (hetero)sexual difference (Edelman 2004: 139). However, *The Birds'* narrative trajectory opens out to an uncertain future in which "heterosexual meaningfulness" is left insecure but not entirely obliterated. At the film's end, the birds attack and seriously wound Melanie. Mitch succeeds in removing the family from the house and into the car, after which point the film ends with a shot of their departure from the property. Yet this sequence is far more ambiguous than *North By Northwest*'s ending. Mitch's family must abandon their home as the birds mass around the car, claiming what was formerly the space of the heterosexual family and suggesting the possibility of another attack. At the same time, the film pays close attention to his mother as she comforts the injured Melanie, showing a newfound warmth toward her rival. The mother's behavior intimates a future for the Couple and a resolution of the maternal jealousy a common reading of the film takes to precipitate the birds' attack. The birds do not stop the car from driving away, and its apparently successful departure suggests that the heterosexual family has not been obliterated but rather relocated and consolidated. With Melanie's life in danger, however, one is left with a sense of uncertainty about their future. Moreover, unlike the ending of *North By Northwest* in which the Couple's triumph is secured by Leonard's elimination, *The Birds*' *sintho*mosexuals offer reprieve to the family while holding their newly claimed terrain and continuing to attack other towns. The film thus ends with the sense that neither the Couple nor the *sintho*mosexuals are yet victorious. The ambivalence at play in the final sequence of *The Birds* mimics the state initially induced by fantasy's traversal: not that of having no future, but that of not yet having established its coordinates.

Edelman remarks upon the film's "deliberately disorienting conclusion," arguing that it "raises meaninglessness as a possibility" while using reproductive ideology as a context to place "a particular meaning on such meaninglessness" (Edelman 2004: 118–20). He rightly observes that *The Birds*' ending "declines to affirm *as certain* any future at all" (Edelman 2004: 118, emphasis added). However, there is a world of difference between refusing to affirm *certainty* about the future—that is, to be assured of specific details in advance—and indulging in the apocalyptic repudiation of the very *idea* of a future to which Edelman's title, *No Future*, points. It is in light of this distinction that we must view his reliance upon Lacan. In the clinical context, traversing the fantasy does not lead to the wholesale abandonment of the idea of having a future, but rather clears ground for previously unimaginable ways of inhabiting it.

No Future misses this point even as Edelman rightfully criticizes Butler and mainstream gay and lesbian politics for turning on imaginary and symbolic appeals for recognition and coherence. His de Manian critique of meaning informs this stance, which approaches history as a "rhetoric or poetics rather than as the ongoing dialectic of meaning's eventual realization through time" (Edelman 2004: 135). In describing irony as "synchronic" and allegory as "diachronic," de Man speaks of two different ways literature can organize temporality and signification (de Man 1983: 226). He does not, however, repudiate the idea of a future in the sweeping way Edelman assumes. Rejecting a dialectical view of historical progress in favor of a "rhetorics" or "poetics" does not require that one jettison more open-ended ways of thinking about history or the future.

Ironically, Edelman's reading of *The Birds* ultimately engages in more of a dialectic than he acknowledges. Though he argues earlier in the chapter that *The Birds* offers a narrative undercutting the "narrative covenant of futurity" it appears to embrace, his reading's privileging of the film's end reflects a conventional approach to narrative he aligns in Chapter Three with reprofuturity and its order of illusory meaning. *No Future*'s logic culminates in the future offered by this final scene, which envisions an accumulation of queers whose *jouissance* promises to undo reproductive futurism's and (hetero)sexual difference's tyranny. Thus Hitchcock's *The Birds* offers *No Future* a future— albeit a highly ambiguous one—that Edelman's interpretation of Lacan refuses. Whereas Edelman's *sintho*mosexual revels in *jouissance* without transforming the symbolic via the Real, Hitchcock's film offers something closer to fantasy's traversal: a future in which the future offered by reproductive futurism and its prop, (hetero)sexual difference, is left open by the birds' swelling numbers and ever more powerful assaults on Bodega Bay's residents.

Traversing the Fantasy of (Hetero)sexual Difference: Figuring the Future

In *Sex, or the Unbearable* (2014), Edelman continues to stress "the necessity of recognizing the importance of addressing structural antagonisms in any analytic of the social," and for the first time acknowledges the potential "the negativity of relation" holds for "making transformation possible" (Edelman in Berlant and Edelman 2014: xii, 29, 29). These are claims with which Dean and Ruti would likely agree. Edelman also labels sexual difference "contingent," arguing that "Lacan's well-known assertion that 'there is no sexual relation' resists the imperative to resolve the structural antagonism of the symbolic" that is "given a contingent expression in heteronormativity's sexual binarism" (Edelman in Edelman and Berlant 2014: 1–2). Nonetheless, he declines to imagine what lies beyond the subjective "undoing" prompted by fantasy's traversal: to offer alternatives to the "contingent" fantasy of (hetero)sexual difference whose oppressive vision *No Future* rightfully targets (Edelman in Berlant and Edelman 2014: 1).

Edelman's refusal of all modes of addressing the future is troubling because it downplays the transformative aims of fantasy's traversal. Those who voluntarily enter into psychoanalysis are *seeking* transformation, and in its clinical form, traversing the fantasy *is* futurally oriented, though it offers no guarantees of a better future. But if, as Ruti observes, psychoanalysis's goal is to expand the analysand's options, it is difficult to accept Edelman's assertion that all futural orientations are dangerous (Ruti 2008a: 498). His version of traversing the fantasy exclusively emphasizes subjective destitution, suggesting that queers embrace the figure of the *sintho*mosexual to abandon imaginary misrecognitions and the symbolic order of illusory meaning sustaining them. Yet Edelman disavows the way embracing the role of the *sintho*mosexual and traversing the fantasy creates an opening for a future, even though its contours are not immediately apparent.

Whereas Edelman's argument leaves the *sintho*mosexual suspended in a place of *joussiance* that does not challenge the symbolic's coordinates, Tim Dean observes that the anti-social thesis, with its goal of "shattering... the civilized ego," promises "not the end of sociality but rather its inception" (Dean 2006: 827).[8] The only participant in the 2006 *PMLA* forum to engage Edelman's use of psychoanalysis, Dean attributes *No Future*'s negativity to its author's inflexible interpretation of the drive, which is far more unpredictable—and far more capable of constructive as well as destructive effects—than Edelman allows. Tim Dean backgrounds *Beyond Sexuality*'s Lacanian arguments, noting that "[t]he symbolic law of reproductive futurism is not as encompassing or determinative as Lacanians like Edelman seem to think" and using the work of Sigmund Freud, Lacan, Guy Hocquenghem, and Bersani to launch his own account of "new forms of sociability... not grounded in imaginary identity or the struggle for intersubjective recognition" (Dean 2006: 827). Unlike Edelman, whose *sintho*mosexual embraces the death drive, Dean argues that in psychoanalytic terms it is impossible to embrace a drive, which "never can become an object of consciousness" (Dean 2008: 208). The drive "is amenable to sublimation yet constitutively unavailable for individual or collective identification": though "it never can be embraced or deployed for political purposes," it can underpin politics (Dean 2008: 208). Dean also conceives of the drive as "oriented as much toward an underdetermined future as toward an always already determined past," and as not "opposed to *every* form of social viability" (Dean 2008: 195, 204). Even though for Dean, "human drives... do not unequivocally support our well-being or even our survival," they are "not purely destructive," for they also prompt "inventiveness" (Dean 2008: 206). I am interested in developing the implications for fantasy's traversal of the idea that subjective destitution need not involve permanently repudiating the social.

Dean's account of the drive's unpredictability suggests that fantasy's traversal is initially experienced as a field of immanent possibilities rather than as a new topography mapped out in advance. Ruti, too, finds in the Real a negativity pointing not to subjectivity's permanent obliteration but to its renewal (Ruti 2008b: 114). Though I concur with Ruti's view of the Real's generativity, she does not address *No Future*'s political implications—questions that are particularly pressing for queer theory. Nonetheless, her and Dean's arguments reveal that Edelman's work is not the only viable account of fantasy's traversal. In neither Dean nor Ruti's accounts does traversing the fantasy entail the wholesale repudiation of politics, signification, and futurally oriented thinking Edelman promotes. Though he is right to criticize Butler's excessive emphasis on the symbolic, for resignifying its terms and transforming the imaginary do not dislodge the kernel in the Real that keeps constrictive fantasies in place, his thoroughgoing rejection of all signification distorts psychoanalytic theory and overstates the case against her. In so doing, Edelman undermines his own effort to traverse the fantasy of reproductive futurism, even though Lacan's work still holds significant potential for feminist and queer theory.

Traversing the Fantasy of (Hetero)sexual Difference: Embracing the *Sinthôme*

This difficulty with Edelman's argument is a consequence of Lacan's having never fully developed the accounts of the *sinthôme* and fantasy's traversal that *No Future* grafts into queer theory. The *sinthôme* is an antiquated word for "symptom," though Lacan distinguishes between these two concepts. Roberto Harari offers a useful explication of this distinction despite his reliance upon an orthodox understanding of Lacanian sexual difference. The "symptom," which produces "[m]etaphor" and "remains within the order of the signifier" (Harari 2002: 241), consists of the anxiety-inducing and "'rotten' jouissance" of "meaning" (Harari 2002: 235). By contrast, the "*sinthome*," which enacts "nomination" and "works by means of the letter" (Harari 2002: 241), entails an "'opaque' jouissance" that "privileges what is heard over what is meaningful" (Harari 2002: 235). Associating the symptom with the signifier and the *sinthôme* with the letter—which Lacan describes as the "material medium [*support*] that concrete discourse borrows from language"—Harari stresses the transformative potential of "identification with the *sinthome*" (Harari 2002: 358; Lacan 2006c: 413). Whereas unhappy subjects wish to alleviate symptoms, those who embrace their *sinthômes* and traverse the fantasy can experience profound change (Harari 2002: 348–9).

For Lacan, the fundamental fantasy sustains desiring subjectivity and is supported by all three orders, tied together by the *sinthôme*. Traversing the fantasy enables a new *sinthôme* to emerge, reinaugurating and reorienting the subject. However, this theory develops gradually as Lacan's seminars progress, and does not take a consistent form. Because explorations of fantasy's traversal eventually cede to theories of identifying with the *sinthôme*, it is unclear whether the two theories are distinct or whether the latter merely elaborates the former. Lacan addresses traversing the fantasy at length in *Seminar XI*, in a discussion building to the problem of that process's "beyond" (Lacan 1977: 273). He writes that the question of how "a subject who has traversed the radical phantasy experiences the drive" has "never been approached," although it points to "the beyond of analysis" (Lacan 1977: 273). Later, in *Seminar XXIII*, he uses a reading of James Joyce's experimental writing to rework the question of psychoanalysis's aim, suggesting that it ends when the analysand identifies with the *sinthôme*. *Seminar XXIII* concludes by reprising the question of the treatment's "beyond," leaving it up to his audience's response in the same way Joyce's texts track their protagonists' epiphanies and simultaneously provoke different revelations in readers.

Though scholarship in *Seminar XXIII*'s wake offers rudimentary maps of the psychoanalytic treatment's beyond, Lacan's writings do not offer evidence that definitively settles such disputes. Contemporary theorists have been left to develop the beyond's potential consequences for subjectivity, identifying several prospects for what might follow fantasy's traversal. These developments all hinge on the *sinthôme*, yet published versions of *Seminar XXIII* are unreliable. Reflecting "what was heard by those responsible for the transcription (and very often repeated unquestioningly by translators)," these texts are beset by "contradictions and obscurities" complicating interpretation (Harari 2002: 40).

These "unconcluded" aspects of Lacan's work are nonetheless generative, inviting "new inventions of his own reinvention of Freudian psychoanalysis" to emerge as scholars refine the concept of the *sinthôme* (Chiesa 2007: 189). Though Lacanian scholarship from the 1990s all too often takes the form of internecine disputes in which orthodox hardliners oppose those who offer more flexible interpretations of the master's sacred texts, debates over the *sinthôme* cannot be settled through such constrictive rhetoric. The permanently open question of "the beyond of analysis" is salutary, attuned to the spirit of fantasy's traversal: the point of which is to clear the ground for a future whose contours are not available in advance (Lacan 1977: 273).

Current scholarship nonetheless suggests several possibilities for fantasy's "beyond." Yannis Stavrakakis argues that for Lacan it is only by embracing the *sinthome* and "accepting... an impossible representation... that it is possible to 'represent' the impossible or rather to identify with the impossibility of its representation," traversing the fantasy (Stavrakakis 1999: 134). Lorenzo Chiesa notes that one possible outcome of fantasy's traversal is that the subject will actively engage in politics by "*nam[ing] a movement*, promot[ing] a new Symbolic—resymbolized through one's individual Master-Signifier/*sinthôme*—and struggle politically to establish its hegemony" (Chiesa 2007: 191).

In these accounts, the *sinthôme* would reconfigure the imaginary, symbolic, and Real, supporting them with a new fundamental fantasy.[9] This reconfiguration need not be understood as defeat. Although Butler and others claim that the Lacanian symbolic regulates subjectivity, Carlson observes that the symbolic instead "enables structure to be operationalized" and used creatively by the subject (de la Torre 2018: 6). So understood, the symbolic does not constrain but rather "sustain[s] the subject in the exercise of desire or freedom" (de la Torre 2018: 4). The establishment of a new symbolic could therefore provide support for a subject taking a new direction after fantasy's traversal. These new directions could be driven by fantasies dispensing with or operating beside (hetero) sexual difference: or granting other axes of identity such as race, ethnicity, and nationality equal or greater importance than gender or sexuality.

Other thinkers find reason to believe fantasy's traversal could lead to something more radical than a reconfiguration of the three orders and a new fundamental fantasy. Such an outcome would entail a new form of subjectivity dispensing with the desire for recognition in the Other. Both Ed Pluth and Ruti argue that after fantasy's traversal, the subject is no longer mired in imaginary misrecognitions or illusory symbolic meanings but has achieved an open-ended relationship to signification. Pluth views traversing the fantasy and embracing the *sinthôme* as a process of "voiding of the Other" and supplanting the subject's previous "investment in fantasy" with a more "direct investment in signifiers as such" (Pluth 2007: 163). I similarly see Lacan's later work—for instance, *Seminar XI* and *Seminar XX*—as less invested in recognition or a structuralist account of the symbolic as in a more expansive account of signification in the Other. These theories of the psychoanalytic treatment's end are all potentially useful for queer theory—far more so than Edelman's bleak version of Lacan. Moreover, by implicitly challenging (hetero)sexual difference's status as the fundamental antinomy animating subjectivity, they make intersectional theorizations of the psychoanalytic subject possible.

Rearticulating the Fundamental Fantasy

One contemporary interpretation of the psychoanalytic treatment's "beyond" assumes that embracing the *sinthôme* knots the subject, rendering the imaginary, symbolic, and Real functional. For both psychotic and non-psychotic subjects, the *sinthôme* works as what Lacan describes in *Seminar XXIII* as "the fourth ring" tying together the Borromean knot he previously described as a triad comprised of the real, imaginary, and symbolic (Lacan 2016: 3, 12). Although the knot's three circles are usually inseverably locked, because "a knot is something that can be botched" in some cases "a mistake" in the triad's construction leaves it potentially separable and the subject at risk for psychosis (Lacan 2016: 80, 76). Lacan claims that evidence from the "unconscious" reveals "piles of" such "botched cases" (Lacan 2016: 80). To exemplify a "mistake," he claims that Joyce's unconscious fused with the Real and split from the ego in a rupture that freed the imaginary, making it dispensable (Lacan 2016: 134). To account for the fact that relatively few cases culminate in psychotic breaks, in *Seminar XXIII* Lacan replaces the aforementioned triad with a tetrad—"the imaginary, the real, the symptom... and the symbolic"—whose new element, the *sinthôme*, creates "the possibility of binding" the other terms together and staving off psychosis even when the knot is "botched" (Lacan 2016: 12, 12, 80). Lacan says that

> Should the symbolic thereby come free, as I once noted it would, we have a way of mending it, which is to fashion what I defined for the first time as a sinthome. This is the item that enables the symbolic, the imaginary, and the real to go on holding together, even though here none of them are actually holding on to any of the others anymore due to the two mistakes.
>
> (Lacan 2016: 77)

He further specifies that the *sinthôme* is "that which enables the trefoil knot, not to go on forming a trefoil knot, but rather to maintain itself in a position that *looks like* it is forming a trefoil knot" (Lacan 2016: 77). This ability to create the appearance of a knot despite a "mistake" makes the *sinthôme* a potentially effective means through which "the Borromean link" can "be mended" and the real, imaginary, and symbolic realigned (Lacan 2016: 76).

In all cases, whether psychotic or non-psychotic, the *sinthôme* appears accidentally; it is not willed into existence. Yet to say that a particular *sinthôme* is a "mistake" does not necessarily indicate that it is pathological, for all subjects are constituted through the errors their unique *sinthômes* suture (Lacan 2016: 134). Chiesa nonetheless argues that for non-psychotic subjects, traversing the fantasy is akin to a temporary psychosis that undoes the fundamental fantasy to clear ground for a different fantasy's emergence. By contrast, actual psychosis involves "the subject's fundamental fantasy being undone once and for all," creating a "partially individuated symbolic" enabling the person to function (Chiesa 2007: 184, 189).

Chiesa claims that Joyce is one such "non-triggered psychotic" whose position "in between neurosis and psychosis" obviates the "need to traverse any fundamental fantasy" to produce a "partially individuated symbolic" (Chiesa 2007: 189). Chiesa asserts that the writer's example offers nothing more than an idiosyncratic, personal, and apolitical solution: one in which, by creating his "founding Master-Signifier" to avoid psychosis, Joyce has "*become his own name*, develop[ed] his own *sinthome*, while coexisting with the hegemonic Other" (Chiesa 2007: 191). Moreover, in a particularly panicky instance of slippery slope reasoning, Chiesa speculates that "a hypothetical society of fully *sinthomatic* beings of language... would *inevitably*" be catastrophic because of the resultant "fragmentation of the symbolic into many symbolics" (Chiesa 2007: 191, emphasis added). However, Lacan is unclear on this point.

It is easy to discern in Chiesa's explanation a structuralist assumption from Lacan's *Seminar III*: that to avoid psychosis, the subject must accept a master signifier to knot the imaginary, symbolic, and Real. However, as I argue in *Insane Passions* (2006), *Seminar III* is problematic for feminist and queer theory because it insists that the subject accept the Name-of-the-Father or risk psychosis. This argument mandates compliance with the patriarchal order of (hetero)sexual difference and leads to the orthodox Lacanian conflation of transgender with psychosis Grace Lavery critiques in Chiesa's 2016 *The Not-two* (Lavery 2019a: 143–4).

However, Lacan's later work gives queer and trans theory cause for optimism because it presents traversing the fantasy as a way of detaching from what Chiesa calls "hegemonic fundamental fantasies" and reconstituting subjectivity along the lines of a different fantasy (Chiesa 2007: 189). In my view, (hetero)sexual difference is a fundamental fantasy available for such a traversal. Afterwards, symbolic inscription could be achieved through the acceptance of a master signifier other than the Name-of-the-Father.

Raul Moncayo stresses that the Name-of-the-Father is only one of many ways of reattaching the three orders to reformulate the fundamental fantasy and reinaugurate the subject (Moncayo 2016: 47). He emphasizes that the subject is not a voluntaristic agent who can single-handedly change their *sinthôme* but rather that which is intuited on the basis of the knot in the Real. Tying the three orders enacts "the binding of the drive," though it also has "unbinding properties" (Moncayo 2016: 46–7). According to this view, the subject is a retroactive effect of the knot rather than its self-authorizing creator.

In "Is There a Cause of the Subject?" Žižek (1994a) similarly presents the subject as retroactively constructed by the three orders. As I argue in Chapter 1, his work highlights the symbolic order's availability for transformation. For Žižek, traversing the fantasy leads not to the permanent repudiation of futurity but to the emergence of a new *point de capiton* grounding a newly configured imaginary, symbolic, and Real. In *The Sublime Object*, he argues that politics takes place through "symbolic rearticulation via the intervention of the Real of an act" targeting the *point de capiton* and replacing it with a different signifier (Žižek 1989: 262). This act's ground-clearing negativity is followed by a new order's emergence.

Drawing on *The Sublime Object*, Stavrakakis observes that "Going through the fantasy entails the realization of the lack or inconsistency in the Other which is masked by fantasy, the separation between *objet petit a* and the Other" (Stavrakakis 1999: 134). Traversing the fantasy does not abolish all sociality, but does symbolically recognize "the impossibility of social closure" (Stavrakakis 1999: 134). Stavrakakis defines politics as this paradoxical gesture of putting the void into language (Stavrakakis 1999: 135). He claims that it is only during a "brief moment, after the collapse of an order and before the articulation of another one," that one can "attest to the visibility of the hole in the big Other" (Stavrakakis 1999: 135). For him, the basic structure of the imaginary, symbolic, and Real remains intact after fantasy's traversal, although their contents can shift to accommodate a new regime. Although Žižek similarly argues that traversing the fantasy can initiate profound political transformation, he denies that the Name-of-the-Father could be replaced with another master signifier. Nonetheless, as I argue in Chapter 1, his theory opens up this possibility despite his resistance to it.

Whereas Žižek and Stavrakakis graft the concept of the Real into Marxist theory (Žižek 1999; Butler, Laclau, and Žižek 2000), Edelman rejects politics and the social altogether.[10] Though his neologism—the *sinthom*osexual—puts a void into language, he denies that gesture's political implications. Equating all forms of politics and structural rearticulation with Butler's work, he presents his theory of the *sinthom*osexual's refusal of reprofuturity as an alternative to her argument in *Antigone's Claim* (2002) that structural change can be achieved by resignifying the symbolic. He asserts that "Butler's Antigone conduces to futurism's logic of intelligibility by seeking no more to widen the reach of what it allows us to grasp" and "moves, by way of the future, toward the ongoing legitimation of social form through the recognition that is said to afford 'ontological certainty and durability'" (Edelman 2004: 107). By contrast, "*sinthom*osexuals would insist on the unintelligible's unintelligibility, on the internal limit to signification and the impossibility of turning Real loss to meaningful profit in the Symbolic without its persistent remainder: the inescapable Real of the drive" (Edelman 2004: 106–7). Though I agree with Edelman's insistence that intervention take place in the Real *and* the symbolic, his formulation implodes sexual difference and reproductive futurism while refusing to develop viable alternatives.

Edelman states that "*Sinthom*osexuals could not bring the symbolic order to crisis since they only emerge, in abjection, *to support the emergence of Symbolic form*" (Edelman 2004: 106–7, emphasis added). This position reflects Dominiek Hoens and Pluth's argument that the *sinthôme* provides "the grounding principle of the Symbolic" and, as such, "enjoyment not outside of but inherent to the Symbolic" (Hoens and Pluth 2002: 14). Lacan, too, claims that "because the subject is what one signifier represents relative to another signifier, ... it is in the symptom that one of these two signifiers from the symbolic derives its support" (Lacan 2016: 15). In elevating the *sinthom*osexual for refusing to engage the symbolic producing him, Edelman suggests that queers should simply abandon attempts at structural change.

He concedes that Butler shows that "the norms of the social order do, in fact, change through catachresis, and those who once were persecuted as figures of 'moralized sexual horror' may" gain "a place on the public stage" (Edelman 2004: 107). However, he also insists that this "redistribution of social roles doesn't stop the cultural production of... *sinthom*osexuals" (Edelman 2004: 107). Though I agree with Edelman's Žižekian assertion that there will always be a "persistent remainder" erupting from the Real no matter what shape the symbolic may take, he overlooks the most promising implications of Lacan's intertwining of the symbolic with the imaginary and Real: that a traversal of the fantasy that intervenes at the level of the symbolic *and* the Real could change the *point de capiton*, making something other than sexual difference the constitutive antagonism governing their operation.[11]

Edelman reaches this impasse and fails to move beyond it because he frames rearticulation in Butlerian terms—as solely symbolic—and not in the terms of Žižek's *The Sublime Object*, according to which rearticulation can more profoundly intervene in both the symbolic and the Real through the kinds of acts I describe in Chapter 1. In Žižek's, Chiesa's, and Stavrakakis' accounts, we *cannot do without* the imaginary and symbolic, no matter how illusory and prone to failure they may be, and however dependent they may be on the Real of the *sinthôme*. Edelman, by contrast, assumes that if we traverse the fantasy by embracing the position of the *sinthom*osexual, we can dispense with the imaginary and symbolic along with the ideologies of reproductive futurism and sexual difference they support.

For Žižek, on the other hand, the subjective destitution involved in traversing the fantasy is not a permanent state but rather a temporary, ground-clearing movement opening the way for a new *point de capiton* reconfiguring the imaginary, symbolic, and Real. If a politicized version of Lacan is dependent on grafting into the social his theory of the Real's constitutive antagonism by proposing that the symptom is "that which is ideologically thought to introduce disharmony in a society that would otherwise be harmoniously unified under a certain utopian ideal," then it is important to remember that this antagonism is structural (Stavrakakis 1999: 133). For queer theory, this means that homosexuality is neither inherently disruptive nor inherently anti-social. It only appears as such in homophobic fantasies. Edelman clearly recognizes this point. But if he is right to suggest that embracing the *sinthom*osexual's position is a viable strategy for traversing the fantasies of reproductive futurism and (hetero) sexual difference, he is wrong to assume that this obviates sociality or futurity. Because the Real of antagonism is "constitutive of the social" and structurally unavoidable, traversing the fantasy does not provide an escape from sociality or disharmony, nor does it permanently suspend futurity (Stavrakakis 1999: 133). In attempting to make of the "brief moment" following fantasy's traversal a permanent state of *jouissance*, Edelman suspends his challenge to reproductive futurism and sexual difference outside of time and space, precluding another order's emergence (Stavrakakis 1999: 135). By contrast, for Stavrakakis and Žižek, traversing the fantasy involves repudiating the current order by creating a temporary void to patch with a new régime. This account of traversing the fantasy offers a way of reorganizing the positive contents of the imaginary, symbolic, and Real rather than obliterating their structural functions. Even though Žižek resists this possibility, such a traversal could replace (hetero)sexual difference with another constitutive antagonism governing subjectivity.

A Politics of the Signifier, A Politics of the Real

The second interpretation of the psychoanalytic treatment's "beyond" comes from a more radical reading of Lacan's *Seminar XI*, *Seminar XX*, and *Seminar XXIII*. The latter two seminars extensively engage Joyce's postmodern fragmentation and open-ended signification, marking a move away from the symbolic. This shift in emphasis is legible as early as *Seminar XI*, which gives sustained attention to the Real but emphasizes the signifier and Other rather than the symbolic. Lacan writes that "The Other is the locus in which is situated the chain of the signifier that governs whatever may be made present of the subject—it is the field of that living being in which the subject has to appear" (Lacan 1977: 203). This process constitutes and splits the subject. Lacan explains that "The subject is born in so far as the signifier emerges in the field of the Other. But, by this very fact, this subject—which, was previously nothing if not a subject coming into being—solidifies into a signifier" (Lacan 1977: 199). After the birth of the subject comes "separation," and

> By separation, the subject finds, one might say, the weak point of the primal dyad of the signifying articulation, in so far as it is alienating in essence. It is in the interval between these two signifiers that resides the desire offered to the mapping of the subject in the experience of the discourse of the Other he has to deal with, let us say, by way of illustration, the mother. It is in so far as his desire is beyond or falls short of what she says, of what she hints at, of what she brings out as meaning, it is in so far as his desire is unknown, it is in this point of lack, that the desire of the subject is constituted. The subject—by a process that is not without deception, which is not without presenting that fundamental twist by which what the subject rediscovers is not that which animates his movement of rediscovery—comes back, then, to the initial point, which is that of his lack as such, of the lack of his *aphanisis*.
>
> (Lacan 1977: 219)

As Lacan's casual reference to the mother suggests, *Seminar XI* continues to describe gender roles and familial configurations in antiquated ways. While *Seminar III*'s explicit homophobia is absent from *Seminar XI*, the latter still figures desire heterosexually. *Seminar XI* also claims that "the field of the Other" is, "strictly speaking, ... the Oedipus complex"—a concept long discredited by feminist and queer theory (Lacan 1977: 204).

Nonetheless, *Seminar XI* suggests that it is possible for the subject to traverse the fundamental fantasy and release him or herself from the ideologies of (hetero)sexual difference on which Lacan's own exposition relies. Because the Other is the realm of the signifier, his texts should be understood as clusters of signification available for challenge and transformation. He writes, "What the subject has to free himself of is the aphanisic effect of the binary signifier and, if we look at it more closely, we shall see that in fact it is a question of nothing else in the function of freedom" (Lacan 1977: 219). Shortly thereafter, he begins to discuss the way analysis can help the analysand traverse the fundamental fantasy. Doing so targets the imaginary, symbolic, *and* Real—so the subject's process of shaking off "the aphanisic effect of the binary signifier" goes beyond the symbolic resignifications advocated by Butler (Lacan 1977: 219).

Moreover, in *Seminar XX*, Lacan asserts that "the apparent necessity of the phallic function turns out to be mere contingency" (Lacan 1998: 94). This statement differs significantly from his notorious claim in "The Signification of the phallus" that the phallus is "the privileged signifier of that mark in which the role of the logos is joined with the advent of desire" (Lacan 1998: 287). While that essay notes that a subject's "anatomical" "sex" does not determine their position with respect to the phallus, *Seminar XX* goes farther by marking it as contingent (Lacan 1998: 282). *Seminar XX* also emphasizes that the Other is not systematically organized. Lacan writes, "[T]here is no Other of the Other. The Other, that is the locus in which everything that can be articulated on the basis of the signifier comes to be inscribed, is, in its foundation, the Other in the most radical sense. That is why the signifier, with this open parenthesis, marks the Other as barred" (Lacan 1998: 81). This differs markedly from the language he uses to discuss the symbolic order in *Seminar III*. And while the ideology of (hetero)sexual difference *does* continue to pervade *Seminar XX*, which elaborates the supposed antinomy between the masculine and feminine, that seminar's open-ended account of signification and explicit assertion of the phallus's contingency suggest that subjectivity and desire need not require accepting the Name of the Father or the phallus. Even though Lacan's own reasoning does not go so far, *Seminar XX* makes it possible to imagine structures of desire and signification that are not anchored by the phallus or governed by the fantasy of (hetero)sexual difference.

Others similarly suggest that release from a symbolic governed by a master signifier could be salutary rather than catastrophic. Pluth's *Signifiers and Acts* (2007) offers an interpretation of Lacan's work on the *sinthôme* and traversing the fantasy that does not require a new Master-Signifier. Dispensing with the need for a newly configured fundamental fantasy, Pluth frames the "beyond" of fantasy's traversal in a way that suggests that refusing to acquiesce to a symbolic grounded in paternal law is not necessarily psychotic. Pluth draws heavily on *Seminar XI* to describe fantasy's traversal as leading to a subjectivity of "the act" distinct from the form of subjectivity preceding it (Pluth 2007: 118).[12] Unlike the latter, which is supported by fantasy, the former entails an engagement with signifiers that is not totalizing and not motivated by the desire for recognition in the Other.

Pluth emphasizes that the "subject of the act" uses signifiers, but not to demand recognition (Pluth 2007: 155). Joyce's punning neologisms—to which Lacan pays careful attention—exemplify the more inventive uses of signifiers possible for the "subject of the act": they engage "in something like a reinvention of the Other" (Pluth 2007: 155).[13] Paul Verhaeghe and Frédéric Declercq further explain that in *Seminar XXIII*, Lacan supplanted his earlier emphasis on the way the symbolic order is secured by the Name-of-the-Father with "the opposite idea: that there is no Other of the Other" (Verhaeghe and Declercq 2002: 71).

By *Seminar XXIII*, the key element is the *sinthôme*'s or master signifier's "function"—"separation—and its operative character, meaning that the operative function is a signifier" that has an individual and idiosyncratic—rather than an universal—form (Verhaeghe and Declercq 2002: 71). Even though "In Freud's time," the master "signifier was linked to the real father, . . . this is a mere historical contingency" (Verhaeghe and Declercq 2002: 71).[14] Although Lacan offers Oedipus and the Name-of-the-Father as examples of *sinthômes*, he opens up the possibility of replacing them with others (Lacan 2016: 13). He thereby "invites everyone to follow Joyce's example and to create their own *sinthome* at the place of the lack of the Other" (Verhaeghe and Declercq 2002: 75). According to Juliet Flower MacCannell, this "creative act" "transforms the traditional symptom and the symbol alike into a new hybrid form: a linguistic, or linguistically modeled, formation that somehow permits *jouissance* to flow through it rather than be repressed and hidden by it" (MacCannell 2008: 53; Verhaeghe and Declercq 2002: 75).

This mode of subjectivity is not necessarily inscribed in the symbolic and subject to a master signifier simply by engaging in signification. The closing passages and diagrams of Lacan's *Seminar XXIII* invoke the unconscious, ego, imaginary, and Real, but do not include the symbolic. Pluth therefore argues that even though Lacan ceases to speak of the act and traversing the fantasy in his final seminars, emphasizing instead the need for the analysand to embrace and enjoy the *sinthôme*, those texts raise the question "of what remains of the Other after the act, and what can be done with . . . a de-Othered symbolic"

(Pluth 2007: 163). He observes that "[w]hat happens after the voiding of the Other is that rather than an investment in fantasy, which is mediated by the Other, there is a direct investment in signifiers as such; and it is on this basis that a partnership with the Other, on the level of enjoyment, is forged" (Pluth 2007: 163). Pluth considers this outcome to be equally the case for the "subject of the act" (of fantasy's traversal, derived from seminar XI) as for the subject that has come to enjoy their *sinthôme* (Pluth 2007: 155).

By allowing for a new politics of the signifier that intervenes in the Real, *Signifiers and Acts* implicitly counters Chiesa's false assumption that politics are impossible from Joyce's position as a subject embracing their *sinthôme*. Chiesa's presumption surprisingly overlooks several decades of scholarship documenting the way Joyce's (and other modernist writers') experimental language does not evade but rather offers a fresh approach to political questions. The politics of language and gender animate the psychoanalytic feminist approaches to Joyce that Cixous and Kristeva initiated in the 1970s; the politics of Irish resistance to British domination drive the postcolonial approaches to Joyce pioneered by Vincent Cheng (Cheng 1995) and Emer Nolan (Nolan 1995).[15] As MacCannell notes, in *Seminar XXIII*, Lacan approaches Joyce's wordplay as a form of resistance conditioned by his situation as an Irishman subject to Imperial English (MacCannell 2008: 47). She reminds us, too, that Cixous—whose research on Joyce was well under way by the time she met Lacan—served as his assistant during the initial stages of the work that would eventually lead to *Seminar XXIII*. Ruti further observes that Cixous' "The Laugh of the Medusa" uses "the annihilation of the normative order as a means for constituting new forms of sociality, generosity, and love," and goes on to find similarly productive energies in Lacan's seminar on the *sinthôme*—even though Ruti surprises by downplaying the two theorists' most significant differences (Ruti 2008b: 116). Pluth's book, too, appeals to Lacan's reading of Joyce to emphasize the more generative approach to signification distinguishing Lacan's "subject of the act" from that of fantasy, allowing the former a new mode of political engagement (Pluth 2007: 155). Whereas scholars such as George Haggerty (2006), Lynda Hart (1994), and Valerie Rohy (2000) rightfully argue that homophobic societies stage queerness as the impossible Real, Pluth's account of the Lacanian act—with its ability to touch the Real and bring its impasses into signification—offers the possibility of shifting the terrain. Though Stavrakakis and Žižek do this too, Pluth theorizes outcomes other than another fantasy's emergence.

These thinkers' ground-shifting acts are distinct from Edelman's embrace of the abject position of the *sinthomo*sexual, who is bound by a strict interpretation of Lacan equating all signification with the politics of the symbolic *No Future* refuses. Though the *sinthom*osexual's *jouissance* brings the drive's workings into representation, and so seems as if it could lead to a viable politics, Edelman's refusal of *all* politics denies the value of taking up queers' cause. His reading of Lacan equates all signification with a politics that would change the symbolic without touching the Real. Though traversing the fantasy could open up the prospect of a régime other than that of reproductive futurism and (hetero)sexual difference, Edelman's rejection of all signification—of *any* politics involving the signifier—pre-empts this possibility.

Edelman's stance is not the only viable reading of Lacan's theory of the *sinthôme*. Harari observes that in Joyce's case, "without" the *sinthôme* "the signifier would not have functioned properly" (Harari 2002: 210). Although "the *sinthome* does not demand meaning," and is not itself a signifier, its dependence on the letter makes signification possible (Harari 2002: 210, 241). The *sinthôme* creates what Dylan Evans describes as "a signifying formulation beyond analysis, a kernel of enjoyment" that is "unique," takes place in the Real, and remains "immune to the efficacy of the symbolic" (Evans 1996: 189). Hoens and Pluth thus describe the *sinthôme* not as a refusal of meaning but as an investment in "enjoyment-in-meaning," in the sense of poetic language's "production of meaning" (Hoens and Pluth 2002: 11). Though they note that "[T]he *sinthome* is not concerned with the meanings produced, but with the activity of production itself," what is important is that the *sinthôme* does not reject all signification but creates a novel relationship to signifiers (Hoens and Pluth 2002: 11). As Ruti insists in response to *No Future*, if we read Lacan while allowing "for the possibility that the signifier does not invariably obey the dictates of the normative symbolic—that it is capable of poetic and innovative interventions"—then "it becomes necessary to rethink the relationship between the symbolic and the real; it becomes conceivable that the unruly energies of the real can sustain and revitalize, rather than merely weaken, the signifier" (Ruti 2008b: 119). And while some might be tempted by a common but misguided critique of deconstruction to shift the blame for Edelman's nihilism from Lacan onto de Man, the queer theorist's repudiation of signification comes from neither the French psychoanalyst nor the Belgian deconstructionist. Neither the former, in noting the symbolic's failure to achieve full meaning, nor the latter, in insisting on its indeterminacy, rejects all forms of signification. These theorists insist, rather, on signification's unpredictability. While Edelman similarly identifies the desire for meaning's *closure* as an especially problematic feature of the fantasy of reproductive futurism, he makes it seem as if this impossible desire renders *all* significations futile.

To the contrary: as Pluth suggests, it is possible to have a relationship to signification and even to the future that is neither psychotic nor driven by the kind of perpetually unfulfilled desire Edelman rightfully rejects. Pluth's and Ruti's willingness to engage the signifier is a helpful counterpoint to *No Future*, which—despite some nods to fighting for equal rights and embracing the position of the *sintom*osexual—would abandon all attempts at signification because the closure of meaning is impossible. Pluth reminds us that for Lacan, "an act does not just involve doing something, it involves doing something with signifiers" (Pluth 2007: 101). Edelman, by contrast, makes the same mistake with which Pluth (overly hastily) charges Žižek: making the "act" involved in traversing the fantasy "a negation of any relation to signifiers whatsoever" (Edelman 2004: 132).[16]

Whereas Edelman would have us dismiss all attempts at legal change as bids for recognition, Pluth demonstrates that the politics of the signifier does not necessarily constitute a demand for recognition from the Other. He observes, "An act is certainly using signifiers in some way… and is thus bound up with the Other as a site of signifiers in general. But the Other as mere site of signifiers should not be confused with the Other as a site capable of granting recognition and guaranteeing identity and meaning" (Pluth 2007: 117). In rightfully targeting the latter uses of signifiers, Edelman overlooks the way other deployments of them could be felicitous, taking queer theory and politics in directions that remain open to considering sexuality's intersection with other areas of experience.

Another Scene's Emergence

Though all of these accounts of the "beyond" of fantasy's traversal undermine Edelman's argument that it leaves queers with no future, traversing the fantasy is not a surefire way of achieving structural transformation, nor are we guaranteed that changes will be for the better. Chiesa observes that in traversing the fantasy, "the subject's encounter with the real lack beneath his ideologized fundamental fantasy forces him to assume the lack in the universal" (Chiesa 2007: 191). However, the subsequent "resymbolization of lack is… always carried out at the level of the particular" (Chiesa 2007: 191). Though I have challenged his capitulation to *Seminar III* and claim that Joyce's resymbolization has no political efficacy, Chiesa's larger point stands: individual traversals of the fantasy might or might not reconfigure the symbolic (Chiesa 2007: 191). Some traversals may be individual solutions with no political force, while others may engage in politics.

As I suggested earlier, Edelman's *No Future* advocates a mode of fantasy's traversal with a vexed relationship to politics. de Lauretis rightfully observes that one can discern in his rhetoric "the intimation of a political project" both "affirmed and denied" through the simultaneity of the book's call to *jouissance* and critique of Butler's politics of the signifier (de Lauretis 2011: 257). de Lauretis finds in Edelman's irony—"The dissonance between [his] tone and words"—the trace of "two contrary impulses toward affirmation and negation" (de Lauretis 2011: 257). On the one hand, his polemic enacts a queer "manifesto" against reproductive futurism and literality, and so participates in politics; on the other hand, the negativity of its persistent irony undoes the illusory order of literal meanings on which politics depends (de Lauretis 2011: 257-9).

Distinguishing between *No Future*'s figurality and what she erroneously presumes to be political discourse's literalism, de Lauretis claims that as a "figure of negativity," Edelman's writing differs from pure referentiality by undercutting language, making words "mean something else or displac[ing] them onto another scene" (de Lauretis 2011: 259). Reflecting in 2011 on *No Future* and other books that followed in the wake of her 1990 conference and 1991 *differences* issue on "Queer Theory"—which she considers both "critical and political"—she uses the distinction between the figurative and the literal to raise newfound doubts about queer theory's compatibility with politics (de Lauretis 2011: 257). Yet we might consider a more expansive definition of "politics" than she proposes when she claims that "literality, or referentiality, is a mainstay of political discourse" and that "rhetoric is primarily instrumental" (de Lauretis 2011: 257). Scholars have long found in experimental writers' figural language, rhetorical performances, punning, and reworking of established genres a deep engagement with politics. Nor is the realm of politics purely referential, as de Lauretis assumes. To the contrary: everyday political discourse is saturated with metaphors and other figures of speech; psychoanalytic feminists such as Cixous have reworked the manifesto in ways that are highly political *and* proliferate signification beyond referentiality. Though I concur with de Lauretis that *No Future* gains its theoretical purchase from a figurality undercutting and displacing referential meaning, I see no reason to deny that this is, in and of itself, a form of politics.

In *Sex, or the Unbearable* Edelman responds that instead of what de Lauretis describes as a "radical incommensurability" between politics and "the drive," the two are intimately entwined (Edelman in Berlant and Edelman 2014: 70). As he rightfully insists, political language's illusory meanings are no more stable than those of any other discourses. He emphasizes that because politics "already bears within it the pressure of the drive," meaning's "solidity... is no more than a rhetorical effect" (Edelman in Berlant and Edelman 2014: 70). By ironizing rather than uncritically reproducing "fantasy," politics enacts "the insistence of a structural antagonism that undoes the totalization of meaning to which it seems to aspire" (Edelman in Berlant and Edelman 2014: 70).

However, in *Sex, or the Unbearable* Lauren Berlant labels Edelman's emphasis on "[s]tructural consistency" as itself "a fantasy," pointing to prospects for "transforming the dynamics and the costs of our negativity and its appearance" by working with "what's movable in the situation" (Berlant in Berlant and Edelman 2014: 124–5). Edelman overlooks the salutary results that could come from what he ungenerously understands as superficial modifications to "the scene" or "our objects"—changes he insists cannot "change our subjection to" the "framework" arising from "the specific imperative of" the subject's "fundamental fantasy," which supposedly "drives those changes with the goal of *preserving* those attachments" and reproducing "the unbearable" (Edelman in Berlant and Edelman 2014: 104–7). He stresses the need for "changing, ... undoing, the subject rather than the subject's scene" by "encountering what is truly unbearable, attempting to push through the barrier of ourselves," "approaching the medium of fantasy as the medium of desire," and "finding ourselves in the movement of the drive that *structures* our changes of scene" (Edelman in Berlant and Edelman 2014: 107–8). This allows the subject to shed "the self's immobilized form as well as... the fantasies that freeze-frame the self in relation to desire" (Edelman in Berlant and Edelman 2014: 28).

I agree: genuine transformation is only possible by traversing the fundamental fantasy, passing through subjective destitution, and starting anew. However, there is no reason changes to one's "scene" and "objects" could not prompt such a traversal. As in *No Future*, in *Sex* Edelman refuses to imagine what might lie behind transformative "undoing," which—he insists—"doesn't free" the subject "from determination by structure, repair its incoherence, or liberate it from fantasy" (Edelman in Berlant and Edelman 2014: 107). The alternative readings of Lacan I have explored in this chapter suggest otherwise, proposing that the subject's fundamental fantasy could either be supplanted by a less destructive one or be replaced by an open-ended "investment in signifiers as such" (Pluth 2007: 163).

The reinaugurated subject Pluth sees as enjoying open-ended signification strikes me as especially hospitable to Berlant's elastic theory of fantasy. Although Edelman is right that the subject must traverse the fantasy and engage the drive to enable radical subjective transformation, Berlant offers a compelling account of strategies for prompting fantasy's traversal and of the expanded options available afterwards. Whereas Edelman conceives of the object as Lacan's *objet a*—as cloaking lack by appearing as desire's illusory cause—Berlant presents it via Jean Laplanche as "also… a scene, a setting for actions, a discontinuous space that appears navigable for moving around awkwardly, ambivalently, and incoherently" (Berlant in Berlant and Edelman 2014: 100). She views "'structure' less as the insistence of the Real and more as that which organizes diverse and contradictory systemic forces" (Berlant in Berlant and Edelman 2014: 100). Within this unbound "setting," it is possible for people "to make do and to flourish in the awkward, riven, unequal, untimely, and interesting world of other beings, abstractions, and forces" (Berlant in Berlant and Edelman 2014: 100, 116).

Advocating a conceptual "loosening of the subject that puts fear, pleasure, awkwardness, and above all experimentality" in the foreground, Berlant's theory offers more supple forms of relationality than a new configuration of the symbolic, imaginary, and Real would allow (Berlant in Berlant and Edelman 2014: 117). By emphasizing relationality, she offers a psychoanalysis that could capture the vicissitudes of Eve Kosofsky Sedgwick's "beside," in all its "desiring, identifying, representing, repelling, paralleling, differentiating, rivaling, leaning, twisting," and "mimicking"; "withdrawing, attracting, aggressing," and "warping" (Sedgwick 2003: 8). Berlant's relational approach also refuses the orthodox Lacanian privileging of (hetero)sexual difference that subordinates areas of experience such as class, race, ethnicity, or nationality to gender and sexuality. Stressing "experimentality," her theory enables intersectional accounts of the psychoanalytic subject.

Grounded in Freud and Laplanche rather than Lacan, de Lauretis' *Freud's Drive* (2008) also makes a compelling case for the drive's generativity. Whereas *No Future* deploys rhetoric and figuration in the service of Edelman's call to identify with the drive by embracing the figure of the *sintho*mosexual, *Freud's Drive* reveals that the drive's own figural potential opens up possibilities Edelman's more tightly bound framework forestalls. Exploring the unpredictably figural properties of the drive's negativity, de Lauretis builds on Laplanche's idea that fantasy dramaturgically stages the psyche and praises Edelman for displacing queer politics "onto another scene" (de Lauretis 2011: 259). She stresses that the drive *itself* has a figural capacity whose similarity "to the most highly wrought forms of writing" suggests that "a theory of the drive might well allow the figural dimension of writing into the space of thinking and suspend the demand for rational, scientific, referential coherence" (de Lauretis 2008: 84). In *Sex*, Edelman concurs with this characterization of the drive even as he rightfully challenges the distinction de Lauretis makes between it and politics. Nonetheless, she is right to observe that despite her and Edelman's projects' uncanny similarities, they "diverge" because she declines to make a "programme," an "ethical position," of embracing the death drive (de Lauretis 2008: 87). This allows her to take a more open-ended approach than Edelman to the drive's potential consequences: to show that despite his book's efficacy in pointing to the possibility of "another scene," Edelman does not help us imagine an alternative to the fantasy of (hetero) sexual difference (de Lauretis 2011: 259).

Nor does the "other scene" prompted by *No Future* necessarily take the form of the "heterotopia" whose capacity to be "disturbing" de Lauretis praises (de Lauretis 2011: 259). Whereas Foucault characterizes "heterotopia" as the "*incongruous*... linking together of things that are inappropriate" and share no common ground, *No Future*'s tightly woven argument is anything but fragmentary (Foucault 1970: xvii). Other kinds of queer theory may well produce the heterotopias de Lauretis imagines, but *No Future* offers no guarantees. While I welcome the heterotopic figurations of the drive de Lauretis envisions, and while I find much to admire in psychoanalysis's Freudian and Laplanchian modes, I nonetheless see queer theory's Lacanian inflection as prompting something different: a traversal of homophobic and transphobic fantasy that clears the ground for a new fundamental fantasy, or even a new relationship to signifiers altogether.[17] Though it is conceivable that a newfound relation to signifiers could entail a heterotopia, it could take many other forms as well: the results of fantasy's traversal are never clear in advance.

Instead, after eviscerating the ideology of reproductive futurism and its prop, (hetero)sexual difference, Edelman leaves us with nothing: with pure negativity. de Lauretis—who recognizes this—therefore suggests that *No Future* may be as "unreadable" as Edelman's neologism, the *sinthomo*sexual: "A word, a book, a task without a future" (de Lauretis 2008: 258). Although she rightfully compares *No Future*'s effect to that of Valerie Solanas' *SCUM Manifesto*—a text shot through with a "charge of negativity" exposing a new "critical space" for view— this effect does not resemble Foucault's vision of heterotopia. Although that is surely one among the many possibilities that could follow fantasy's traversal, there is no guarantee that it would come to exist or that the connections it might entail would be productive.

Despite Edelman's vehement repudiation of futurity—which he admits to be impossible—*No Future* points to the possibility of a future of pure negativity beyond fantasy's traversal. However, his refusal to engage any notion of a future leaves readers ill-equipped to imagine a world organized otherwise or, more modestly, to be able to navigate its uncertain terrain. Edelman's argument only leads to "coexist[ence] with the hegemonic Other"—to ironizing rather than supplanting the symbolic and Real (Chiesa 2007: 191). Edelman's thoroughgoing rejection of the symbolic and its illusory meanings forestalls any future for the signifier that the collective embrace of his *sinthôme* might otherwise provoke. Even though he recruits Lacan's emphasis on imaginary and symbolic failures for a polemic that hyperbolically calls for us to refuse *all* politics and signification—not just a politics such as Butler's that fails to intervene in the Real—it is also possible to read Lacan elsewise: as promising both the displacement *and* the renewal of queer politics.

Edelman's extremist stance is unhelpful for queer theory because it does not address the more practical problems a heterosexist and cissexist symbolic order presents for LGBTQI persons. As Salamon demonstrates by reading Lacan's essay on "The Instance of the Letter in the Unconscious" against legal documents, Lacan's argument that the Law of the Father grounds the symbolic cannot account for the complexities created by the various legal constructs of "sex" leading to discrepancies between city, state, and local documents indicating gender: for example, to the impossible situations created for the transperson who holds some documents indicating "male" and others indicating "female" (Salamon 2010: 171–93). Those in same-gender relationships, too, encounter numerous problems brought about by the inscription of sexual difference as the "letter of the law," from denial of medical benefits and hospital visitation rights to immigration injustices forcing couples either to live apart or to break the law to remain together. In the face of these problems it is no help whatsoever to claim, as do some Lacanians, that the ideology of sexual difference does not oppress queers because its logic is independent of biological sex, or to assert, as does Edelman, that queers should embrace the structural position of the *sinthom*osexual that is produced by and actively maintains a homophobic symbolic. For those encountering such problems, a politics that can alter the symbolic via the Real is vital. Though it is certainly true that some people seek personal validation through legal recognition—a mode of mainstream gay and lesbian politics Edelman rightfully challenges—other queers might be motivated to change the legal system for more pragmatic reasons, such as living in the same country as one's partner or eliminating the problems created by inconsistent gender assignments on legal documents. Political efforts to alter the "letter of the laws" oppressing queers and transpeople are not necessarily motivated by "the governing fantasy of achieving Symbolic closure" and gaining recognition in the Other, as Edelman assumes (Edelman 2004: 14).

In my view, queer and trans theories need not abolish all signification. Rather, they can engage the Lacanian *sinthôme* to prompt fresh significations that will insist, like letters in the unconscious, not only on the displacement of the current fantasy but also on another scene's emergence, whether that entails the constitution of a new fantasy or the production of new significations not seeking recognition in the Other. Freeing theory from the fantasy of (hetero) sexual difference, refusing "Symbolic closure" and tapping into the signifier's most generative potentialities: this other scene entails not the refusal but the renewal of politics (Edelman 2004: 14).

Literature and film are especially amenable to queer politics' renewal because they foster experimentation. As I will argue in Chapters 5 and 6, the last four decades have provided numerous examples of texts that play with language, narrative, and genre to facilitate new sexualities' and genders' emergence. Monika Treut's *The Virgin Machine* (1988), John Cameron Mitchell's *Hedwig and the Angry Inch* (2001), Gloria Anzaldúa's *Borderlands/La Frontera* (1987), and Andrea Lawlor's *Paul Takes the Form of a Mortal Girl* (2017) all feature immigrant or mixed-race subjects who traverse the fantasy of (hetero)sexual difference and emerge in open-ended relation to identity, signification, and the future. Highlighting the roles performance, activism, and care can play in reorienting and supporting queers after fantasy's traversal, these works exemplify ways traversing the fantasy can produce "moments when an established temporal order gets interrupted and new encounters consequently take place," reformulating queer politics and the temporalities—futural or otherwise—on which they depend (Freeman 2010: xxii).

To prepare for those reformulations, Chapters 3 and 4 will consider Lacanian theories of transgender, examining ways orthodox Lacanian accounts of (hetero) sexual difference have either hindered or been rewritten in the service of affirmatively theorizing transsubjectivities. Trans-affirmative rewritings of Lacan, I argue, must continue to press forward in ways that reinterpret "the letter" of his texts: refusing to remain locked into the 1970s vocabulary of "men" and "women" animating orthodox accounts of (hetero)sexual difference; embracing instead a linguistic elasticity enabling contemporary trans vocabularies and genres to reframe his account of gender embodiment for the present and future.

Notes

1. Lacan outlines his theory of the *sinthôme* at greatest length in *Seminar XXIII* (Lacan 2016).
2. Dean (2008), Ruti (2008b), and Ruti (2017) offer the most detailed assessments of Edelman's psychoanalytic methodology to date.
3. See Butler (1990), Butler (1993), Butler (1994), Butler (1998), and Butler (2004) for different iterations of the argument to which Edelman responds.
4. See Edelman (2006) for more about the antagonism's significance in his work.
5. For an opening into such an inquiry, see Gayle Salamon's reading of Freud's comments on bisexuality and intersex in *Three Essays on the Theory of Sexuality* (Salamon 2010).
6. For example, see Copjec (2010).
7. For critiques of Kristeva's figuration of female same-gender desire as pre-Oedipal, see Butler (1990), Butler (1993), and Coffman (2006).
8. Approaching an earlier version of Edelman's argument from the perspective of political theory, John Brenkman similarly asserts that "Queerness is not outside sociality; it is an innovation in sociality" (Brenkman 2002: 180). Though Brenkman's follow-up piece rightfully insists that neither the social nor the political is as totalizing as Edelman's reading of the symbolic assumes, the former nonetheless does not fully answer the latter's insistence upon the figurality of his call for queers to embrace the death drive. By contrast, Dean's and Teresa de Lauretis' subsequent psychoanalytic interventions push the discussion toward a more precise assessment of *No Future*'s inscription of the drive.
9. See, for instance, Žižek (1989), Žižek (1999), Žižek (2000a), Žižek (2000b), and Žižek (2000c).
10. For Žižek's take on fantasy's traversal, see Žižek (1999), Žižek (2000a), Žižek (2000b), and Žižek (2000c).
11. It must be noted, however, that Žižek resists the idea that sexual difference could be anything other than a fundamental antagonism. See Chapter 1 for my response to this resistance.
12. See especially Pluth (2007: 130–2) for a discussion of Lacan's theory of traversing the fantasy in *Seminar XI* (1977).
13. See Pluth (2007: 107–14) for an extended discussion of Lacan's analysis of puns.
14. Given Verhaeghe's and Declercq's recognition of the Name-of-the-Father's contingency, it is unfortunate that they conclude what is otherwise a forward-thinking

article by reiterating Lacan's arguments in *Seminar XX* about the respective positions taken by "[t]he man" and "Woman" (Verhaeghe and Declercq 2002: 76). *Seminar XXIII*'s theory of the *sinthôme*, though clearly connected to Lacan's view of the impossibility of sexual relationship, diverges from the conceptions of masculinity and femininity that continue to dominate Lacanian scholarship.

15 See especially Cixous (1972), Cixous (1991), Kristeva (1980), and Kristeva (1984).
16 Pluth's (2007) criticism of Žižek glosses over the different stages of his thought and overlooks the point at which he theorizes traversal of the fantasy as holding the potential to rearticulate the symbolic via an act in the Real. For more about this aspect of Žižek's work, see Chapter 1.
17 De Lauretis' argument in *Freud's Drive* (2008) is less persuasive regarding Lacan: she concedes too quickly to Laplanche's view of Lacan as making, through an "accent" on "the signifier, nothing more than a new accentuation of the death drive" (LaPlanche qtd. in de Lauretis 2008: 83). This runs parallel to the excessively negative reading of Lacan I critique in Edelman's *No Future* (2004) and Pluth's (2007) reading of Žižek.

3

Žižek's Antagonism and the Futures of Trans-Affirmative Lacanian Psychoanalysis

Over the last decade Slavoj Žižek has loudly resisted trans-affirmative rewritings of Lacan, even those grounded in orthodox understandings of (hetero)sexual difference: a fantasy he seems unwilling to give up. In 2016, his essay "The Sexual Is Political"—which makes transpeople objects of his long-standing disdain for North American multiculturalism—elicited justifiably unfavorable responses. "The Sexual Is Political" reiterates and rearticulates claims that will sound familiar to frequent readers of Žižek's work. For instance, he explains—and hardly for the first time in his *oeuvre*—that

> The reason for this failure of every classification that tries to be exhaustive is not the empirical wealth of identities that defy classification but, on the contrary, the persistence of sexual difference as real, as "impossible" (defying every categorization) and simultaneously unavoidable. The multiplicity of gender positions (male, female, gay, lesbian, bigender, transgender…) circulates around an antagonism that forever eludes it.
>
> (Žižek 2016c)

The first sentence in this passage does not advance a claim that will be new to those familiar with Lacanian theory. It is the explanation of sexual difference animating every one of Žižek's books. And it is also the account behind Shanna Carlson's query, in the initiatory 2014 issue of *TSQ*, about "What happens when we take a trans look at the formulas" of sexuation through which Lacan reformulates sexual difference in *Seminar XX*, without assuming "the formulas' positions to be occupied by (only) the 'men' and 'woman' of normative imaginings?" (Carlson 2014: 169). This is a good question: one about which Žižek, in 2016, appears to be in agreement with the trans theorists he claims to oppose.

However, as Che Gossett points out, "The Sexual Is Political" does not even try to engage the burgeoning field of trans theory. Gossett rightfully asks how

Žižek dares "to write about trans subjectivity with such assumed authority while ignoring the voices of trans theorists (academics and activists) entirely" (Gossett 2016). This refusal to consider transpeoples' perspectives is part of a larger pattern for Žižek. Rather than carefully investigate and respond in an informed fashion to the North American debates to which he so often refers, Žižek typically reacts superficially and sensationalistically. In "The Sexual Is Political," he avoids engaging recent Lacanian scholarship on transgender by intellectual peers such as Carlson, Sheila Cavanagh, Patricia Gherovici, Oren Gozlan, and Gayle Salamon, drawing instead on Wikipedia to construct an inaccurate and superficial genealogy conflating transgender with "so-called postgenderism." And in one of his follow-up pieces, "A Reply to My Critics," Žižek continues to assert that "the universal fluidification of sexual identities unavoidably reaches its apogee in the cancellation of sex as such" (Žižek 2016a). Žižek's conflation of "transgender" and "postgender" makes these slippery-slope claims unconvincing (Žižek 2016a). Through this strategy, he treats transpeoples' lives as mere manifestations of North American "political correctness" run amok and misses the opportunity to explore ways his Marxist rearticulation of Lacanian psychoanalysis could serve rather than negate trans theory's claims.

Žižek's continued attempts to engage trans materials have proven even less constructive than "The Sexual Is Political." In a May 2019 essay called "Transgender dogma is naïve and incompatible with Freud," Žižek engages trans discourse while continuing to ignore the work of trans-affirmative Lacanian psychoanalysts. Using a film and an advertisement to argue that transgender and psychoanalytic discourses are fundamentally "incompatible," he concludes with a claim with which many queer and trans-affirmative Lacanians would likely agree: that "psychic sexual identity is a choice, not a biological fact"—not "a conscious choice" but rather "an unconscious choice which precedes subjective constitution and which is, as such, formative of subjectivity" (Žižek 2019b). Yes: and this is an understanding of "psychic sexual identity" upon which viable theories of transgender embodiment can be built—indeed are already being built. Moreover, Žižek's penultimate conclusion—that the "unconscious choice" that is "formative of subjectivity… entails the radical transformation of the bearer of the choice"—is likewise a statement with which trans-affirmative psychoanalysts would likely agree (Žižek 2019b). This claim backhandedly acknowledges a point Žižek and other orthodox Lacanians have been vehemently resisting for several decades: that "radical transformation" can be achieved by traversing the fundamental fantasy of (hetero)sexual difference.

Given the pattern of disavowal at work in Žižek's refusal to engage trans-affirmative psychoanalysis, a reasonable response would be to ignore him and thereby reduce his power: to throw his writings in the "GENERAL WASTE" bin to which, in one of the most objectionable analogies in "The Sexual Is Political," he compares those people hailed by the "+" in the formulation "LGBT+" (Žižek 2016c). In Chapter 1, I demonstrated that queer people are among those Žižek has "not deemed useful enough to be preserved or retained"—albeit not in the way Judith Butler thinks (Ahmed 2019: 20). In this chapter, I contend that Žižek does that to transpeople too. Yet I also offer an alternative to simply throwing away his work: one that, acknowledging and pushing back against his capacity to get under our skin, interrogates the ways his thinking is tripped up by transgender phenomena and the reasons for which trans-affirmative psychoanalysts are so tripped up by him. Examining these issues reveals that what is at stake in the way Žižek spins diversity issues is not only the desire to provoke the kinds of controversies fueling academic celebrity but also the very terms through which he apprehends gender. Žižek's misguided comments about transpeople reveal aporias within his philosophical system and therefore ways some of his ideas can be rearticulated in the service of an intersectional, trans-affirmative mode of Lacanian psychoanalysis.

Žižek's Antagonism

In the past, Žižek and trans-affirmative psychoanalytic thinkers have parted ways not over the many socially constructed genderings Judith Roof (2016) describes as operating independently of Lacanian sexual difference but about what—until recently—he has presumed to be the latter's fundamental intractability as the constitutive antagonism setting gender multiplicity into motion. In Chapter 1, I expose the internal contradictions within Žižek's thought and develop their potential for queer and trans theory. I demonstrate that, contrary to Žižek's claims in various writings from 1989–2012 about sexual difference's intransigence, his positing of class struggle as an antinomy analogous to Lacanian sexual difference reveals that both are contingent and available for "ideological struggle and transformation" (40). Žižek repeats this move in "The Sexual Political," claiming that "the other great antagonism is that of classes"—a formulation granting both antagonisms equal importance (Žižek 2016c).[1] Reiterating this assertion with a difference in the second of two replies to "The Sexual Is Political," he acknowledges the multiplicity of antagonisms by defining "class struggle" as comprised not only of "the workers' struggle" but also of "Third World crises" and "the plight of immigrants and refugees" (Žižek 2016b).² In so doing, Žižek confirms my argument despite himself.

Despite his prior insistence that sexual difference is transhistorical and unchangeable, in 2016 Žižek finally concedes that "The LGBT trend is right in 'deconstructing' the standard normative sexual opposition, in de-ontologizing it, in recognizing in it a contingent historical construct full of tensions and inconsistencies" (Žižek 2016c). Thus, without admitting it, he accepts a point Butler repeatedly makes in *Bodies That Matter* and *Contingency, Hegemony, Universality* despite his vehement resistance throughout the 1990s. Yet even in Žižek's 2016 reformulation, he acknowledges the contingency of "the standard normative sexual opposition" without admitting that it is a fundamental fantasy available for traversal (Žižek 2016c).

Herein lies the problem with Žižek's subsequent claim that "transgenderism is ultimately an attempt to avoid (the anxiety of) castration," which he presumes exclusively to concern sexual differentiation (Žižek 2016c). He formulates its cause as the worry that "Whatever choice I make, I will lose something, and this something is NOT what the other sex has" (Žižek 2016c). This wording implies that there are only two possibilities for sexual differentiation. Yet as Roof explains, "if we dismiss Freud's Oedipal chamber drama and understand castration more figuratively as the moment individuals begin to recognize difference—that they are separable and perpetually separated from their environment and from others around them—castration... signals the point when a polymorphous lack of differentiation gives way to differences and taxonomies" that are "multiple," provisional, and changeable (Roof 2016: 59–60). Roof's argument demonstrates that the proliferation of genders and sexualities in the United States—which Žižek accounts for in Lacanian terms with a "+" symbolizing the "one exceptional element which clearly does not belong to it and thereby gives body to +"—is compatible with Lacan's thinking (Žižek 2016c). Žižek, however, overlooks the fact that violence is disproportionately directed at those who defy the gender binary, and unjustifiably asks them to bear the burden of this positioning in ways others do not.

Lacan need not be interpreted this way. As Kaja Silverman demonstrates, castration is fundamentally linguistic rather than sexual (Silverman 1992: 112). And as Mari Ruti explains, "Language generates lack," which "in turn generates desire" (Ruti 2008a: 488). Because desire circulates around the *objet a*, an endlessly deferred phantasmatic object, the "subject... lacks not simply some locatable object [e.g., a penis] but... lacks being as such," as Carlson elaborates (Carlson

2010: 51). Castration does not necessarily lead to the dramas of Oedipalization or the theatres of the phallus so commonly revived in mainstream psychoanalytic writing, but rather to our most fundamental existential condition: what Ruti calls "ontological lack" (Ruti 2008a: 485). Thus if, as Silverman argues, the Name of the Father is only "one" among many possible "signifiers that impart a retroactive significance to the lack introduced by language," that signifier could be replaced by another (Silverman 1992: 112). As I argue in the first two chapters, an authentic act in the Real—rather than Butlerian resignification—could replace the Name of the Father with another signifier and thereby render sexual difference either incidental or irrelevant to subjectivity. In other words, the "antagonism" in the "real" to which Žižek refers may be "unavoidable," but its consequences are not inalterable, nor need the difference it concerns necessarily be sexual. Instead, the "antagonism" may have to do with something else altogether—such as race, ethnicity, nationality, or social class—or with a mixture thereof. Nor need trans be understood as "ultimately an attempt to avoid (the anxiety of) castration," as Žižek claims (Žižek 2016c). Instead, it can be understood as just one of myriad responses to existential lack.

Traversing the Fantasy

Trans-affirmative Lacanian psychoanalysis has not yet explored the implications of the possibility that an act in the Real might rearticulate the constitutive antagonism mobilizing a variety of genders. Carlson, for example, explores one possibility for trans theorizing available within a conventionally Lacanian account of sexual difference. Reinflecting the arguments through which strict Lacanians such as Žižek and Joan Copjec conceive of sexual difference as Real and therefore unchangeable, Carlson argues that

> with respect to sexual difference, we must insist on the ways in which, for Lacan, the terms *masculine* and *feminine* signal two different logics, two different modes of ex-sistence in the symbolic, two different stances with respect to desire, and (at least) two different types of *jouissance*. Nothing here indicates "gender" as we might more conventionally conceive of it.
>
> (Carlson 2010: 64)

This distinction implies that although every subject must come to occupy either the masculine or feminine position, a person's positionality does not constrain their gender expression. Carlson has since nuanced this explanation, using Willy Apollon to argue that Lacan's theory of sexuation allows that "a subject may be either all or not-all under the phallic function—'not both'—*and* encounter the distinct ethical exigencies of both masculinity and femininity" (de la Torre 2018: 112).

As this recent turn in Carlson's work confirms, Lacan's theory of sexual difference enables her to make the case that the subjectivity of the transperson who "strives to pass *and/or*… identifies with one gender or another with an apparent degree of certainty" is "psychically no different than any other subject who lines up under one banner or the other" (Carlson 2010: 64). This argument underpins her important observation that transgender "is not in and of itself any more extreme a type of symptom than is 'man' or 'woman'" (Carlson 2010: 64–5). For Carlson, "the transgender subject—as someone who is not necessarily or only very strategically invested in 'passing' as one gender or another…, as someone who may be invested in embodying a gender that would attest to what he or she may define as the constructedness of gender… —would be the human subject as such" (Carlson 2010: 65). Clearly, there are powerful possibilities for trans-affirmative theorizing available even within strict interpretations of Lacan.

Salamon's *Assuming A Body* (2010) also works within a conventional reading of Lacan. Invoking the Real to argue that Jay Prosser's *Second Skins* (1998) underestimates the implications for trans embodiment of Lacan's account of split subjectivity, she stresses that transsubjectivity entails the production of a sense of "bodily coherence" through symbolic and imaginary "recognition" and "misrecognition" (Salamon 2010: 24). Underscoring the dangers of Prosser's insistence "that the transsexual body is 'unimpeachably real,'" Salamon charges that this claim "ends up landing him squarely in the Real," in all its "plenitude and fullness," leaving the transperson "outside of language, outside of meaning, outside of the symbolic, outside of relation, outside of desire"—in a space of "radical abjection and death" (Salamon 2010: 41). Although I concur with her critique of Prosser, find her Lacanian account of trans embodiment powerful, and share her desire for a reading of Lacan situating transgender within rather than outside of "language" and "relation," I also see possibilities for altering the terms of the Real (Salamon 2010: 41).

Carlson hints at such a possibility when she argues that Stephen Whittle, in the Foreword to the first *Transgender Studies Reader*, implicitly positions transpeople as engaging in what Žižek calls the "ethical act" (Carlson 2010: 68). To make this claim, Carlson equates what Ellie Ragland describes as "the suffering of hysteria," with its refusal to accept that "[e]ither one is masculine or one is feminine," with Whittle's statement about the sacrifices made by Trans Studies' pioneers: "it has been through this articulation of the imposition of gendering on us by others that the position of suffering of those with trans identities has been heard" (Carlson 2010: 67-8; Whittle 2006: xv). However, by valorizing femininity's potentially revolutionary potential—and Lacan's association of it with hysteria—to theorize the transperson's questioning of gender ("Am I a man, or am I a woman, and what does that mean?"), Carlson implicates her analysis in some of his more questionable assertions about femininity (Carlson 2010: 65). These claims become especially problematic when she quotes Ragland's statement that the hysteric's self-questioning puts her "at risk of being overtaken by the real in both the symbolic and the imaginary" (Ragland 2004: 67). Although Carlson finds in the hysteric's and transperson's "suffering" the beginnings of the "ethical act"— and therefore the seeds of "social transformation"—her argument reproduces Lacan's pathologization of femininity, illustrating the continuing need for trans theorists to challenge his underlying assumptions (Carlson 2010: 65-8).

I see less pathologizing and more expansive ways for trans theory to conceive of the capacity of the "ethical act" to initiate "social transformation" (Carlson 2010: 65-8). Žižek's work, which grafts Lacan's theory of the constitutive antagonism into other contexts such as class struggle, reveals—despite his denials—how generative further rearticulations of Lacan could be. As he and others argue, Lacan's later writings suggest that through an ethical act, it is possible to traverse the fundamental fantasy. The resulting "disbanding of fantasies... allows us to begin to imagine alternative ways of living and relating," enabling new forms of subjectivity to emerge (Ruti 2010: 1).

Embracing the Sinthôme

As I noted in Chapter 2, Lacan argues that to traverse the fantasy, the subject must embrace the *sinthôme*, the individual mode of *jouissance* linking the imaginary, symbolic, and Real. This *sinthôme* "is not concerned with the meanings produced, but with the activity of production" (Hoens and Pluth 11). Functioning as what Lacan calls a "letter," the *sinthôme* creates new ways of using signifiers without being a signifier itself (Harari 2002: 241). In *Seminar XXIII*, James Joyce serves as Lacan's primary example of a subject who has knotted the three orders back together through the *sinthôme*—in his case, experimental writing—and successfully staved off a psychotic break. However, in *Horsexe* (1983), Catherine Millot uses this theory of the *sinthôme* to pathologize transpeople. This is the theory to which Žižek responds when he claims, inadequately, that he doesn't "think that the idea to conceive transgender identity as a 'sinthom' in Lacan's sense is of great use" (Žižek 2016b). While he is right to refuse to "see transgender individuals as potential psychotics who avoided psychosis by creating a sinthome," in his rejection of this theory's most transphobic formulation he overlooks possibilities for its trans-affirmative reformulation (Žižek 2016b).

For Lacan, staving off psychosis is not the only use to which the *sinthôme* can be put; it is also available to those whose Borromean knot has not been "botched" (Lacan 2016: 80). The *sinthôme* is merely "neurotic" in the latter cases (Lacan 2016: 42). In *Seminar XXIII*, Lacan identifies "the father" as a "sinthome" that is "*im-ply-cated*" in the "enigmatic bond between the imaginary, the symbolic, and the real" (Lacan 2016: 11). As Ragland explains, this development in Lacan's thinking implies that—unlike in *Seminar III*—"The Father's Name signifier need not be the 'imaginary daddy' of contemporary conceptualization... It can also be a signifier such as 'the outsider,' or a river god, rather than the actual progenitor, or even the mother's brother," among many possibilities (Ragland 2004: 120). The father is only one of many signifiers that could anchor subjectivity.

This change in Lacan's thinking has important consequences for queer and trans theory. First, his identification of "the father" as replaceable revises his claim in *Seminar III* that the subject needs to accept the Name of the Father as master signifier to become a subject rather than a psychotic (Lacan 2016: 11). By superseding this argument in *Seminar XXIII*, Lacan eliminates *Seminar III*'s homophobic and transphobic elements. Second, when Lacan identifies "the father" and "the Oedipus complex" as *sinthômes* in *Seminar XXIII*, he suggests that they could be supplanted by other formations (Lacan 2016: 11-13). Such an act could mobilize novel possibilities for desire and embodiment.

Gherovici therefore employs Lacan's theory of the neurotic *sinthôme* to critique Millot and affirm transpeoples' desire to transition. Arguing that transitioning is an "art that can allow someone to love, work, desire" (Gherovici 2014: 258-9), Gherovici defines the *sinthôme* as "a creative knotting together of the registers of real, symbolic, and imaginary": "the trace of the unique way someone can come to be and enjoy their unconscious" (Gherovici 2012: 261; Gherovici 2014: 253). Stressing that "Lacan defines the *sinthome* as an artifice... a creation, an invention," she observes that it offers a valuable contribution to trans theory "because it offers a novel way to think about sexual difference" independently of "the phallus or the Name-of-the-Father" (Gherovici 2012: 261-7).

The *sinthôme* also affords Gherovici a means of understanding writings about transition as examples of the "*Künstlerroman*, a novel of the artist," which enable transpeople to "embody sexual difference" (Gherovici 2012: 266-7). The act of "writing the memoir" engages the "unsymbolizable"—the Real—and "grants a different form of embodiment in which the body finds its anchor in the sea of language" (Gherovici 2014: 255, 255, 262). Writing becomes the means through which transpeople find their "creative *sinthome*" and offer themselves up "for deciphering" by others (Gherovici 2012: 279–84).

Through this reading of the *sinthôme*, Gherovici reworks Lacanian theory to "argue for a depathologization" of transgender that repudiates Millot's claims and animates subsequent trans-affirmative work by Cavanagh and Gozlan (Gherovici 2014: 258). Encouraging transpeople to identify their "creative *sinthome*," Gherovici enables them to reconfigure the imaginary, symbolic, and Real (Gherovici 2014: 262). However, her argument suggests that transpeople must alleviate suffering by finding a new way of inhabiting a symbolic constituted through Lacanian sexual difference. She asserts, for instance, that "the body is marked by the conundrum of sexual difference" rather than by existential lack (Gherovici 2014: 262). Her argument—and the form of transsubjectivity for which she advocates—thus remains governed by (hetero)sexual difference.

Transpsychoanalysis would therefore benefit from a theory of traversing the fundamental fantasy of (hetero)sexual difference. As I noted in Chapter 2, existing scholarship suggests that in some cases, embracing the *sinthôme* can suture breaches of the Lacanian triad that might otherwise lead to psychosis. This is not a strategy for fantasy's traversal but rather for preventing a psychotic break (as in Joyce's situation). In other instances, embracing the *sinthôme* allows non-psychotic subjects to traverse the fundamental fantasy, profoundly altering subjectivity's unconscious underpinnings. One way of doing so involves creating a temporary void that is quickly covered over by a reformulated version of the Lacanian triad alleviating non-psychotic forms of suffering (as in Gherovici's example of the "creative *sinthome*" whose inventiveness enables transpeoples' transitions) (Gherovici 2014: 262). Gherovici's theory accounts for transitioning subjects who use the *sinthôme* to reposition themselves within sexual difference by moving from one side of the gender binary to the other.

An advantage of Gherovici's approach is that it enables transpeople to reconfigure but not abolish the Lacanian triad. Ruti notes that despite Lacan's otherwise powerful critique of ego psychology and fantasy's "narcissistic" elements, it is sometimes vital to "reconstitute the ego" after it has been "profoundly injured" by oppression (Ruti 2008a: 493). As Salamon demonstrates, transpeople often rely upon recognition from others to live out novel embodiments in contexts risking symbolic erasure. Although in keeping with Lacan's account of the imaginary she acknowledges that recognition always entails *mis*recognition, Salamon makes a compelling case for the capacity of the imaginary and symbolic to support transgender embodiment, despite the misprisions and inconsistencies they engender. Yet Ruti also observes that the "act" prompting fantasy's traversal "is essentially an encounter with the real which jolts the subject beyond the social coordinates of its existence, potentially allowing it to rupture the parameters of whatever is oppressing it" (Ruti 2010: 12). Her account suggests that by engaging the Real, traversing the fundamental fantasy can shift the symbolic's most oppressive terms while maintaining the underlying structure of the Lacanian triad that provides psychical support for vulnerable subjects. Unlike Prosser's transperson, whose subjectivity is permanently bereft of imaginary and symbolic support, the subject who traverses the fantasy only temporarily experiences subjective dispossession. The brief "passage through 'symbolic death'" that takes place by traversing the fundamental fantasy allows the subject to alter and thereby reanimate their position within "language," "meaning," "the symbolic," "relation," and "desire" by engaging the Real alongside the other orders (Salamon 2010: 41; Žižek 1999: 262).

I thus see considerable potential for transpsychoanalysis in a theory of traversing the fantasy that enacts "a radical reconfiguration of the normative order" but retains the Lacanian triad's underlying structure (Ruti 2010: 11). Another, more radical approach to fantasy's traversal would provide a different account of transsubjectivity that does not require a reconfigured imaginary, symbolic, and Real. This theory holds that "everyone" may "create their own *sinthome* at the place of the lack of the Other" (Verhaeghe and Declercq 2002: 52). Dispensing with symbolic anchorage, this subject replaces an "investment in fantasy" with a "direct investment in signifiers as such" (Pluth 2007: 163). This second approach enables theorizations of transsubjectivities that permanently cross from one side of the gender binary to the other as well as non-binary subjectivities that move within or beyond the gender binary.

Both of these approaches to fantasy's traversal go beyond Carlson's positioning of sexual difference as the constitutive antagonism and see it as potentially subject to transformation. Moreover, by going beyond the fantasy of (hetero)sexual difference, both of these outcomes of fantasy's traversal open up possibilities for theorizing transgender's crossings with race, ethnicity, nationality, and social class. The forms of transsubjectivity that are best sustained through the symbolic and imaginary recognitions Salamon describes can be effectively theorized through a theory of traversing the fundamental fantasy that emphasizes the emergence of a reconfigured symbolic, imaginary, and Real. Those that require fewer supports—especially non-binary subjectivities—could proliferate within the open-ended and postmodern approach to signification that no longer depends upon recognition in the Other.

I expand on these possibilities in Chapter 4. For now, I will note that the latter solution offers another route to Carlson's insight that "there is something transgendered about the human subject, and that this transgenderism transcends notions of gender" (Carlson 2010: 66). Her argument demonstrates the transgender potential inherent in orthodox readings of Lacan in which sexual difference names the "impasses" existential castration sets into motion (Carlson 2010: 66). The grounds for such interpretations are legible in *Seminar XX*. Although *Seminar XX* relies upon formulations such as "[a] woman seeks out a man" and "[a] man seeks out a woman" to stake out sexual difference's terrain, Lacan also claims that "[m]en, women, and children are but signifiers," underscoring their status as discursive constructions (Lacan 1998: 33). He implies something similar in "The Instance of the Letter in the Unconscious" when he relays the famous anecdote about a brother and sister who, while sitting opposite one another in a train, look from different vantages at a station's restroom and dispute whether they have arrived at "Ladies" or "Gentlemen" (Lacan 2006d: 416). Although orthodox Lacanians usually use this passage to demonstrate that sexual difference is an intractable antinomy, Lacan stresses (hetero)sexual difference's contingency. He prefaces the diagram with an acknowledgement that it "exaggerates the incongruous dimension psychoanalysts have not yet altogether given up, because of their justified sense that their conformism derives its value from it alone" (Lacan 2006d: 416). Moreover, he follows the illustration by emphasizing that "GENTLEMEN and LADIES" are arbitrary designations, observing that if they "were written in a language [*langue*] with which the little boy and girl were unfamiliar, their quarrel would simply be more exclusively a quarrel over words," albeit ones "ready to take on signification" (Lacan 2006d: 420). Because they could just as well be two other words, "GENTLEMEN and LADIES" are replaceable and the antinomy between masculinity and femininity is contingent.

Thus at his most radical, Lacan hints at sexual difference's contingency. These ideas, which remain undeveloped in his own texts, have been drawn out in more recent psychoanalytic thought. Carlson insists that anybody can occupy the masculine and feminine positions, and Roof elaborates that "Lacan's theory of subjective sexuation" offers "multiple possibilities for individual positioning in relation to" Lacanian sexual difference—possibilities "that interpret this difference through vectors that simultaneously define difference as binary and leave the binaries behind" (Roof 2016: 60). Whereas Gherovici and her followers argue that transpeople embrace the *sinthôme* to situate themselves within sexual difference, I contend that (hetero)sexual difference is a fundamental fantasy available for traversal: a movement that further mobilizes and thereby "transcends" gender (Carlson 2010: 66).

Žižek's Disavowals

As a strategy for moving beyond Žižek's ideologically contingent antagonism between masculine and feminine, Lacan's theory of traversing the fundamental fantasy has much to offer trans psychoanalysis. Yet given Žižek's defensive provocations and apparent unwillingness to engage serious psychoanalytic scholarship in trans studies, further elaboration of these claims would best be served by detaching itself from his discourse. Though in 2016 he finally acknowledges sexual difference's contingency, he continues to defend against that insight's implications.

Žižek's valorization in *The Indivisible Remainder* of the example of a man who "dress[es] up as a woman and commit[s] suicide in public" as his "best candidate" for the authentic act that would prompt fantasy's traversal offers an illustration of its potential perils, stressing that its outcome is not always positive and could even be destructive (Žižek 1996: 170). Similarly, "The Sexual Is Political" discusses a case from 1926 Turkey—the execution of the "very masculine-looking" Şalcı Bacı for wearing a fedora in defiance of the Hat Law (Žižek 2016c). Asserting that "[r]ather than undermin[ing] sexual difference," Bacı "stood for this difference as such" by embodying "the impossible-Real of antagonism," Žižek uses Bacı's situation to argue—contra Butler—that "the formula of sexual antagonism is not M/F (the clear opposition between male and female) but MF+, where + stands for the excessive element which transforms the symbolic opposition into the Real of antagonism" (Žižek 2016c). In "A Reply to My Critics," Žižek repeats this argument while clarifying that "[i]t is not transgender people who disrupt the heterosexual gender binaries; these binaries are always-already disrupted by the antagonistic nature of sexual difference itself" (Žižek 2016a). However, unlike the suicidal person in *The Indivisible Remainder*, Bacı does not exemplify a subject who traverses the fundamental fantasy. Instead, Žižek uses Bacı's "impossible-Real" positioning to support the claim that not sexual difference but "the fantasy of a peaceful world where the agonistic tension of sexual difference disappears" can be traversed (Žižek 2016c). This argument rests on an orthodox account of sexual difference.

This line of thinking is reiterated in *Sex and the Failed Absolute* (Žižek 2019a: 133-4) and runs counter to Carlson's 2010 article "Transgender Subjectivity and the Logic of Sexual Difference," which argues that "'transsexuality' is not in and of itself any more extreme a type of symptom than is 'man' or 'woman'" (Carlson 2010: 65). For Carlson, "transgenderism," too, "figures not as a solutionless solution to the impasses of sexual difference, but rather as an expression of the logic of sexual difference" (Carlson 2010: 65). Although I advance a Lacanian theory according to which transgender is not necessarily "a feminine solution," I concur with Carlson's assessment that trans need not be positioned as any more exceptional than "'man' or 'woman'" (Carlson 2010: 65). Rather, these are all options among the varied "differences" that can emerge through desire's dialectic (Roof 2016: 60). Although Žižek contends in *Sex and the Failed Absolute* that "the total transgender 'fluidification' of gender, the dispersal of sexual difference into multiple configurations—is... false" because the "poles" of masculinity and femininity "both miss sexual difference as the real/impossible of an antagonism," there is no reason that other differences could not function similarly (Žižek 2019a: 134).

Yet even more worrisome than Žižek's positioning of transpeople as emblematic of sexual "difference as such" is the echo in "The Sexual Is Political" of *The Indivisible Remainder*'s tacit approval of violence against transpeople (Žižek 2016c). In the context of an essay that exploits—by purporting to address—North American political movements seeking to secure transpeoples' safe access to public restrooms, Žižek's inability to see the injustice at work in Bacı's fate reveals his argument's limits. Although he is right that apparently "'normal' heterosexuals" also "often find it difficult to recognize themselves in prescribed sexual identities" because of the incommensurability subtending all forms of subjectivity, he misses the ways those who differ *openly* from heteronormative genders and sexualities are systematically at risk for violence in ways others are not (Žižek 2016c). His ending assertion of the need to go beyond "the fantasy of a peaceful world where the antagonistic tension of sexual difference disappears" avoids confronting the issues of social justice that trans activists raise (Žižek 2016c).

In "A Reply to My Critics," Žižek rightfully observes that some of his opponents, too, make themselves unpersuasive by operating within the narrow intellectual confines of "tweet culture," which relies upon superficial "snaps," "retorts," and "outraged remarks" rather than lengthier and more thoughtful forms of "argumentation" (Žižek 2016b). Moreover, it is noteworthy that although he continues to decry his interlocutors' "self-righteous Political Correctness," his replies are devoid of the callous dismissals characterizing his initial response in "The Sexual Is Political" to political contestation over transpeoples' need for safe access to public restrooms (Žižek 2016b, Žižek 2016a). Both of Žižek's follow-ups to "The Sexual Is Political" offer analysis explicitly demonstrating his growing recognition that transpeople are regularly faced with injustices emerging from "the violent imposition of gender norms" (Žižek 2016a).

Nonetheless, Žižek continues not to see that transpeople are disproportionately burdened with these violences because they are structurally coerced into emblematizing the "antagonism" at work in even the most "normative" manifestations of sexual difference (Žižek 2016a). Although he concedes in response to his critics that he "fully support[s] the struggle of transgender people against their legal segregation" and is "deeply affected by their reports of their suffering," he does not admit that his own philosophical system risks compounding their problems (Žižek 2016a). Instead, he transforms their suffering into an ethics, asserting that "the ethical greatness of transgender subjects resides precisely in the fact that they" embody "the deadlock of subjectivity even more radically than other more 'normalized' subjects" (Žižek 2016b). These claims reveal Žižek's need to traverse the fantasy of (hetero)sexual difference—a movement that would relieve transpeople of the disproportionate burden they bear for what he rightly describes as an "universal" existential condition (Žižek 2016a).

Rethinking Embodiment through Stryker's Traversals

In "A Reply to My Critics," Žižek insists that "[t]ransgender people... bring out the antagonistic tension which is constitutive of sexuality" in all its modalities, and that because they "bring out the anxiety that underlies every sexual identification," their "message is universal" (Žižek 2016a). When Carlson similarly observes that "there is something transgendered about the human subject, and that this transgenderism transcends notions of gender," she distinguishes between different kinds of transpeople using psychoanalytic arguments I would not (Carlson 2010: 66). Yet her universalizing formulation importantly extends Žižek's thinking while sidestepping its greatest dangers. Her insistence on the "transgendered" element of all subjectivity tacitly acknowledges his point that even apparently heteronormative subjects experience the incommensurability of the masculine and feminine (Carlson 2010: 66). At the same time, her articulation of a Lacanian theory of transsubjectivity provides Lacanians with a way of seeing it as viable rather than as a misguided "attempt to avoid (the anxiety of) castration" (Žižek 2016c).

Both Žižek and Carlson remain faithful to Lacan's argument that sexuation mobilizes only masculine and feminine positions, however. By contrast, Susan Stryker's prolific work in trans studies offers compelling examples of such rearticulations' efficacy in traversing the fantasy of (hetero)sexual difference. Whereas Žižek argues that transpeople achieve "ethical greatness" by refusing to embrace the *sinthôme*, undergo temporary "depersonalization," and traverse the fantasy of (hetero)sexual difference, Stryker's introduction to the 1998 "Transgender Issue" of *GLQ* implicitly presents one way of achieving transsubjectivity by traversing that fantasy (Žižek 2016b). Viewed through *Queer Traversals*' argument, the passage Stryker grafts from Lacan's "The Freudian Thing" into her 1998 introduction now shines in a different light. Stryker rips the passage from its original context, in which Lacan stages "the impulsive leap into reality [*reel*] through the hoop of fantasy" as an ineffective means of acting out in the imaginary (Lacan 2006b: 357). In the context of the 1998 *GLQ* issue, however, this passage offers Stryker's own transition as an *avant-la-lettre* example of an act in the Real (Stryker 1998: 151). She builds up to the citation from Lacan with the explanation that in the 1990s,

> Informed by S/M and drag praxis as well as my graduate school exposure to speech-act theory, I began to see transsexuality not as an inauthentic state of being but rather as yet another communicational technology through which I could attend to the care of my self. It was a medico-scientific, juridico-legal, psychotherapeutic apparatus for generating and sustaining the desired reality effects of my gender identifications through the manipulation of bodily surface, thereby extending those effects beyond dungeons or drag bars into more widely shared social spaces. Audience, I finally decided, was everything, and transsexual technology would be my vehicle for which Jacques Lacan called, in another context, "an impulsive leap into the real through the paper hoop of fantasy." Becoming "a transsexual" implied nothing more than the willingness to engage with the apparatus for one's own purposes.
>
> (Stryker 1998: 151)

Here, Stryker reframes the passage from "The Freudian Thing" as a metaphor for the way her transition has enabled her to traverse the fantasy and reconfigure her relationship to the symbolic. One can make a similar observation about Stryker's 1994 "My Words to Victor Frankenstein above the Village of Chamounix," another initiatory text for trans studies. Describing the 1994 essay as a work "of Lacanian psychoanalytic theory dragged in rock-and roll garb" (Lavery 2019b), Grace Lavery observes that Stryker draws upon "rage" to performatively enact trans embodiment (Stryker 1994: 244). I see this "rage" as accompanying Stryker's act of embracing the *sinthôme* and prompting fantasy's traversal.

As Yannis Stavrakakis argues, traversing the fundamental fantasy by engaging the *sinthôme* requires that one take on "an impossible representation" so as "to 'represent' the impossible or rather to identify with the impossibility of its representation" (Stavrakakis 1999: 134). And as Lynda Hart argues in a Lacanian analysis of lesbian S/M, the impossible "'Real' … is precisely the possibilities of the imaginary that are located at the very limits of representation. Or, what representation fails to limit" (Hart 1998: 67). She argues that S/M offers one way of accomplishing this task: it engages the border between the imaginary and the Real, simultaneously mobilizing the "mirroring gaze of the lover"—who "promises to 'fix' us, to offer us constancy and coherency"—and pushing representational limits to provoke an encounter with the Real that could prompt fantasy's traversal (Hart 1998: 160). Hart's theory assumes that the oppressed subject needs a fantasy to provide imaginary and symbolic support for their being but figures S/M as a theatre in which to challenge its boundaries.

Similarly, Stryker's 1998 autobiographical anecdote in *GLQ* stresses the importance of "S/M and drag praxis" in shaping her transsubjectivity (Stryker 1998: 151). These practices allow her to see "transsexuality" as part of an "apparatus for generating and sustaining the desired reality effects of my gender identifications through the manipulation of bodily surface" (Stryker 1998: 151). Stryker's formulation resonates with Hart's assertion that

> Lacan's "Real" is impossible, but through psychoanalytic time, it becomes the "real-impossible." For if the "Real" is a psychic space that cannot be occupied, it is because it is not ocular. That is, it does not take place in the time or space of the ideological illusion called "reality" because it exceeds a specular economy. Nonetheless, it does produce "reality-effects," but in spite of but due to its extra-metalinguistic status.
>
> (Hart 1998: 161)

Thus, if the theatres of drag and S/M set an encounter with the Real into motion, it is not to render the Real visible. These practices' "reality-effects" are observable, but only as second-order phenomena. Stryker's narrative reveals that transgender embodiment can be thought of as emerging in the gap between what Hart calls "the body" and "the flesh" (Hart 1998: 10). Both "illusions," the "'body' keeps us anchored in the worlds we have constructed in 'reality'" and the "'flesh' is a place toward which we reach that always exceeds our grasp" (Hart 1998: 10). This formulation nuances Salamon's claim in her analysis of Lana Tisdell's remark in Kimberly Peirce's film *Boys Don't Cry* (1999) that she has seen Brandon Teena "in the full flesh." Salamon uses Maurice Merleau-Ponty's phenomenology to observe that Lana is referring not to her perceptions of Brandon's anatomy but to her recognition of his subjective sense of maleness. However, from a Lacanian perspective it is important to realize that trans embodiment does not simply emerge as a phenomenon propped up through imaginary and symbolic (mis)recognition—as Salamon suggests—but rather subsists in the interstices of the imaginary, symbolic, and Real (Salamon 2010: 58).

This means that engagement with the Real does not permanently consign Stryker to the dreaded realm of "abjection and death" Salamon associates with Prosser's argument "that the transsexual body is 'unimpeachably real'" (Salamon 2010: 41). Instead, Stryker inscribes herself within a reconstituted network of "language," "meaning," "the symbolic," "relation," and "desire" (Salamon 2010: 41). In so doing, she exemplifies Lacan's account in *Seminar XX* of embodiment's emergence through the process of coming to enjoyment through signification. Lacan explains that this subject "enjoys itself only by 'corporizing' (*corporiser*) the body in a signifying way"—a dynamic in which "[e]njoying (*jouir*) has the fundamental property that it is, ultimately, one person's body that enjoys a part of the Other's body" and in which "that part also enjoys" because "the Other likes it more or less" (Lacan 1998: 23). As Ragland notes, this theory connects "the body to language by way of unconscious fantasy," suggesting that "language creates one's imaginary body and defines one as a signifier that represents a subject for another signifier in a chain of articulations" (Ragland 2004: 43). Moreover, there is "a certain Sadian flavor" to this dynamic: "an ecstatic, subjective flavor suggesting, in fact, that it is the Other who enjoys" (Ragland 2004: 23–4). When read in the context of queer expansions of Lacanian sexuation, rather than through the heterosexist vocabulary animating Lacan's *Seminar XX*, this argument resonates productively with Hart's and Salamon's work. By suggesting that significatory play renders flesh incarnate, Lacan's thinking affords a way of theorizing trans embodiment as emerging through the encounter with the other via the Other.

Lacan also provides a way of understanding the role fantasy's traversal plays in achieving trans embodiment. As Ragland explains, "Insofar as certain *sinthomes*—identificatory *sinthomes* that are real knots—create the 'self' as a series of knots concerning the mother's unconscious desire and the place of the

Father's Name signifier in the social realm, they can be undone. Lacan called this 'using the symbolic to work on the real'" (Ragland 2004: 190–1). For Hart and Stryker, S/M provides a way of traversing the fundamental fantasy, undoing the knots between the three orders, and creating a new *sinthôme*—one that, in the latter case, enables trans embodiment.

Irreducible to the Real even as it is encountered via the Other, this process of embodiment partakes of the "body" and "flesh" as Hart defines them (Hart 1998: 10). If we understand the "flesh" as "a place toward which we reach that always exceeds our grasp"—and as that which one can (but need not necessarily) bring into closer alignment with one's "body"—this theory can account for the varied decisions transpeople make with regard to contemporary options for physical and hormonal transition (Hart 1998: 10). I use the phrase "bring into closer alignment," rather than claim that the subject can fully align the "flesh" with the "body," to underscore the importance of Lacan's argument that the subject is always split and subtended by internal divisions (Hart 1998: 10). Theorized in this fashion, transgender need not be understood as a search for "ontological consistency," as Žižek claims (Žižek 2016c). Nor need transgender embodiment be understood as "unimpeachably real," as Prosser would argue (Prosser qtd. in Salamon 2010: 41). Instead, it could be seen as yet another modality of split subjectivity.

In *Seminar XX*, Lacan asserts that "there's no such thing as a sexual relation. It's only speaking bodies... that come up with the idea of the world as such" (Lacan 1998: 126). Thus, his argument that the subject is split and desire is driven by an antinomy does not preclude social inventiveness or the creation of new modes of embodiment. Damon Young and Joshua J. Weiner advance a similar idea when they complicate queer theory's "so-called anti-social thesis" by stressing those forms of "incommensurability" that foster worldmaking (Weiner and Young 2011: 224). Lacan emphasizes that embodiment, too, is achieved by inventing the very "idea of the world as such," even as his exclusive references to "men" and "women" offer an impoverished sense of the gendered worlds it could entail (Lacan 1998: 126).

By contrast, Stryker's prolific work with word and image in Trans Studies uses signification to create new worlds of gender embodiment. What she formulates as a "communicational technology" Gherovici understands as an "art" through which "writing" touches the "unsymbolizable" to remake "embodiment" (Gherovici 2014: 255–62; Stryker 1998: 151). Whereas Gherovici's argument is grounded in trans memoir—a genre also featuring prominently in Prosser's archive—my expanded account of the potential the Lacanian *sinthôme* holds for trans studies also provides a means of reading the forms of embodiment at work in what Pamela Caughie calls the "transgenre" (Caughie 2013: 503). Building on Sandy Stone's 1991 suggestion that transpeople be considered "a *genre*—a set of embodied texts" who promise "disruption" of existing constructs—Caughie offers a model of "transsexual life writing" whose "temporality of embodiment" differs from that offered in Lili Elbe's 1931 memoir *Man Into Woman* (Caughie 2013: 503, 519). Caughie's argument—that Virginia Woolf's novel *Orlando* (1928) offers a trans inflection of Elizabeth Freeman's "queer vision of how time wrinkles and folds"—positions Orlando as a figure of "future embodiment": "as the deliberate shaping of a narrative of a life that might be lived, and liveable" (Caughie 2013: 519). I propose that fantastic narratives such as *Orlando* can be as effective for figuring trans potentialities as the trans memoirs Gherovici considers. Defying the realist conventions typically grounding autobiography; shuttling back and forth in time to facilitate the imagination of hypothetical worlds: texts such as Woolf's allow for the perpetual reinvention of possibilities for gender embodiment—possibilities that may or may not be grounded in bodily transitions or in the limited language of masculinity and femininity that has heretofore dominated Lacanian psychoanalysis.

However one might describe the "art" of trans embodiment, written or elsewise, Lacanian approaches to transsubjectivity stress the importance of engaging the signifier to touch the Real (Gherovici 2014: 255–62). This engagement with the Real can also entail traversing the fundamental fantasy. As Stryker observed during her remarks at the Opening Session of the 2016 Trans* Studies conference at the University of Arizona, "Trans people know about deep change" (Stryker 2016). As do transpsychoanalytic accounts of fantasy's traversal, Stryker's writings from the 1990s to the present point to the way transitioning entails profound subjective transformation and to the way those who transition trenchantly challenge received ideas about gender, sex, sexual difference, and sexuation. As Lavery's description of Stryker's 1994 essay as "Lacanian" suggests, Stryker engages in transpsychoanalytic analysis *avant la lettre* (Lavery 2019b). Lavery concludes her tribute to Stryker with a compelling example of the promise and uncertainty of such a traversal, writing that "[a]t a certain point, transgender rage recedes as transfeminine life becomes impossible not to live: in the ruins of grace, in the absence of certainty, in the mouth of hell" (Lavery 2019b).

Because of its stress on "deep change," transpsychoanalysis is ideally positioned to engage in a transformative rethinking of Lacanian sexuation that goes beyond the limited vocabulary animating the claim that "men and women are sexuated psychically, not biologically" (Ragland 2004: 179). Whereas orthodox Lacanians such as Žižek consider sexual difference to be an intractable antinomy, Stryker demonstrates that it is not. Traversing the fundamental fantasy and engaging in "deep change" reveal the contingency of (hetero)sexual difference and the formulae of sexuation Lacan elaborates in *Seminar XX* (Stryker 2016). These kinds of transformations create myriad opportunities for "undoing" and redoing not only gender but also sexuation and sexual difference: ways we can understand not only "men" and "women" but also many other ways of being "sexuated psychically" as viable possibilities for desiring subjectivity (Butler 2004; Ragland 2004: 179).

Transpsychoanalysis should therefore take the process of returning to Lacan's texts not as a mandate worshipfully to recite the Master's mantras in antiquated vocabularies unresponsive to contemporary concerns but rather as an opportunity to mobilize repetitions of his ideas with twenty-first-century differences. If we graft Carlson's observation that "there is something transgendered about the human subject, and that this transgenderism transcends notions of gender" into the context I offer in this chapter—one in which Lacanian sexual difference is a fundamental fantasy available for traversal and need not permanently remain the only antinomy animating possibilities for gender and desire—both her observation and Stryker's account of "deep change" resonate anew (Carlson 2010: 66). As Ruti observes, "the aim of Lacanian analysis" is to "loosen" constrictive "fantasies in order to create space for alternative life plots and directions, and in so doing expand the subject's repertoire of existential options" (Ruti 2008a: 498). Rather than insisting upon the intractable and "antagonistic nature of *sexual* difference"—as do orthodox Lacanians such as Žižek—we need to focus on "the antagonistic nature of... difference" as the constitutive antagonism driving desire, class division, ethnic division, and a variety of other social processes (Žižek 2016a, emphasis added).

This chapter has highlighted Woolf's *Orlando* and Stryker's transition as examples of traversing the fantasy of (hetero)sexual difference to achieve profound subjective transformation. In Chapter 5, I discuss gender embodiment in John Cameron Mitchell's *Hedwig and the Angry Inch* (2001), a film that shares with Monika Treut's *The Virgin Machine* (1988) traversals of fantasies animating queer German migration to the United States. In Chapter 6, I will examine (hetero)sexual difference's traversal in Gloria Anzaldúa's mixed-genre texts *Borderlands/La Frontera* (1987) and *Light in the Dark/Luz en lo Oscuro* (2015), which theorize a multiethnic "new consciousness of the *mestiza*" whose hybridity extends to queer and trans subjects (Anzaldúa 1987: 80); and Andrea Lawlor's novel *Paul Takes the Form of a Mortal Girl* (2017), which uses a *sinthom*estizx—a mixed-race, shape-shifting artist named Robin—to prompt protagonist Paul's traversal of the fantasies animating dominant 1990s queer sexualities and gender embodiments. These works illustrate different trajectories for fantasy's traversal as well as a variety of strategies—activism, art, performance, and care—that foster progressive outcomes after "deep change."

Setting the stage for Chapters 5 and 6, Chapter 4 examines recent trans-affirmative readings of Lacan that challenge the orthodox understanding of (hetero)sexual difference animating Žižek's antagonism toward transgender. Building on work by Carlson, Cavanagh, Gherovici, and Gozlan, I insist that trans-affirmative psychoanalysis take an elastic approach to the language of "men" and "women" Lacan employed in the 1970s. In so doing, I argue for a Lacanian psychoanalysis that enables affirmative theorization of non-binary subjectivities as well as those transsubjectivities that involve transitioning from one side of the gender binary to the other. Such a theory would account for the sorts of "deep change" exemplified in this chapter by Stryker's transition as well as those illustrated in the films and literary texts I discuss in Chapters 5 and 6.

Notes

1 This claim is followed by a series of preposterous analogies between sexual identities and class positions that only confirm Žižek's lack of familiarity with LGBTQ issues in North America.
2 Žižek's claim that there is a "lack of contact" or "antagonism even" between "the struggle for sexual liberation" and these other struggles is baffling given the currency of intersectional feminist and queer analysis (Žižek 2016b).

4

Cavanagh and Gherovici: Toward a Transfeminist Theory of Embodiment

Despite pathologizing tendencies within mainstream psychoanalysis lingering even today, Trans Studies has always engaged in deeply psychoanalytic work. In a 2019 blog post, Grace Lavery describes Susan Stryker's 1994 "My Words to Victor Frankenstein above the Village of Chamounix" as an "essay of Lacanian psychoanalytic theory dragged in rock-and roll garb" (Lavery 2019b) drawing upon "rage" to performatively enact trans embodiment despite its "pathologization" (Stryker 1994: 244). I cannot help but agree with Lavery's assessment, which aligns with my own argument in Chapter 3 that Stryker's introduction to the 1998 "Transgender Issue" of *GLQ* reinterprets Lacan to stage her transition as a Lacanian act engaging all three orders—not just the imaginary and symbolic—to traverse the fantasy of (hetero)sexual difference and achieve trans embodiment. Trans studies has always been psychoanalytic even if mainstream psychoanalysis has been slow to trans its paradigms.

Although Stryker elaborates her account of transition through a rereading of Lacan's "The Freudian Thing," over the last several decades Lacanians have struggled to theorize transgender subjectivities and embodiments without pathologizing them. Catherine Millot's *Horsexe*, which conflates transgender with psychosis, stimulated several decades of such thinking.[1] However, in the last ten years, trans-affirmative psychoanalysts such as Shanna Carlson (2010, 2014), Sheila Cavanagh (2015, 2016, 2018), Patricia Gherovici (2010, 2012, 2014, 2017, 2019a, 2019b), Oren Gozlan (2015), and Gayle Salamon (2010, 2016) have reworked Lacan to theorize a wide range of gender embodiments.

The dogma of (hetero)sexual difference nonetheless continues to be repeated so insistently within the secondary literature that it is easy to miss the ways trans-affirmative readings of sexuation, sexual difference, and gender embodiment are invited by Lacan's texts. Although interpretations of *Seminar XX* stress Lacan's presentation of sexual difference as an antinomy between masculine and feminine, that text also acknowledges that "[m]en, women, and children are but signifiers" (Lacan 1998: 33). In "The Instance of the Letter in the Unconscious," Lacan similarly qualifies his account of the divergent perceptions a boy and girl seated opposite one another on a train have of a station's bathroom signage, visible to one as "Ladies" and the other as "Gentlemen" (Lacan 2006d: 416). If the signs were "written in a language [*langue*] with which the little boy and girl were unfamiliar," he observes, "their quarrel would simply be more exclusively a quarrel over words" that are "ready to take on signification" (Lacan 2006d: 420). These formulations suggest that Lacan's words—including those for sexual difference—are potentially interchangeable and that his theories are potentially adaptable to today's gender subjectivities and embodiments. Even his famous declaration in *Seminar XX* that "there's no such thing as a sexual relation"— which is usually taken to stage the masculine and feminine as an antinomy— is quickly qualified with an explanation that should be interpreted far more flexibly: "It's only speaking bodies... that come up with the idea of the world as such" (Lacan 1998: 126). This formulation opens space to theorize contemporary trans embodiments.

To fully realize what Gherovici has recently called a "new ethics of psychoanalysis" affirming transgender people, transpsychoanalysis needs to continue to offer alternatives to orthodox understandings of Lacanian sexuation (Gherovici 2019b: 146). Cavanagh, Gherovici, Gozlan, and Salamon all offer trans-affirmative reworkings of Lacan, but have yet to move past Lacan's emphasis on the phallus and the need to choose between masculine and feminine positions. As a consequence, they have not provided a satisfying account of non-binary subjectivities.

Moreover, only two trans-affirmative psychoanalysts—Salamon and Cavanagh—have put their theories into dialogue with the work of psychoanalytic feminists who have been challenging Lacan's phallogocentric repression of female embodiment for decades. The former offers a trans-affirmative rereading of Luce Irigaray's *An Ethics of Sexual Difference*; the latter builds on the writings of psychoanalytic feminist visual artist Bracha Ettinger to understand trans embodiments (Salamon 2010: 131–44). Ettinger presents a feminist alternative to strict Lacanianism by theorizing a womb-inspired "matrixial borderspace" standing alongside the phallic order without negating it (Ettinger 2006a: 152). In my view, Hélène Cixous' work is also useful because she would smash the phallogocentric order altogether. If, as Cixous contends, Freud's and Lacan's theories repress the female body, that suppression also informs psychoanalysis's past occlusion of transgender embodiments.

In this chapter, by examining psychoanalysis's historical blind spot with regard to transgender embodiment, I argue for a psychoanalytic transfeminism that is not anchored by the phallus and that traverses the fantasy of (hetero)sexual difference informing the view that one must choose between masculine and feminine positions. This fantasy underpins not only works of orthodox Lacanians such as Joan Copjec and Slavoj Žižek but also trans-affirmative books such as Gherovici's *Please Select Your Gender* (Gherovici 2010) and Gozlan's *Transsexuality and the Art of Transitioning* (Gozlan 2015), which offer supportive approaches to transition while pathologizing non-binary and genderqueer subjectivities.[2] Moreover, this fantasy—which positions sexual difference as primary and other forms of difference as secondary—obscures the significance of factors such as race, ethnicity, nationality, and economic class for subjective formation. A psychoanalytic transfeminism that traverses the fantasy of (hetero)sexual difference will help reach beyond these impasses to provide a groundwork for theorizing a wide range of genders, sexualities, races, ethnicities, nationalities, and classes.

Ettinger's Matrixial Borderspace: Beyond the Fantasy of (Hetero)sexual Difference

Ettinger's concept of the matrixial borderspace has been especially useful for trans-affirmative psychoanalysis because it pushes beyond the theory of the antinomy between masculine and feminine that Lacan articulates in a 1970s vocabulary in *Seminar XX* (Lacan 1998). Her concept of the "matrixial borderspace," the centerpiece of Cavanagh's theory of transgender embodiment, stakes out a space for femininity in the womb (Ettinger 2006a: 152). Ettinger introduces the matrix to get past the "impasse" of (hetero)sexual difference Lacan presents as a function of castration when he argues that "the sexual relationship... does not exist" because the masculine and feminine are incommensurate (Ettinger 2006a: 106; Lacan 1998: 63). Delineating stances anybody can occupy regardless of anatomy, he claims that "it is through the phallic function that man as a whole acquires his inscription (*prend son inscription*)" and arrogates universality, whereas the feminine is "not-whole" and does "not allow for any universality" (Lacan 1998: 79–80). For Lacan, this antinomy animates divergent ways of desiring. Whereas masculine subjects' desire is structured around unattainable *objets a*, for feminine subjects, "something other than object *a* is at stake" (Lacan 1998: 63). Because the feminine subject is "not-whole, she has a supplementary jouissance" rather than phallic *jouissance* (Lacan 1998: 69).

Refusing the misogynist logic that then leads Lacan to assert that "Women content themselves (*s'en tiennent*)" with "being not-whole" and experiencing a "supplementary" feminine "jouissance" enabling them to control men, Ettinger goes beyond his antinomy between masculine and feminine (Lacan 1998: 69). Unlike Irigaray, who challenges Lacanian phallogocentrism by exploring female anatomy's implications, Ettinger derives her theory of femininity from the subject's experiences in the womb.[3] Much as Lacan notes that anybody can occupy the phallic position because sexual difference is linguistic rather than anatomical, Ettinger observes that feminine sexual difference is "not a result of having/not having an organ" (Ettinger 2006a: 193).[4] Femininity is available to all subjects irrespective of anatomy because the matrixial results from the subject's openness to the other within the womb, where the incipient subject first experiences a "matrixial unconscious sphere" entailing "a borderspace of simultaneous co-emergence and co-fading of the *I* and the uncognized *non-I*" (Ettinger 2006a: 139). In contrast to Lacan, who stages masculinity and femininity as an antinomy determining that there is "no such thing as a sexual relation," Ettinger's matrix is relational and connective (Lacan 1998: 126). Fostering "relation-without-relating," the matrix is "a dynamic borderspace of active/passive co-emergence, with-in and with-out the unrecognized other, that inscribes joint existential ontogenesis, a becoming-memory in relation to a feminine-Other desire" through a process Ettinger calls "metramorphosis" (Ettinger 2006a: 109, 109, 69).

These arguments shift Lacan's theories in important ways. As Griselda Pollock observes, Ettinger's matrix provides "a nonphallic, non-Oedipal, nongendering redefinition of a subjectivizing apparatus that is, nonetheless, sexuate and sexuating" in ways different from those articulated in Lacan's formulas for sexuation (Pollock 2006: 13). Exposing the blind spots in his understanding of non-phallic subjectivities, Ettinger credits the "matrixial borderspace" with a "primary" and "originary feminine difference that doesn't confront, submit to, or fight the phallic difference," on which "[i]t is in no way dependent" and to which it "bears no comparison" (Ettinger 2006a: 183).

Because the matrixial "is not derived from the exchange of signifiers and does not refer to the phallic field and to the rift of castration," metramorphosis works in sideways relation to "phallic subjectivity" rather than being derived from, submerged by, or subordinated to it, as is Julia Kristeva's pre-Oedipal (Ettinger 2006a: 183).[5] Moreover, unlike the pre-Oedipal, the matrixial does not remain "unintelligible, invisible, and presymbolic"; instead, metramorphosis engages the real, imaginary, and symbolic, transforming them "from within"

(Ettinger 2001: 125). A "nonphallic *erotic co-response-ability*," metramorphosis "accompanies the phallic subjectivity all along its voyage in time and place, even if its sources are in the 'pre-'" (Ettinger 2006a: 143, 182). Because the "borderspace" is "supplementary" to rather than in competition with the phallus, the matrix's movements cause the symbolic to be "shifted or returned, rather than overturned" (Ettinger 2006a: 152; Pollock 2006: 2, 5). Pointing to "the beyond-the-phallus," the "matrixial is generative" of new forms of relationality, visual art, and writing (Ettinger 2006a: 66, 111).

Ettinger's thinking therefore offers an alternative to considering subjectivity an effect of "castration," challenging assertions of its primacy (Ettinger 2006a: 69). Critiquing Lacanian psychoanalysis's phallogocentric bias, Ettinger observes that

> "Oedipal castration" is only one of the prisms—that of the male viewpoint of the difference between the sexes—through which the passage to the symbolic field occurs... The matrixial passage by metramorphic borderlinking precedes and transcends phallic castration and Oedipal gender difference... These different passages to the Symbolic (*phallic castration* and *matrixial metramorphosis*) indicate two *variations* of repression and two different kinds of complexes behind repression... The phallic sexual difference is therefore not the only unconscious sexual difference.
>
> (Ettinger 2006a: 69)

Instead, metramorphosis immerses the subject in a space of "desire that must be differentiated not only from phallic desire, but also from *material* or *female* desire as defined in the phallic universe" (Ettinger 2006a: 66). This "poietic-artistic process" involves "*jouissance*, traumas, pictograms, phantasies, and affects" in "death-drive oscillations" between "originary difference and... its transforming potentiality" (Ettinger 2006a: 140). Using "co-emergency and co-fading as meaning," metramorphosis is unpredictably generative (Ettinger 2006a: 140).

Ettinger's theory of matrixial difference presents a valuable alternative to Lacan's phallogocentric understanding of sexuation, fantasy, and desire. Arguing that "[t]he matrixial complex of fantasy is linked to the sexual nonphallic difference deriving from the late prenatal traumatic encounter in the Real," she conceptually detaches the feminine from the masculine, dispensing with the Lacanian fantasy of (hetero)sexual difference (Ettinger 2001: 123). As Pollock argues, Ettinger's ability to go "beyond the phallic" antinomy of "masculine/feminine, phallic/other" helps us to "imagine a theoretical space beyond the limits of phallic logic within which the feminine is merely the other term of its masculine-consolidating binary" (Pollock 2006: 5).

However, just as for Lacan "the phallus would be nothing without the penis," for Ettinger the matrix would be nothing without the womb (Butler 1993: 84). Although she frequently describes the matrix as "feminine," from a transpsychoanalytic perspective the womb prompting metramorphosis might be that of a woman, a transperson, or a non-binary person (Ettinger 2006a: 183). And despite the matrix's grounding in anatomy, Ettinger contends that her matrixial "feminine... difference is not the effect of social structuring (Gender) nor an essentialist datum or deterministic result of a biological difference" but something "woven in a human relation and therefore in some human language" involving "bodily signs" and "affective channelings" (Ettinger 2006a: 183). These unpredictable energies are accessible to anyone because they derive from experiences in the womb.

Joining Cixous in critiquing psychoanalysis's repression of feminine desire, Ettinger argues that Lacan's theorization of (hetero)sexual difference as an "impasse" derives from his inability to understand the "passions of the daughter and her partial drives rooted in matrixial incest" except insofar as they support "patriarchy" and the "desire to have children in heterosexually regulated units of society" (Ettinger 2006a: 106). Whereas the daughter's "drives" remain the "silenced and unthought par excellence" within the Lacanian symbolic, in Ettinger's "matrixial paradigm it is metramorphosis, not the knot, that accounts for feminine relation, *jouissance*, and desire in the subject" (Ettinger 2006a: 106). Because "[e]rotic or traumatic *jouissance* does not totally evaporate from matrixial desire," metramorphosis works as "a passage-lane through which matrixial affects, events, intensities, resonances, and modes of becoming infiltrate the nonconscious margins of the Symbolic" (Ettinger 2006a: 109, 180). Operating alongside the phallus, the matrix mobilizes a formerly "silenced matrixial desire" that endangers "patriarchy" while connecting to others (Ettinger 2006a: 106). This process promises genders and desires unbeholden to the sexist, cissexist, and heterosexist paradigms that have governed so much Lacanian scholarship (Sedgwick 2003: 8). As such, Ettinger's work opens up important new directions for psychoanalytic queer and trans theory, going beyond the fantasy of (hetero) sexual difference.

Moreover, Ettinger's claim that "The phallic sexual difference is therefore not the only unconscious sexual difference" has even more implications than she theorizes (Ettinger 2006a: 69). Unlike the Lacanian subject, her matrixial subject is not forced to choose between masculine and feminine positions. And unlike Lee Edelman's *sintho*mosexual, who embraces a *jouissance* defined through Lacanian sexual difference while failing to subvert it, the matrixial subject unpredictably—queerly—goes beyond (hetero)sexual difference, generating myriad relations. Finally, metramorphosis's sideways relation to "phallic subjectivity" makes it possible to think of difference as multiple: comprised of differences that might include gender, sexuality, race, ethnicity, nationality, or economic class (Ettinger 2006a: 183). As Eve Kosofsky Sedgwick notes, being "beside" can entail many different relationalities, from "desiring, identifying, representing, repelling, paralleling, differentiating, rivaling, leaning, twisting," and "mimicking" to "withdrawing, attracting, aggressing," and "warping" (Sedgwick 2003: 8). These relationalities may engage many forms of difference: not just (hetero)sexual difference.

Ettinger's Matrixial Borderspace: Beyond the Lacanian *Sinthôme*

Ettinger also complicates Lacan's account of the *sinthôme* by calling attention to the feminine's role in its production. She observes that "[w]hen the Real, the Imaginary, and the Symbolic intercoil around a feminine encounter according to the parameters of the Real, the knot 'goes wrong,' it appears as a 'slip of the knot' (as one would say a 'slip of the tongue')" (Ettinger 2006a: 190). As a result, "[a] 'supplementary' feminine sexual 'rapport' that the signifier has not blasted and castration has not inflated is, in moments, drawn out of—and swept back into— Lacan's thinking" about the *sinthôme* (Ettinger 2001: 119). Thus, Gherovici notes, "[t]hanks to the 'sinthome,' we can rethink sexual difference without the... phallus": without presuming that its absence from or subordination within an individual's psychical economy is evidence of psychosis (Gherovici 2017: 8, *sic*). Ettinger argues that despite Lacan's argument in *Seminar XX* that "[s]exual nonrapport is the result of the phallic equivalence between the sexes," he later posits that there is "another level," one "of nonequivalence, in which a sexual rapport should become possible" because of the *sinthôme* (Ettinger 2001: 119). This "'feminine' rapport" does not entail "a traumatic return onto the real corporal past event but" rather "a transformation" suggesting "nonphallic sublimation" (Ettinger 2001: 120). Consequently, when "[t]he phallus fails, or this feminine-other thinking fails" within "the phallic order, ... an-other sense, based on originary feminine difference, emerges" (Ettinger 2006a: 190).

However, Ettinger notes that within Lacan's thinking this difference's emergence "is not enough to shift the phallic paradigm" (Ettinger 2006a: 191). She observes that for him, "the *sinthôme* is still the phallic failure to tie" the three orders back together; its "knots enigmatically account for the failure to inscribe feminine desire" (Ettinger 2006a: 191, 193). By contrast, for Ettinger "'woman' is not just a failure of/in the phallus, not even as it is taken up by the poetics of the *sinthôme*" (Ettinger 2006a: 191). Rather, "a matrixial *sinthôme*" appears when "[k]nowledge is released from blanks and holes in the Real by the metramorphic process of webbing and wit(h)-nessing, the metramorphic process of exchange of affect and phantasy based on the conduction of/in trauma or *jouissance* in jointness, and the metramorphic process of transmissions-in-transformation of phantasy" (Ettinger 2006a: 193). This "intersubjective" feminine *sinthôme* "releases/creates/invents/reveals, from a feminine side, potential desires whose sense, which does not depend on the signifier, will be revealed in further encounters" (Ettinger 2006a: 192–3). Going beyond Lacan's economy of lack into the Sedgwickian "beside," Ettinger's feminine *sinthôme* produces novel forms of desire and relationality that extend beyond Lacanian (hetero)sexual difference and may implicate other factors, such as race, ethnicity, nationality, or economic class (Sedgwick 2003: 8).

In all of these cases, Ettinger's "matrixial *sinthôme*" engages the matrix's "transitivity"; it can appear in an analysand's speech or "in writing as a work of art" (Ettinger 2006A: 190–94). This artwork's origins are "co-poietic" because "the matrixial sexual difference, linked to another experience and another body, gives supplementary connections between libidinal and erotic action, effect and traces, subject and object, Other and desire" (Ettinger 2006a: 193, 137). Capable of provoking a wide range of responses—"desiring, identifying, representing, repelling, paralleling, differentiating, rivaling, leaning, twisting," and "mimicking"; "withdrawing, attracting, aggressing," and "warping"—the matrixial subject's sideways connectivity is unpredictably creative, capable of connecting multiple aspects of subjectivity (Sedgwick 2003: 8). Through a "metramorphic process of intersection and interchange," Ettinger's subject "embraces and discharges unthought subknowledge from the knotted Real into meaningful co-inscription in artwork," generating aesthetic innovations and novel forms of subjectivity offering alternatives to the fantasy of (hetero)sexual difference (Ettinger 2006a: 102).

Transsubjectivity and the *Sinthôme*

The most compelling recent psychoanalytic theories of trans embodiment are based on the *sinthôme*, which provides subjects with the opportunity to create alternatives to Lacanian sexual difference. Cavanagh, Gherovici, and Gozlan all emphasize that art and writing allow transpeople to form unique *sinthômes* grounding embodiment. As Gherovici observes, for transpeople the *sinthôme* is "a singular invention allowing someone to live" when they otherwise might perish (Gherovici 2017: 9). Unlike Millot, who believes that transpeople psychotically use the *sinthôme* to raze "the frontiers of the *real*" of "sexual difference" by linking only the imaginary and symbolic, Cavanagh, Gherovici, and Gozlan understand the *sinthôme* as a fiction enabling transpeople to anchor their embodiments in all three orders (Millot 1990: 15).[6] The *sinthôme* itself is not gendered, and need only be consistent in linking the three orders, as are the tics Gherovici discusses in *Please Select Your Gender* (2010).[7] Her, Cavanagh's, and Gozlan's examples of *sinthômes* knotting trans embodiments include the written word—especially autobiography—and bodily writing such as scar tissue from gender reassignment. Jeanne Vaccaro's "woolly ecologies" extend this understanding of trans writing to include "wood, wool, skin, sweat, rubber, foam," and "cloth," which offer creative modes of subjective inscription (Vaccaro 2015: 276). These artforms function "by means of the letter" rather than the signifier to anchor transgender embodiment in all three orders, regardless of whether a transperson utilizes bodily technologies for gender reassignment (Harari 2002: 241).

Whereas Gherovici and Gozlan employ Lacan's *sinthôme*, Cavanagh builds on Ettinger's argument that the feminine *sinthôme* works within the matrixial borderspace to generate novel modes of desire, embodiment, and subjectivity. Writing that "[t]he matrix is an Other axis of sexual difference accessible to us all, regardless of trans status and is not reducible to femininity or to gender identity," she clarifies that anybody can experience metramorphosis, which results from having been in a womb (Cavanagh 2016: 28). Arguing that "transsexuality... predates phallic sexuation as theorized by Lacan," Cavanagh uses Ettinger's theory that the matrixial operates alongside rather than rejects the phallus to argue that transpeople do not ignore but rather deprioritize it: they "don't register the phallic signifier as a primary signifier (underwriting sexual difference) but only one of others that can be animated and resignified" (Cavanagh 2015: 104; Cavanagh 2016: 38). Noting that "Ettinger's notion of the trans-subjective does not refer to transsexual people per se but rather to" an universal "modality of experience in the matrixial borderspace," Cavanagh contends that transitioning "may be understood... in terms of the matrixial substratum," whose process of metramorphosis "involves changes in borderlines and thresholds" well "suited to conceptualizing a transsexual transition" (Cavanagh 2016: 27–30).

This process is inherently relational. Whereas Salamon (2010, 2016) stresses the importance of social and imaginary recognition to a transperson's sense of embodiment, Gherovici and Cavanagh emphasize the need to link all three orders with a *sinthôme*: which, as Raul Moncayo (2016) observes, can only change when the Other is engaged.[8] As a clinician, he emphasizes psychoanalysis's capacity to prompt such a transformation. Gherovici and Cavanagh argue that art and writing are similarly effective ways to reach the Other and form a new *sinthôme*. The latter describes "transsexual transitions" as "acts of artistry that reassemble a borderspace between the subject and m/Other (the I and the non-I) that enables subjectification" and fosters "a sense of bodily integration" (Cavanagh 2016: 39–40). Gozlan also notes that the trans "body and its narrative are held together by 'sutures', whose visible scars reveal its precarious composition" (Gozlan 2015: 51). Cavanagh emphasizes that in order "to establish subjective limits on the body," "to produce new signifiers and to desire," the transperson must achieve a "sinthomatic knotting between the Real (the flesh), the Imaginery (embodiment), and the Symbolic (gender pronoun)" regardless of whether bodily inscription is accomplished through "a surgical cut" or "hormone injections" (Cavanagh 2016: 40 sic). The subject must also be able to initiate "new significations, new discourses and fantasies about his or her gender, sex embodiment, and relationship to the Other" so as "to live productively with the impossibility of ever finally signifying sexual difference" (Cavanagh 2016: 38).

Because this process is relational and entails creating a new *sinthôme*, it goes beyond the phallic order and the fantasy of (hetero)sexual difference. It therefore has the potential to implicate many different kinds of difference: not just sexual difference. Race, ethnicity, nationality, and economic class could take on primary rather than secondary roles in the formation of transsubjectivites grounded with Ettingerian *sinthômes*.

Transing Embodiment, Transing Sexual Difference

These path-breaking theorizations improve considerably over Millot's inadequate approach to transsubjectivities by offering new ways of utilizing the radical potential of Lacan's theory of embodiment. This concept, which Charles Shepherdson introduced in 2000, offers an alternative to notions of anatomical "sex" and "gender role" (Shepherdson 2000: 112). Trans-affirmative psychoanalysts have retained Shepherdson's emphasis on embodiment while correcting his overreliance upon Millot's pathologization of transition.

Lacan does not define embodiment by observing the body's material contours; he understands it as a subjective experience arising through *jouissance*. He states that psychoanalysis "presumes that desire is inscribed on the basis of a corporal contingency" and that "[i]t's only speaking bodies... that come up with an idea of the world as such" (Lacan 1998: 93, 126). Describing "the substance of the body... as that which enjoys itself" through "'corporizing' (*corporiser*) the body in a signifying way" (Lacan 1998: 23), he argues that "what appears on bodies in the enigmatic form of sexual characteristics—which are merely secondary— makes sexed beings (*êtres sexués*). No doubt. But being is the jouissance of the body as such" (Lacan 1998: 6). This formulation positions embodiment as a secondary byproduct of *jouissance* "marked... by the impossibility of establishing as such, anywhere in the enunciable, the sole One that interests us, the One of the relation 'sexual relationship' (*rapport sexuel*)" (Lacan 1998: 6–7). Psychical and material, embodiment is achieved through signification and *jouissance*.

Lacan presents this theory of embodiment in the context of his thesis in *Seminar XX* that there is no "sexual relationship" between "man" and "woman"— that is, through a heterosexual example (Lacan 1998: 7). He argues that "[m]an and a woman... are nothing but signifiers" who "derive their function from this, from saying (*dire*) as a distinct incarnation of sex" and in so doing demonstrate that "[t]he Other... can thus only be the Other sex" (Lacan 1998: 39). From this perspective, embodiment is achieved by aligning oneself with either the masculine or the feminine. A subject's position need not match up with their anatomy but is defined through the antinomy of (hetero)sexual difference.

Built on these assumptions, Gozlan's theory of trans embodiment construes gender as "a phantasy" connected to "the real of sexual difference" and bound up in the impossible quest to recover the *objet a* (Gozlan 2015: 26). Achieved by assuming a position with respect to sexual difference, the process of coming into gender is "a universal challenge" rather than "a problem" only experienced by transpeople (Gozlan 2015: 89). He insists that all genders emerge by grappling with the "enigma at the heart of subjectivity": "the fact that there is no signifier for sexual difference in the unconscious" (Gozlan 2015: 12). He also notes that "As the word 'engenderment' suggests in its double meaning of 'bringing into existence' and 'coming to gender,' gender is deeply tied with the subject's fantasy of origin" (Gozlan 2015: 76). He thus speculates that "gender is an artifact or invention, an embodiment of phantasies of origin weaved in our narratives of sexuation and desire" (Gozlan 2015: 76). Subjectivity "rests on the loss of an imagined cohesiveness that only exists as a retroactively constructed phantasy" (Gozlan 2015: 27). Gozlan understands transition as one strategy for undoing gender's phantasmatic underpinnings and starting anew. He observes that "[t]ranssexual surgery may... signify an 'act' that traverses phantasy": it offers "a means to claim one's desire, altering the body for further elaboration over the course of life" (Gozlan 2015: 47).

However, for Gozlan, the route "through which one comes to assume a particular sexual embodiment occurs through the simultaneous registration and repudiation of" Lacanian "sexual difference" (Gozlan 2015: 13). Claiming that "[g]ender constitutes both a disruption and a solution to the trauma that founds subjectivity," he argues that although "the real of sexual difference remains forever inaccessible, its articulation through the phantasy-framework of gender materializes the regime of sexual difference that defines our symbolic universe" and grounds "subjectivity" (Gozlan 2015: 86, 74). Because "femininity and masculinity" are "psychic positions in relation to the unknown of desire," embodying "a gender signifies an acceptance of an answer regarding one's place in the symbolic order" (Gozlan 2015: 6). However, these "psychic positions... exceed symbolic articulation" and "fail to contain the real of sexual difference" (Gozlan 2015: 6). This "incommensurability between the symbolic articulation of gender and the real of sexual difference" is intrinsic to "unconscious differentiation" (Gozlan 2015: 13).

Within this logic, genders beyond the binary remain unsymbolizable consequences of contending with the feminine, which "stands in helpless relation to the Real," whereas "gender certainty" claims "phallic mastery and power" (Gozlan 2015: 6). Although Gozlan understands this "mastery" as illusory, arguing that people are easily destabilized by visibly transgender people's challenges to "gender certainty," he also prescribes it as the solution to transpeoples' ill ease (Gozlan 2015: 6). Observing that "[t]he fiction of coherence that gender provides us with constitutes a source of certainty that defends against the traumatic real of sexuality," he argues that transitioning entails a Lacanian "act" successfully reconfiguring a transperson's embodiment (Gozlan 2015: 73, 6).

Many aspects of this theory are salutary, understanding transsubjectivity as life-affirming rather than psychotic. And even though Gozlan does not acknowledge as much, his ideas can be extended to theorize other forms of transsubjectivity, whether those involving living as a gender other than that assigned at birth without the assistance of surgical or hormonal technologies, or those entailing refusing to choose between the identities of "man" and "woman." However, from a feminist perspective, Gozlan's routing of transsubjectivity through the masculine position is problematic because it is androcentric and does not challenge the fantasy of (hetero)sexual difference.

This fantasy has a stronger hold on thinkers writing in Lacan's wake than it does on his own formulations, which are amenable to revision. For instance, Lacan clarifies that the fantasy of (hetero)sexual difference is contingent rather than necessary when insisting in *Seminar XX* that "[m]an" and "woman" are "nothing but signifiers" (Lacan 1998: 39). The meaning of his claim that "[t]he Other... can thus only be the Other sex" is therefore subject to interpretation (Lacan 1998: 39). Lacan argues that "the jouissance of the body" underpinning embodiment is fundamentally "asexual (*asexué*)," and that signification in the Other involves the exchange of the "*a*-sexual (*a-sexué*)" and phantasmatic "object *a*" (Lacan 1998: 6, 127, 127). Tim Dean therefore observes that Lacan offers queers a theory of sexuality leaving desire "independent of gender" (Dean 2006: 216).[9] Yet to be more precise, Lacan's description of the *objet a* and *jouissance* as "*a-sexué*" suggests that they are not sexuated. Although the word "*a-sexué*" resonates with the English word "asexual"—typically connoting a person not sexually attracted to others—Lacan's language should be translated in light of his theory of sexuation. His statement that "[i]n the psyche, there is nothing by which the subject may situate himself as a male or female being" indicates that the psyche is not sexuated, and his remarks that the *objet a* and *jouissance* are "*a-sexué*" should be interpreted similarly (Lacan 1977: 204). The *objet a* lures the subject with desire's dialectical deferrals; *jouissance* registers the drive's ecstasy in the Real; but neither is intrinsically tied to sexual difference.

There are therefore many different ways to read Lacan's statement that "[t]he Other presents itself to the subject only in an *a*-sexual form. Everything that has been the prop, substitute-prop, or substitute for the Other in the form of the object of desire is *a*-sexual" (Lacan 1998: 127). These unsexuated *objets a* are culturally and historically contingent. Although Lacan claims at one point that "[t]he Other... can... only be the Other sex," Ellie Ragland observes that the big Other's imaginary and symbolic representations are a function of "time and place" (Lacan 1998: 39; Ragland 2015: 16). His theory thus might apply to the "[m]en" and "women" he names in a 1970s vocabulary as well as to today's wide range of genders: and to other aspects of difference—such as race, ethnicity, nationality, and economic class—appearing in the Other (Lacan 1998: 33).

Paul Verhaeghe's reading of Lacan's argument that *jouissance* is "asexual" further supports this expansive theory of embodiment (Lacan 1998: 6). Cavanagh observes through Verhaeghe that because *jouissance*'s "traces are originally not sexual ones, their sexual character being secondary," gender is a "compromise formation" defending the subject against "anxiety" stemming from "lack" (Cavanagh 2016: 31; Verhaeghe 2001: 14; Verhaeghe 2002: 112). When "the primordial loss at the level of the organism is reinterpreted as a phallic lack in the relationship between the subject and the Other," gender emerges (Verhaeghe 2002: 133). Achieved by "sticking a signifier to the part of the Real for which originally there was no signifier," gender appears after "the phallus enters the scene, together with the father," whom the subject erroneously credits with the lacking organ (Verhaeghe 2001: 14). As Verhaeghe notes, the phallus's contingency implies that "the relationship between man and woman… is nothing but a defensive elaboration of an underlying problem": sexual difference is "secondary" and mobilized by "an original lack," where "the drive enters the scene" and stands "beyond gender as such" during sexuation (Verhaeghe 2001: 7). Because "the body is constructed" through phallicization and the onset of the Oedipus complex in cultures dominated by heterosexual families, "the body that we have (not the body that we are)" is "clothed in an ever-secondary gender identity" (Verhaeghe 2002: 135). In societies organized elsewise, the phallus and Oedipus would have little to no sway over embodiment; other factors might be more significant.

Thus when Lacan claims that "[t]he Other… can… only be the Other sex," his wording simply suggests that there needs to be difference and signification (Lacan 1998: 39). It does not necessarily imply, as commentators often assume, that sexual difference can only take the form of a fundamental antinomy between the masculine and feminine, or that embodiments need be limited to male and female. Other forms of sexual difference—such as Ettinger's matrixial—remain possible, as do the modes of transgender embodiment theorized by Cavanagh, Gherovici, and Gozlan. Furthermore, other sorts of differences—of race, ethnicity, nationality, or social class, for example—might be as important to embodiment as sexual difference. Remaining open to the varied "differences" Lacan would reduce to "difference" allows to us theorize the diverse forms of embodiment that can emerge through signification (Roof 2016: 60).

Thinkers working at the cutting edge of transpsychoanalysis have begun to make it possible to do so. As Gherovici stresses, "in matters of sexual difference, one proceeds from one's own authorization" and makes an "ethical decision" to position "oneself as a man, woman, or something else altogether" within language (Gherovici 2019b: 146). This formulation acknowledges that the subject may opt into one of the positions offered within orthodox Lacanian sexual difference or may instead push its limits by becoming "something else altogether" (Gherovici 2019b: 146). This, Gherovici insists, is "a new ethics of sexual difference" refusing to limit subjectivity to the masculine and feminine positions Lacan originally theorized (Gherovici 2019b: 146).

Transgender psychoanalysis is primarily concerned with this "new ethics of psychoanalysis": with instances in which sexuation has produced a person who—feeling at odds with the gender assigned at birth—seeks to change their gender assignment and, in many cases, their body (Gherovici 2019b: 146). If sexual difference and gender identity are "secondary" formations responding to the subject's confrontation with their own lack, they are alterable constructs rather than transhistorical and unchangeable aspects of the psyche (Verhaeghe 2001: 7). Thus understood, Lacanian psychoanalysis sounds much like Judith Butler when she claims that "[i]f the inner truth of gender is a fabrication and if a true gender is a fantasy instituted and inscribed on the surface of bodies, then… genders can be neither true nor false, but are only produced as the truth effects of a discourse of primary and stable identity" (Butler 1990: 136). Lacanians would formulate these fantasmatic "truth effects" as products of lack rather than "discourse," and would argue that transforming all three orders via the *sinthôme*—rather than resignifying gender in the symbolic—promises transformation. Such accounts of transsubjectivity go beyond the orthodox Lacanian fantasy of (hetero)sexual difference, enabling embodiment to be rethought in ways that take seriously many kinds of difference.

Theorizing Non-Binary and Genderqueer

Much trans-affirmative psychoanalysis focuses on those who cross from one side of the gender binary to the other by tapping the *sinthôme*'s creativity. When Carlson observes that "a subject may be either all or not-all under the phallic function—'not both'—*and* encounter the distinct ethical exigencies of both masculinity and femininity," she suggests a way of theorizing non-binary subjectivities within orthodox Lacanian sexuation (de la Torre 2018: 112). I see additional possibilities for theorizing non-binary and genderqueer subjectivities by adapting Cavanagh's reworking of Ettinger. Positioned as "something else altogether," these subjectivities foreground gender flux rather than fixity (Gherovici 2019b: 146). Ettinger's matrix mobilizes the Sedgwickian "beside," affording multiple modes of relationality amenable to shifts in gender (Sedgwick 2003: 8). Anchoring subjectivity in the imaginary, symbolic, and Real, the matrixial *sinthôme* grounds subjects in ways allowing identifications, self-inscriptions, and embodiments to shift without risking hysteria or psychosis.[10]

Reinterpreting Sigmund Freud's assertion that "the ego is first and foremost a bodily ego," Cavanagh offers a promising approach to such transformations

(Freud 1961: 26). As she observes, Freud's claim implies that "the bodily imago is not determined by an actual reflection so much as it is determined by an external identification with the gaze of the Other," inscribed upon the body (Cavanagh 2016: 33).[11] As a result, "[g]ender identity and sexed embodiment" are "structured by the Other's traces, by language and our psychically invested projections" (Cavanagh 2016: 33). Moreover, "the ego's attachments to gender identity are somatized and have a sexuating corporeal component that must, in turn, be signified"—especially when trans "identity is not reliably recognized and thus symbolically validated" within cultures promoting Oedipalization (Cavanagh 2016: 33).

Cavanagh also observes that "matrixial relations bear upon bodily ego functioning in ways that are highly individual" because of each person's history (Cavanagh 2016: 33). Because these "libidinal processes" are secondary, it is possible to intervene in them "at the level of the signifier" (Cavanagh 2016: 36). When transpeople find unique *sinthômes* to ground their embodiments, they gain imaginary recognition and symbolic sanction while tapping into the Real. Cavanagh notes that for transpeople, "the sinthome may be somatized and understood as a corporeal appendage" emerging through a process of "metramorphical becoming" (Cavanagh 2016: 34, 42). Yet because "[e]veryone identifies with an externalizing reflection from the position of the Other," there is no difference between "transsexuality" and "cisgender (non trans) identifications at the level of the bodily imago (or schemata)" (Cavanagh 2016: 32). This formulation could be extended to include all transsubjectivities, including non-binary (Cavanagh 2016: 32).

In Cavanagh's analysis, "*transsexuality*" encompasses "trans men and trans women," including "those who transition using medical and surgical interventions and also those who transition without such interventions" (Cavanagh 2016: 28). However, her adaptation of Ettinger is best equipped to understand subjectivities grounded in a fixed gender identity. This is especially clear whenever she reproduces Lacan's reliance upon the language of "men" and "women." She notes that the matrixial "feminine preexists phallic sexuation where (and when) it is possible to talk about men and women," and therefore "is relevant to those sexuated as men (as well as women) and… to transsexuals (those identifying as trans men and trans women alike)" (Cavanagh 2016: 28). Cavanagh's references to "trans men" and "trans women" imply—perhaps unintentionally—that the transperson needs to secure a new place within the binary gender system other than that assigned at birth (Cavanagh 2016: 28). Cavanagh's inclusion of the "gender pronoun" among those elements transpeople need "to establish subjective limits on the body" creates a similar impression (Cavanagh 2016: 40).

However, because Cavanagh understands the "libidinal processes" undergridding gender "identifications at the level of the bodily imago (or schemata)" as changeable, there is no good reason not to extend her claims about transgender embodiment to non-binary and genderqueer subjects (Cavanagh 2016: 32–6). Although Millot claims in *Horsexe* that psychosis leads people to position themselves as "outsidesex," she erroneously assumes that everybody seeking to go beyond (hetero)sexual difference has a similar subjective structure: one in which the *sinthôme* links the imaginary and symbolic but not the Real (Cavanagh 2016: 65).[12] Trans-affirmative psychoanalysts' argument that there are other uses of the *sinthôme*—many of which do connect all three orders— offers possibilities for theorizing non-binary and genderqueer subjectivities as healthy and viable. Cavanagh's emphasis on Ettinger's matrixial *sinthôme* is especially promising as it enables theorizations of gender flux.

Theorizing Nonbinary and Genderqueer *Sinthômes*

Lacanian psychoanalysis understands the body not as a material given but as sexuated and libidinalized through the signifier's failure to symbolize the Real. When Cavanagh observes that transition offers an option for resignification, she makes a point relevant to transgender people who assume a singular gender identity as well as those non-binary and genderqueer individuals who undergo gender reassignment. The concept of embodiment pertains equally to individuals who transition and those who neither do so nor "aim towards a coherent gender presentation" at all (Pellegrini and Saketopoulou 2019). As Ann Pellegrini and Avgi Saketopoulou observe, some non-binary people "may not approach gendered embodiment as a matter of aligning bodily morphology to gender" and instead "may treat their gendered body as inhabiting multiple, distinct zones that don't cohere into a unified presentation" (Pellegrini and Saketopoulou 2019).

Pellegrini and Saketopoulou also observe that "gender is not the only way to organize and 'cohere' the body" (Pellegrini and Saketopoulou 2019). Although Cavanagh does not discuss non-binary and genderqueer people, her Ettingerian approach to anchoring embodiment with a *sinthôme* offers a way of understanding how non-binary embodiments might turn on gender multiplicity or something other than gender. Except in dramatic personal transformations prompted by fantasy's traversal, which generate new *sinthômes* and fundamentally reorganize subjectivity, a person's *sinthôme* remains consistent. Because the *sinthôme* need not be gendered, some individuals' gender identifications, self-inscriptions, and embodiments may shift without risking psychosis. This is the case for non-binary and genderqueer people, whose subjectivities are neither grounded "in assigned sex" nor oriented through "a cohesive gender presentation" (Pellegrini and Saketopoulou 2019).

Gherovici understands nonbinary and genderqueer people as those "who do not think that they are in the wrong body but feel that the gender binary does not fit them"; her wording suggests that they do not experience conflicts in the imaginary—at the level of the body image—but in the symbolic (Gherovici 2017: 33). This may not be the case: some embodiments may involve fluctuating body images, as Pellegrini and Saketopoulou suggest, and some non-binary and genderqueer people do pursue gender reassignment. Moreover, Gherovici questionably distinguishes nonbinary people from other transpeople, noting that Lacan's "model of sexual difference" posits "only one logical operator, which is the phallus," even though "some individuals are placed in a position in which the phallus is not operative" and "seem to be able to deal with sexual difference without fully relying on the phallus" (Gherovici 2017: 33). For Gherovici, monogender subjectivities require assumption of a stance with respect to the phallus, whereas non-binary and genderqueer subjectivities decline to orient themselves around it. While it makes sense to claim that not everybody shares the same position with regard to the phallus—and that some people might dispense with it partially or entirely—Gherovici draws too sharp a distinction between stances. Because assuming an embodiment involves embracing an idiosyncratic *sinthôme*, doing so might take subjects in far more directions than Gherovici imagines.[13]

Ettinger's matrix—whose unpredictability mobilizes the Sedgwickian "beside"—provides a better way of understanding contemporary gender embodiments because it offers a wider range of options than Gherovici's sharp distinction between phallic and non-phallic logics (Sedgwick 2003: 8). Operating alongside rather than seeking to obliterate the phallus, the matrix is relational and generative, enabling a wide variety of embodiments involving "multiple, distinct zones" that may or may not be gendered (Pellegrini and Saketopoulou 2019). Distinct from the Lacanian *sinthôme*, Ettinger's "matrixial *sinthôme*" is transitive, amenable to transitions from one side of the gender binary to the other and to the flux often involved in non-binary and genderqueer embodiments (Ettinger 2006a: 193–4). Moreover, the matrix's connectivity enables theorizations of links between trans embodiments and other axes of identity, such as race, ethnicity, nationality, and class.

Theorizing Pronouns, Theorizing Naming

Along with the *sinthôme*, pronouns and names play important roles in subjectivity and embodiment. Using orthodox Lacanian terms, Gherovici describes "sexual positioning" as "a symptom," explaining that "[b]eing a 'he' or a 'she'" is an "attempt to 'make up' for the disharmony between the sexes" (Gherovici 2017: 149 sic). This argument underscores pronouns' importance in inscribing divergent sexual positions as well as the urgency of respecting transpeoples' pronouns, which many—though not all—transpeople consider vital anchors for gender subjectivity.

However, Gherovici's identification of "she" and "he" with "masculine and feminine subject positions" reveals that they are changeable constructs rather than requirements for successful subjective inscription (Gherovici 2017: 149). Just as (hetero)sexual difference is a fantasy available for traversal, the pronouns supporting it are alterable. Whereas Gherovici's *Transgender Psychoanalysis* deploys a wide range of pronouns, Cavanagh does not address whether her theory accounts for new choices—such as the increasingly common use of singular they/them pronouns—and the expansion of the gender system beyond the categories "man" and "woman." This aspect of Cavanagh's theory needs to be developed to account for non-binary and genderqueer people, some of whom employ they/them pronouns and others of whom accept a shifting array of designations.

Lacan's writings most frequently focus on the role of the gender-neutral "I" in inscribing and decentering the ego; he does not stress pronouns' importance for successful subjective inscription.[14] One need only embrace the "I" to be a speaking subject; it does not matter whether a non-binary or genderqueer person's pronouns shift so long as a *sinthôme* links the imaginary, symbolic, and Real. This theory is well suited to understanding the subjective division and multiplicity foregrounded in non-binary and genderqueer identities. Refusing to choose a single pronoun—even "they"—embraces rather than masks subjectivity's multiplicity.

Moreover, Lacanian psychoanalysis underscores the importance of using a transperson's chosen name and of avoiding dead-naming. Moncayo observes that we comprehend the name's "function when we have grasped the subjective or emotional response to any alteration of the name" (Moncayo 2016: 70). "Naming" confers "bodily identity," providing a psychical orientation and sense of the ego's integrity (Moncayo 2016: 15).[15] Because names are frequently "linked to a relative, the desire of the Other, a particular destiny, a cultural ideal," a person's last "name and forename... are usually bound up with his or her plans, likes and dislikes, choices, moods, opinions, and so on" (Moncayo 2016: 70). Although Moncayo addresses the experiences of individuals satisfied with their given names and objecting to their misuse, his arguments can be extended to understand the passionate intensity often accompanying the desire to change one's assigned name.

Moncayo's study of the *sinthôme* strictly adheres to Lacan's vocabulary and *Seminar III*, affirming that the neurotic must submit to the phallus, the Name of the Father, and castration to avoid psychosis. However, Moncayo admits that the Name of the Father could be replaced with another master signifier, as is common "within Queer, anarchist, or feminist discourses" taking "the patronymic as a sign of patriarchal domination" (Moncayo 2016: 72). Although he rightfully observes that the broader problem of "the imposition of language cannot be so easily done away with" through alternatives to the Name of the Father, as humans depend upon language and naming to situate themselves within discourse, it is important that oppressive usages sustaining patriarchy or constraining options for socially viable gender identities be challenged so that all peoples' lives are livable (Moncayo 2016: 72). When transpeople are at odds with their assigned genders and refashion themselves by engaging the *sinthôme*, recognizing their chosen names is important for securing their subjectivities and embodiments.

For some transpeople, this may involve choosing a new pronoun; for non-binary and genderqueer people, it might or might not. Whereas a person transitioning from one side of the gender binary to the other may change both their name and pronoun, non-binary and genderqueer people might adopt a variety of stances. Some may change their names and ask to be called "they"; others may keep their given name and adopt a gender-neutral pronoun; others may retain the pronoun assigned at birth but claim a gender-neutral abbreviation of their given name. In all of these examples, a person's linguistic self-inscriptions might or might not be accompanied by surgical or hormonal interventions.

What is crucial, however, is that the trans subject link the three orders with a *sinthôme*—which may or may not be gendered—and inscribe themselves as an "I" with a name. Moncayo's account of naming's importance puts the stakes of transpeoples' requests into relief, countering Lacanian scholarship dismissing recognition's importance.[16] Early Lacanian commentary on trans all too often decries what Shepherdson, drawing on Millot, calls transpeoples' imaginary "demand" for recognition that would "short-circuit... the symbolic order" (Shepherdson 2000: 101) and psychotically override the Real by avoiding what

Dean calls the "experience of symbolic subjectivity" (Dean 2000a: 65).[17] Yet when one understands gender reassignment as a strategy for anchoring subjectivity in all three orders via the *sinthôme*, it is clear that transpeople are engaging all three orders rather than trying to avoid contending with the Real. The name has "so much significance" neither because it fosters delusions nor because it is strictly symbolic but because it functions as "a letter of a singular jouissance" anchoring subjectivity and holding great personal importance (Moncayo 2016: 70).

Transing the Other: Between Transitivity and Relationality

Engaging the Other creates the conditions within which it is possible for a new *sinthôme* to emerge and for subjectivity to be renewed. Pointing out that transgender, non-binary, and genderqueer embodiments flourish in affirmative contexts such as intimate relationships and queer bars, Salamon's *Assuming a Body* provides several examples of forms of relationality through which these negotiations can take place (Salamon 2010: 69–93). Whereas *Assuming a Body* offers a pioneering trans-affirmative rereading of Irigaray's *An Ethics of Sexual Difference*, Salamon's recent reworking of Freud argues that castration should be understood as experienced through the loss of a breast rather than a penis and that sexual difference is not an antinomy but relational. Reading Nick Krieger's memoir *Nina Here Nor There* (2011), Salamon concludes through analysis of scenes in which Nina looks at transmasculine roommates that "gendered senses of self develop in relation to other gendered bodies" and that "masculinity... is conferred through the absence of breasts" (Salamon 2016: 317–18, 318). This argument for sexual difference's relationally expands psychoanalytic thinking about gender embodiment.

Notably, Salamon describes Bec—the roommate fascinating Nina the most—as sliding between the gender binary's poles and evading "pronouns altogether" (Salamon 2016: 315). Nina is captivated by Bec's masculine self-presentation, especially Bec's propensity to display "faded chest scars" by going shirtless (Krieger 2011: 20). These details persist throughout the memoir, prompting Nina's reflections on gender identity, scarring from athletic injuries, and eventual top surgery. Although in many ways *Nina Here Nor There* exemplifies the genre of the trans memoir whose firm grounding in the (small "r") real has attracted transpsychoanalytic analysis since Jay Prosser's *Second Skins* (1998), Krieger's stress on scarring also illustrates Cavanagh's, Gherovici's, and Gozlan's shared contention that transpeople creatively use *sinthôme*s such as scars to anchor trans embodiment in all three Lacanian orders (Cavanagh 2015, 2016; Gherovici 2012 and 2014; Gozlan 2015; Prosser 1998). In Krieger's memoir, scars are creative self-stylizations constituting *sinthômes* grounding Bec's and Krieger's gender embodiments not only in the imaginary and symbolic orders (which Salamon emphasizes) but also in the (large "R") Real.

Engaging the imaginary's and symbolic's imbrication with the Real in transsubjectvity's constitution, Cavanagh builds on Ettinger's concept of the matrixial *sinthôme* to argue that "at the level of the bodily imago," gender involves identification "with an externalizing reflection from the position of the Other" (Cavanagh 2016: 32-6). Although this claim is compatible with Salamon's theory of relationality, Cavanagh claims that cisgender and transgender people experience sexual difference in fundamentally different ways. Discussing those who move from one side of the gender binary to the other but not non-binary and genderqueer people, she claims that "[t]hose who are cisgender (non trans) tend to apprehend sexual difference between themselves and others in an intersubjective relation," whereas "transsexuals animate and reinscribe (literally, on the body) a subterranean matrixial zone where sexual rapport is and was a possibility and underwrite the phallic signifier with a change of address (or, rather, a transition) that introduces another axis (or mapping) of difference, one that is transitive (not intersubjective)" (Cavanagh 2016: 37). By stressing that "[t]ranssexual identifications with the other sex can be total" and viable, driven by novel ways of using the *sinthôme* to anchor subjectivity in all three orders, Cavanagh rightfully corrects Millot's conflation of transgender with psychosis (Cavanagh 2016: 37). Yet in so doing, Cavanagh overlooks ways alternative uses of the *sinthôme* could also successfully ground non-binary and genderqueer subjectivities.

Cavanagh's claims about transitivity do not map as neatly onto those people, even though she and Ettinger acknowledge that anybody can experience the matrixial. For Lacan, transitivity implies identification and therefore a lack of distance between the other and the ego.[18] By contrast, relationality entails a clear distinction between self and other. Ettinger considers both transitivity and relationality to be possible within the matrix. Her borderspace is especially conducive to theorizing non-binary and genderqueer subjectivities and embodiments, which refuse to be fixed and are often explicitly invested in breaking down boundaries imposed by binary thinking. Generating and connecting in unpredictable and non-phallic ways, the matrix transforms the symbolic, going beyond orthodox Lacanian terms. Ettinger's feminine *sinthôme* derails and transforms Lacan's, appearing through "blanks and holes in the Real" to produce "potential desires whose sense... does not depend on the signifier" (Ettinger 2006a 193). As Cavanagh shows, Ettinger's *sinthôme* can anchor transsubjectivities because it is feminine only within Lacan's logic of sexuation. It therefore stands to reason that the matrixial *sinthôme* can ground non-binary, genderqueer, and monogendered trans embodiments alike.

Yet if, as Cavanagh suggests, "The incorporation of sexual difference within the self is a distinguishing feature of transsexuality," non-binary and genderqueer people may instead experience sexual difference both transitively and relationally (Cavanagh 2016: 37). Ettinger's matrixial *sinthôme*, which works alongside rather than in opposition to the phallus, is open-ended and unpredictable in ways that are especially amenable to the forms of creativity driving non-binary and genderqueer embodiments. The "matrixial surfs beneath/beside the phallic," dismantling phallogocentrism "while itself never emerging as another, hence phallic, contender" (Pollock 2006: 5). Unconfined to a single position, mobilizing the unpredictably queer relationalities of Sedgwick's "beside," Ettinger's matrix is mobile and capable of prompting structural change (Sedgwick 2003: 8).

This open-endedness is well suited to theorizing queer and trans sexualities *and* embodiments. It also calls into question whether cisgender and transgender subjectivities can be distinguished as sharply as Cavanagh claims—and whether my additional distinction between them and nonbinary subjectivities should be taken as anything more than provisional. All modes of embodiment involve embracing an idiosyncratic *sinthôme*, yet unlike the Lacanian *sinthôme*, which quilts the three orders, Ettinger's matrixial *sinthôme* generates more unpredictable effects: ones that arguably cannot be mapped neatly onto gendered divisions between transitivity and relationality or reduced to gender at all. Instead, in keeping with the Sedgwickian "beside," this *sinthôme* might take the subject in many different directions. This might entail forging new genders; it might also involve forming new connections to other aspects of embodied experience, such as sexuality, race, ethnicity, nationality, and economic class.

Trans-cending (Hetero)sexual Difference

Even though Ettinger's concept of the "matrixial borderspace" enables robust theorizations of gender subjectivity and its connections to other aspects of embodied experience, her rewriting of Lacan's theory of the *sinthôme* does not entirely abandon its phallogocentrism. Although she provides a means of detaching from the phallus, she does not entirely obliterate it. Similarly, Cavanagh's use of

Ettinger to theorize transgender does not dispense with the phallus. At one point, Cavanagh observes that "Ettinger supplants Lacan's equation 'Phallus = Symbol' with 'Phallus + Matrixial' (+ possibly other concepts) = Symbol" (Cavanagh 2016: 32). While these theories innovate by placing the masculine and feminine side by side, rather than staging them as a binary opposition or an antinomy, the latter continues to supplement the former, which remains intact. Feminine and transgender subjectivities may present alternatives to (hetero)sexual difference, but they do not entirely obliterate it.

Whereas Ettinger's work rests on the troubling premise that patriarchy must be tolerated rather than overthrown, another feminist interpretation of Lacan would take things further and stress the way his theory of the *sinthôme* makes it possible to dispense with the phallus and the Name of the Father altogether, going beyond the fantasy of (hetero)sexual difference. At his most radical, Lacan argues that anything quilting the imaginary, symbolic, and Real can become a *sinthôme*. These *sinthômes* need not take any predetermined form; they need only be functional. They can bypass the phallogocentric symbolic, traversing the fantasy that subjectivity must be predicated on (hetero)sexual difference to avoid psychosis.

Other strains of psychoanalytic feminism openly reject Lacan's phallogocentrism, striving to smash patriarchy and its supporting apparatus, the symbolic. Cixous, for example, does not supplement but obliterates the phallic order. Thus far she has been left out of trans-affirmative rereadings of psychoanalysis, most likely because she grounds her strategy for overthrowing the phallogocentric symbolic in a reclamation of the female body's diverse libidinal capacities. Even though at one point "The Laugh of the Medusa" acknowledges that "[t]here are some men" such as Jean Genet "who aren't afraid of femininity," I see this as a limitation of Cixous' work for transpsychoanalysis (Cixous 1991: 342). Whereas Ruti does not remark upon this problem in praising Cixous' approach to signification as more generative than Edelman's, I see possibilities for expanding and rewriting Cixous for trans-affirmative ends (Ruti 2008b: 116).

In "The Laugh of the Medusa," Cixous contends that writing the female body will free it from symbolic repressions and dismantle phallogocentrism. When extended to include transgender embodiments, Cixous' argument points to a way to replace Lacanian accounts of sexual difference as an antinomy with an explicitly trans-affirmative psychoanalytic theory of embodiment as a plurality of differences. Such a theory does not claim that trans is inherently feminine but rather that (hetero)sexual difference's governing distinction between masculinity and femininity can be abolished by dispensing with the phallus.

However, a trans-affirmative rewriting of Cixous requires relinquishing her implied claim to female embodiment's uniqueness. Starting with such a premise, Cixous famously advocates that woman "must write her self" and create a "*new insurgent* writing" that returns to the repressed female body, reanimates pleasures previously suppressed by the phallus, and prompts her "unconscious" to "spring forth" (Cixous 1991: 337–8). Both writing and speaking make woman "the taker and initiator... in every symbolic system" and release her "non-phallic" drives from the symbolic (Cixous 1991: 338).

This argument goes beyond Ettinger's in striving to "transform" rather than supplement the phallic order (Cixous 1991: 339). Although Cixous retains the penis as a potential site of pleasure, she strips the phallus of its symbolic importance (Cixous 1991: 347). This enacts a symbolic decolonization of the body, freeing woman's "libido" to generate novel sexualities (Cixous 1991: 339). Insisting that women "don't pledge allegiance to the negative" characterizing the phallic economy of lack, Cixous presents their drives as "prodigious" and generative, exemplified by the exclamations of "'And yes,' ... 'I said yes, I will Yes'" with which Molly Bloom closes James Joyce's *Ulysses* (Cixous 1991: 339–41). As Ruti observes, Cixous' theorization of the drives' productive capabilities sharply contrasts to Edelman's emphasis on their destructiveness (Ruti, 2008b: 116). Whereas Edelman's narrow approach to the drive "bypasses and, by bypassing, eradicates, trans identification"—as Lavery notes—Cixous' insistence on the drives' generativity offers a potentially trans-affirmative alternative (Lavery 2019a: 148n11).

As I argue in Chapter 2, the drives' generativity makes it possible to embrace the *sinthôme* and go beyond the fantasy of (hetero)sexual difference: either by grounding a new version of the Lacanian triad or by tapping the unpredictable generativity of a "direct investment in signifiers" unbeholden to the phallic order (Pluth 2007: 163). Moreover, as I have shown in this chapter, Cavanagh and Gherovici demonstrate that embracing a new *sinthôme* can successfully ground trans embodiments. Cixous' argument for the drives' generativity can also be reinflected to theorize and affirm trans embodiments.[19]

One approach would be to read transgender as undoing the body's subjection to phallogocentrism. Much as Joyce's texts resist Britain's domination of Ireland, Cixous' "The Laugh of the Medusa" is driven by a decolonizing energy targeting not French rule of her native Algeria but patriarchal colonization of the female body.[20] Cixous writes that because of the body's colonization, "Almost everything is yet to be written by women about femininity: about their sexuality, that is, its infinite and mobile complexity, about their eroticization, sudden turn-ons of a certain miniscule-immense area of their bodies" that "articulate the profusion of meanings that run through it in every direction" (Cixous 1991: 342). In *Ulysses*, this decolonizing feminine writing is emblematized by Molly Boom's feminine "yes" but in other contexts it could also register the forms of desire and embodiment experienced by a wide variety of people, regardless of their initial gender assignment.

Moreover, Cixous' 1975 essay heralds both pansexuality and contemporary understandings of bisexuality as an openness to lovers of all—not just binary—genders. Defying the "false theater of phallocentric representationalism," what Cixous calls the "*other bisexuality*" taps into "the presence... of both sexes" in everyone to facilitate the "multiplication of the effects of the inscription of desire, over all parts of my body and the other body" (Cixous 1991: 341). Although this formulation invokes the outdated notion of androgyny, at other points Cixous stresses the capacity of "vatic bisexuality" to decolonize the body (Cixous 1991: 341). What she calls "vatic bisexuality... doesn't annul differences but stirs them up, pursues them, increases their number" (Cixous 1991: 341). Trans theory positions us to see consequences of this fluidity that Cixous does not envision. Fluidity renders embodiment mobile: going beyond binary gender to produce novel forms of desire; connecting to other aspects of embodied experience such as race, ethnicity, nationality, and economic class.

However, such a reading must complicate the underlying assumptions about prediscursive materiality at work in Cixous' argument that undoing phallogocentrism would liberate the female body, deterritorializing its drives. As Salamon argues in response to Prosser's insistence that the trans body is "unimpeachably real," "[a]ny insistence on a bodily materiality outside and opposed to discourse about bodies" is unpsychoanalytic (Salamon 2010: 40–1). As she explains, psychoanalysis understands the process of "bodily assumption, and hence subject formation itself," as "a constant and complex oscillation between narcissistic investment in one's own flesh and the 'necessary self-division and self-estrangement'... that is the very means by which our bodies are articulated" (Salamon 2010: 41). For Lacan, "self-division and self-estrangement" come from the imaginary and symbolic, which mediate subjects' embodiments through the Other (Salamon 2010: 41). And as trans-affirmative Lacanians further clarify, the *sinthôme* anchors embodiment in all three orders.

Thus if—as Cixous contends—the phallus can be obliterated as master signifier, the subject's constitutive repressions can be undone and the subject reconstituted: but not by liberating the body from discourse. Instead, traversing the fantasy by embracing the *sinthôme* can reconstitute embodiment in ways that make life more liveable. Unlike Edelman's *sinthom*osexual, who embraces the drive's pure negativity without going beyond the orthodox Lacanian fantasy of (hetero)sexual difference, those traversing that fantasy may take new directions. Whether by repositioning themselves within sexual difference, grounding a new Lacanian triad with a new master signifier, or embracing the open-ended unpredictability of a "direct investment in signifiers" unbeholden to the symbolic, the reconstituted subject embraces the *sinthôme* and uses signification to start anew (Pluth 2007: 163).

Challenging orthodox Lacanian claims to (hetero)sexual difference's primacy by undoing the phallogocentric order's repressions, Cixous stresses women's ability to become a "body without end, without appendage, without principle 'parts'" (Cixous 1991: 344 sic). Noting that if woman "is a whole, it's a whole composed of parts that are wholes, not simple partial objects but a moving, limitlessly changing ensemble, a cosmos tirelessly traversed by Eros," she emphasizes this deterritorialized body's eroticization in ways not governed by the phallus (Cixous 1991: 344–5). Although her formulation implicitly focuses on women's bodies, it can be expanded to include all forms of gender embodiment. For Cixous, writing deterritorializes the body and deploys signifiers to re-establish subjectivity and embodiment: whether by reconfiguring gender or by implicating other aspects of embodiment such as race, ethnicity, nationality, or class.

Such a feminist transpsychoanalysis could connect to trans work deploying the concept of "transitivity" in its most expansive sense. Whereas Ettinger focuses on transitivity's capacity to break down boundaries within a feminized "matrixial borderspace" standing alongside the phallic order, Cixous' thoroughgoing deterritorialization of the body opens up even more forms of transitivity (Ettinger 2006a: 152). These modes go beyond transitivity's psychoanalytic definition as the "identification with the imago of one's semblable" sparking "the drama of primordial jealousy" (Lacan 2006e: 79) and motivating "aggressive competition" (Lacan 2006f: 92). Instead, deterritorialization's effects are "multiply transitive" in the way Sedgwick understands the word "queer" and Stryker, Paisley Currah, and Lisa Jean Moore position the prefix "Trans-": unattached and open to many future directions (Sedgwick 1993: xxii; Stryker, Currah, and Moore 2008: 11). Rejecting these thinkers' "kaleidoscope of verticality and horizontality in favor of pure potentiality," Abraham L. Weil clarifies via Félix Guattari that transitivity entails "mobility, creativity, and self-engendering" (Stryker, Currah, and Moore 2008: 14; Weil 2017: 642). As "pure potentiality," trans is "explicitly relational": "open-ended" and untied to "any single suffix" (Stryker, Currah, and Moore 2008: 11). It embodies the many vicissitudes of Sedgwick's "beside" (Sedgwick 2003: 8).

This mobility animates diverse trajectories within trans theory, such as Lucas Cassidy Crawford's challenge to metronormative narratives of transgender self-realization (Crawford 2013); José Esteban Muñoz's analysis of desire's provocation in Vaginal Crème Davis' disidentificatory performances (Muñoz 2013: 82–3); Vaccaro's feminist analysis of felt's implications for trans embodiment (Vaccaro 2013); Riley Snorton's analysis of blackness's implications with transness (Snorton 2017: 9); and Salamon's phenomenological examination of bodily orientation in Latisha King's murder (Salamon 2018). These far-ranging examples are far from exhaustive, asking us to understand trans in ways ranging well beyond the orthodox Lacanian fantasy of (hetero)sexual difference.

These divergent trajectories are all potential outcomes of fantasy's traversal. Earlier in this book, I argue that traversing the fundamental fantasy can result in the emergence of a novel *sinthôme* reconnecting the three orders and renewing subjectivity. I also describe two divergent paths these reorganized subjectivities could take. Whereas the first entails the emergence of a new fundamental fantasy grounding subjectivity, the second involves not the production of a new fantasy but a "direct investment in signifiers as such" (Pluth 2007: 163). Many transpeople pursue the former, seeking recognition by utilizing technologies for gender reassignment and asking that they be addressed using suitable names and pronouns. Cavanagh, Gherovici, and Gozlan show that when supported by *sinthômes*, these actions and requests are salutary, situating transsubjectivities within new fundamental fantasies that make trans lives livable. Other transpeople take the second path, embracing unique *sinthômes* and authoring novel forms of subjectivity that do not depend upon the kinds of recognition provided by pronouns or gender reassignment. These, too, are effective ways to create livable lives.

All of these vectors of transsubjectivity range well beyond the gender binary. Theorized through Ettinger—who emphasizes the experience of being open to another in ways ungoverned by the Lacanian antinomy between masculine and feminine—trans embodiments stand as evidence of tectonic shifts within the logic of sexual difference (Ettinger 2006a: 152). Thus understood, sexual difference is not a field defined by (hetero)sexual difference but rather an open horizon: a space of possibility through which contemporary genders come into being and future genders can continue to emerge.

Arguing that the speaking subject is both oriented and lost through subjective inscription, Lacan observes that

> I identify myself in language, but only by losing myself in it as an object. What is realized in my history is neither the past definite as what was, since it is no more,

nor even the perfect as what has been in what I am, but the future anterior as what I will have been, given what I am in the process of becoming.

(Lacan 2006c: 247)

This argument elucidates the temporal complexity of transsubjectivities, which involve a person taking on a new public self-presentation while continuing to remember the past: a dilemma trans philosopher Jacob Hale (Hale 1998) addresses in "Tracing a Ghostly Memory in My Throat: Reflections on FtM Feminist Voice and Agency." As Hale's metaphor of haunting suggests, transsubjectivity entails both inscription and loss.

Joshua Jennifer Espinoza's poem "Things Haunt" (2018) similarly employs the metaphor of haunting to explore transsubjectivity's dislocations of identity. "Things Haunt" opens with the observation that "California is a desert and I am a woman inside it. / The road ahead bends sideways and I lurch within myself." After staging the category "woman" as a construct produced by an impoverishing "desert" so uncomfortable it must be fled, the persona states that "When you ask me am I really a woman, a human being, / a coherent identity, I'll say No." This response exposes identity categories as constructs, points to their shiftiness, and declines their illusion of stability. Simile, however, provides the poem's persona with room to move. After refusing to assume the subject position "woman," she acknowledges that "*I'm something else/like that though*." She then insists that "the weight of her voice" remind that "things haunt" and continue to "exist long after they are killed." Staging identities as necessarily discomfiting fictions, Espinoza's poem dramatizes the temporal paradox at the heart of all forms of transsubjectivity, whether grounded in or defiant of identity claims. This paradox asks transpeople to contend with the implications of their gendered pasts, even as courageous acts of creativity have enabled them to traverse the fantasy of (hetero)sexual difference, reject socially assigned gender identities, and find more livable ways of being.

In Chapters 5 and 6, I explore ways the protagonists of John Cameron Mitchell's film *Hedwig and the Angry Inch* (2001) and Andrea Lawlor's novel *Paul Takes the Form of a Mortal Girl* (2017) do so. I also gesture toward gender's mutual implication with sexuality, geography, and race: concerns connecting Mitchell's and Lawlor's works to Monika Treut's film *The Virgin Machine* (1988) as well as Gloria Anzaldúa's mixed-genre *Borderlands/La Frontera* (1987) and *Light in the Dark/Luz en lo Oscuro* (2015). Each illuminating a different trajectory of queer becoming, these texts are driven by the relationality and transitivity of Ettinger's matrix and Sedgwick's beside, breaking down boundaries and leaving their subjects open to the many possibilities for self-invention lying beyond (hetero)sexual difference's traversal.

Notes

1. See Chiesa (2016), Tim Dean (2000a), Gherovici (2010), Millot (1990), Morel (2000), and Shepherdson (2000).
2. Although Gozlan recognizes that homophobic interpretations of Lacan have hindered trans-affirmative thinking, he does not extend this point to non-binary and genderqueer subjectivities (Gozlan 2015).
3. For examples of this aspect of Irigaray's thought, see *This Sex Which Is Not One* (Irigaray 1985a) and *Speculum of the Other Woman* (Irigaray 1985b).
4. See Lacan (2006g) and (1998).
5. See Ettinger (2006b) for an explanation contrasting the matrixial borderspace to concepts readily recognizable as Kristeva's pre-Oedipal.
6. See Cavanagh (2016) for an extensive critique of Millot's overreliance upon Freud's Schreber as exemplary of all transpeople rather than as an unusual case of transgender fantasies symptomatizing psychosis. See Moncayo (2016) for a technical elaboration of neurotic versus psychotic *sinthômes* that turns on the distinction between repression and foreclosure.
7. Gherovici (2010) offers case studies underscoring the importance of a *sinthôme*'s consistency in anchoring subjectivity.
8. See Moncayo (2016) for a technical explanation of the process through which the Borromean knot is written and the *sinthôme* emerges.
9. However, Gherovici and Cavanagh rightfully complicate Tin Dean's claim, via Millot, that transpeople seek to resolve their gender identities at the level of the imaginary while bypassing the other two orders (Tim Dean 2000a: 86).
10. Gherovici problematically argues that hysteria underlies non-binary and genderqueer subjectivities (Gherovici 2010; Gherovici 2017).
11. Freud's claim that "the ego is first and foremost a bodily ego" is also important to the work of earlier trans-affirmative psychoanalytic thinkers such as Prosser (Freud 1961: 26; Prosser 1998). Whereas Cavanagh's argument reflects Lacan's view that embodiment is formed through imaginary and symbolic representations, Prosser—responding to Butler—uses the work of Freud, Didier Anzieu, and Oliver Sacks to argue that embodiment arises from awareness of bodily sensations (Prosser 1998: 34–45, 65, 78–80).
12. Although Millot concedes that the female-to-male transpeople she encountered did not display "any sign of psychotic symptoms" (Millot 1990: 117), she ultimately—and questionably—concludes that they share with male-to-female transpeople a similar "relation to the phallus," "identification with its incarnation of outsidesex," and reliance upon "demand" rather than "desire" (Millot 1990: 140–2).
13. This is further evidence that the distinction between transgender and transsexual—whose importance in Jay Prosser's (1998) psychoanalytic trans theory Salamon

challenges (2010)—continues to operate in trans-affirmative psychoanalysis in ways that unnecessarily constrain theorizations of non-binary and genderqueer subjectivities.

14 Lacan's *Écrits: The First Complete Edition in English* includes numerous essays focusing on the "I," including Lacan (2006b, 2006c, 2006d, and 2006e).
15 See also Harari (2002) for an explication of naming's importance.
16 Much Lacanian hostility to transgender was prompted by Butler (1990 and 1993), who emphasizes the imaginary and symbolic while misunderstanding the Real's nature and function. However, these responses to Butler present sexual difference as intractably Real rather than a secondary formation emerging through subjects' failed attempts to symbolize the Real.
17 Dean's reading of Jennie Livingston's 1990 film *Paris Is Burning* questionably assumes that its trans subjects are operating solely at the level of imaginary demand (Dean 2000a: 89–91).
18 Lacan's *Écrits: The First Complete Edition in English* includes several examples of transitivity: see Lacan (2006e: 79); and Lacan (2006f: 147).
19 See Ruti (2017) for an extended version of this argument.
20 See Cheng (1995) and Nolan (1995) for postcolonial readings of Joyce.

5

Traversing the Atlantic, Traversing (Hetero)sexual Difference

Queer and trans fictional narratives have long featured traversals of the fantasies of (hetero)sexual difference and romantic love, from German filmmaker Monika Treut's 1988 *The Virgin Machine* (*Die Jungfrauenmachine*) to American John Cameron Mitchell's 2001 *Hedwig and the Angry Inch*. Both of these films are driven by their German protagonists' transatlantic migrations. We initially meet Treut's Dorothee in Hamburg and follow her move to San Francisco; we first encounter Mitchell's Hedwig in communist East Berlin and track their band's tour through the North American heartland to New York City. Both narratives traverse fantasies of (hetero)sexual difference and romantic love while also engaging those motivating their protagonists' migrations. Whereas *The Virgin Machine* refuses to present immigration as utopian and repudiates the fantasy of a rootless queer nation, *Hedwig* rejects its protagonist's initial fantasy that leaving the Eastern Bloc would be inherently liberating.

Traversing the Fantasy of Reproductive Futurism in *The Virgin Machine*

The Virgin Machine opens in Germany and follows Dorothee's sexual exploits as she traverses the Atlantic Ocean. The film's first half reveals her early influence by heteronormative and reproductive temporalities, cutting together references to Dorothee's absent mother; shots of her research into animal reproduction for an article on romantic love; and scenes of her affairs with her lover, Heinz, and brother, Bruno. The film's second half is set in California and tracks the ways Dorothee's desires expand through her encounter with late 1980s San Francisco's radically sex-positive cultures.

Much 1990s scholarship on *The Virgin Machine* is grounded in Judith Butler's *Gender Trouble* (1990), emphasizing the ways Dorothee eventually goes beyond essentialist conceptions of gender and sexuality figured in the opening scenes' investigation of biological sexual theories.[1] In my view, the film also does more: it tracks Dorothee's traversal of the fantasy of (hetero)sexual difference that orthodox Lacanians posit as structuring desire; challenges what Lee Edelman calls "reproductive futurism" and its prop, the pre-Oedipal search for the mother; and shows the protagonist distancing herself from, but not ultimately rejecting, what Chris Straayer describes as the "romantic illusions" animating desire's fantasmatic structure (Edelman 2004: 28; Straayer 1993: 25).

The Virgin Machine's opening section tracks Dorothee's research into biological paradigms driven by heterosexually reproductive temporalities. The film's style mocks and undermines such notions, preparing her to reject them. Marcia Klotz notes that the film's German segment cuts in images of clogged drains with shots of Dorothee's "leering" boyfriend "Heinz blowing his nose"; Treut intersperses these scenes with clinical images of semen and animal reproduction (Klotz 1998: 68).[2] These sequences' "polemic against the ideology of love" and its "imperative to couple" mock patriarchal and heteronormative ideas about sexual release (Klotz 1998: 68).

Moreover, these sequences mock masculinist accounts of sexuality that do *not* valorize coupledom, such as male chimpanzees' practice of sharing sexual access to a female in heat. This system is propelled by a serial temporality rather than by reproductive futurism. Early in the film, Dorothee writes an article combining anthropological language with the heterosexual pornographic trope of the gangbang to describe the chimpanzees' behavior. She presents the "female chimpanzee" as encountering "the male horde only when in heat, handed from male to male… cementing brotherly love." This analysis calls attention to patriarchal structures' reinforcement by claims that sexuality is driven by the biological imperative to reproduce. From these animals' example, Dorothee concludes that "To discharge his millions of sperm is man's biological impulse." Later, her research into love's hormonal underpinnings takes her to a disgusting professor who picks at food, informs her that everyone wants to return to the oceanic experience of the mother's womb, and inappropriately discloses his own desire to do so. Inducing revulsion, these opening sequences use Dorothee's research to encourage viewers to distance themselves from reproductive futurism even as she remains in its grip.

After Dorothee's relationships with Heinz and Bruno devolve, she departs for San Francisco in search of her lost mother. After facing hostility at her mother's last known address, Dorothee encounters the city's radically sex-positive culture. Interactions with two of its representatives—sex educator Susie Bright (a.k.a.

Susie Sexpert) and sex worker Ramona—prompt Dorothee to traverse the fantasies animating her life in Hamburg and quest for reunion with her mother. This transformation leads her to direct herself toward a broader range of sexual objects and to reject reproductive heterosexuality's temporalities for a more open-ended relationship to desire.

The first of these encounters is with Susie, whom Dorothee meets outside a strip joint on Market Street. When Dorothee discloses that she has come to San Francisco to find her mother, Susie encourages her to abandon the search, telling her that "you're too old to worry about a momma any more, aren't you? You're a grown-up girl." As Andrea Reimann observes, this statement redirects the narrative of "Dorothee's personal maturation" away from the Freudian "psychoanalytic model" focusing on familial dynamics, in particular "the mother-daughter relationship" (Reimann 2003: 185). Her desire rerouted, Dorothee follows Susie across town to hear about the feminist potential of pornography, erotic performance, and sex toys.

The second such encounter is Dorothee's involvement with an escort named Ramona, who first appears in a television commercial offering therapy to people "addicted to romantic love." Interpellated by the advertisement, Dorothee calls Ramona and identifies herself as a "German journalist." Receiving no response, Dorothee soon finds Ramona performing for women as a drag king stripper. Ramona's show lays on the sleaze, mockingly undermining phallic masculinity by concluding with a beer bottle ejaculation conveying the same message as the clogged drains and disgusting men in Hamburg. As Gerd Gemunden points out, this scene "ends with Ramona's boxer shorts open and empty, suggesting" both "castration and female empowerment" (Gemunden 1998: 185). The performance leads Dorothee to approach Ramona to schedule a date, which takes them through San Francisco's varied nightlife and back to Dorothee's hotel room for a highly stylized and aesthetically distanced sexual encounter. The next morning, Ramona hands Dorothee a bill, clarifying that the previous night had been a commercial transaction rather than the beginning of a romance. This revelation forces Dorothee to confront her continued investment in romantic fantasy. As Dorothee's fantasy crumbles, she reacts not with tears but with what Gemunden calls "liberating laughter" (Gemunden 1998: 181). Shortly thereafter, we see her performing as a femme stripper in the club where Ramona had appeared in drag.

Stripping for her female friends' gaze, Dorothee's desire is routed away from heterosexuality as she traverses the fantasies of reproductive futurism and (hetero)sexual difference as well as the pre-Oedipal bond to the mother. Most existing scholarship on *The Virgin Machine* asserts that this transformation has definitively "cured" Dorothee of her "romantic illusions," as Straayer puts it (Straayer 1993: 25).³ Indeed, as Klotz observes, Ramona pitches her services as meant to induce such a "cure" (Klotz 1998: 68). An exchange with a cocktail server after Dorothee's strip show also suggests that she has entirely relinquished her romantic aspirations. When the server asks about her dreams, she responds that they're gone.

However, the film's closing scene suggests that San Francisco has done more than prompt Dorothee to abandon romantic fantasy. As she shreds photographs from her past and scatters them under the Golden Gate Bridge, she asks, "Next time I fall in love what will happen then?" Her question suggests that although she has disentangled sexuality from reproduction and romance, she has not rejected love. Instead, she has gained critical distance from romantic constructs that may continue to structure her desire: from what Julia Knight calls "dreams of romance" holding out "the promise of happiness" (Knight 1995: 44). Dorothee's migration from Germany to California has separated her from but not thoroughly disabused her of such dreams, even as it has opened her to a wider range of possibilities—sex for fun; sex or love with both men and women; sex with toys or sex workers—than are available in the fantasy of reproductive heterosexuality structuring the film's first half.

The Virgin Machine also complicates common late 1980s fantasies of a utopian queer nation. Klotz rightfully observes that *The Virgin Machine* enacts a "radical queer" politics transcending lesbian-feminism (Klotz 1998: 65). However, this move does not substitute a queer utopia for a lesbian utopia—as Klotz claims—but rather transnationally reroutes radical queer politics (Koltz 1998: 75). If *The Virgin Machine* reveals a world in which gender and sexuality are sites of play rather than bound by fixed identities such as "woman," "man," or "lesbian," that world's most radical possibilities are elaborated through Dorothee's episodic wanderings.

Dorothee is not the only of Treut's characters to migrate across national boundaries. Shortly after her arrival in San Francisco, her dour look on a beach near the Golden Gate Bridge leads another woman, Dominque, to identify her as German. Dominique herself is marked as "neither American nor German," as Gemunden observes (Gemunden 1998: 194). Although Dominique never discloses her national origins, she reveals that she has lived in Uruguay, Germany, and the United States; she speaks German with Dorothee and mentions that she misses Munich.

Whereas Dorothee's encounters with Susie and Ramona reorient her position within sexual cultures, her friendships with people such as Dominique further direct her attention away from heteronormative, familial models and toward a chosen family of transnational migrants. Gemunden rightfully describes Dominique as one of the most important facilitators of Dorothee's "transformed identity and sexual discovery" (Gemunden 1998: 194). As a migrant, Dominique's movements are not defined by linear progress through space and time, but rather—like Dorothee's—are open to unpredictable futures. Nor are the spaces though which these women wander presented as utopian sites of freeplay dissolving all difference. As Sunka Simon points out, Treut's work "does not... deny the historically specific problematics of race and class, or national identity" (Simon 1998: 393). Instead, *The Virgin Machine* undercuts Dorothee's utopian imaginings about San Francisco, as Reimann argues (Reimann 2003: 189). Dorothee is shown navigating situations that present the potential for violence, including the seedy Tenderloin distinct and her mother's last known place of residence, where she attracts hostile treatment as an outsider (Reimann 2003: 189).[4] Dorothee's and Dominique's migrations loosen rigid constructs of sexual and national identity, but their experiences do not erase their personal histories. The film's attention to these factors is transnational, avoiding the problematic claims to universal queer identity underpinning the internationalist assumptions of Gemunden's and Alice Kuzniar's approaches to the film.[5]

Dorothee is nonetheless transformed by San Francisco's expansive sexual possibilities and role as a hub for transnational migration. Dominique's unreadable nationality is echoed in her apparent asexuality, understood both in the contemporary English-language sense of not being sexually attracted to others and in the Lacanian sense I discuss in Chapters 2 and 4 of not being subject to sexuation (at least as orthodox Lacanians understand it). As Kathrin Bower notes, Dominique's gender presentation and sexuality remain "uninscribed" throughout the film (Bower 2000: 35). Whereas Dorothee is consistently feminized until the closing scene and has sex with both men and women, the "frumpy" Dominique styles herself with long hair and women's skirt suits but does not wear make-up or accessories that would mark her as masculine or feminine (Bower 2000: 35). Nor does Dominique express sexual desire. When Dorothee reveals that she is studying romantic love, Dominique discloses that it does not interest her and that she lives with her sister.

Dominique unsurprisingly declines to accompany Dorothee on her first visit to the women's strip show, yet appears as a supportive friend for her performance: the first of two scenes in the film's second half showing the protagonist renegotiating rather than transcending national and sexual identities as a self-described "German girl in America" ("Ein Deutsches Mädchen in Amerika") after Ramona disabuses her of romantic fantasy. Dominique's multiple positioning as a multilingual person who has lived in a variety of nations makes her role at Dorothee's performance crucial. This event, from which men are excluded, enables a play between the look and the gaze going beyond hegemonic heteronormative visual regimes.[6] Praising the performance by telling Dorothee that "Du hast das gut gelebt" ("you have lived well"), the otherwise asexual Dominique becomes the temporary conduit for an approving lesbian gaze. Her history of migration further twists the scene's visual economy, complicating the play between the gaze and various looks in the American nightclub. By the film's end, Dominique and her international group of women friends form a non-heteronormative gaze providing Dorothee with an alternate way of viewing her life that depends neither on lovers nor on biological family.

The scene in the club is less unanimously affirmative, however. Dominique's frumpiness sharply distinguishes her appearance from the other clubgoers' trendy 1980s fashions and subcultural lesbian styles, marking her as an outsider. After she hugs Dorothee to congratulate her for a successful performance, the film cuts to an image of a glowering butch-femme punk couple, lingering on them in a resignification of Brassaï's atmospheric black-and-white photographs of 1930s Parisian lesbian clubs.[7] The punks look notably different from other patrons: they sit silently and sullenly at a back table, whereas the others are dressed in mainstream 1980s styles and enthusiastically engage the performance from seats close to the stage. Even though the rest of the crowd cheers Dorothee on, this couple's image is cut into the sequence in a manner suggesting disapproval of the migrants. The punks distance themselves from the spectacle, glaring at Dorothee's warm interaction with Dominique. The couple's hostile looks complicate the gaze at play in the club by casting a negative light on the migrants' destabilization of gendered, sexual, sartorial, and national trends. By twisting the gaze, *The Virgin Machine* calls attention to San Francisco's queer potentialities but also to its forms of normativity and internal division.

Thus, while the film positions the encounter with San Francisco as the impetus behind several crucial changes in fantasies structuring Dorothee's desire, Treut does not idealize the city as purely liberatory. *The Virgin Machine* instead positions San Francisco as a site of productive dislocation for migrant subjects. Brassaï—the heterosexual man whose photographs of early twentieth-century Parisian subcultures are referenced in the cinematography used to show Dorothee's performance—was also an immigrant: a Hungarian who migrated to Paris. His camera constructs queer venues not through a dominant Parisian gaze but through that of a recent arrival. Treut similarly presents San Francisco's queer community through migrants' eyes.

Unlike Brassaï's heterosexual gaze on Parisian queer milieux, however, Dorothee's encounters with San Francisco include observation of and participation in its queer life. Dorothee's active engagement with the city is transformative. Although the closing scene shows her in a leather cap, suggesting her assimilation to late 1980s North American lesbian subcultural styles, the film also underscores her continued identification with Germanness. As she shreds photographs of her family and former lovers to scatter them into the Pacific Ocean under the Golden Gate Bridge, she identifies herself as "A German girl in America." San Francisco does not erase her Germanness but rather transforms it, divorcing it from her family line and rearticulating it through a community of diasporic migrants in California. Despite Kuzniar's reading of Treut's films as advocating "an allegiance to queerness" transcending national divisions to form "a truly queer nationhood," I read *The Virgin Machine* as insisting on Dorothee's difference from American norms, whether national or sexual (Kuzniar 2000: 169). If, as Gemunden claims, her "encounter with American culture presents the need for change," this prompts a re-envisioning of rather than a disidentification from Germanness (Gemunden 1998: 177). And if Reimann is right that in *The Virgin Machine*, "the destruction or at least destabilization of 'the self' provides the condition for a revaluation of how nationality shapes identity," that process does not lead to a wholesale rejection of "identification with nation" but to a more complicated destabilization of identification (Reimann 2003: 186). Dorothee's transnational migration has left the question of what it means for her to be "A German girl in America" as open as the future of her desire.

Driven episodically rather than by a coming out story's conventional narrative arc, *The Virgin Machine* does not bring closure either to Dorothee's narrative or to the question of her sexual identity. Rather, it creates an opening to a future in which neither her desire nor its temporality is scripted in advance.[8] Although Bower argues that by the film's end, Dorothee's "romantic dream is displaced by the emancipatory consciousness of her own power to fantasize and create herself in and as desire," this statement overlooks unconscious psychical dimensions that undercut and thereby complicate agency (Bower 2000: 27). While the encounter with Ramona makes Dorothee more aware of her "power to fantasize," it does so by exposing the ways fantasy structures desires whose origin lies somewhere between compulsion and volition (Bower 2000: 27). By asking "Next time I fall in love what will happen then?," Dorothee underscores her romantic trajectory's unpredictable future and her openness to fantasies whose contours are neither fully volitional nor determined in advance.

"Something Beautiful and New": *Hedwig*'s Traversals

Mitchell's *Hedwig and the Angry Inch*—a cinematic rendition of a play by the same name—tracks the story of a person, assigned male at birth, who grows up in East Berlin and moves to the United States upon marrying an American soldier, Luther. To leave East Germany, the title character takes the name "Hedwig" and undergoes gender reassignment, but the operation is "botched" and an "angry inch" remains between their legs. Scholars have debated whether *Hedwig* is a gay male film (because Hedwig has surgery to leave East Germany with a male lover rather than to act upon the desire for female embodiment) or a transgender film (because Hedwig, once operated upon, must negotiate life as a person whose body defies binaries; until the film's final scenes, Hedwig presents as high femme and has a Croatian transmasculine lover, Yitzhak). However, the film's engagement with gender and sexuality is far more complicated than both of these readings suggest.

As Caridad Svich observes of the stage version of *Hedwig*, "physical trauma serves as the psychological core of the show," staging "Hedwig's multiply traumatized self" as the origin of "sex" well "before the term 'genderqueer'" became widely familiar (Svich 2019: 44). Instead of hewing to orthodox Lacanian accounts of (hetero)sexual difference's supposedly originary trauma, Mitchell's narrative makes Hedwig's queerness foundational and tracks their assumption of genderqueer embodiment. In so doing, *Hedwig* also interrogates the relationship between gender, desire, fantasy, and love.

Hedwig approaches these questions by taking up the theoretical tension between Butlerian undercutting and genderqueer proliferation of genders.[9] Mitchell's narrative follows a protagonist who straddles "East and West, slavery and freedom, man and woman," yet ultimately moves past those terms.[10] To do so, the film uses national border-crossing as a metaphor for crossing gender and sexual boundaries. Yet as Svich observes, *Hedwig* does not accurately portray homosexuality's history in East Germany, which "had significantly more lenient sodomy laws and accepted the demands of gay activists with greater alacrity than its democratic neighbor on the West" (Svich 2019: 28). Nor does the film—despite its engagement of multiple musical traditions—acknowledge the role of the "East German punk music scene" in "social protest" leading "to the fall of the Berlin

Wall" (Svich 2019: 28).[11] Instead, *Hedwig* uses borders as metaphors for subjective division. The film's attention to the Berlin Wall's construction and destruction situates all identities as constituted through—and split by—historically and ideologically contingent forces rather than through what orthodox Lacanians consider to be the transhistorical antinomy of sexual difference.

The film also includes a song, "The Origin of Love," featuring two same-sex couples and one opposite-sex pair. Repeated throughout the film with animated illustrations, this song is based on Aristophanes' mythological account of love's origins and structures the romantic fantasy of finding "my other half" propelling Hedwig across the Atlantic Ocean. By the film's end, however, Hedwig and their band have traversed the fantasy of (hetero)sexual difference structuring the assumption that one must be either "man or woman" as well as the fantasy that romantic love makes people whole. To do so, Hedwig embraces a genderqueer version of the Lacanian *sinthôme*, using "creativity" to shape what Svich calls a "newly assembled identity" (Svich 2019: 48).[12] Hedwig thereby sheds the belief that their "angry inch" is a sign of ruinous failure and comes to understand their body as a "bridge" between genders. By the end of the film, spectators are left with the realization that "the binary of the sexes has succumbed to the same fate as that of the Berlin Wall" (Gherovici 2017: 29). Hedwig's peregrinations also go beyond the fantasy whose equation of the Eastern bloc with slavery and the West with freedom motivates their desire to leave for the United States.

Mitchell's film uses visual metaphors to signal Hedwig's traversals of the fantasy. At a key moment in the middle of the narrative, Hedwig is shown in a cheap chain steakhouse called "Bilgewater's Baltimore" dissociatively floating over hostile middle American crowds—as if flying past conventional assumptions about gender and national identity—while performing the song "The Angry Inch." Directly following a flashback to the moment at which Hedwig is operated upon in Berlin, the show in Baltimore bears the weight of their physical and geographical traumas. Yet unlike many narratives of transition, Hedwig's operation does not end with the relief of physically realizing their internal sense of gender identity. Rather, the operation is traumatic—a literalization of Hedwig's division by dualistic constructs of gender and nation.

Hedwig's performance in Baltimore draws on punk anti-aesthetics to register these traumas. "The Angry Inch" describes the operation in detail, emphasizing that Hedwig's genitalia exceed binary gender. Moreover, as Don Dingledine argues, the film draws on tropes from surrealism to depict Hedwig's body (Dingledine 2009). Anticipating a later song with an explicitly surrealist title—"Exquisite Corpse"—"The Angry Inch" includes a line describing Hedwig's "one-inch mound of flesh" as having "a scar running down it like a sideways grimace on an eyeless face." Associated with negative affect, this "eyeless face" anticipates the film's attention to vision.

"The Angry Inch" thereby develops themes introduced in "The Origin of Love," which posits that people originally had "two faces peering out of one giant head so they could watch all around them as they talked while they read," but were split into two-eyed, two-legged creatures after angering the gods. After the split, the gods threatened that if the people didn't "behave" they would be "cut… down again" through the middle and left "hopping round on one foot/ And looking through one eye." The gods' strategy for quashing rebellion is to reduce peoples' mobility and vision. Moreover, "The Origin of Love" suggests that love is motivated by the desire to reunite the "two faces" that were blissfully "peering out of one giant head" before division by the gods. Although at first glance *Hedwig* seems to be caught up in this romantic fantasy of finding one's "other half," the film ultimately challenges it. The simile comparing Hedwig's genital scarring to "a sideways grimace on an eyeless face" points to their initial interpellation by yet eventual exclusion from this narrative.

At the early performance at Bilgewater's Baltimore, Yitzhak steps up to defend Hedwig when their reference to their genitalia's "sideways grimace on an eyeless face" prompts an enormous male member of the audience to roar "faggot!" and charge the band. As the performance devolves into a fistfight and then a restaurant-wide brawl, Hedwig stops singing and dissociates. As the band continues to play and sing, Hedwig's back is to the camera; they slowly walk away from the stage, diving into the air to soar above madcap chefs and food-fighting families. At first glance this scene appears to figure Hedwig's transcendence of a hostile environment governed by the ideology of (hetero)sexual difference. However, the camera looks upward at Hedwig's floating body, which remains under the Bilgewater's bland ceiling and generic recessed lights. They land in a bleak trailer park in Kansas, only to discover that Luther has left them for a twink and that the Berlin Wall has fallen. At that moment, traversing the fantasy does not change Hedwig's life for the better.[13]

Only later in the film does Hedwig successfully traverse the fantasy of (hetero) sexual difference structuring the assumption that one must be either "man or woman." In so doing, they go beyond the dualistic assumptions about gender embodiment—as well as the homosexual and heterosexual trajectories— mobilized in "The Origin of Love." Mitchell's protagonist is initially interpellated into this story's gay male version, only to become Hedwig by attempting to embody its heterosexual variant. After Luther leaves, Hedwig gradually sheds these narratives while coming to terms with their genderqueer embodiment and engaging in two relationships: first with a teenage future rock star named Tommy, then with the transmasculine Yitzhak. Hedwig's relationship with Yitzhak comes to an end in the film's concluding scenes, set in New York City's Bilgewater's Times Square. At that venue, Hedwig dons glam-rock garb and performs two numbers in sequence. The first—"Hedwig's Lament"—speaks to their origin in "a town ripped in two" by geopolitical divisions that "cut" their body "into parts." However, this song is followed by a piece entitled "Exquisite Corpse" whose performance allows Hedwig to move beyond their trauma and the fantasy of (hetero)sexual difference.

"Exquisite Corpse" opens by depicting Hedwig as "[A]ll sewn up" in "a hardened razor-cut scar map across my body"; they are "A collage/All sewn up/A montage/All sewn up." As Dingledine argues, the song invokes the surrealist parlor game of "exquisite corpse," in which a body is constructed not by a sole artist striving for a preconceived ideal but by a group randomly stringing together words and images. Because the "exquisite corpse" is a "collage," it enables Hedwig "to transcend the binaries that violently restrict our definitions of gender identity and sexuality" and thereby "be liberated" (Dingledine 2009: 258). Dingedine's argument is problematic, though, for relying on Janice Raymond's transphobic claim that gender reassignment reifies gender categories. As Jason Cromwell argues, trans bodies queer rather than stabilize dualistic genders and sexualities (Cromwell 1999). Dingledine also uses surrealist leader André Breton's work without critiquing his misogyny or the way his *"primordial androgyne"* blends rather than challenges the putative antinomy between masculinity and femininity (Dingledine 2009: 267).

In my view, *Hedwig* ultimately uses the "exquisite corpse" to transform early twentieth-century surrealist accounts of gender. It is not, as Dingledine claims, that Hedwig *"transcends* gender," but that they traverse the orthodox Lacanian fantasy that gender is a secondary formation set into motion by a fundamental antinomy between masculine and feminine (Dingledine 2009: 267). By the film's end, Hedwig comes to view their body not as a failure to achieve a culturally dominant ideal but as an "exquisite corpse" representing "something beautiful and new." The latter phrase, sung by Hedwig's ex-lover Tommy Gnosis, mobilizes what Jack Halberstam calls a "transgender look" affirming the transperson's gender (Halberstam 2005: 86).

The looks circulating in "Exquisite Corpse" similarly help Hedwig see their body in a positive light and validate their gender. Both the soundtrack's and film's versions of "Exquisite Corpse" depict Hedwig as a "hollowed out" "tornado body with a hand grenade head"—lines Yitzhak sings in a high voice, foreshadowing the subjective dispossession that ensues while traversing the fantasy of (hetero)sexual difference. Hedwig, too, eventually embraces the state of being an "exquisite corpse" after being encouraged to view their embodiment positively. In the soundtrack's rendition of "Exquisite Corpse," Hedwig and the band react to an unnamed "you" that only sees bodily "decay and ruin." Using a collective "I," they respond that "I tell you 'No, no, no, no/You make such an exquisite corpse'"—one causing "[t]he whole world" to begin "unscrewing/As time collapses and space warps." Mobilizing a "transgender look" encouraging Hedwig to view their gender affirmatively, these lyrics figure the "exquisite corpse" as a *sinthôme* anchoring genderqueer embodiment (Halberstam 2005: 86).

Michell's film, however, replaces this stanza (and the remainder of the song) with a montage mixing Hedwig's punkish display of guitar-smashing rage with scenes from their past, such as their molestation by their father and failed relationship with Tommy. In the film, this sequence—which begins when Hedwig sheds their wig and rips off their bra to reveal their chest—does the work of the lyrics used in the soundtrack version of "Exquisite Corpse," and bears the weight of their subjective dispossession. The montage's end is dominated by shots of Tommy rehearsing songs plagiarized from Hedwig for performances to stadium-sized crowds. These images bridge to an exchange of looks between Tommy and Hedwig standing in for soundtrack lyrics in which the band collectively affirms Hedwig's "exquisite corpse."

Hedwig's and Tommy's final encounter takes place during a scene in which a bare-chested Hedwig watches a bare-chested Tommy practice a reprise of "Wicked Little Town," which Hedwig also sings earlier while trapped in the trailer park. Tommy's rendition, sung to apologize for having jilted Hedwig and stolen their songs after failing to understand that they were "more than a woman or a man," transforms the song by affirming Hedwig's body as "something beautiful and new." Much like the "unscrewing" of the "world" in the soundtrack's version of "Exquisite Corpse," Hedwig's tears and grimaces during Tommy's performance of "Wicked Little Town" visually represent the subjective destitution entailed in traversing the fantasy.

As the camera circles Hedwig's face and upper body, Tommy's song disabuses Hedwig of the fantasy underpinning their quest for love's origin, stating that "there's no mystical design, no cosmic lover preassigned." Hedwig breaks down when Tommy points to their estrangement by the displacements wrought by that fantasy: "with all the changes/you've been through,/It seems the stranger's always you,/Alone again in some new/Wicked little town." The song continues, telling Hedwig that "when you've got no other choice/You know you can follow my voice/Through the dark turns and noise/Of this wicked little town." However, after "follow my voice," Tommy stops voicing the lyrics as he and Hedwig look at one another.

By the end of this scene, Hedwig has shed the fantasies of romantic love and (hetero)sexual difference structuring the assumption that one must be either "man or woman." Yet this time, Hedwig is propelled forward—rather than stuck—at the song's end by the vision that their gender may not be a hardship but something "beautiful and new." Hedwig has embraced their *sinthôme* and "newly assembled identity" (Svich 2019: 48). Although the film's substitution of Tommy's for the band's validation of Hedwig's gender appears to transform communitarian into individual support, "Wicked Little Town" is followed by a scene in which Hedwig and their band enable Yitzhak, too, to traverse the fantasy of (hetero)sexual difference. As Hedwig sings "Midnight Radio," they pick up their wig and hand it to Yitzhak, who dons it and falls backward into the crowd, transformed into a high femme with make-up and shaved legs. In contrast to Hedwig's flight above the hostile scene at Bilgewater's Baltimore, Yitzhak's traversal is supported by the hands of a cheering crowd. Later in "Midnight Radio," cartoons from "The Origin of Love" reprise to show various lovers' reunions and redivisions. Viewers finally see Hedwig—naked, back facing the camera—tentatively walking down a poorly lit New York alleyway toward a street.

This closing scene suggests that the protagonist has gone beyond dualistic understandings of sex, gender, and sexuality to create "something beautiful and new." Yet what will come after Hedwig's and Yitzhak's traversals remains uncertain. The closing song, "Midnight Radio," falls prey to the fantasy of wholeness, declaring that "your blood… /Knows that you're whole," yet differs from "The Origin of Love" by declining to position Hedwig as needing completion in a romantic partner. Whereas the animated sequence preceding Hedwig's emergence into the alleyway features half faces "[t]rying to shove" themselves "back together" to fit the narrative offered in "The Origin of Love," Hedwig's nude body features a tattoo of a face with a straight line for a nose and two differently styled eyes: one open, the other shut. This tattoo suggests that Hedwig has solved the problem "The Angry Inch" depicted by describing their genitalia through the simile of "a scar running down it like a sideways grimace on an eyeless face." The tattoo implies not that Hedwig is now whole but that they have come to terms with their subjective splitting and non-binary embodiment. The eyes differ from one another and suggest visual limitations, even as Hedwig has gone beyond the fantasies structuring and constraining their past.

Thus, in keeping with Hedwig's traversals, "Midnight Radio" ends the film with an expansive opening that—unlike romantic love—has no predetermined direction. Unsurprisingly, the many students to whom I have shown this film have offered radically different readings of the alleyway scene—suggesting, perhaps, that *Hedwig*'s power lies in mobilizing multiple desirings and genderings. Although one is left with the sense that Hedwig and Yitzhak have freed one another from structures of desire and identity compelled by the ideology of (hetero)sexual difference, they have not gone beyond gender altogether. Rather, the film's ending leaves their options for gender more varied and the futures of their desires more open than ever before.

Moreover, the closing scene—the last of Hedwig's geographical displacements—suggests that they have gone beyond the supposed antinomy between "East and West, slavery and freedom" with which the film opens. Though the Berlin Wall is a metaphor for Hedwig's and Yitzhak's division both by the cold war East-West opposition and dualistic gender ideologies, the film also engages another putative divide: that between the Western metropolis and its others, whether America's heartland or the former Eastern Bloc. Although Hedwig flees East Berlin for the US seemingly greener pastures, they hate life in Junction City. Nor is New York City—the venue for Yitzhak's traversal and Hedwig's naked emergence—an unambiguous space of freedom. As Scott Herring observes, New York is often figured as "the be-all and the end-all of modern queer life," as the site of liberation from the heartland's "wicked little towns" (Herring 2010: 1, 10). Yet Mitchell's film does not unambiguously promulgate "metronormativity" (Herring 2010: 17). When Hedwig's band tours the United States they attract a ragtag group of fans from queer communities in parts of the country that are often misrepresented as uniformly hostile. Moreover, the film ends shortly after Hedwig arrives in New York, leaving open the question of whether they will be happy there.

By including these and other details, the film interrogates and ultimately traverses the fantasy of American freedom structuring Hedwig's desire to leave East Berlin. As the narrative builds to "Hedwig's Lament," "Exquisite Corpse," and "Wicked Little Town," the band plays an out-of-tune version of "America the Beautiful" repeating the film's opening soundtrack. While the band's uglification of America's beautiful and spacious skies represents, on the one hand, a slight against the negatively stereotyped regions of the United States that Hedwig toured earlier, it also represents—more constructively—a questioning of the ideological fantasy that compels them to leave East Berlin with an American.

Thus if *Hedwig* employs New York City as the space in which Hedwig traverses the fantasies of romantic love and (hetero)sexual difference, what will happen next remains uncertain. Viewers are left to wonder whether the Big Apple will be as liberating as queer metronormativity claims. Even though the film ends after Hedwig walks naked into a New York alleyway, freed from (hetero)sexual difference and romantic love, Tommy's reprise of "Wicked Little Town" suggests that New York might be no more liberatory than other places. Going beyond the fantasy that things are better elsewhere, Hedwig emerges into Manhattan with no guarantees: yet with an opening to many possible futures.

Notes

1. See, for example, Kuzniar (2000) and Reimann (2003).
2. See also Simon (1998) for analysis of mucus's role in this part of the film.
3. In addition to Straayer (1993), see Bower (2000), Klotz (1998), Knight (1995), and Reimann (2003) for different versions of the argument that Dorothee is ultimately disabused of romantic illusions. See Gemunden for an argument that the film stages romantic love's "impossibility" (Gemunden 1998: 180).
4. Neither Reimann (2003) nor Simon (1998) uses the term "transnational," though they point to transnational aspects of the film.
5. See Cohler (2008) regarding differences between internationalist and transnationalist approaches to sexuality. In reading *The Virgin Machine* as transnational, I challenge Gemunden's characterization of Treut's films' queer "internationalist frame of reference" as well as Kuzniar's argument that they illustrate "a truly queer nationhood" transcending national boundaries (Gemunden 1998: 194; Kuzniar 2000: 169).
6. For differently inflected arguments about the film's complications of heterosexist visual economies, see Alter (1998), Bower (2000), and Simon (1998). Whereas Bower notes the film's "mobile treatment of the gaze," Alter uses scenes featuring Susie Bright to argue that Treut's film achieves a "simultaneously triangulated and distriangulated vision" implicating spectators and characters alike (Alter 1998: 21; Bower 2000: 32).

   I use Lacan (1977) to distinguish between the "look" (the act of looking) from the "gaze" (the field of vision mobilized to invite looking); see Silverman 1996 for further discussion of this distinction and its muddying in translation.
7. See Brassaï (2001).

8   See Straayer (1993) for analysis of the differences between *The Virgin Machine*'s narrative structure and conventions of the "coming out story."
9   See Svich (2019) for another reading of Hedwig as genderqueer.
10 I thus use gender-neutral pronouns to reflect Hedwig's positionality.
11 See Svich (2019) for extended analysis of *Hedwig*'s engagement of multiple musical traditions.
12 See Chapter 4 of this book for discussion and genderqueer extension of Lacanian arguments by Cavanagh (2015, 2016, 2018), Gherovici (2012, 2014, 2017), and Gozlan (2015) that viable transsubjectivities may be anchored in the imaginary, symbolic, and Real orders by a creative *sinthôme*.
13 See Chiesa for a Lacanian argument that the outcome of fantasy's traversal is unpredictable.

6

Traversing North America, Traversing (Hetero)sexual Difference

The idea that traversing the fantasy of (hetero)sexual difference allows queer subjects to start anew animates three mixed-genre texts—Gloria Anzaldúa's *Borderlands/La Frontera* (1987) and *Light in the Dark/Luz en lo Oscuro* (2015); Andrea Lawlor's *Paul Takes the Form of a Mortal Girl* (2017)—that use mythological shape-shifters to explore the subjectivities of queers from ethnically mixed backgrounds. Whereas *Borderlands* takes an intersectional queer and feminist approach to the historically contested US-Mexico borderland to highlight its capacity to stimulate subjective transformation, Paul uses a protagonist living at the borders of gender, sexuality, and ethnicity to undermine the notion that coastal metropolises such as Boston, New York, Los Angeles, and San Francisco are the only viable places for queers. *Borderlands* creates an opening by complicating the multiple vectors of identity produced at the US-Mexico border; Paul's travels free him from "metronormativity" and constrictive identity constructs (Herring 2010: 6). By tapping queers' creativity, both texts offer examples of what Anzaldúa calls the formation of a "new consciousness" and what I have been calling the subjective transformation that can arise from traversing the fundamental fantasy (Anzaldúa 1987: 80).

Beyond the Fantasy of Border Divisions: Gloria Anzaldúa

In *Borderlands/La Frontera* and *Light the Dark*, Anzaldúa argues that "*mestiza* consciousness" offers a way of "healing the split that originates in the very foundation of our lives," achieving "wholeness," and transcending the pain of the borderlands (Anzaldúa 1987: 80; Anzaldúa 2015: 89).[1] She explains that in crisis, "[a] gap ... or abyss opens up between" a person's "desires and what occurred" to create "disorientation" that prompts reconsideration of "the situation and the people involved," allowing consciousness to be transformed by "[m]ourning... wounds and losses" (Anzaldúa 2015: 87–8).

Posthumously published in an edition edited by Analouise Keating, *Light in the Dark* wavers with regard to personal transformation. Keating's volume foregrounds parts Anzaldúa finished and places portions "that would not have met her publication standards but would have been further revised or entirely deleted" in "endnotes and appendices" (Keating in Anzaldúa 2015: xx). At some points, Anzaldúa argues that subjects seek "integration, completeness, and wholeness" by surmounting fragmenting external forces (Anzaldúa 2015: 50). At others she eschews such teleologies, open-endedly underscoring the "healing" possible by reassembling "the pieces" after "disintegration" (Anzaldúa 2015: 29). And at her most radical, she abandons dialectic altogether in favor of flexible negotiations refusing binaries and embracing open-ended connectivity.

However, Antonio Viego rightfully critiques Anzaldúa for "operating a theory of the border subject that replicates an ego- and social psychological conception of human subjectivity" focused on imaginary recognition (Viego 2007: 128). Offering a counterpoint to those parts of her argument that assume dialectical synthesis to produce a higher level of consciousness, Lacan's theory of subjective splitting challenges the fantasy of psychical reunification underpinning the search to restore "wholeness" (Anzaldúa 2015: 50). Although Viego proposes "a more Lacanian, psychoanalytic-language-based account" of "the border subject," he overlooks Anzaldúa's deep engagement with language's shaping of the psyche, apparent in her use of linguistic mixing to enact *mestiza* consciousness (Viego 2007: 129). I doubt she would disagree with his claim that we should "understand the bordering and splitting of the subject as not only predominantly social, cultural, and historical in its origins and effects but as additionally linguistic and psychical" (Viego 2007: 129). The difficulty with Anzaldúa's theory arises not from a refusal to engage linguistic accounts of the psyche but from her capitulation to ego psychology.

Anzaldúa rightfully identifies linguistic bias as oppressive, bringing psychoanalytic queer theory's attention to gender and sexuality into dialogue with linguistic, ethnic, and religious differences to identify remediable internal divisions produced by oppressive external forces. Yet Lacanian psychoanalysis considers language itself—not just its oppressive uses—to be implicated in the subject's "ontological lack," which is formed through "privative and generative effects of language" independent of sociocultural forces (Ruti 2008a: 483; Viego

2007: 128). As Viego observes, a Lacanian approach to the "border subject" compels consideration of "those losses attributable to the unequal distribution of social and material resources" as well as those "that constitute subjectivity as such" (Viego 2007: 129). Anzaldúa considers sociolinguistic causes of the subject's "circumstantial lack" but not language's implication in its "ontological" dimensions (Ruti 2008a: 494m11, 483).

Nonetheless, Anzaldúa's argument for a "new consciousness" offers an approach to subjective transformation that corrects Lacanian queer theory's oversights (Anzaldúa 1987: 80). As Jack Halberstam notes, studies such as Lee Edelman's *No Future* (2004) turn on a narrow range of examples illustrating Lacanian theory's unmarked whiteness (Halberstam 2006). Whereas Lacan assumes that desire is inevitably constituted through and driven by the antagonism of sexual difference, Anzaldúa considers the psychical consequences of multiple differences. She thereby brings language, culture, ethnicity, and religion into dialogue with gender and sexuality in ways that can make psychoanalysis more inclusive.

Beyond the Fantasy of Dialectical Synthesis

Cross-reading Anzaldúa with Lacanian queer theory nuances psychoanalytic approaches to lack, which she and Lacan present as dialectical yet take in radically different directions. Anzaldúa frames her project as remediating oppression's psychically divisive consequences by "recognizing and legitimizing" the "excluded," such as "women, people of color, queer, and othered groups" (Anzaldúa 2015: 6). In *Borderlands* and *Light in the Dark*, she argues that dialectical oppositions can move the divided subject toward "synthesis" and "wholeness" (Anzaldúa 2015: 89; Anzaldúa 1987: 79).

For Lacan, by contrast, dialectic exacerbates rather than overcomes subjective division. In "The Signification of the Phallus," he argues that "demand annuls (*aufhebt*) the particularity of everything than can be granted" and that "the particularity thus abolished" will "reappear *beyond* demand" as a gap—or "*Spaltung*"—that desire's deferrals impossibly try to fill (Lacan 2006g: 580). Desire's dialectic does not culminate in a higher level of consciousness resolving the subject's internal conflicts; instead, it produces a residue of signification sending the subject off in pursuit of objects *a*. These objects—phantasmatic screens for lack concealing the subject's "alienation" and "misrecognition"—support the subject's constitutive nexus of fantasy and desire (Lacan 2006h: 681, 690, 691).

Because Lacan's dialectic never stops, his account of subjectivity undermines Hegel's theory of recognition and transcendence. Because the desiring subject "is not identical to himself," "desire can never be satisfied with reciprocity of any kind between egos" and recognition is illusory: nothing but *mis*recogniton (Borch-Jacobsen 1991: 90). Moreover, as Ellie Ragland explains, for Lacan "the obverse face of lack is desire," whose significations impede self-understanding by concealing and perpetuating subjective division (Ragland 2015: 16). Lacan therefore replaces Hegel's dialectical "upward movement" with the three orders' triadic relationship, refusing the imaginary illusions and "cognitive satisfactions" of synthesis, as Malcolm Bowie notes (Bowie 1991: 96, 120–1). Rather than moving the subject forward, Lacanian dialectic traps the subject in misrecognitions and deferrals.

It is therefore insufficient to use dialectic to create synthesis and transcend oppressive forms of consciousness, fueling subjects' fundamental fantasies. Ragland observes that such "[f]antasies come from the Other of a given time and place as created by images and signifiers that represent a subject for another signifier"; they conceal lack by providing "identifications, images, and *sinthomes* that knot together the real, symbolic, and imaginary" (Ragland 2015: 16). Race, gender, and sexual orientation are all bound up in historically and culturally contingent fantasies that must be dislodged for the subject to transform.

Kalpana Seshadri-Crooks argues that "[t]he fantasy of wholeness" operates as one such "fundamental fantasy" (Seshadri-Crooks 2000: 5). Hewing to the orthodox Lacanian line that sexual difference is foundational, she contends that "the order of racial difference" is a component of the psychical "logic of difference" functioning as a second-order cover "for sex's failure in language" in the Real (Seshadri-Crooks 2000: 7, 3, 7). She therefore sees "[t]he fantasy of wholeness" as "entirely predicated on sexual difference," defining "the trajectory of the subject of 'race'" (Seshadri-Crooks 2000: 5). Similarly, James Penney makes supposedly "less materially significant... differences of race, religion and ethnicity" secondary to class and "sexual difference" (Penney 2014: 105).

However, as Jan Campbell notes, feminist and postcolonial psychoanalysts such as Luce Irigaray and Frantz Fanon challenge the "exclusionary politics of the phallic metaphor" founding sexual difference, and propose more inclusive ways of theorizing differences (Campbell 2000: 197). I see fantasy's traversal, too, as capable of prompting the subject to think more expansively. Doing so does not involve overcoming lack or achieving "wholeness" but repositioning the subject to establish a new relationship to the Other: to those historically and culturally produced forms of oppression producing the wounding Anzaldúa describes (Anzaldúa 1987: 79). Seeking synthesis of conflicting viewpoints would not solve oppressed subjects' problems but instead return the subject to desire's deferrals: to the misrecognitions of ego psychology Viego critiques. By contrast, fantasy's traversal—a process Viego leaves unaddressed—can undo oppressive fantasies dividing people on the basis of race, gender, sexual orientation, and other traits, enabling them to change direction.

Anzaldúa, too, notes the subject's potential to undergo subjective destitution. Breaking from ego psychology, she states that "[t]o be healed we must be dismembered, pulled apart": she explains that "[t]he healing occurs in disintegration, in the demotion of the ego as the self's only authority" (Anzaldúa 2015: 29). Her emphasis on razing subjective structures to start anew shares the same goal as fantasy's traversal. Embracing Anzaldúa's intersectionality can thus take Lacanian psychoanalysis in a new direction: one that relinquishes damaging orthodoxies about the putative universality and intractability of (hetero)sexual difference; gives up fantasmatic distinctions between "us" and "them" animating volatile racial, ethnic, and national divisions; and traverses the fantasy of (hetero)sexual difference along with its implication in racism, nationalism, and ethnocentrism.

"Towards a New Consciousness" in *Borderlands/La Frontera*

In the "Preface" to *Borderlands/La Frontera*, Anzaldúa notes that she will consider the interplay between an "actual physical borderland" at "the Texas-U.S. Southwest/Mexican Border" and another set of "borderlands": those "psychological borderlands, ... sexual borderlands and ... spiritual borderlands" that "are not particular to the Southwest" (Anzaldúa 1987: n.p.). *Borderlands* draws on multiple linguistic, cultural, and spiritual traditions to position a feminine figure, the *mestiza*, as the exemplar of the "new consciousness"; to argue that her "struggle ... is above all a feminist one"; and to argue that she "and the queer" enact mixing (Anzaldúa 1987: 80–5). Anzaldúa stresses that the *mestiza*'s "struggle is inner" and transpires regardless of an individual's background (Anzaldúa 1987: 80, 87). Everybody's "psyches resemble the bordertowns and are populated by the same people ... Nothing happens in the 'real' world unless it first happens in the images in our heads" (Anzaldúa 1987: 87).

This call for change to happen "in the images in our heads" exemplifies Anzaldúa's argument that a "new consciousness" can alter actions and material realities (Anzaldúa 1987: 87, 80). Doing so requires disabling the binaries confining people to narrowly defined identities. One way is to abandon the idea that there is "a split" between "mortal combatants" engaging in a binary "duel of oppressor and oppressed"; another is to "disengage from the dominant culture" (Anzaldúa 1987: 78–9). Both responses represent progress but create new challenges for the *mestiza*, whose "enemy within" continues to adhere to "rigid habits and patterns" grounded in singular identities (Anzaldúa 1987: 79). The "new *mestiza* copes by developing a tolerance for ambiguity" turning her unsettling state of "perpetual transition" into an embrace of the "ambivalence" of "contradictions" enabling new ways of being (Anzaldúa 1987: 79). While generative, "ambivalence" does not move the *mestiza* past the dialectical "impasse[s]" tormenting her (Anzaldúa 1987: 79, 4). Only "an… emotional event" involving "intense pain" will provide the "third element"—the "new consciousness"—that will work "subconsciously" to prompt "a synthesis" realizing "*mestiza* consciousness" (Anzaldúa 1987: 79–80). Dismantling "the subject-object duality that keeps her a prisoner to show in the flesh and through the images in her work how duality is transcended," Anzaldúa's mestiza transcends oppression through synthesis (Anzaldúa 1987: 80).

The resulting "consciousness" is both imaginative and bodily, characterized by dynamic movement and a "continual creative motion" envisioning "a new mythos… a change in the way we perceive reality, the way we see ourselves and the ways we behave," that builds more livable lifeworlds (Anzaldúa 1987: 80). Transforming the *mestiza* from a "sacrificial goat" into "the officiating priestess at the crossroads," the "new mythos" endows her with the ability to reshape materiality (Anzaldúa 1987: 80). Using "cultural figures to intervene in, make change, and thus heal colonialism's wounds," Anzaldúa invokes mythological shape-shifters to figure the *mestiza*'s profound self-transformation (Anzaldúa 2015: 44). Offering readers an explicitly feminist, queer, and trans-friendly version of Mesoamerican myth, her metaphorical invocation of the supernatural powers of the "priestess" builds to the claim that the *mestiza* becomes "a nahual, able to transform herself into a tree, a coyote into another person" (Anzaldúa 1987: 80, 82–3).

Navigating Nepantla in *Light in the Dark/Luz en lo Oscuro*

Although Anzaldúa draws on spiritual tradition to describe her mythopoetics as "magical thinking," her arguments underscore her approach's potential efficacy (Anzaldúa 2015: 4). It depends not only on "intentions" but also on refusing to engage oppressive modes of interaction and engaging otherwise (Anzaldúa 2015: 5). It hinges, too, on careful consideration of "interests": divergent concerns brought up as differences are negotiated (Anzaldúa 2015: 5). Stressing that *Light in the Dark* simultaneously enacts thinking, creativity, and action, Anzaldúa states that she will "show (and not just tell) how transformation happens": she will not only "interpret or describe realities but" also "create them through language and action, symbols and images" (Anzaldúa 2015: 7). Like *Borderlands*, *Light in the Dark* does what it describes.

Whereas Anzaldúa's emphasis on reworking myth offers revised imaginary and symbolic representations, *Light in the Dark* theorizes a process called "nepantla" that taps into the Real by profoundly altering a subject's "habitual perspective" after "trauma" (Anzaldúa 2015: 86, 86, 131). Anzaldúa explains that "[w]hen we experience bodily and boundary violations, border shifts, and identity confusions, a flash of understanding may sear us, shocking us into a new way of reading the world" and causing "[i]deological filters" to "fall away" (Anzaldúa 2015: 86). Taking "9/11" as her example, she writes that "choque shifts us to nepantla, a psychological, liminal space between the way things had been and an unknown future. Nepantla is the space in-between, the locus and sign of transition" prompting "different, often contradictory forms of cognition, perspectives, worldviews, belief systems" (Anzaldúa 2015: 16–17). Successfully navigating nepantla—the "Nahuatl word for an in-between space, el lugar entre medio"—leaves one "between worldviews," "between realities" (Anzaldúa 2015: 28, 150, 150).

This intermediary space invites "psychological and spiritual transformations" (Anzaldúa 2015: 150). Thrown into "crisis" and moving through the "*seven stages of conocimiento*," a person is "exposed, open to other perspectives," positioned "to examine the ways" to "construct knowledge, identity, and reality, and" to "explore how some... constructions violate other people's ways of knowing and living" (Anzaldúa 2015: 121–2). This process is recursive: going through the "*stages*," the "internal transformation tries to keep pace with each rift," but "each reenactment" of the underlying "trauma" causes one to lose "ground" (Anzaldúa 2015: 121, 131–2). Eventually, "[i]n the seventh space, the critical turning point of transformation," one changes "realities; develop[s] an ethical, compassionate strategy with which to negotiate conflict and difference within self and between others; and find[s] common ground" (Anzaldúa 2015: 123).

Anzaldúa calls people who work through this shock "nepantleras" and positions them as change agents: they shed damaging worldviews, fundamentally transforming themselves and the world around them (Anzaldúa 2015: 93). As she explains, "In nepantla we undergo the anguish of changing perspectives and crossing a series of cruz calles, junctures, and thresholds, some leading to a different way of relating to people and surroundings and others to the creation of a new world" (Anzaldúa 2015: 17). This passage departs from Anzaldúa's earlier focus on borderlands. Although she acknowledges that "nepantla" involves the "anguish" of division, she also directs readers to new connections at crossings and "thresholds" (Anzaldúa 2015: 17).

Anamorphosis emerges from the resulting change in "our perceptions of the world" (Anzaldúa 2015: 16). She states that "[t]o become nepantleras, we must *choose* to occupy intermediary spaces between worlds" and to "perceive… from multiple angles" (Anzaldúa 2015: 93). Doing so "creates a split in awareness that can lead to the ability to control perception, to balance contemporary society's worldview with the nonordinary worldview, and to move between them to a space that simultaneously exists and does not exist" (Anzaldúa 2015: 28). Embracing this state is "real 'nepantla'"; plays of perception are at the heart of its transformative potential (Anzaldúa 2015: 28). Anzaldúa writes that "[w]hen two or more opposing accounts, perspectives, or belief systems appear side by side or intertwined a kind of double or multiple 'seeing' results"—a person experiences "continuous dialectical encounters with… different stories, situations, and people" (Anzaldúa 2015: 125). This dialectic prompts efforts "to critique your own perspective and assumptions" as well as to "understand" others (Anzaldúa 2015: 125). This experience of "[l]iving between cultures results in 'seeing' double, first from the perspective of one culture, then from the perspective of another," so "those cultures" become "transparent" and transcendable (Anzaldúa 2015: 127).

In contrast to Lacan, who subverts dialectic by arguing that a "split" between "[t]he eye and the gaze" creates a gap covered by the *objet a*, Anzaldúa draws on Carl Jung's understanding of perspectival dialectic to argue that "[t]o make meaning from your experiences you look through an archetypical psycho-mytho-spiritual lens" (Anzaldúa 2015: 139; Lacan 1977: 73–7). Invoking the nahual, she notes that anamorphosis prompts inner change. She writes that "[a]ccording to nagualismo, perceiving something from two different angles creates a split in awareness" that "engenders the ability to control perception"; "if you hold" these "opposites long enough without taking sides, a new identity emerges" (Anzaldúa 2015: 127). By "reversing the polarities, erasing the slash between them, then adding new aspects of" herself, the nepantlera transforms (Anzaldúa 2015: 139). As her "perceptions" and "emotions shift," she regains inner control, reaches "a new understanding of… negative feelings," and emerges from "depression"

(Anzaldúa 2015: 131). However, "[t]here is never any resolution" to nepantla's turmoil, only "the process of healing" (Anzaldúa 2015: 20).

Invoking Aztec mythology, Anzaldúa takes "the Coyolxauhqui state of dissociation" as a "symbol for" nepantla's transformative pain (Anzaldúa 2015: 17). Coyolxauhqui illustrates "the necessary process of dismemberment and fragmentation, of seeing that self or the situations you're embroiled in differently," and the "reconstruction and reframing... that allows for putting the pieces together in a new way" (Anzaldúa 2015: 19–20). She explains that "Coyolxauhqui also represents the 'me' tossed into the void by traumatic events (an experience of the unconscious). I disintegrate into hundreds of pieces, hundreds of separate awarenesses," multiplying perspectives (Anzaldúa 2015: 50). At some points, she states that that this "making and unmaking" remains perpetually in process (Anzaldúa 2015: 20). At others, she argues that "while experiencing the many, I cohere as the one reconstituted and restructured by my own unconscious urge toward wholeness" (Anzaldúa 2015: 50).

This language reveals differences between Anzaldúa and Lacan, even though both understand anamorphosis as dialectical. Whereas she sees nepantla as mobilizing divergent viewpoints that eventually combine and restore the subject's sense of "wholeness," he views anamorphosis as illustrating the split between the look and the gaze (Anzaldúa 2015: 50). For Lacan, anamorphosis "makes visible" that "the subject" is "annihilated" by "castration, which... centres the whole organization of desires through the framework of the fundamental drives" (Lacan 1977: 88–9). Yet Anzaldúa implies that individual perspectives' limitations can be overcome by achieving a higher state of awareness accommodating their multiplicity: recognizing all viewpoints facilitates negotiation and synthesis. Lacan, by contrast, argues that recognition is impossible. If all recognitions are nothing but illusory *mis*recognitons, there can be no synthesis or transcendence; the subject remains trapped in desire's infinite deferrals. The only way out is to traverse the fundamental fantasy.

If we reconceptualize nepantla as mobilizing different perspectives that need not necessarily build to synthesis, that process could be understood as a way of prompting fantasy's traversal. Anzaldúa's emphasis on creativity supports such a reading. In Chapter 2, I described two potential outcomes of traversing the fantasy: the emergence of a reconfigured triad of the imaginary, symbolic, and Real grounding a new fundamental fantasy; or what Ed Pluth calls a more "direct investment in" the creativity of "signifiers as such" (Pluth 2007: 163). For both Anzaldúa and Lacan, artists exemplify subjective transformation. Whereas Lacan offers James Joyce as an example of a writer whose linguistic experimentation taps the *sinthôme*, Anzaldúa highlights the importance of "border artists" (Anzaldúa 2015: 57). She writes that when we are "[i]n nepantla, ... Nepantleras such as artistas/activistas help us mediate these transitions, help us make the crossings, and guide us through the transformation process" (Anzaldúa 2015: 17). Considering "[c]reativity" to be "a liberation impulse, an activity that transforms materials and energy," she sees artmaking as submission to "the creative process, the creative urge" enabling "the story/artwork to be channeled" after one "has exhausted everything" else (Anzaldúa 2015: 40). Seen through a Lacanian lens, the nepantlera acts as what Viego calls a "*sinthomestiza*": she enacts subjective transformation by engaging in "the production of meaning not so much for meaning's sake, but for production's sake" (Viego 2007: 151–2).

For Anzaldúa, "mestizo border artists" best exemplify nepantla: they "partake of the traditions of two or more worlds," they "may be binational," and their work produces "a new artistic space, a border mestizo culture" that need not culminate in synthesis (Anzaldúa 2015: 57). They contest "neat separations between cultures," making "[t]he border... the locus of resistance, of rupture, and of putting together the fragments"; that is, of dynamic creativity (Anzaldúa 2015: 47). Both nepantleras and artists employ a "'connectionist' or web-making faculty" hinging on the flexibility of "less structured thoughts, less rigid categorizations, and thinner boundaries" (Anzaldúa 2015: 83). This open-ended connectivity seeks "similarities instead of divisions" (Anzaldúa 2015: 83). Anzaldúa extends this argument to all artists, whose creativity makes "nepantla" their "natural habitat" (Anzaldúa 2015: 57). Although this argument for the nepantlera's "connectionist" capacity contrasts to Lacan's claim that communication is impossible, her "web-making faculty" enables unpredictable, open-ended signification after fantasy's traversal (Anzaldúa 2015: 83).

Traversing the Fantasy, Transcending Identities

Recognizing that "[m]estizas live in between different worlds, in nepantla," Anzaldúa explains that "[w]e are forced (or choose) to live in categories that defy binaries of gender, race, class, and sexuality," operating in "negotiation mode" (Anzaldúa 2015: 71). She extends her argument to situations comparable but not identical to the nepantlera's. Noting that her aim is to move from theorizing "a sexed, racialized body to a more expansive identity interconnected with its surroundings," she acknowledges that there are "[o]thers" not from geopolitical border zones "who find themselves in this bewildering transitional space," such as "people caught in the midst of denying their projected/assumed heterosexual identity and coming out, presenting and voicing their queer, lesbian, gay, bi, or transgendered selves" (Anzaldúa 2015: 66, 56, 56, 56). Presenting *mestizas* as "[p]eople who refuse to pick sides and identify exclusively with one group," she states that they "trouble the majority, disturbing the dominant discourse of race, just as bisexuals trouble that of sexuality, transpeople confound that of gender" (Anzaldúa 2015: 73). But by moving through nepantla, the nepantlera can form a "new hybrid, the new mestiza, a new category of identity" beyond binaries (Anzaldúa 2015: 66).

Like other queer theorists, then, Anzaldúa rejects singular identities. She sees nepantla's shock as implicating "identity and life purpose": as a constructive "identity crisis" leaving people "open to other ways of identification" (Anzaldúa 2015: 86). Writing that "[t]o bridge the fissures among us, to connect with each other, to move beyond us/them binaries (men and women, queer and straight, able and disabled), we must dismantle the identity markers that promote divisions," she challenges simplistic identity politics with intersectionality (Anzaldúa 2015: 77). She writes that "Like queer and bisexual people who must live in both straight and gay worlds, or like rural people living in cities—stuck between the cracks of home and other cultures"—*mestizas* "experience dislocation, disorientation" and "are forced (or we choose) to live in spaces/categories that defy gender, race, class, sexual, geographic, and spiritual locations" (Anzaldúa 2015: 82). While uncomfortable, this "dislocation" acquaints the *mestiza* with multiple perspectives allowing her "to negotiate the cracks between worlds, to accommodate contradictory identity positions and mutually exclusive, inconsistent worlds": "to reconfigure" herself "outside the us/them binary" (Anzaldúa 2015: 82). She is "[s]hifting and fluid," able to "accommodate all identities," seeking "a hybrid consciousness that transcends the us versus them mentality of irreconcilable positions" (Anzaldúa 2015: 105, 79). Her multiplicity goes beyond border divisions.

Moreover, like Hélène Cixous—who engages psychoanalysis to go beyond patriarchal divisions—Anzaldúa emphasizes that writing is embodied. She asks, "Where does the work of naguala take place?," and responds, "In the body. All emotions and ideas pass through it; writing is nothing if not a bodily act. An image produces a physiological reaction experienced in strong feelings (desire, hate, fear) and manifests itself in neuromuscular, respiratory, cardiovascular, hormonal, and other bodily changes" whose "emotion" prompts re-creation (Anzaldúa 2015: 105). Yet like Cixous, Anzaldúa sometimes references "[t]he material body" as if it were prediscursive, as does Campbell when she praises Irigaray and Fanon for refusing "to separate thinking with the mind, from thinking the body" (Anzaldúa 2015: 5; Campbell 2000: 197). Gayle Salamon challenges such claims, stressing that psychoanalysis emphasizes "bodily assumption": embodiment's formation through imaginary and symbolic mediation (Salamon 2010: 41). Others argue that transpeople fashion embodiment through the *sinthôme*, tapping all three orders.[2] Like transpeople, Anzaldúa's nepantlera undergoes profound subjective transformation affecting her embodiment and connections to others. Taking this process of subjective "making and unmaking" in new directions by undoing externally imposed forms of ethnic oppression and opening herself to new connections, her nepantlera exemplifies an explicitly intersectional reconfiguration of embodiment (Anzaldúa 2015: 20).

Although Anzaldúa states that nepantla does not result in "resolution," she argues that "[t]he creative process" allows neplanteras to harmonize "conflicting impulses and ideas" through flexible negotiation rather than dialectical "synthesis" (Anzaldúa 1987: 79; Anzaldúa 2015: 20, 40, 40). Instead of pitting opposites against one another, *Light in the Dark* accretes them. Anzaldúa notes that the *nepantlera* can "shift from one position to another, listening to all sides" (Anzaldúa 2015: 82). Because "[t]he nepantla mind-set eliminates polarity thinking where there's no in between, only 'either/or,'" it abandons division and "reinstates 'and'" (Anzaldúa 2015: 82). Going beyond dialectic, Anzaldúa uses connectivity to achieve the "higher awareness and consciousness" experienced by artists immersed in creation (Anzaldúa 2015: 40). And unlike the orthodox Lacanian subject, imprisoned by (hetero)sexual difference, Anzaldúa's nepantlera is inclusive: she is open to "diverse others and does not depend on traditional categories or sameness" (Anzaldúa 2015: 151). Instead, she employs a non-teleological "mode of connecting similar to hypertexts' multiple links" (Anzaldúa 2015: 151). Like a Lacanian subject who has traversed the fundamental fantasy, Anzaldúa's nepantlera frees herself of oppressive constructs, embraces the signifier, and uses creativity to make herself anew.

Traversing Genders, Traversing Sexualities: Lawlor's *Paul*

Like Anzaldúa's books, Lawlor's *Paul* mixes genres to go beyond constrictive constructs of gender, sexuality, ethnicity, and nationality, complicating monolithic understandings of North American LGBTQ cultures. Lawlor's eponymous protagonist, Paul Polydoris, is a twenty-two-year-old shape-shifter whose ability to change embodiment at will enables him to explore a variety of genders and sexual identities.[3] Moreover, he is of mixed ethnic heritage. Born on Cyprus to an Irish-American expatriate, his father may be either Greek or Turkish; he isn't sure. Caught between multiple identities, navigating internal conflicts, Paul functions as a *sinthom*estizx whose embrace of the *sinthôme* breaks down stable categories of gender, sexuality, and ethnicity.

Unlike Anzaldúa's *mestiza*, Paul is not rooted in his birthplace. Whereas the *mestiza* is geographically grounded but internally divided by her region's colonial history, Paul's identity is unsettled by his mother's and his own wanderings. Yet his situation as a migrant differs from those of the German immigrants to the United States in *The Virgin Machine* (Monika Treut, 1988) and *Hedwig and the Angry Inch* (2001). After a childhood spent in Troy, New York—a town near Albany emblematizing the normative equation of "[h]eterosexuality = marriage = death" exemplifying the ideology of "reproductive futurism" Paul flees—he uses his shape-shifting ability to experience varied embodiments and LGBTQ communities in the early 1990s United States (Edelman 2004: 28; Lawlor 2017: 152).

After briefly attending SUNY Binghamton and escaping to New York City (a stretch of time revealed only through flashbacks), Paul lives as a bisexual man in Iowa City, a lesbian in Provincetown, and a gay man in San Francisco. In these locales, he encounters a wide range of LGBTQ personae. Shorter trips to the Michigan Womyn's Music Festival and Chicago's Boystown further broaden his experience. Through these movements, Paul traverses locales often opposed to one another in North American queer imaginaries. Narratives of domestic movement frequently reflect the ideology Scott Herring calls "metronormativity" by following young, oppressed, rural, white queers fleeing to liberating big cities (Herring 2010: 6). *Paul* invokes the gay male imperative to go "west, as the Pet Shop Boys" say, while complicating metronormativity (Lawlor 2017: 233). Critically interrogating metronormative understandings of "queer subcultures," Lawlor's novel nuances Christopher Nealon's argument that queer communities are no longer "isolated" but "networked across urban centers" attracting domestic and international LGBTQ "migration" (Nealon 2001: 9). Going beyond Nealon's emphasis on the "urban" into smaller locales such as Provincetown and the Michigan festival, *Paul* shows that neither rural nor urban spaces are fully emancipating.

Paul also engages in what Elizabeth Freeman calls "erotohistoriography," employing "the body as a method" and figuring "historical consciousness as something intimately involved with corporeal sensations" (Freeman 2010: 96). Paul's malleability enables him to access a wide range of queer sexual cultures and for the novel to register "historicity... as a structure of *tactile* feeling, a mode of touch, even an erotic practice" (Freeman 2010: 120). A self-described "omnivore," he relishes a diverse array of fantasies crossing genders and sexualities (Lawlor 2017: 40). A budding filmmaker and author of the zine *"Polydoris Perversity"*—which puns on Freud's concept of "polymorphous perversity" from *Three Essays on the Theory of Sexuality*—he uses queer spaces to facilitate sexual encounters and fall in love (Lawlor 2017: 107). The novel opens with a flurry of exploration in Iowa City, from his opening encounter as Polly with a butch punk singer for whom he dresses as "the girl he wanted to fuck" (Lawlor 2017: 12) to the handjob he gives to heroin-dealing Maisie at a party (Lawlor 2017: 25–7) to the fellatio he performs on a straight writer in a car (Lawlor 2017: 28–31) to the unenjoyable blowjob he gives as Polly in a stinky back alley (Lawlor 2017: 142). Over the course of the narrative, Paul tries on two gay male relationships and one lesbian relationship, but none fully suits him.

Lawlor also emphasizes that naming defines Paul and allows him to redefine himself (Lawlor 2017: 7). The novel's epigraph from Gertrude Stein's "Poetry and Grammar" asserts that *"People if you like to believe it can be made by their names. Call anybody Paul and they get to be a Paul…"* (Stein qtd. in Lawlor 2017: 7). Despite this utopian declaration, Paul encounters institutions and practices that make his self-redefinitions more difficult than they initially seem. Gender markers and naming conventions create challenges to navigate while living beyond the binary. Whereas the lack of a need to show an identity card ("with its laminated M, its *Paul Polydoris*") for an under-the-table job facilitates Polly's arrival in Provincetown, the need for a telephone number slows down Paul's entrance into San Francisco's queer economy (Lawlor 2017: 173). Acknowledging these dilemmas, Paul praises "Stevie Nicks's voice… the promise of her name, a secret way around the problem of what to be called" and how to be recognized (Lawlor 2017: 129).

By the novel's end, Paul has arrived at a different solution to this problem. By traversing the fantasy of (hetero)sexual difference, he goes beyond several intertwined fantasies serving as its prop: romantic love; normative understandings of gender and ethnicity; heteronormativity, homonormativity, and metronormativity. Paul's traversals show that queer communities can enable livable lives even though they come with new constraints. His eventual arrival in San Francisco is not a liberatory triumph but an opening created by rejecting normalcy. He ultimately chooses desire and pleasure over monogamy; gender fluidity over gender stability; and sexual fluidity over sexual identity. Declining idealized normative fantasies, he opens himself to the aesthetic saturation of a place "as good-smelling and various as himself" (Lawlor 2017: 354).

Figuring the Fundamental Fantasy

Lawlor's Queer Foundling

Mixing fantasy and realism, *Paul* intersperses fairy-tale interludes into larger narratives set in realistically depicted early 1990s LGBTQ scenes. Although the novel's fantastic portions provide myths shaping Paul's fundamental fantasy, the book also critiques the idea of structuring one's life in this way. At one point, his lesbian friend Jane asks how "straight people" could "have real friends when their entire lives were an inhabitation of a myth?" (Lawlor 2017: 73). *Paul* considers how to shed unsatisfying life patterns structured through heteronormative *and* homonormative myths. Hinting at the fantasmatic underpinnings of desire and subjectivity, Lawlor introduces short narratives revealing elements of the fantasy Paul ultimately traverses.

These interludes function like *Hedwig and the Angry Inch*'s "The Origin of Love," providing Paul's backstory and revealing his fundamental fantasy as a poor foundling living by his wits in a failing heterosexual world. Lawlor's novel thereby complicates the "foundling" narrative Nealon finds in early-twentieth-century gay and lesbian literature (Nealon 2001: 1). He argues that "foundling" stories offer alternatives to the "inversion model," which views "homosexuals" as "people whose souls are trapped in the body of the 'other' sex," and the "ethnic model," which sees them as "a people with a distinct culture" (Nealon 2001: 1–2). Nealon finds different possibilities in Hart Crane's poetry, Willa Cather's novels, and gay and lesbian popular texts, which envision, "on one hand, an exile from sanctioned experience, most often rendered as the experience of participation in family life and the life of communities and, on the other, a reunion with some 'people' or sodality who redeem this exile and surpass the painful limitations of the original 'home'" (Nealon 2001: 1–2).

Defying dominant identity categories, Paul engages yet ultimately goes beyond these models through traversals of gender, sexual, and ethnic divisions. The text's fairy tales provide Paul with multiple origin stories. Embracing flux rather than "inversion" and rejecting the "ethnic model" of queerness, they undermine stable ontologies of identity (Nealon 2001: 2). Paul—who knows his mother but not his father—blends genders, sexualities, and ethnicities from the outset; he does not experience the "split" between ethnicity and sexuality Nealon sees in the "post-Stonewall literature of queer ethnicity" (Nealon 2001: 10). Lawlor ultimately creates a different type of "foundling" literature than Nealon's (Nealon 2001: 1). Questioning assumptions about what it means for an exiled queer person to find a distinct "people," Paul browses numerous LGBTQ spaces but finds no community fully satisfying (Nealon 2001: 1). It is only when he meets another ethnically mixed shape-shifter—the *sinthom*estizx Robin Suarez—that Paul is able to go beyond the fantasies animating his quest to understand his "nature," locate his "people," and discover in his double a form of queer kinship seeking not to overcome but to embrace internal differences (Lawlor 2017: 206; Nealon 2001: 1).

Paul's Fairy-Tale Origins

Featuring abandoned children and lovers, *Paul*'s fairy-tale interludes foreshadow the protagonist's closing traversals of monolithic fantasies of queer peoplehood. The first four chapters track Paul's movements from Iowa City to Provincetown and from man to woman; the fifth follows him on a westbound train and the sixth shows him settling in to San Francisco. All but the chapter on the train contain one fairy tale apiece, the first three featuring foundlings. The initial story, which appears immediately after Paul fantasizes about a straight Iowa classmate, follows two adopted twins—Paul and Polly—left in the woods after their "bookkeeper" father is "laid off" and can no longer feed them (Lawlor 2017: 49). The "bookkeeper's wife" disapproves and gives Paul, her favorite, "a sharp pocket knife and a compass" (Lawlor 2017: 50). Left at a trailhead and told to use their wits to reach the end, aesthete Paul—having rejected a "drab blue Cub Scout uniform"—assembles an appealing "bouquet of pretty sticks and flowers" while practical Polly builds a campfire in recognition that they "have been abandoned" (Lawlor 2017: 51–2). After Paul declines help from hikers and Polly rejects rides from creepy men, she accepts a lift in "a red convertible" from "[a] young woman in very large sunglasses" who buys them food and offers to take one of them "across the country" to a place "where only women and children live" (Lawlor 2017: 55). Polly saves herself by claiming the opportunity, stating that "Paul will only grow up to become a man, and he will have to leave then," whereas she will "never leave" (Lawlor 2017: 55). Paul, who cannot find a reason to go instead, offers her "the pocketknife and compass" after she tells him he "will be son and daughter to our parents now" (Lawlor 2017: 55).

This explanation, emphasizing Paul's vulnerability as well as his simultaneous assumption of the roles of "son" and "daughter," is followed in the second chapter by another foundling story, this one concerning "a sweet darling young wolf who lived alone in the forest and loved pretty things" (Lawlor 2017: 55, 55,

78). The latter tale, following immediately upon Paul's disclosure to Jane of his shape-shifting abilities, stresses the wolf's foundling status and cross-gender identifications, metaphors for Paul's traversals of gender and sexual identity. Of mixed parentage—"maybe partly coyote on his mother's side, or maybe his father was a fox"—the pup is raised by a "pack" after his mother's death (Lawlor 2017: 78). However, "he knew they did not mind his absence" when he left the "pack," which "found him easier to miss than accommodate" (Lawlor 2017: 78). After the young animal admires a cottager—an "old human woman" with "silver and red hair" who mates with "a bad-smelling woodsman"—an "old fox" teaches him how to mug a young woman for her "gorgeous, expensive-seeming blood-red cloak" (Lawlor 2017: 78–9). Donning it, he touches "his furless soft hands," puts on "the longed-for velvety red cloak, and" goes "to meet his beloved old human woman" (Lawlor 2017: 79). This foundling's cross-species heritage and desires disturbingly combine with his vulnerability, thieving, and sexualized violence to contrast to the first fairy tale's naïve and submissive Paul.

Whereas the second fairy tale uses the metaphor of cross-species mixing, the third uses a changeling to narrate abandonment. "A contractor and his wife" give birth to a long-desired baby, only to have him "swapped out" through fairies' secretive political maneuverings (Lawlor 2017: 102–4). The child they receive is part fairy and "part water sprite," the daughter of a fickle and imperious fairy Queen who has "hidden" her spawn "on an island in the forest lake" to be "raised by a kindly old otter" (Lawlor 2017: 104). Not realizing that their boy has been replaced with a girl, the human parents do not understand why their child becomes cantankerous when clad "in a tiny football costume," believing the resultant "howling" evidences a "temper" that has "spoiled" (Lawlor 2017: 104). The father, thinking there is "something wrong with" the "baby," assigns responsibility to "his wife" because "her family had always seemed odd to him"; he eventually "moves across the sea" to terminate contact (Lawlor 2017: 104–5).

The fate of this "mischievous" child, provided with both animal and human care, contrasts to that of the baby whose birth concludes the fourth chapter's fairy tale (Lawlor 2017: 104). Introduced while Paul is living in Provincetown as Polly, this story features a lonely young fisherman who inhabits a seaside "shack" and accumulates substantial "savings" (Lawlor 2017: 179). One morning the fish are so plentiful that he fills his boat early and remains at sea for pleasure. After a nap, he rescues a "swimmer"—"a beautiful woman, perhaps a few years older than himself," who accepts his invitation to dinner and sticks around, quickly pronouncing him her "husband" and becoming pregnant (Lawlor 2017: 180–1).

Without consulting her, he uses his savings to build "their new family" a home (Lawlor 2017: 182). Not suited to this "cottage on the land where his family's house had been, in the center of town," the fisherman's wife begins "to weep" and asks to "go home" to the shack (Lawlor 2017: 182-3). He asks that they stay and she initially submits, only to flee with the baby in the middle of the night.

This story is followed by other stories mythologizing his origins and explaining his decisions. In the fifth chapter, as he is en route to San Francisco, one such snippet uses realism to provide his mother's backstory. Like Paul, his mother—Theresa—is a wanderer. After a "year" of college, she gives up a "full scholarship" to move to Europe, always taking "the first" opportunities offered (Lawlor 2017: 212-13). Originally planning to settle in Paris, she instead follows Rosalie—an "Italian girl" from Queens—to Italy and Cyprus because her "free" approach to life distinguishes her from the stifled girls of Theresa's childhood (Lawlor 2017: 213). Mimicking the Italian-American, Theresa betrays her for the "English playboy" who "persuaded" them to go to Cyprus and then—after dancing like "Isadora Duncan" in a "new bar for tourists"—is impregnated by a "dark stranger" whose "accent" she isn't "sophisticated enough to identify" but who is "maybe Greek or Turkish" (Lawlor 2017: 213). Once geopolitical developments force Theresa back to the United States, she gives up her job "babysitting" for German "archaeologists" and returns with baby Paul to "the safe lie of home" (Lawlor 2017: 213, 216).

Adult Paul shares his mother's wanderlust, although he does not always accept "the first" jobs and living situations offered (Lawlor 2017: 212). He also differs from his mother—whose "safe lie" includes a failed marriage to a bookkeeper—by rejecting a boyfriend's offer of economic security and gay male normalcy (Lawlor 2017: 216). The open question of Paul's origins amplifies his inhabitation of the cultural "Borderlands," undermining monolithic understandings of national identity and intersecting with his queerness (Anzaldúa 1987: 77).

Paul's queering of gender and sexuality drives the plot of a sketch for a screenplay he drafts in San Francisco. Called "The Uncanny Ex-Man" and set in 1985, the story offers a fantastic spin on his and Theresa's backstories. It begins when a "barrel" filled with a "mysterious radioactive substance" falls from a "Cargo ship off the coast of Cyprus" and spills toxic "fluid" onto a "Moray eel" (Lawlor 2017: 266-7). This "nocturnal, cave-dwelling creature" is "known for its evolutionary cleverness—in a pinch, the Moray eel can CHANGE ITS SEX" (Lawlor 2017: 267). It eventually bites Paul, who—visiting Cyprus with a gay high school friend—probes into its cave to retrieve "a small trinket" given to him by a "Handsome College Boy" interested in a "Pretty College Girl" (Lawlor 2017: 270). After dreaming about being a dress-wearing "girl" invited "to prom" by "Handsome College Boy," Paul "wakes up" the next morning to find that "he IS a girl," but changes back before his friend awakens (Lawlor 2017: 270–1). This origin myth—providing an explanation for Paul's shape-shifting and channeling his desire into a hegemonic romantic script—reveals another fantasy he will traverse in the novel's realistic segments.

After one of the moments sparking Paul's traversal, the novel features a final fairy tale. Refusing national distinctions and stressing inclusion, this story begins when "poor farmers and their beasts" cross a "small mild sea" and are welcomed by the locals, who have "land to spare and a delight in the new" (Lawlor 2017: 317). The "king welcomed newcomers" because his "mother" had been an immigrant "and the lilt of the farmers' speech made him wistful for his childhood" (Lawlor 2017: 317). On a riding excursion, a prince—"the king's eldest son"—gets "tired of his companions" and runs away (Lawlor 2017: 317). His dogs conflict with "another pack" and he drives off the others so his animals may feast on their "freshly slain stag" (Lawlor 2017: 317–18). However, an "unknown king" confronts him and asks the prince to "defeat my rival;" the only "condition" is that the prince must do so by assuming the king's "form" (Lawlor 2017: 318). Once the prince agrees, he suddenly sees himself in the "mysterious king… as if he were gazing in a mirror": he "saw his own thick black hair, his own aquiline nose, his own scarred cheek" (Lawlor 2017: 318). Yet instead of urging the prince into battle, the king asks him to strip, foreshadowing three encounters with Robin that immediately follow. The last of those scenes reveals their shared ability to shape-shift and steers Paul away from the ontological questions driving his experimentation.

Questioning the Fantasy

Questioning Normative Fantasy

In the novel's realistic segments, Paul's peregrinations are driven by the search for an answer to the classic *Bildungsroman* question—"What *was* he?"—that he asks early on; the best comparison "he found was *Orlando*" (Lawlor 2017: 48, 74). Like Virginia Woolf's Orlando and Mitchell's Hedwig, Paul is not a realistic representation of a contemporary transgender or non-binary person; his shape-shifting embodiment makes him unique. He is born into and can initiate changes to his embodiment, whereas Orlando awakens unexpectedly transformed and Hedwig obtains surgery from an incompetent physician.

However, all three characters recreate themselves. Like transpeople, they live as genders other than those assigned at birth and deliberately stylize themselves to navigate their surroundings, finding new challenges in their reconfigured embodiments.

Although Paul's blurrings of binary gender recall Orlando's stay with androgynous gypsies and cross-dressed pursuit of English prostitutes, Paul nonetheless realizes that—unlike Woolf's protagonist—he isn't "some count slash ess who could just instruct the servants in his castle to be cool" (Lawlor 2017: 74). Paul is poor, so he must "think logistically" about survival (Lawlor 2017: 74). Whereas Orlando employs English eccentricity to navigate legal challenges brought on by becoming a woman, Paul does not fall back upon any stock personae. Instead, he insists upon being "willfully eccentric" in a country whose dominant culture aggressively pushes normativity (Halberstam 2005: 1).

Paul's uncertain parentage is also a source of internal and external conflict throughout the novel. As a teenager, he is taunted by classmates from "the model UN," who "coughed 'fag' at him in multiple languages" (Lawlor 2017: 150). This harassment—simultaneously targeting his gender, sexuality, and ethnicity—punctuates his young adulthood: he is frequently asked "What are you, Hispanic? Ay-rab? Are you a boy or a girl?" (Lawlor 2017: 71). On an Iowa City bus, he is bullied by small-town nationalists who treat him like a "freak" and ask if he speaks Spanish (Lawlor 2017: 101). Reflecting on this misattribution, "[h]e wished he had a good comeback, in Spanish or English. What was he going to say, 'Actually I'm half-Turkish, or maybe Greek, but my mom isn't really forthcoming about my biological father and maybe I'm just really dark Black Irish'" (Lawlor 2017: 101). Avoiding *Orlando*'s orientalism, Paul challenges such constructs, asking himself "what if I *was* Latina slash o?" and silently affirming that "by the way, yes, I am a giant queer who threatens your pathetic sense of knowing anything about the world" (Lawlor 2017: 101–2). This "so what?" moment reveals Paul's awareness that mixing can prompt the transformative "new consciousness" Anzaldúa theorizes (Anzaldúa 1987: 80).

By the novel's end, Paul has read widely in LGBTQ literature and learned that Robin is also of mixed heritage (Lawlor 2017: 298). However, Paul has not settled into a heteronormative or LGBTQ ideal of maturity, as typifies the *Bildungsroman*, but instead rejects adulthood's trappings. After romping in Iowa City's student district he visits his girlfriend Diane in Provincetown, noting when he stays on that he might be "growing up" and settling down with someone after having left his New York boyfriend Tony Pinto (Lawlor 2017: 186). But when Diane dumps him, he moves to San Francisco and repudiates this understanding of personal growth. He ironically comments on "adult" living spaces in the Haight and describes Noe Valley lesbians as possessed of "jobs with titles"; he declares himself interested neither in people who retain their religiously motivated self-hatred nor in "normal AT&T gays" (Lawlor 2017: 313, 302, 229). Noting that "[h]e strongly preferred to have sex with or talk to people who *liked* being queer," he declares that he does "not care to assimilate into the power structures of heteropatriarchal white Christian America, was bored and horrified by those who did" (Lawlor 2017: 229).

This rejection of assimilation informs Paul's critique of lesbians and gays whose normative schedules and life patterns capitulate to straight time. Praising San Francisco's "imaginative life schedules," he embraces the nightclubs, restaurants, and retail spaces Halberstam associates with "queer time": those "models of temporality that emerge within postmodernism once one leaves the temporal frames of bourgeois reproduction and family, longevity, risk/safety, and inheritance" (Halberstam 2005: 1–6). These temporalities are apparent from the novel's opening when Paul returns home after a night of Iowa City partying and asks his roommate, Christopher, "'What are you doing up'?" (Lawlor 2017: 19). Christopher retorts that "[i]n some cultures, people go to things called classes or jobs in the morning and sleep in the nighttime" (Lawlor 2017: 19).

Paul's refusal of straight time encompasses a broader critique of mainstream gay and lesbian prosperity. Visiting the Chicago Eagle bar, he ignores men arriving after having "gone home from their brokerage jobs in the Loop, changed into Garanimals-style Hellfire jackets and chaps, and come out to watch next year's International Mr. Leather contestants open bottles of beer" (Lawlor 2017: 57). In Provincetown, he describes the "Atlantic House" ("A-House") bar as identical to "everything else" there: "a stop on some rich person's historical landmark garden tour, with rent boys and leather daddies instead of docents and butlers" (Lawlor 2017: 165). He also derides a vacation home he is hired to paint, dismissing it as the "boxy Commercial Street condo of some closeted Back Bay lawyer" (Lawlor 2017: 183). In San Francisco, he criticizes Pride for catering to the "business gays" and describes his boyfriend Derek's friends as "boys with five-year plans" (Lawlor 2017: 308, 351). Critiquing the class politics of "globalized queer culture," Paul observes that he and Derek "attended and hosted dinner parties made up of other handsome young college-educated gay couples of all nations" (Nealon 2001: 9; Lawlor 2017: 346). Noticing Derek's "not-very-well-hidden embarrassment that Paul hadn't finished college and worked in retail," Paul looks skeptically on his boyfriend's suggestion that he should apply to Berkeley in addition to San Francisco State since he "might as well go to the better school" (Lawlor 2017: 345). These reactions all challenge the queer bourgeoisie's moneyed regularity and upward mobility.

Paul chooses "queer time" instead (Halberstam 2005: 1). Settling into his job at San Francisco's A Different Light bookstore, he notes that whereas "[h]e disliked arriving late, ... no one else minded": "[t]he store, the owners, the workers, the customers—everyone was on Gay Time" (Lawlor 2017: 243). He also visits a "dingy punk club on 16th street" and approvingly takes in its typical "Tuesday night crowd": "bike messengers, waiters, students," and "drug dealers—people who get by outside the work week" and exemplify the personae Halberstam associates with queer temporalities (Lawlor 2017: 223).

A nighttime excursion to one of San Francisco's edgier clubs prompts a particularly startling reversal of Djuna Barnes's association in *Nightwood* (1937) of queerness with misery and the night. Hiding "a packet of notepads" between "the metal bars of a shuttered limousine service office" so he can enter the bar, Paul imagines himself as "Night-Paul the package fairy" leaving gifts for "morning people" who "would feel but not understand the superiority of the night," not realizing that they could "just leave" the "soul-crushing jobs" forcing them up every morning (Lawlor 2017: 258).

Paul's eventual rejection of Derek confirms this repudiation of homonormativity. By the end of the novel, Paul has learned to support himself by his own wits and has found a person like himself, Robin: a shape-shifting, ethnically mixed artist who keeps a schedule as erratic as his own. In this sense, *Paul* is a *Künstlerroman* taking up where Joyce's *Portrait of the Artist as a Young Man* (1916) leaves off. Whereas Joyce's narrative ends with its protagonist's self-imposed exile from Ireland, Lawlor's begins partway through Paul's peregrinations after fleeing Troy. However, Joyce's Stephen Daedalus leaves for continental Europe "to encounter for the millionth time the reality of experience and to forge from the smithy of my soul the uncreated consciousness of my race"—to seek experience that could revitalize colonized Ireland in ways not dependent on racial purity, as Vincent Cheng argues (Cheng 1995; Joyce 1977: 252–3).[4] By contrast, the mixed-heritage, shape-shifting Paul searches for himself in the name of pleasure, love, and variety: not to renew nations or identity-formations but to queerly eschew them. Traversing the fantasies initially available to him, Paul rejects all available subject positions and uses artistry to anchor a mode of subjectivity in which his gender, sexuality, and ethnicity remain in flux.

Navigating the Fundamental Fantasy

Setting the Scene

In the novel's realist portions, Paul samples and rejects all available queer scenes before traversing the fantasy of (hetero)sexual difference. Enjoying these places' pleasures but avoiding their material trappings, he provides a test case for the conflicting theories of fantasy Lauren Berlant and Edelman debate in *Sex, or the Unbearable* (2014). Whereas Berlant argues that profound subjective transformation is possible by changing "movable" aspects of "the situation" (Berlant in Berlant and Edelman 2014: 124–5) and Edelman counters that radical change is only achievable by transforming "the subject rather than the subject's scene," I view *Paul* as exemplifying the way changes in "scene" can prompt the personal revolution Edelman seeks (Edelman in Berlant and Edelman 2014: 107–8).

Before traversing the fantasy of (hetero)sexual difference, Paul improves his life considerably through several changes of scene. Although his fluidity provides access to diverse sexual cultures, even LGBTQ scenes ultimately prove unsatisfactory no matter his location. Nor do his switches of scene—of gender, sexual orientation, lover, venue, domicile—fundamentally alter him. Although these changes position him to fall in love, he rejects romantic fantasy's futural orientation and imaginary props. Frequently confounding love and sex, he treats life as a "game" governed by "a single question: If you had to fall in love with (by which Paul meant have sex with) one person in this elevator, who would it be?" (Lawlor 2017: 36). Readers eventually learn that he has loved three people: Tony, Diane, and Derek. He falls for Tony and Diane by embracing their scenes: the former's AIDS activism in New York City and the latter's womyn-loving-womyn in Michigan and Provincetown. Derek's Castro scene of homonormative upward mobility lacks appeal from the start. These milieux are among many LGBTQ scenes Paul tries on and rejects before embracing the drive and traversing the fantasy of (hetero)sexual difference.

In Iowa City, Paul works multiple jobs that consume his attention and eclipse his studies. Later, he looks back on Iowa and remembers scenes superior to those available in coastal gay Meccas. Waiting for a date in San Francisco, he recalls the creativity he and others employed in the Midwest and realizes that "[h]e misse[s] Iowa, where necessity had mothered such charming invention" (Lawlor 2017: 259). Later, while attending a drag show, he notes that "He'd expected San Francisco fashion to be more daring than that of Iowa City, but the ped mall had been a nonstop fashion safari: punk-rock drag queens and dyke fashion models and boy poets in tight polyester Sansabelts and all those rhetoric or painting graduate students with their unpredictable fabric combinations" (Lawlor 2017: 323). Questioning San Francisco's privileged queer metronormativity, he suggests that "[m]aybe you had to be more inventive in the country; you had to learn to hem and rip and sequin, to sift through the cast-offs of the exotic manual laborers of middle America, those corn-husking teens, cereal factory third-shifters, and Monsanto janitors" (Lawlor 2017: 323). Although Paul has "to admit that he was impressed" by a "herd of space-child androgynes in Angela Bowie jumpsuits" at the drag show, his challenge to coastal queer hegemony reverberates throughout the novel (Lawlor 2017: 323).

At one point, Paul even goes with Jane as Polly to the notoriously transphobic Michigan Womyn's Music Festival to experiment with lesbian cultures. This distinguishes him from fairy-tale Paul, who concedes that he should not join Polly in a place "where only women and children live" (Lawlor 2017: 55). As Paul and Jane settle in at Michigan, he ambivalently evaluates lesbian stereotypes. Looking at the festivalgoers, he imagines himself "a time traveler, a tourist at a gay reenactment—Hidden-from-History-Town" (Lawlor 2017: 84). This formulation—disavowing its revelation of "Hidden" personae—includes "hippies and the sensitive punks from his earlier travels, and a raucous gang of obviously San Franciscan butches and extremely high femmes, but mostly... androgynous 70's lesbians, surprisingly appealing in their labrys necklaces and Rosie the Riveter tee shirts" (Lawlor 2017: 84).

Letting Jane pitch their tent, Paul insists that she is not "a Stepford lesbian just because they were at Michigan and she had all this secret knowledge of tents" (Lawlor 2017: 82). At another moment, he observes that the musical tastes of different LGBTQ populations reveal divergent approaches to women and queerness. Displaying the consciousness of an individual who would name his zine *Polydoris Perversity*, these remarks intervene in debates about sexual difference and queer theory's "anti-social thesis" (Caserio 2006: 819). As Paul recognizes, his "gayboy ideas of women who were *every* woman, women for whom no mountain was too high, women who remembered the way things were," risk idealizing the "Woman with a capital *W* indicating the universal" in Lacan's manner (Lacan 1998: 72; Lawlor 2017: 93). Yet far from capitulating to the phallogocentric idea that "[t]here's no such thing as Woman because... she is not-whole" but castrated, Paul goes on to observe the women around him (Lacan 1998: 72–3). The "hard sneering punks" (Lawlor 2017: 93) who mock his "love" of the band "L7" when he first arrives for his shift at the camp kitchen insist upon Edelmanian queer negativity, whereas mainstream lesbian singers mobilize an Irigarayan plurality of differences, challenging Lacan and Edelman alike (Lawlor 2017: 84). Going on to reflect on the "amber divas of lesbian melancholy," Paul distinguishes between "the woman who was driving away from something upsetting in a fast car, the one who was closer to being fine, the one for whom life was a brook, and all the others" (Lawlor 2017: 93). His observations about the varied festivalgoers—"the tattooed love children, the women's studies professors, the raucous catcallers, the quiet swayers, the breastfeeders, the cliques of the fat-positive and the scent-free, the disability activists and the suburbanites"—position him to question Jane's attitude toward Midwestern women "she imprecisely" dismisses as "softball players" in "labrys jewelry" and "Indigo Girls tee shirts" (Lawlor 2017: 95, 95, 95, 95, 36). Even though he eventually falls back into stereotypes upon their return to Iowa City, imagining Jane "cuddling" at home with a "*barista*" rather than nightclubbing, at the Festival he notices lesbians' diversity (Lawlor 2017: 119).

Jane and Paul both use the Festival to fulfill fantasies, with limited success. Jane, a high femme who feels invisible in Iowa, signs up to work "security in a scheme to meet butches" and quickly meets a "Flat-Top" named "Frog" (Lawlor 2017: 83). Frog, "the star top ... of the Austin SM scene," indulges Jane's desire to "act out" her "best-loved, most-read-about sex-positive feminist fantasies": being "whipped," ordered to engage in "[b]oot-licking," and permitted to participate in a "[p]ublic ejaculation contest" in which she wins "second place" (Lawlor 2017: 99). Nonetheless, Frog fails to enact Jane's fantasy of staying overnight: not "to *cuddle*," she insists, but to get "her brains screwed out ... to be fucked so thoroughly that she couldn't think" (Lawlor 2017: 99). She leaves the Festival unsatisfied.

Paul, on the other hand, meets Diane while working in the kitchen as Polly. Even though he is just at the festival as "a lark, to pass, to pass among all these women, to sleep with a bunch of people," Diane starts "looking at him" expectantly and he quickly develops the kinds of "girl-feelings" that come from not knowing how to interpret her suggestion that they "hang out" (Lawlor 2017: 87–9). After a series of encounters allowing Paul to experience the pleasures afforded by female anatomy—his soft "breasts," his vagina's "pounding thrum," the "sloshy" feeling building to a "violent universal bang" once Diane goes down on him—he realizes that their connection is more than sexual (Lawlor 2017: 89–90). Near the end of the Festival, they share the hope that they will not "die" until they are "very old," and Paul recognizes that he has "never said 'we' to anyone before, not even Tony Pinto" (Lawlor 2017: 98). As he and Jane drive back to Iowa City, he confesses that he "might love" Diane (Lawlor 2017: 99). Their incipient love, formed through sexual experimentation rather than romantic fantasy, hinges on the idea of a future that—remaining uncertain at the Festival's end—eventually takes Diane to Iowa City and Paul to Provincetown.

Gender and Anamorphosis in the Fantasy: Desiring Malleable Genders

As Paul searches for himself and moves closer to fantasy's traversal, his ability to alter his embodiment leads to scenes in which he becomes subject to anamorphic perceptions arising from the gaze. His mixed ethnic background amplifies these visual effects. He elicits a variety of reactions, from the "type of man" who "disapproves of him and will not say why" to the "type of woman… who will reach out and stroke Paul's face" to those who stop him "on the street and ask him" inappropriate questions "straight out": "What are you, Hispanic? Ay-rab? Are you a boy or a girl?" (Lawlor 2017: 71). Deploying what Judith Roof calls "vantage"—the way changes in viewpoints and expectations affect readings of "gender signifiers" in the play between the "look" and the "gaze"—these reactions make Paul a fulcrum of anamorphic perceptions (Roof 2016: 79–81).[5]

As Paul changes into Polly in a bathroom in the Providence bus station on the way to meet Diane in Provincetown, an "elderly lady" initially gives him a "subtle double take" and looks "relieved" when he emerges from a stall "all breasted up," ready to "apply eyeliner and creamy bright pink lipstick" (Lawlor 2017: 154). Returning to the vehicle, he expects somebody to react to the fact that the "*swishy gay boy*" is now wearing an "orange plaid mod sweater dress," but he is left alone (Lawlor 2017: 154). Theorizing that "[p]eople saw what they wanted to see and wanted to see what they expected to see"—that is, that what is seen depends on viewers' positionality—Paul realizes that he "could do whatever he wanted" (Lawlor 2017: 154). It is as if Paul—whose friend Jane reads "book[s] on the Gaze"—intuitively understands that anamorphosis can result from changes in "vantage" (Lawlor 2017: 10; Roof 2016: 79–81).

Shifts in perception also inflect scenes in which Paul displays "malleability" to others (Lawlor 2017: 74). When he reveals himself to Jane to demonstrate his capacity to pass as female in Michigan, she initially believes he is "tucking" (Lawlor 2017: 76). He has to spread his legs, allow Jane to "smell" his genitalia, and show her "his clit" transforming back into "a cock" as his "labia" turn into "a nutsack" to convince her (Lawlor 2017: 76). Once at the Festival, lesbian sex helps Paul coax his body into femaleness. The morning after he first sleeps with Diane, he wakes up with a "piss hard-on" and tries to change "back into his girl body," but can't "get beyond the breasts" (Lawlor 2017: 91–2). In the woods "with his hand covering his half-hard dick," he must ejaculate before urinating; only afterwards does his "vagina return, still dripping piss" (Lawlor 2017: 92). On this occasion, thinking "of Diane" while ejaculating makes him desire "more of whatever" is at the Festival (Lawlor 2017: 92). But later—after having sex all night and surrounding Diane's "tent" with a supply "fort"—Paul is able to hold "his girl body for five days straight" while "sleeping lightly" next to her (Lawlor 2017: 96). One morning, "still in girl form," he gets up to pee and lets "hot urine spill out of somewhere in his vagina, a little turned on by the pressure" (Lawlor 2017: 96). Yet shortly thereafter, he returns to Iowa City and resumes life as Paul.

Anamorphosis also attends Diane's perceptions of Paul when she pursues him in Iowa after having had sex with him as Polly—and she finds those perceptions quite unsettling. Seeing Paul bartending, Diane squints "in confusion" and starts "staring" at him in what he recognizes is "not... a good way" (Lawlor 2017: 122). Fearing "another dramatic revelation scene like the one he'd had with Jane, the kind of scene he always fast-forwarded," he takes Diane outside, shows her his capacity to shape-shift, and invites her to touch his womanly face (Lawlor 2017: 123). Repudiating his claim that "I'm like you," Diane retorts that he isn't because she doesn't "lie" (Lawlor 2017: 123). When he insists that the matter isn't "that simple" and starts to "change back," she looks at him in shock (Lawlor 2017: 123–4). When he comments that "They all just think I do really good drag sometimes," Diane sarcastically replies "Yeah... You're really good" (Lawlor 2017: 124).

Seeing Paul's panic when he returns to the bar, a friend takes over his shift so he can leave with Diane. At home, he admits that he "should've told" her about his embodiment, yet ruminates about the transphobic Festival rules dictating that he "*couldn't*" (Lawlor 2017: 124). After a standoff, Diane reiterates that Paul is "a liar" and states that he "knew" she "wouldn't want to be with a man" (Lawlor 2017: 125). Paul retorts that "I don't *know* what I am—so how is that lying? I mean, I'm obviously not some *man*. Jesus!" (Lawlor 2017: 125). Reiterating that "I'm not what you think," he insists that in another sense, "I *am* what you think, what you thought" in Michigan: "the girl who can't stop thinking about you, the girl who wants to be your girlfriend" (Lawlor 2017: 126).

This conversation resolves their conflict by distinguishing between the material body and subjective embodiment. Paul's body may default to male whenever he is not working to present as female, and others may refer to him with he/him pronouns (rather than they/them pronouns) when he is not being viewed as Polly: but these things do not make him the same thing as a "'*man*'" (Lawlor 2017: 125). Nor does his capacity for male embodiment make him any less of a woman when he is presenting as one. Paul's embodiment literalizes Salamon's distinction between the material contours of a person's body and their subjective sense of embodiment (Salamon 2010).

That is, Paul becomes recognizable as Polly not only because he willfully alters his body's features but also because he experiences himself and is recognized by others as her. Beyond the female embodiment he assumes in Michigan, what attracts Diane to Paul is his subjective sense of femaleness: of being a "girl" seeking lesbian sex and a lesbian relationship (Lawlor 2017: 126). Diane is attracted to the pleasure he takes in being a woman: an attitude matching her own.

This exchange temporarily resolves Paul's and Diane's conflict, strengthening their relationship before it collapses in Provincetown. At one point, examining himself in light of "*Our Bodies, Ourselves*" with "a plastic speculum and a flashlight," he concludes that he has "all the parts just like in the book"—his "vagina" has a "clit, peephole, fuckhole, g-spot" and feels "to his fingers like Diane's insides" (Lawlor 2017: 194). His "vagina did everything advertised but bleed" (Lawlor 2017: 195). Nonetheless, his and Diane's divergent relationships to the fantasy of (hetero)sexual difference eventually reach an impasse.

Paul's ability to remember what it is like to live in different embodiments and change them at will distinguishes him from monogender people. This fluidity and agency distinguish his psyche from those of transpeople seeking to live as a singular gender. His psyche registers his multiplicity. He feels that because "[h]is body did whatever he wanted, … he belonged in all the genders," and doesn't understand the tendency of "[s]traight people" to be "confused by each other": "so anxious to find camaraderie within their gender, so startled by differences between their bodies, always pinning explanations for the inevitable gulf between humans on chromosomes" (Lawlor 2017: 193). Critiquing straight people for believing that unbridgeable differences are anatomical and chromosomal rather than linguistic and cultural, he presents them as symptoms of a larger problem that "confound[s]" him: the way "[m]en and women" are "so rule-bound" (Lawlor 2017: 193). That is, he critiques widespread captivation by the fantasy of (hetero)sexual difference.

Considering Diane to represent a lesbian variation on this theme, he notes that "[s]he never mentioned what she once called" his "body of origin" because she takes women as given, as "the norm" (Lawlor 2017: 193). She seeks the same land as the "young woman" in the novel's opening fairy tale who is driving to a place "where only women and children live" (Lawlor 2017: 55). A way of seeking "camaraderie" within a single "gender," this position represents another mode of normativity (Lawlor 2017: 193).

Paul recognizes that Diane—like straight people—desires a single gender whereas he is attracted to her multiplicity. He eventually admits that "[h]e'd imagined Diane as a boy, and loved her" because she reminds him of "a child sailor, a red-cheeked, creamy-skinned European boy" (Lawlor 2017: 228, 191). Although only Paul's perceptions of Diane are changeable—and not her body itself—his anamorphic view of her reveals his attraction to changeability. Diane, however, is more singular in her attractions and identity.

Complaining that Diane wants him to be her "sidekick" and join him "elsewhere" in a world driven by animal rights activism to which he is indifferent, Paul insists that he prefers to "dress himself variously" for diverse gazes: to engage in gender performances as plural as the embodiments he assumes (Lawlor 2017: 190-2). Although Paul thoroughly explores "lesbianism"—at one point, getting ready to fuck Diane with a dildo, he affirms to himself that "[h]e wanted to do *all* the lesbianism"—it ultimately does not satisfy him, as Diane recognizes (Lawlor 2017: 198). He orgasms during the encounter by "imagining" himself putting "his flesh dick into Diane"; she realizes that he is "really into it" and likely wants to do "it the other way" (Lawlor 2017: 199-200). Shortly thereafter, they break up because Diane has recognized that Paul wishes "to be everything, all the time," whereas she only wants one thing (Lawlor 2017: 206). Citing his desire for mutability, she states that she doesn't want to suppress his "nature," and lets him go (Lawlor 2017: 206). Paul seeks to traverse the fantasy of (hetero)sexual difference in whose lesbian variant Diane remains.

Gender and Anamorphosis in the Fantasy: Policing Malleable Genders

As Diane's rejection of Paul's mutability suggests, normative gender rules sometimes cause anamorphic perceptions to take on an ambivalent or outright unappealing cast. Jane, for example, dislikes Diane, who "never once acknowledged her": an omission that is "at best a violation of the ancient laws of hospitality and at worst a serious misunderstanding of a butch's job" (Lawlor 2017: 134). Paul, too, is unsure how to read Diane's gender. In Provincetown, he observes chivalrous aspects of her demeanor and considers the possibility that

"*She*"—unlike Jane—"thought he was a femme" (Lawlor 2017: 176). He notes that she enjoys watching him wear dresses and that "she liked that he was girlier than her, liked that she was so much bigger than him, liked to do little things for him," yet also "sometimes… did wonder if she liked liking what she liked" (Lawlor 2017: 174). This suggestion that Diane may be suffering from butch self-hatred is echoed by one member of an older butch/femme couple and seconded by "snicker[ing]" college dykes while they are out one evening (Lawlor 2017: 162–3). After a "butch lounge singer" campily asks Diane and Paul "[w]ho is the *man* in your little ménage?" the "glamorous femme comedian" ironically counters that "[t]hey just want to be free" and tells the butch to "leave those nice young people alone" (Lawlor 2017: 162–3).

Paul nonetheless dismisses this suggestion that Diane is playing conflicted butch to his femme. Instead, he decides that they are "tuff girls" after observing her clothing: "tighty whities" under "workpants" (Lawlor 2017: 197, 162). This concept first enters his mind as the letters "t-u-f-f" when he realizes that she rejects butch/femme culture but not the distinction between man and woman (Lawlor 2017: 191). She may renounce (hetero)sexual difference's dichotomized understanding of masculinity and femininity in its heterosexual and lesbian iterations, but considers females "the norm" (Lawlor 2017: 193). Paul, by contrast, revels in expansiveness that eventually takes him beyond the fantasy of (hetero)sexual difference and singular gender identities.

Yet embracing gender malleability does not immunize Paul from the gender policing so common in LGBTQ communities. Words such as "faggy" and "faggotry" appear throughout the novel when divergent expectations mobilize anamorphic perceptions of gender. At Michigan, for instance, Paul and Jane get into an altercation when she declares that he is going to "have to rein in the faggotry" to pass (Lawlor 2017: 92). When he insists that Polly is "femme"—something Diane can see, if not name—Jane retorts that he isn't "a femme… Trust me" (Lawlor 2017: 92). This exchange, turning on divergent lesbian and gay male understandings of "femme," anticipates the way Polly and Diane are received in Provincetown (Lawlor 2017: 92).

Later, in San Francisco, Paul derides a "faggy butch" who works at Café Flore (Lawlor 2017: 299). This phrase first appears when Robin is enthusiastically greeted by a "counterperson," "a faggy butch with… a septum piercing, like a *bull*" (Lawlor 2017: 299). Whereas Paul is attracted to Robin's unreadable gender, he finds the "mincing" of the "counter butch" offputting, interpreting it as "fake" and aesthetically objectionable "gender-bending" (Lawlor 2017: 300). Comparing the latter to a gay man who talks about "football teams" to hide his desire to dress in "a cheerleader uniform," Paul assumes that she is self-hating and cloaking her own masculinity by acting "more campy" than she actually is (Lawlor 2017: 300). Similarly, while chasing Robin at a drag show, he indulges in stereotypes that "[b]utches must be working class, ideally also vaguely alcoholic, with an undercoat of physical menace, whereas femmes could be—maybe even *should* be—from privileged backgrounds, slumming it in collective houses" (Lawlor 2017: 325). At these moments Paul, like Jane, temporarily capitulates to LGBTQ gender norms and fails to consider that the café worker is resignifying gender (Lawlor 2017: 92).

Later at Flore, Paul revises this opinion in light of the politics of queer visibility. Noting the femininity of the "counter girl," he complains that she does "not achieve that true androgyny some butches have, where you look once and see a boy, look again and see a girl, look again for the pleasure of the trompe l'oeil"—that is, for what I have been calling gender anamorphosis (Lawlor 2017: 315). This time, however, Paul recognizes the reason for the girl's self-presentation: she is "one of the many femmes who'd moved to the city and cut off her hair to partake of the urban pleasures" of a city in which a queer woman "with long hair wouldn't register in a quick scan" whereas "[a] dyke with short hair was noticeable even from across the street" (Lawlor 2017: 315). But after distinguishing in detail between butches and short-haired femmes, Paul introduces a new complaint about queer female genders. Remarking that ears with "[o]ne or even two silver piercing hoops could still signify butch," he continues that "then you were also getting into SM territory, and SM butch in some cases = less masculine butch" (Lawlor 2017: 315). Commenting that "[t]here was something a little faggy about someone who made a point to identify as a top, instead of just *being* a top," he compares SM butches to the men he encounters in the gay male leather scene, who also costume for their roles (Lawlor 2017: 315). This commentary—which, at first glance, may look like it is turning a slur on its head and complimenting SM butches—instead shames all SM queers for performing femininity.

As repetitions of Paul's dispute with Jane over his gender presentation at Michigan, these remarks reveal the way conflicts between gay male and lesbian genders can manifest between different members of those communities and from within individual psyches. These perceptual clashes—far more unsettling than the gender anamorphoses attracting Paul—can simultaneously produce visual dissonance and elicit bias. The scenes at Flore show that Paul is not free of prejudices, despite his ability to alter his embodiment and experience multiple LGBTQ scenes.

Gender and Anamorphosis in the Fantasy: Embracing Malleability

Paul's conflicted attitude toward gender resignification resolves when he becomes friends with Robin, who serves as an important nexus of desire and identification throughout the novel. Robin appears in Paul's life as part of the latter's pattern of attraction to the anamorphic spectacle of others' malleable genders. Their interactions spark Paul's traversal of the fantasy of (hetero)sexual difference, prompting him to go beyond normative fantasies animating queer gender policing.

Throughout the novel, Paul chases and stares at the shape-shifting Robin, who initiates their interactions by "staring" at and circling Paul on the dance floor of a Chicago bar (Lawlor 2017: 60). Intrigued by this "elven... boy," Paul follows Robin like "quarry" once the club closes (Lawlor 2017: 60–1). But after the "youth" raises his "eyebrow" at Paul, he comes to believe that Robin is, "without question," a girl (Lawlor 2017: 61–2). Robin later appears in Provincetown and San Francisco in various eye-catching embodiments.

The novel's structure builds on Paul's anamorphic perceptions of Robin, creating the sense that their friendship is fated. Unlike a trans coworker named Franky—whom Paul considers potential kin before realizing that by transitioning, his colleague has chosen "what he wanted forever"—Robin functions as Paul's double throughout the novel (Lawlor 2017: 260). In Iowa, Paul reflects that "[t]he youth" he trailed through Chicago's streets "was like him, must be," and pursues Robin again each time they cross paths (Lawlor 2017: 68).

In Provincetown, Robin appears in the A-house right as Paul is caught up in his desire to be Polly, "to be girls together with" the "hot tomboy" Diane (Lawlor 2017: 166). After an "older bear" helps them obtain drinks from a sexist bartender, Paul notices Robin in a "daddy-boy couple" as a gay male porn star's "boy-toy" (Lawlor 2017: 166–7). In an identificatory moment, Paul realizes that Robin "had definitely been a girl when they'd last seen each other" in Chicago (Lawlor 2017: 167). Flush with desire, Paul is possessed by "free-floating jealousy" of the man monopolizing Robin's "gaze" (Lawlor 2017: 167–8).

Later, in San Francisco, Paul sees Robin in Flore and admits to feeling like "*some clueless straight person*" who cannot tell between "male or female" (Lawlor 2017: 300). After considering Robin's style and looking at "the usual" bodily "tells"—"pores, throat, hands, feet, hips, chest, package, eyebrows, knuckle hair"—Paul admits that his study is "inconclusive" and that his fascination is heightened by Robin's ambiguity (Lawlor 2017: 300). Later, cruising at a drag show, Paul embraces his desire to "plumb the mystery of Robin's sometimes-slitty-sometimes-saucer eyes," whose anamorphic play attracts him like "a mirror looked into from an angle" (Lawlor 2017: 323–4).

These desires for and identifications with Robin intensify as the narrative progresses and crystallize Paul's emergence as a gender-bending, sexually fluid, ethnically mixed artist. Their budding friendship prompts the novel's concluding shift in consciousness. Although at one point Robin teases Paul with a flirtatious question—"I can't decide if we should become lovers or best friends"—it eventually becomes clear that whereas Paul desires Robin, the latter does not reciprocate (Lawlor 2017: 343). Instead, Robin functions as Paul's object *a*, crystallizing his perpetually unfulfilled desire and emblematizing the artistic self-creation for which he is poised at the novel's end.

When Paul and Robin finally talk, Robin calls out Paul for "chas[ing] me through the streets of Chicago" and "staring at me on New Year's at the A-House, with your girlfriend right there" (Lawlor 2017: 311–12). Yet instead of rejecting Paul, Robin recognizes their similarity and befriends him. With a teasing comment that "[y]ou like San Francisco" but are "also hiding here," Robin heightens the air of "mystery" that initially attracts Paul (Lawlor 2017: 312, 313, 323). Paul, in turn, perceives Robin as "a very powerful magician" whose power he desires (Lawlor 2017: 301).

En route to the drag show, Paul imagines that "Robin was more a portal than a person; if Paul could get through Robin he'd know something new on the other side" (Lawlor 2017: 319). Later, when Robin arrives at an ACT UP fundraiser, Paul reacts as if heavenly bells are ringing. He notices that "Robin walked in and the brass section blew its bold angelic chorus, a great unseen remote changed the channel of the universe. Robin walked directly over as if they were friends, as if Robin were meeting Paul here, as if they had an *assignation*" (Lawlor 2017: 328). As this metaphor suggests, Paul is trying to "get through Robin" to traverse the fantasy of (hetero)sexual difference and transform into "something new" (Lawlor 2017: 319).

Traversing the Fantasy, Going beyond the Scene

These encounters with Robin prepare Paul to traverse the fantasy of (hetero) sexual difference; they also reveal his libidinal investment in those who go beyond heteronormative and homonormative genders. Paul's attitude toward the Bay Area shifts as he acclimates. As a new arrival, he takes in San Francisco's varied scenes, his reactions ranging from identificatory approval to disinterest to disdain. Uninterested in the Castro's "would-be daddies" with their mainstream "Dockers and braided belts," he seeks out subcultural spaces (Lawlor 2017: 250). Yet his initial praise of a "dingy punk club on 16th street" showcasing characters embracing "queer time" eventually turns to avoidance of "his roommates, his roommates' friends, the punk rock queers he saw on Mission street, … the muscley bike messenger dykes and the twiggy tattooed fags and bi-curious boys who'd be with the dykes, as cover" (Halberstam 2005: 1, 250–1; Lawlor 2017: 223). Once Paul realizes they might include Diane, these scenes lose appeal and he seeks out edgier "gay bars where the boys he liked wouldn't be" (Lawlor 2017: 251).

Although Paul pursues pleasure in a variety of queer and non-queer venues, his visits to Eagle bars bring him closest to embracing a scene (Lawlor 2017: 251). Eagles enable him to traverse the fantasy and temporarily experience subjective dispossession. He initially caters to but eventually distances himself from sceney aspects of leather bars, focusing on using them to tap into the *jouissance* of the Real in ways that are foreshadowed during his time in Iowa City. Paul and Jane encounter the concept of *jouissance* as students: she reflects on Leo Bersani's account of its role in bottoming; he praises its figuration on album covers during a fantasized seduction of a straight classmate and then travels to Chicago to fulfil his desire to be "rent" by leathermen (Lawlor 2017: 59).

The trip to Chicago would best be described as Midwestern sex tourism: upon arriving, Paul goes directly to Boystown "looking for the gays" (Lawlor 2017: 56). Paul seeks out the Eagle because he wants to be mentored: "to see what leather guys did with leather guys… to find a hot young top who would show him how to be" (Lawlor 2017: 56–7). On his way to the Eagle, he stops at a café to stash his backpack and transform into "a taller, more muscled, and slightly hairier version of himself" (Lawlor 2017: 56). He also places a copy of Michel Foucault's *Discipline and Punish* in "his pocket" where "any guy who saw it would assume it was porn" (Lawlor 2017: 56). Paul's self-stylization works: the staff at the Eagle don't "even card him" because he looks "so right" (Lawlor 2017: 56). Finding himself among older gay professionals in blue-collar clothing, he cannot find the back room, complains to himself that "[n]o one was being flogged," and reflects on his disproven assumption that "a leather bar in Chicago would be populated exclusively by young Henry-Rollins-looking firemen and stevedores who'd immediately invite him to the dungeon" (Lawlor 2017: 57). Ignoring the cliquish customers, he uses a generous tip to express interest in the "barman," whose "Marlon-Brando-in-*The-Wild-Ones* hat, leather vest with no shirt, and leather chaps over a yellowed jock strap" appeal (Lawlor 2017: 57).

Fucked by the bartender in the back room as numerous patrons watch, Paul observes to himself that "[h]e *wanted* this feeling of being rent" (Lawlor 2017: 59, emphasis added). He *desires* the encounter with the Real that would prompt subjective destitution (Lawlor 2017: 59).

After being fucked, Paul exits "into the feral night of Boystown, where beefy accountants and tender satyrs" mix "on the sidewalks on their way to the next wild time" (Lawlor 2017: 59). In a bar catering to a young crowd, his body morphs back into its regular proportions. The next time Paul enters an Eagle, he is in San Francisco and doesn't change his appearance to fit a fantasy about the scene. Saying "[f]uck it" to the idea of morphing his body or costuming himself to fit BDSM culture, "[h]e didn't bother to make himself into a big hot cub or a dirty boy scout or a young dad type" (Lawlor 2017: 251). Whereas in Chicago, Paul's visit to the Eagle dethrones fantasies about leather life, leading him to submit to the drive and experience subjective dispossession, in San Francisco Paul uses the Eagle to go beyond mainstream and subcultural queer fantasies: to give himself over to the imaginative opening that emerges once he relinquishes bodily control.

However, to access this experience, Paul must first navigate the Eagle's hostility to newcomers. He arrives not dressed in any of the gay male leather subculture's uniforms but in an outfit marking him as an indie dyke. Recognizing that he is not "even dressed right," he looks at "[h]is Levi's… cords and… old Revolution Girl Style Now!" T-shirt, beginning to suspect that his appearance is offputting because it reminds the daddies of their "teenage daughters" (Lawlor 2017: 252). Initially ignored by staff and patrons alike, he is eventually hailed as "*miss*" and pre-emptively admonished by the bartender that the Eagle doesn't "serve lite beer" (Lawlor 2017: 252). Responding by ordering a Jack Daniels, Paul reflects on the bullying hypermasculinity of the "big tough leathermen," who try "to act how they thought construction workers would act" by "pissing in troughs, beating each other up and off, drinking shitty beer, and hazing" him (Lawlor 2017: 252). Denying his attraction to these personae, he tries unsuccessfully to gain their attention. After butching up with a Marlboro Red, he grows "his cock" (Lawlor 2017: 252–3). Realizing that "[n]o one was looking at him" despite his newfound bulk, he fills up on water, goes to the bathroom, and heads to a urinal to display himself (Lawlor 2017: 254). After his splattering attracts attention from several men who praise his "[h]oly" cock, he receives free drinks at the bar (Lawlor 2017: 254).

Later, in the back room, Paul gives himself over to the other patrons, allowing his "body" to become "a product to be constructed by" an "assembly line of deft fingers" (Lawlor 2017: 255). Foreshadowing the novel's closing passage, he loses himself in the experience. Extending the subjective destitution he achieves in Chicago, he experiences no pain and achieves a dreamlike state. Remembering that he has already paid rent and is unencumbered by possessions, he realizes that he is "free" and allows himself to "float" while imagining himself a beauty supported by "*Belle et la Bête* hands" (Lawlor 2017: 255). Fond recollections of his bohemian Alamo Square home—his bedroom's "blue walls" and "morning sunlight," the house's "lemon tree in the backyard," the neighborhood's "honeysuckle alleys" and "taco cart on the corner"—eventually give way to memories of his room's coldness, and he realizes that "he'd go sleep there later tonight or tomorrow," in his thrifted "sleeping bag," "alone and cold," because "no one had heat in San Francisco" (Lawlor 2017: 255). Nonetheless, warmed by the leathermen's touch, which emerges only after "hazing," Paul imagines himself as a queer project under construction (Lawlor 2017: 252). Going beyond his experience of subjective dispossession in Chicago, whose Eagle he enters at the price of tolerating the "loss" of his backpack, Paul's dreamlike traversal of fantasy in the San Francisco bar sets the stage for the opening offered in the novel's final scene (Lawlor 2017: 56).

It is in these two Eagles that Paul most overtly submits to the drive and engages the Real, embracing submission but vacillating about taking pleasure in pain. Late in the narrative, he complains about "chaps" as a signifier of "the BDSM lifestyle" and specifies what he will and will not accept: "Fetish, yes; outfits, yes! Pain, no" (Lawlor 2017: 305). He suggests that he selectively embraces specific BDSM stylizations, but that he doesn't "believe in doing something painful in order to get a pleasure reward," as would a masochist—or so he claims (Lawlor 2017: 321). Ambivalence is evident in his trip to Chicago to be "rent" by the leatherman and in his admission of pleasure in being the receptive partner in "anal sex" with Tony (Lawlor 2017: 59, 321). Of the latter, he explains that "the pain did feel sort of good, ... partly because he also felt Tony Pinto's good feeling" (Lawlor 2017: 321). This response to anal sex registers the drive's multiplicity.

The specificity of Paul's tastes is less important than the way the novel uses BDSM to figure an otherwise unfigurable drive. Refusing to be bound by binaries, he takes himself beyond all available scenes. Becoming far more than the *sinthom*osexual he plays in Eagles, *sinthom*estizx Paul traverses the fantasies figured through those scenes and embraces subjective destitution. Simultaneously entailing symbolic death and rebirth, unraveling reinvigorates his capacity for life. These moments of dispossession stay with him throughout the novel.

Traversing the Fundamental Fantasy: From Scene to Drive and Back

Embracing the Drive's Vicissitudes

After Paul's experiences of subjective destitution in Eagles, the drive's vicissitudes continue to push the narrative forward while leaving unresolved questions. Paul's lust for life propels his movements yet also cloaks the possibility of his untimely death: of his undoing by HIV. Paul is well aware of this threat, his reason for leaving New York City for the supposedly safer Midwestern pastures he initially "scorn[s]" (Lawlor 2017: 153). Lawlor stresses his attention to managing risk: in Provincetown, he notes that "[h]e'd taken all the tests, plenty of times" and learned so many "times" that "[h]e was negative, negatory" that "he was positive he was not positive" (Lawlor 2017: 196). These hyperbolic disavowals foreshadow Paul's denials of the lapses occurring throughout the novel's second half (Lawlor 2017: 196).

Paul's denial comes to a head in San Francisco. Thinking that "New York was punk, harder, more fatal," he asks himself, "[W]hat bad thing could happen to a person in San Francisco" while evading "the eyes of the wasting men who took the bus up to the free clinic in the Haight" (Lawlor 2017: 255–6). Asking, "[W]as he immune or did he want to die," he reflects on his night at the San Francisco Eagle and reassures himself that while he "let some man touch him, suck him," he "didn't touch" others: "[y]ou couldn't catch anything from getting blown or fondled," he tries to tell himself, "[n]o matter what the flyers said" (Lawlor 2017: 256). He will be fine, he believes, because "[h]e refused to fuck anyone… or to get fucked… or to blow anyone" (Lawlor 2017: 256).

Shortly after these denials, Paul breaks his self-imposed rules on a date with Franky. Although Paul's reflections initially mix his reservations about Franky with worries about an increase in Tony's "strangely formal" messages, Paul eventually penetrates Franky without protection, but denies it (Lawlor 2017: 261). Subsequent scenes show Paul continuing to refuse to return calls from Tony, the only man with whom Paul had anal sex before his encounter with the Chicago bartender. Finally listening to Tony's messages one night while drinking heavily, Paul assumes that Tony wants him to "come back" (Lawlor 2017: 272). Paul fantasizes about returning to Tony, but instead of calling goes on an all-night bender ending with public sex and then breakfast with a hippie. Returning home, Paul finds a message from Tony's mother, prompting a question culminating in disavowal: "Why was Tony Pinto's mother calling?

He knew and he didn't know" (Lawlor 2017: 283). Paul immediately phones the Pintos. When Tony's gruff father answers that "[t]here's no Tony here" and hangs up, Paul imagines that Tony is "in deep shit" because his father has "found out he was gay" (Lawlor 2017: 284). Calling back and getting Tony's mother, Paul learns that his ex-lover is dead.

Tony's death sparks guilt-ridden memories revealing vulnerabilities Paul remains unwilling to admit. Comparing himself unfavorably to black sex radical Samuel Delany and to a New Yorker named Rainier who had cared for his dying boyfriend, Paul admits that he "abandoned his first love to the stinking deck of the beautiful plague ship" and "fled in cowardice" (Lawlor 2017: 296). Whereas "Delany at nineteen had seen hundreds of men fucking and had jumped in, had been pure body, Paul at nineteen had seen hundreds of people lying down in the streets, dying-in, and had run away" (Lawlor 2017: 298). At this point Paul's lies, denials, and evasions become apparent. Recognizing "that he had failed," he asks himself, "[W]hat do you do after you fail the test and you're still alive?" (Lawlor 2017: 297). Paul responds by recentering his life around reading and working. When his roommate Ruffles observes, "[Y]ou're a changed man," Paul responds, "I'm not a man" (Lawlor 2017: 298). This response insists on Paul's malleability by repeating his insistence to Diane that "I'm obviously not some *man*" and—for the first time—acknowledges the downside of his Halberstamian refusal of adulthood: his failure to come through for others (Lawlor 2017: 125).

However, even this loss and the realization that Ruffles and his friends "were all going to die" do not stop Paul from imagining that he is immune from HIV; he continues to insist that, "full of grace," he will not become infected (Lawlor 2017: 326). Given the naïveté Paul exhibits with regard to a question answered in the book's title—which labels him a "*Mortal Girl*"—one cannot help but sense that the death drive is covertly implicated in what is in so many other ways his desire for life.

Concluding by stressing the drive's double-edgedness, Lawlor's novel goes beyond queer theory's polarized debates about the "anti-social thesis" (Caserio 2006: 819). As Tim Dean observes, the drive may be destructive, constructive, or some combination thereof. It may raze lifeworlds or spark creative new modes of "sociability… not grounded in imaginary identity or the struggle for intersubjective recognition" (Dean 2006: 827). Similarly emphasizing the drive's unpredictability, *Paul* suggests that there is no avoiding the foundational violence inaugurating queer self-creation, and that its consequences—whether positive, negative, or a mixture thereof—cannot be known in advance. Whether scripted or unscripted, setting oneself in a new direction requires, first, that one obliterate the subjective positions made available by heteronormative and homonormative cultures; and second, that one forge new modes of subjectivity and relationality. Having given himself over to leathermen in Eagles, Paul has embraced the drive and the Real, traversing the fantasies structuring his travels across North America.

Traversing the Fantasy, Forming a New *Sinthôme*

Despite offering no guarantees, the novel's final episodes give readers cause for optimism by highlighting Paul's budding friendship with Robin. After an ACT UP fundraiser, Robin observes that Paul has been "hiding in plain sight" and takes him home (Lawlor 2017: 331). Pushing Paul to reveal himself—to traverse the fantasy motivating him to pass as one gender or another—Robin gently insists that "we both know what we are" (Lawlor 2017: 331). Paul responds by retreating to the bathroom twice: first to change into a teenage boy; second to morph into a much older man (Lawlor 2017: 331). After Robin asks, "[W]hat else can you do?" Paul responds by opening "his workshirt" and growing large "breasts" visible underneath "the ribbing of his A-shirt" before retracting his "facial hair, body hair, cock," and "balls" (Lawlor 2017: 332). Robin does the same, "but sweeter, more feminine" (Lawlor 2017: 332). Paul changes his body into that of a "leatherman," with "darker arm hair, a bulge in his crotch, muscles popping"; Robin reacts by transforming into a "slight but wiry... young matador" whose "soft presence of a penis" arouses Paul (Lawlor 2017: 332).

Paul wants "to say *but what* are *you*," but does not (Lawlor 2017: 333). When Robin asks, "Can you look like someone else? Can you look like me?" Paul says he can't: just as he says "I don't think I can do that" to Diane right before they split up (Lawlor 2017: 333, 187). But Robin, like a therapist, pushes him further. After an exchange about their respective ethnicities reveals that Robin is a mixture of "Cuban" and "Irish," Robin begins "to sprout freckles" and then "lighten by barely a shade" (Lawlor 2017: 333). Asked to do the same, Paul allows "his own freckles" to "sink deep into his skin"—something he has "never done... before" (Lawlor 2017: 333-4). After Robin tells him he's "close," Paul claims that he "can't," only to find that he has turned into Robin and vice versa (Lawlor 2017: 334). Made "dizzy" by the experience—characterized by the same time lag accompanying Orlando's recognition that she has woken up a woman—Paul must touch himself to confirm that "he had switched bodies with Robin and *was* looking at himself" (Lawlor 2017: 334). During the experience, he tells Robin it is "amazing," falls back on cultural references so "mainstream and earnest" they prompt "shame," and then abruptly leaves as soon as they "changed back" (Lawlor 2017: 334). Paul—who has "never seen anyone else change" before and "could watch the manifestations of Robin all day, revel in Robin's mystery"—has, at Robin's prompting, traversed the fantasy (Lawlor 2017: 333).

After this encounter, Paul accepts an invitation to visit Robin's studio but cannot bring himself to verbalize his "burning questions—why are we like this? are there others? can we get sick?" (Lawlor 2017: 341). After he indicates that he wants to ask something, he falls back into silence. Robin supplies the question—"[w]hat are we?"—and answers it by saying, "[W]e're like everybody else, only more so" (Lawlor 2017: 342). For Paul, this is an important and validating moment countering Diane's rejection and reframing in positive terms what she cannot countenance: his desire "to be everything, all the time" (Lawlor 2017: 206). Robin's remark shows that Paul creatively combines and intensifies forms of experience that heteronormative and homonormative cultures oppose to one another.

However, Robin also prompts Paul to reorient himself, noting, "We're just what we are" and stating, "You're asking the wrong questions, Polly" (Lawlor 2017: 342). Dismissing the *Bildungsroman*'s ontological questions, Robin suggests that Paul should abandon the quest to find the truth about himself. In so doing, Robin suggests ignoring the question Jane engages when she worries that her tendency to "attribut[e] phenomena to the unseeable (hormones, pheromones)" might betray a lingering question—"Was biology destiny, in fact?"—that could compromise her social constructionist dissertation (Lawlor 2017: 72). Similar essentialisms animate Diane's assertion that Paul's mutability represents his "nature" (Lawlor 2017: 206). Robin encourages Paul to abandon such thinking.

The novel is nonetheless structured around the premise that Paul's inherent mutability fuels his sexual voracity. Robin offers him an alternative to this fantasy by modeling a means of anchoring subjectivity through self-creation. Silently admiring "how sui generis" and "effortless" his friend looks during their final interaction, Paul sees Robin—consummate *sinthom*estizx—use art as a *sinthôme* grounding a mode of subjectivity going beyond divisions of gender, sexuality, and ethnicity (Lawlor 2017: 341). When Robin concludes Paul's visit to the studio by offering him a Cuban candy and remarking that "I can't decide if we should be lovers or best friends," Paul enthusiastically embraces the former only to hear that "Of course that's what you'd say" (Lawlor 2017: 343). Unlike others Paul pursues, Robin never becomes his lover. Instead, Robin's gentle refusal reroutes Paul's subjectivity: first, toward settling down with Derek, to whom he never reveals his shape-shifting capabilities; later, toward embracing the role of the mixed-race, shape-shifting artist, which represents a successful traversal of the fantasy.

Repudiating the "inversion model" and "ethnic model" of queer identity, Robin suggests that Paul need not seek to understand what he is or why he is that way; he need just use his multiplicity to perceive and create (Nealon 2001: 2). This emphasis on self-creation makes *Paul* an unique "foundling" narrative (Nealon 2001: 1). At the end of the novel, Paul is like the transgender subjects described by Cavanagh, Gherovici, and Gozlan: positioned to use artistry to form a new *sinthôme* and reorient himself. Yet unlike these psychoanalyts' clients, Paul does not settle into a singular gender identity. Whereas Cavanagh, Gherovici, and Gozlan argue that gender transition involves traversing the fantasy, rejecting one's initial gender assignment, and restabilizing embodiment on the opposite site of the binary with a new pronoun and *sinthôme*, Robin helps Paul see that he can use the *sinthôme*'s creativity to embrace fluidity.

The novel's closing segment highlights Paul's capacity to recreate himself. After agonizing and wishing that he didn't "have to choose anything," Paul passes Robin on the street (Lawlor 2017: 353). Prompted by Robin's example to refuse to "choose" a single gender, Paul rejects a birthday check from Derek that would "pay off" his Iowa State "tuition" and free him to transfer to a Bay Area university (Lawlor 2017: 352–3). In declining Derek's offer, Paul successfully traverses the fantasies he has been questioning from the outset: heteronormativity, homonormativity, and metronormativity; romantic love; singular understandings of gender, sexuality, and ethnicity.

This act, echoing Paul's submission in Eagle bars, reveals his decision— shedding yet another scene, rejecting yet another lover and normative identity—to begin investing in his own creativity by forming a new *sinthôme* promising reorientation. The resultant broadening of Paul's horizon is evident in his attention to the skyscape that emerges as he wanders through San Francisco, "looking up at the attic windows and roofs of renovated Victorians, the treetops," and "the big Western sky" (Lawlor 2017: 353). He allows his body to be inundated with "sunlight," cascading "into his head, ... down through his eyes, down his throat, and spreading out" until he reaches "Duboce Park" (Lawlor 2017: 353). A rapture of sensation heightens his ability to perceive life around him. Embracing visual detail, he takes in humans, dogs, even the "violet" he notices "pushing up through a disintegrating Muni transfer," and is saturated by his sensory environment (Lawlor 2017: 354). The novel thereby ends not with another change of scene reconfiguring the imaginary, symbolic, and Real but with a more radical outcome of fantasy's traversal: a "direct investment in signifiers" constituting another type of scene, in the word's broadest sense (Pluth 2007: 163).

Prompted by encounters with the gender-bending, sexually fluid, and ethnically mixed Robin, Paul's transformation enacts Anzaldúa's "new consciousness" promising an end to the fantasy of (hetero)sexual difference as well as the ethnic and national divisions implicated in it (Anzaldúa 1987: 77). Observing the visual world around him, Paul is saturated by the "various" forms of life in Duboce Park (Lawlor 2017: 354). This positions him to be creative: to continue to write screenplays, to work with the ways his experience living beyond the binaries of gender, sexuality, and ethnicity might reshape the drive. Paul is poised, that is, to craft a new *sinthôme*, whatever it might bring.

Obtaining Queer Care: Before and after Fantasy's Traversal

And so at the novel's end, we find Paul embracing the polymorphous perversity animating his zine. This concept invokes the drives' unpredictability: a capacity that can be generative yet also leave subjects without a safety net. For Paul, the moment after fantasy's traversal is both exciting and perilous: perilous because of lingering questions about his physical vulnerability and exciting because of the creative future that might emerge. But what will come next? Providing no easy answers, Lawlor leaves Paul at an opening to an undefined future. As he has traversed normative fantasies, he has repudiated dominant life patterns such as romantic love, marriage, monogamy, and child-rearing. And at the novel's end, he finds himself in a familiar position, having rejected a dissatisfying scene governed by an uncompelling fantasy and prepared himself to start anew.

At this point, Paul is well positioned to reorient himself by drawing on the same resources that helped him before: on informal acts of queer acculturation, care, and mentoring providing alternatives to established institutions. His varied interactions with established queer people exemplify strategies making unscripted lives viable for subjects who have traversed the fantasy and fundamentally transformed themselves. By calling attention to queer care's availability, Lawlor's novel suggests that Paul may draw on it again—and perhaps even provide it for others—now that he has traversed the fantasy of (hetero) sexual difference and embraced his creative *sinthôme*.

The acts of queer care supporting Paul as he tries on different LGBTQ scenes exemplify the strategies he might use to regain direction after traversing the fundamental fantasy of (hetero)sexual difference at the novel's end. These supportive encounters—however brief—orient him to new places and point him to resources. His material needs met, he is able to relinquish hegemonic fantasies such as reproductive futurism and upward mobility that otherwise might tempt him. Other queers' guidance also substitutes for the parenting whose lack informs the novel's foundling myths. Paul embraces the idea that care can be provided through informal means, as it is to Polly in the first fairy tale and the foundling wolf in the second.

Upon moving to Provincetown to be with Diane, for instance, Paul (as Polly) joins her shared household and is given a tour of town by their housemate, Zoe, when Diane is at work. Shortly thereafter, Paul accepts Zoe's offer to join her for "under the table" job "prepping rentals for the season," which allows him to support himself in Provincetown (Lawlor 2017: 172). In San Francisco, too, strangers provide guidance. Upon his arrival, his "lost boy routine" nets information about nightclubs and jobs from Oscar, a punkish gay waiter who serves him at a diner (Lawlor 2017: 223). A subsequent hangout and threesome with Oscar and his boyfriend disabuse Paul of the idea of supporting himself as a bartender or drag performer. He instead takes Oscar's suggestion to approach the bookstore. Although Paul and the couple quickly part, his longing for care is clear during their interactions when he imagines himself as "Teen Runaway Paul" who is "adopted by a wealthy but liberal older gay couple" and is able to "start life over" on a trajectory leading to success in "high school" and "a scholarship to NYU for film" (Lawlor 2017: 221).

Queer care's ready availability in San Francisco is equally apparent when Paul makes Flore his "temporary office" to search for a home with a telephone number he can enter on his job applications (Lawlor 2017: 233). After rejecting an unappealing offer, Paul returns to Flore and, schmoozing the staff, is handed a phone number with the name "Ruffles" (Lawlor 2017: 235). When Paul visits, he quickly agrees to respect the household's rules, consents to the possibility of overhearing "SM-related noises," and returns with the requested "money order" (Lawlor 2017: 237). Because this affordable sublet allows him to save for other expenses, he knows he will "make it after all" (Lawlor 2017: 237).

Later, looking to older queers for guidance, Paul allows men he meets "at the bookstore" to "take him out to dinner" and "give him career advice, in the time-honored way of older fags," without expecting "sex" (Lawlor 2017: 256–7). Identifying with Paul, they act as "mentors" and tell "him what they thought they would have liked to have heard" (Lawlor 2017: 257). Some advise him to become a professional; others encourage him to follow his "dreams" (Lawlor 2017: 257).

The novel's closing episodes suggest that Paul will choose his dream of becoming a filmmaker and that he may be more attentive to others' needs in the future.

He also notices the example set by Ruffles, who exemplifies everyday practices of queer self-care and survival. Paul immediately recognizes that the "cool" but standoffish Ruffles is "*not* the kind of gay who rescues puppies," but eventually realizes that HIV has emotionally and physically exhausted him (Lawlor 2017: 235–7). Observing "how Ruffles kept so many plants in the living room, watered them and kept them alive," Paul comments that "[t]he air smelled better than normal air" and makes the entire household a positive living environment (Lawlor 2017: 353). Concluding that Ruffles is "a good person" who does what he can to sustain life despite illness, Paul—grieving Tony's death—realizes that he has failed to care for others (Lawlor 2017: 353). Despite Lawlor's emphasis on Paul's justifiable skepticism toward forms of heteronormativity and homonormativity that are mistaken for maturity, the novel suggests that he may be on the cusp of moving past the irresponsibility that caused him to avoid caring for others or responding to Christopher's bills.

Paul's appreciation of queer care contrasts to his dismissive attitude toward heteronormative and homonormative parenting. When he sees Diane with a new lover—a single mother—he initially flares with envy. However, after asking himself, "[H]ow could he compete with a *mother*?," he realizes that he does not "*want* to be a mother… Or a father… Wasn't the whole point that he didn't have to do those normal things?" (Lawlor 2017: 250). Rejecting homonormative fantasies, he embraces queer self-creation.

Exemplifying a different kind of care, Robin's emergence as a role model in the novel's concluding episodes further suggests that Paul will embrace artistry. Unlike those who help him earlier in the novel, Robin does not facilitate access to material resources. Instead, Robin offers Paul an even more valuable form of care: friendship with a well-established person like himself. Much as Paul is able to settle into Provincetown and San Francisco with the help of queers he has just met, he is able to traverse the fantasy and reject singular identities because he has seen through Robin's example that he has an option that does not confine him to a singular pronoun, gender, sexuality, or ethnicity. It is as if Robin responds to Paul's "who are you/who am I ?" with the most open of answers: "I am I and I am an artist," without further explanation. And so we find Paul at the novel's end rejecting a dominant Bay Area homonormative fantasy in favor of genderqueer creativity, looking out with a filmmaker's eye: freed from fantasy, saturated with signifiers, observing the many lives in a scene "as good-smelling and various as himself" (Lawlor 2017: 354).

Notes

1. See Campbell (2000), pp. 210–15, for a reinflection of Frantz Fanon's critique of Jung's racism.
2. See Cavanagh (2015, 2016, and 2018), Gherovici (2012, 2014, and 2017), and Gozlan (2015).
3. Paul's extrapolation in Provincetown that in "five years" he would be "twenty seven" and his girlfriend Diane would be "twenty-eight" establishes his age (Lawlor 2017: 206). I will use the name "Paul" along with he/him pronouns for Lawlor's protagonist, whose time in Provincetown as a lesbian named "Polly" is conveyed by using "Paul" to indicate his role as the subject of a sentence and "Polly" to figure others' perceptions of him.
4. See Nolan (1995) and Cheng (1995) for two different accounts of ways Joyce repudiated early-twentieth-century Irish nationalism while contributing to the project of decolonizing (Nolan) and internationalizing (Cheng) Irishness. Cheng argues that Joyce reworks the concept of the Irish "race" to repudiate essentialist notions of racial purity.
5. See Chapter One of Coffman (2018) for further elaboration of the ways "vantage" can transgender the visual field.

Coda

Traversing the Fantasy of Authoritarian Patriarchy

Andrea Lawlor's *Paul Takes the Form of a Mortal Girl* (2017), which concludes Chapter 6, highlights the promises and dangers of traversing the fantasy of (hetero) sexual difference by embracing *jouissance* in the Real. Whereas Paul's budding friendship with Robin offers an example of the way traversing the fantasy and embracing the *sinthôme* can prompt creativity that sets a subject on a promising new life direction, the novel's treatment of the AIDS pandemic's central role in early 1990s queer culture reminds readers that the drive that brings life may also bring death. Writing in 2020–1, during the coronavirus pandemic, I cannot help but feel for Lawlor's protagonist not only the joy I felt in 2018 upon first reading the novel but also a newfound fear, grounded in an awareness of the potential cruelty of optimism (Berlant 2011), that is tempered only by an insistence on refusing to relinquish it. Finishing *Queer Traversals* in the midst of a pandemic, as a democratic centrist wrestles the US presidency away from a right-wing authoritarian patriarch, I continue to maintain this dual awareness of the drive's perils and potentialities.

The Covid-19 pandemic emerged during a global resurgence of right-wing authoritarian patriarchy spanning from former US president Donald Trump to Hungary's Viktor Orbán, India's Narendra Modi, Poland's Andrzej Duda, and Turkey's Recep Tayyip Erdoğan, to name just a few examples. Writing in *Why War?* (1993) about an earlier cohort of right-wing leaders such as US president Ronald Reagan and British prime minister Margaret Thatcher, Jacqueline Rose observes that "right-wing fantasy... draws on some of the earliest formations of the drives" (Rose 1993: 68). In a feminist revision of Wilhelm Reich's 1933 *The Mass Psychology of Fascism*, she proposes that "the symbolic order is gendered, and that right-wing ideologies thrive on and strain against the furthest limits of psychic fantasy" (Rose 1993: 42–3). She argues that the symbolic is constituted through "the violence of sexual difference itself, meaning both the trauma of its recognition and the worst forms of its social enactment in the real" (Rose 1993: 42–3). Whereas Rose is concerned with the limit of the social that Thatcher (who supported the death penalty) and Ruth Ellis (who was executed for murder) embody as aggressive women, male authoritarian leaders' rise in the second decade of the twenty-first century reveals the social's continued implication in patriarchy.

Along with Reagan, Thatcher gained power in the 1980s, during neoliberalism's rise. As Wendy Brown shows in *In the Ruins of Neoliberalism* (2019), policies initiated by these leaders (and furthered by subsequent US presidents) created the conditions for anti-democratic patriarchal authoritarianism's emergence, even though canonical neoliberal thinkers such as Friedrich Hayek did not pursue that goal. As twentieth-century "nihilism" made "wreckage... of conscience" and neoliberal regimes gained footholds in democracies, markets began to serve as "both reality principle and moral truth" (Brown 2019: 170, 168). Overtaking individual "[c]onscience" and "guilt" as agents of "thought," "action," and morality, markets rendered "capitalism... necessity, authority, and truth rolled into one" (Brown 2019: 168). This logic permeated "every sphere and" left capitalism "immune from criticism, despite its manifest devastations, incoherencies, and instabilities" (Brown 2019: 168). Trump's 2016 election as US president and failed 2020 reelection bid were fueled by these long-term consequences of 1980s politics.

Brown argues that although these developments did not directly cause contemporary "white nationalist authoritarian" rage from "the economically abandoned and racially resentful," neoliberalism nonetheless set the stage for it (Brown 2019: 8). Implicitly responding to Lee Edelman's *No Future* (2004), her final chapter—"No Future for White Men"—uses Herbert Marcuse's theory of "repressive desublimation" and Friedrich Nietzsche's theory of "ressentiment" to account for white male rage at "dethroned privilege" to which Make America Great Again and other slogans appeal (Brown 2019: 165, 174, 5). Brown argues that whereas Nietzsche describes "the revenge of the weak"—"who suffered in a value system affirming strength power and action," they countered with "a new value system in which strength" is "reproached as evil and weakness lofted as good"—since the 1980s a new "politics of ressentiment" has animated appeals of "the historically dominant" who have felt their "dominance ebbing" and have interpreted their "suffering... as wrongful victimization" (Brown 2019: 174).

Contemporary ressentiment revels in spectacles of limitless white male power and entitlement recalling Freud's myth of the primal father. Writing in the wake of the 2016 election, Robert Samuels argues "that what happens in blind love, fascism, and hypnosis is a regression to the state of the primal horde" (Samuels 2016: 66). Trump's authoritarianism recalled its "primal leader," who "was totally free" of obligations to "others… he loved no one but himself," engaging "other people only as far as they served his needs" (Samuels 2016: 66). As Peter E. Gordon insists, this style is not simply an individual character flaw: not "the political precipitate of a psychological disposition," as is implied by media references to the *DSM* (Gordon 2018: 67). Rather, as "a generalized feature of the social order itself," this style is an "*introjection* of an irrational society" fueled by citizens' "identification" with Trump's behavior (Gordon 2018: 64–7). Brown observes that his posturings played to people whose anxiety "about their ebbing place and privilege" led them to identify with "Trump's crass sexual entitlement to all women, the crude contractualism of his marriage, and for that matter, all of his crude conduct and flaunting of law and the protocols of the presidency" (Brown 2019: 173–4).

Since the 2019 publication of Brown's book—which contextualizes Trump's behaviors without excusing him—neoliberalism's ravages were compounded by the his administration's reaction to the Covid-19 pandemic, which foregrounds the drive's deadliness. Trump took his own positive Covid-19 test not as a reason to stress prevention but as an opportunity to assert his perceived invulnerability and viewpoint that the best response is to refuse to fear going maskless. For Brown, this posture turns on "repressive desublimation," which mixes with nihilism to liberate people "from the restraint, self-blame, and self-abuse that conscience imposes" (Brown 2019: 164–5). People provided with "satisfactory liberties" come to tolerate "misdeeds of society" that appear to be "freedom" but instead perpetuate "the domination of the status quo" (Brown 2019: 167).

As Trump's white nationalist supporters saw a simulacrum of liberty reflected in his image as the limitlessly entitled primal father, they mirrored his behavior with "wild, raging, and even outlaw expressions of patriotism and nationalism" (Brown 2019: 168). In summer 2020, Trumpsters' violent defiance remained unpunished as he turned the National Guard against Black Lives Matter protesters; in late November, MAGA demonstrations re-emerged—again unchecked—to support lawsuits and other forms of resistance he used to rage against the "dethroned privilege" of losing the presidency (Brown 2019: 5). On January 6, 2021, this fury culminated in a failed coup after Trump incited a white supremacist riot at the US Capitol. These vicissitudes of "desublimated, wounded white masculinity" exemplify the "new levels and perhaps even new forms of violence" that "repressive desublimation" can provoke through its "compression or concentration of erotic energy" (Brown 2019: 171, 168, 168, 168).

In other words, at the heart of Trump's irresponsibility to himself and others lay the death drive, whose centrality to his politics was also apparent in the violence his regime enacted yet attempted to obscure through cultural division. Rose describes paranoid "politics" as operating through "a logic of fantasy in which violence can operate as a pole of attraction at the same time as (to the extent that) it is being denied" (Rose 1993: 64). She explains that "[o]ne of the things that Margaret Thatcher was doing... was to make this paradox the basis of a political identity so that subjects could take pleasure in violence as a force and legitimacy while always locating 'real' violence somewhere else—illegitimate violence and illicitness increasingly made subject to the law" (Rose 1993: 64). Trump similarly displaced violence onto "others," albeit without Thatcher's rational posturing. Instead, *ir*rationality—the open contradictions and resilience to fact characterizing Trump's image as the unbridled primal father—drove his aggressive displacements.

This authoritarian, patriarchal style animated the aggression Trump directed at what he claimed to be the United States' external and internal threats. Writing about Thatcher, Rose argues that "one of the fundamental psychic tropes of fascism... acts out" what Jacques Lacan's early work describes as the paranoid "structure of aggressivity, giving name and place to the invisible adversary which is an inherent part of it, and making fear a central component of strategy" (Rose 1993: 62). As John Rajchman points out, Lacan developed this theory of aggressivity "in the thirties, when fascism was on the rise in Europe" (Rajchman 1991: 18). His 1949 essay "The Mirror Stage," initially drafted in 1936, concludes by calling fascism "madness... that deafens the world with its sound and fury" (Lacan 2006e: 80).[1] Similar aggression is also evident now, as authoritarian leaders exploit social divisions by pitting their countries' populations against putative "others" in the name of national coherence and purity. These regimes focus on the perceived need to barricade themselves against external "others" and regulate internal "others," such as women, transpeople, and people of color.

Trump's regime illustrated these dynamics. At the same time as his administration imprisoned migrants, deployed the National Guard against antiracist protesters, and insisted on reopening the economy during the pandemic at the expense of essential employees who are disproportionately women and people of color, he also attempted—though not entirely successfully—to roll back rights for women and transpeople.[2] A similar aggressivity placed the death drive at the center of his re-election campaign as the Trumps used virulently xenophobic invective during the 2020 Republican National Convention to avoid taking responsibility for the United States' many deaths from Covid-19. Even though Trump embodies authoritarian patriarchy's current global resurgence, he refused in the name of American freedom to impose potentially life-saving measures, such as masking and lockdowns, that successfully contained the pandemic elsewhere. Instead of admitting the administration's failure to contain the virus, the Trumps blamed China. This rhetoric escalated into conspiracy theories after the election as they refused to accept defeat, alleged fraud, and incited violence.

This scapegoating recalls the discursive construction of AIDS patients as "exotic" during the early years of that pandemic, when "gay" men, "prostitutes," and "African" women were portrayed as the only victims (Treichler 1999: 20). Similar dynamics emerged during the coronavirus pandemic as social media platforms facilitated shaming of small subsets of stigmatized populations to advance public health goals many of those people support. In summer 2020, users shared images of residents of the Ozarks packing local beaches as well as ravers in Berlin and queers partying on Fire Island amidst a deadly pandemic.[3] Because crowded gatherings raise legitimate concerns about the high risk of coronavirus transmission and the difficulty of contact tracing, they hardly represent events I or many other queers would endorse. However, these seemingly disparate images share the same pernicious consequence: stigmatizing and shaming "hillbillies," "ravers," and "queers." Staging these populations as *sinthom*osexuals whose death drives threaten society, these images deflect attention from the Trump administration's failures of leadership during the pandemic.

Figuring a drive for pleasure pursued at risk of death, these *sinthom*osexuals obscure the capitalist drive for profit motivating the many deaths of essential employees sacrificed on the reopened economy's altar. As Samuels pointed out even before the pandemic, "the neoliberal ideology of consumer capitalism" drives "fantasies" that "provide an Imaginary solution to the conflict between civilization and individual desire," offering a "social foundation for absorbing the social economic system into a personal experience" (Samuels 2016: 89). Disenfranchised blue-collar voters' aspirations explain their willingness to act against their material interests by supporting a candidate whose policies advantage the one percent at workers' expense. Scapegoating *sinthom*osexuals deflects attention from the pandemic's imbrication in this dynamic, obscuring the implications of ordinary citizens' capitalist desires. The drive subtends the actions not only of those who spend money on beach vacations, raves, and circuit parties despite their risks; and not only those who generate revenue for social media companies by sharing images shaming *sinthom*osexuals for risky behavior;

but also—and most importantly—those from across the political spectrum who avoid either of those traps only to fall otherwise into consumerism's clutches.

Discussing "The Capitalist Death Drive," Samuels observes that the theory of "the death drive" recognizes "that people have an unconscious sense of guilt, anxiety, and the need for punishment, and at the same time, ... engage in compulsive, self-destructive activities to efface their guilt and anxiety" (Samuels 2016: 92). This theory holds that "the initial relationship between the helpless child and the all-powerful parent creates a fundamental fantasy that," conflating "love with the need to be punished," is "taken up by the death drive as people find enjoyment in their own self-destruction" (Samuels 2016: 92). One of many forms of addiction fueling this process, consumerism encourages people to "engage in compulsive buying as a way of reducing anxiety through" an "illusion of control over an object or social relationship" that ultimately proves futile (Samuels 2016: 92).

The Trump administration's response to Covid-19, focused on the pandemic's threats to economic growth, enabled the country's capitalist fantasies to continue while damaging public health, fueling a vicious cycle that began with the sacrifice of frontline employees in essential businesses during lockdown and extended to many others. Workers and customers navigated often maskless crowds in the service of consumption. Anxieties over taboos and disease made basic life needs such as toilet paper and cleaning supplies initial foci of panic, which later extended to other consumer goods. At their worst, ordinary people risked others' lives to exercise their right to the "satisfactory freedom" of shopping or dining maskless (Brown 2019: 167). All the while, the United States failed to recognize peoples' imprisonment by "The Capitalist Death Drive," which "takes advantage of the sexual drives by providing opportunities for compulsive behavior" (Samuels 2016: 92). *Sinthom*osexuals disproportionately bore the burdens of collective anxieties brought on by the pandemic, serving as scapegoats for the general population's compulsions. Seemingly uncontrollable, these *sinthom*osexuals became objects of demands that stigmatized groups—rather than the entire populace—be controlled through right-wing legal and policy decisions.

This paranoid logic also animated divergent fantasies driving Trump's supporters and detractors. On the one hand, his campaign promulgated xenophobia, offering his base a (false) sense of unity; on the other hand, this scapegoating incited fierce forces of resistance, ultimately leading to his defeat. These contradictions emerge from the drive's duplicitous unpredictability. Rose credits Jacques Derrida with first registering the drive's "*unheimlich* presence (as binding and repetition) inside the very process of life," whose variability paranoia strives unsuccessfully to contain (Rose 1993: 102). Drawing on Julia Kristeva, she argues that "the sacrificial nature of the social order 'orders violence, binds it, tames it,'" but also "*repeats* it" by "scapegoating its victim... to expel violence out into the real and so end it" (Rose 1993: 63). This binding has a double effect. Although "right-wing ideology" forms "the basis of social cohesion" by "act[ing] out its most fundamental symbolic economy," this spectacle also "threatens the social by making that economy too blatant—the object of a renewed investment by the very drives it was intended to regulate or keep underground" (Rose 1993: 63–4). Trump's style, which flaunts this paradox, elicited polarized responses precisely because it unsuccessfully strove to suppress the drives' plurality. His drive challenged yet also mobilized the vehement forces of resistance that led to his failed bid for a second term.

The behavior animating Trump's political rise and fall echoes Lacan's theory from the 1930s "that our relation to what is 'ideal' in us, to our ideal-egos as well as our ego-ideals, derives from a fundamental violence or 'alienation'" entailing aggression (Rajchman 1991: 18). "The Mirror Stage" describes the ego as "a fortified camp, or even a stadium—distributing, between the arena within its walls and its outer border of gravel-pits and marshes, two opposed fields of battle where the subject bogs down in his quest for the proud, remote inner castle whose form (sometimes juxtaposed in the same scenario) strikingly symbolizes the id" (Lacan 2006e: 78). Similarly, Anna Freud understands "the id-ego relation as a protracted struggle over territorial domain and boundaries... through which self and other, identity and alien, are performatively brought into being and negotiated... within the subject" (Brown 2010: 140).

These "intrapsychic battle[s]" animate calls for border walls, which Brown views as modes "of national psychic defense" enacting an "ideological disavowal of a set of unmanageable appetites, needs, and powers" (Brown 2010: 140–2). She contends that "nation-state walling responds in part to psychic fantasies, anxieties, and wishes... by generating visual effects and a national imaginary apart from what walls" unsuccessfully "purport to 'do'" (Brown 2010: 121). Stressing walling's "narcissistic and defensive" elements, Samuels notes that because people "seek to defend" their "identifications," some treat "the Imaginary borders of a nation to be an extension of the self... to be defended at all costs" (Samuels 2016: 81). Brown emphasizes that these ego-formations protect nationalists' self-images from anything "that disturbs the ego's conceit of itself," including "encounters with the id's own aggression or hostility" (Brown 2010: 141). Defensive "blocking" allows "the ego to split off from the id to construct an identity of virtue and goodness," purging "both its identification and its imbrication with what it is walling out" (Brown 2010: 141).

Though *Walled States, Waning Sovereignty* was first published in 2010, well before Trump's presidency, Brown's description of the ego's determination to project "goodness" while disavowing its aggressivity aptly describes the posturing he used to promote development of the US-Mexico border wall. Brown's stress upon "the gendered dimensions of the anxieties these defenses are managing" further explains these dynamics' imbrication with Trump's image as an authoritarian patriarch (Brown 2010: 142). She notes that "walling" is "a defense against anxieties about need, vulnerability, and penetrability" grounded in "the desire for sovereign containment and protection against such vulnerability" (Brown 2010: 142). Because "[v]ulnerability and penetrability are almost universally coded as feminine," whereas "sovereign supremacy and powers of containment and protection are coded masculine," the contemporary politics of "walling appears to defend against a sovereign failure to protect a penetrable (penetrated) nation (always referred to with a feminine pronoun)"—a "failure" symbolically rectified through "[h]e heterosexual coupling of the feminized nation and the masculine sovereign state" whose authority the leader's "imago" reinstates (Brown 2010: 143).

As Brown's analysis suggests, the explicitly patriarchal, homophobic, and transphobic character of contemporary forms of xenophobic nationalism is no coincidence. She argues that the figure of a presumably white, heterosexual, and Christian "nation lost… drew on a mythical past when families were happy, whole, and heterosexual, when women and racial minorities knew their place" (Brown 2019: 5). Defending against the "loss of horizons, order, and identity attending the decline of state sovereignty" and other forms of stability, walling furthers "fantasies of innocence, protection, homogeneity, and self-sufficiency" inaccurately imagined to characterize the past (Brown 2010: 119). So do legal initiatives targeting LGBTQ people: an operation of fantasy James Penney overlooks in critiquing mainstream US queer activism.

Perhaps because *After Queer Theory* was published in 2014—before Trump's 2016 election brought the United States' white heterosexual supremacist ideologues onto the nightly news and made visible their implication in a global resurgence of patriarchy and homophobia—Penney's critique of the white gaystream's all too frequently unexamined economic privilege fails to note that money leaves queers unprotected from legal disenfranchisement: the reason LGBT activists seek to counter it. Protection from discrimination in employment, housing, and healthcare all came under threat during the Trump administration in ways that risked harming the well-off white queers whose economic privilege Penney critiques and also—and even more alarmingly—diverse queers of more modest means. Their losses have further compounded during the Covid-19 pandemic, which has had a disparately negative impact on precariously employed queers and ethnic minorities in the United States. The United States' marketization of health care—which must be purchased at high cost if not provided by employers—also disproportionately burdens these populations.

Focusing exclusively on well-heeled white queers, Penney argues that it is "impossible to pretend that unfettered capital and 'traditional family values' are mutually enforcing social forces," and offers "[t]he radical queer millionaire Internet pornographer who organizes 'sex-positive' sex toy parties in his spare time" as "one of the best emblems of contemporary capitalism" (Penney 2014: 105–6). Although this is a fair point, free-market capitalism has also provoked the re-emergence of virulent forms of domestic xenophobia that have harmed queers, ethnic minorities, and immigrants from those parts of the world Penney cites in his critique of privileged queers from the United States. Moreover, right-wing attacks on public education have driven political and fiscal crises targeting academic programming fostering diversity, from public complaints about classes to attempts to cut entire ethnic studies, gender studies, and sexuality studies programs or colleges.

These material conditions create problems for those who do the "*identitarian*" work that Penney—in a particularly inflammatory passage—compares to that of France's "xenophobic and crypto-fascist... *Front national*" (Penney 2014: 178). We might therefore evaluate his analysis in light of the situations of black and queer academics, whose economic privilege and cultural capital do not always protect them from discrimination and overburdening. Recruited to enhance institutional diversity, saddled with additional housework in its service, and then made vulnerable to politically motivated attacks on teaching and writing: the situations of many minoritized faculty disprove Penney's claim that gender, sexual orientation, "race, religion and ethnicity" are secondary, whereas class difference and sexual difference are primary (Penney 2014: 105). Queer theorists and scholars of color do not universally exemplify the forms of dangerously "*identitarian passion*" with which Penney charges them; instead, they are all too frequently neoliberal xenophobia's targets (Penney 2014: 178).

The clash between xenophobic political fantasies and growing forces of resistance to them illuminates an interlocking set of issues at the heart of *Queer Traversals*: the intersection of forms of sexual orientation and gender embodiment mobilized by the putative antinomy of (hetero)sexual difference with ideologies about national, racial, and ethnic identity hinging on similar divisions. Much of this book has argued that traversing the fantasy of (hetero)sexual difference can broaden our possibilities for sexualities and genders. Viewing these formations intersectionally—rather than through Penney's distinction between primary and secondary social antagonisms—shows that fantasy's traversal could take us beyond the forms of xenophobia at work in authoritarian patriarchy as well.

Samuels effectively identifies the fantasies that structured the United States' political divides under Trump. Noting that psychoanalysis reveals "how fascism is structured in the same way as hypnosis, and hypnosis itself replicates blind love," he argues that we should short-circuit the resulting cycle of "identification, idealization, projection, splitting," and "repression" (Samuels 2016: 64, 77). Instead of a politics turning on "recognition" of "the suffering and identity of other groups," Samuels advocates "a mode of subjectivity and solidarity that" moves "from Imaginary rivalry to Symbolic identification" (Samuels 2016: 88, 77, 64).

However, this solution risks reproducing the false unity that galvanized Trump's supporters in 2016 and mobilized his opponents to unseat him in 2020 (Samuels 2016: 77). Although I agree that politics should move beyond "Imaginary rivalry," I have argued throughout this book that deep-seated political change cannot be achieved solely through imaginary and "Symbolic" mediation (Samuels 2016: 77). One must also engage the Real, whose implication with the drive constitutes the psyche's greatest source of resistance.

Samuels' reluctance to engage the drive and the Real is understandable given the nihilistic interpretations of these concepts in much current theory. The destruction wrought by the Trump administration and other authoritarian regimes reveals problems with Edelman's argument that queers should embrace the drive's most destructive aspects to prompt fantasy's traversal. This argument's dangers are apparent in Slavoj Žižek's infamous 2016 endorsement of Trump. Despite professing to be "horrified" by him, Žižek argued that his election would force the Republican and Democratic parties to "rethink themselves" and enact a "big awakening."[4] Although Žižek's claim sounds like an argument for fantasy's traversal, Trump's embrace of the death drive only further entrenched those fantasies by making the country's divisions worse.

Writing about two different consequences of "the rancor and rage" characterizing the "ressentiment" bred by "lost entitlement," Brown demonstrates that embracing the death drive alone is unlikely to have constructive effects (Brown 2019: 177). In her first scenario—in which "rancor and rage are not developed into refined moral values," but remain "stuck"—"ressentiment" is "unable to 'become creative'" and find a "way out" (Brown 2019: 178). In her second scenario—in which "values... emerge from the ressentiment of those suffering the lost entitlements of historically conferred power"—the situation is no better, especially for those who have historically had little access to "power," because "dethroned entitlement... denounce[s] equality and even merit in order to affirm its supremacy based on nothing more than traditional right" (Brown 2019: 179). For Brown, this assertion of "supremacy... as a raw entitlement claim... converges powerfully with neoliberalism's assault on equality and democracy, the social and the political" (Brown 2019: 180). Trump's lawsuits contesting Joe Biden's 2020 election exemplify Brown's second scenario and have been widely decried as open attacks on democracy's foundation.

Nonetheless, I fear that the unity both Samuels and Biden advocate—while less aggressive than MAGA tactics—may be no more likely than Trumpism to dislodge the fantasies structuring contemporary US political divisions. Although the attention-seeking contradictions characterizing Trump's chaotic leadership style have ceased as Biden has brought calmness and competence to the Oval Office, the country's problems will likely still fester until the underlying structure of its political discourse is transformed. To dislodge those forms of "right-wing fantasy" bound up with "the drives" (Rose 1993: 68)—including the rage over "dethroned privilege" Trump's imago falsely promises to rectify—one must engage the imaginary, symbolic, *and* Real (Brown 2019: 5). Doing so would deflate the destructive fantasies driving Trump's paranoid politics and fundamentally transform individuals' psychical investments in reactionary ideological formations.

To move beyond current political divides, we must reject the drive's destructive elements writ large in Trump's aggression and grasp hold of the equally powerful—and far more generative—drives that have motivated resistance to his administration. Throughout *Queer Traversals*, I have noted the riskiness of traversing the fantasy by engaging the Real: an act whose consequences might be either destructive or constructive and cannot be predicted in advance. I have also noted that to facilitate progressive change, those prompting fantasy's traversal must proactively fill the gaps opened by the emergence of a "hole in the big Other," providing fresh forms of sociality to replace the dysfunctional symbolic that fantasy's traversal razes (Stavrakakis 1999: 135). In the 2020 election, as Trump's proponents voted for more of the same and his opponents turned out in even greater numbers to thwart him, those whose energies of resistance were set in motion by the 2016 election successfully risked engagement with the drive's destructiveness to mobilize its constructive capacities.

The resistance's success illustrates a claim I have made throughout this book: that the drive need not be that of the *sinthom*osexual nor lead to death. As Lacan stresses in his twenty-third seminar, there are numerous—and highly individual—options for tapping into the drive and finding a new *sinthôme*: far more constructive options than Edelman envisions. As Joshua J. Weiner and Damon Young contend, queers' "'slantwise' ... relation to existing social structures" offers both "symbolic disruption" and "relational inventiveness," producing a "gay play drive" entailing both "antisocial negativity" and "a joyful recombination of forms" (Weiner and Young 2011: 225). And as I showed in Chapter 4, Sheila Cavanagh, Patricia Gherovici, and Oren Gozlan theorize the *sinthôme*'s capacity to ground novel forms of gender embodiment. They demonstrate that the drive can be inventive: capable of taking subjects in many directions and even of saving subjects' lives. Traversing the fantasy does not inevitably lead subjects to a place without a future; instead, it may lead them to a better future.

Traversing the fantasy nonetheless offers no guarantees. Therein lie the drive's and *sinthôme*'s promises and dangers. Yet queer culture offers numerous strategies for cultivating progressive rather than regressive outcomes after fantasy's traversal. David France's documentary film *How to Survive a Plague* (2012) emphasizes ACT UP's role in the fight for changes in the government's and the health-care system's responses to the AIDS pandemic, suggesting that activism can constitute a constructive rather than destructive way of approaching the drive even in the face of death. By tracking AIDS activists—some of whom died, others of whom survived as their work made better medications available—France's film reminds us of the importance of fighting to prevent mass deaths from pandemics and social marginalization.

Moreover, just as Lawlor's *Paul* shows informal assistance making Paul's queer life more livable, David Weissmann's film *We Were Here* (2011) stresses the vital role queer care played during the AIDS pandemic. Although this documentary uses historical footage of protests to acknowledge the LGBTQ community's justifiable anger about the government's and health care establishment's response to AIDS, the film also stresses the community's mourning and caregiving: the grief of doctors who lost their patients; the agonizing choices of LGBTQ caregivers who crossed ACT UP picket lines to comfort mourners.

These examples, like *Paul*'s scenes of AIDS activism and queer care, illustrate that even though traversing the fantasy of (hetero)sexual difference does not guarantee any particular outcome, there are nonetheless ways of countering the drive's most deathly elements and harnessing its creative capacities to create a better future. To achieve the "new consciousness" Gloria Anzaldúa's border theory and Lawlor's novel exemplify, those undergoing fantasy's traversal must first raze unnecessary divisions set in motion by (hetero)sexual difference and xenophobic nationalism (Anzaldúa 1987: 80). Second, they must embrace new *sinthôme*s with the generativity modeled for Lawlor's Paul by the shape-shifting, mixed-race Robin. Inspiring Paul to embrace his artistic vocation, Robin functions not as a death-driven *sinthom*osexual but as a life-giving *sinthom*estizx whose creativity shows us how to make the world anew.

Notes

1. See Marini (1992: 143) for discussion of this essay's compositional history.
2. Trump's unsuccessful attempts to roll back abortion rights affect women and many transpeople assigned female at birth; see https://www.nytimes.com/2020/06/29/us/supreme-court-abortion-louisiana.html At the same time as the Supreme Court affirmed anti-discrimination protections for LGBTQ workers, Trump erased transpeoples' protections against discrimination in health care; see https://www.nytimes.com/2020/06/15/us/gay-transgender-workers-supreme-court.html and https://www.nytimes.com/2020/06/12/us/politics/trump-transgender-rights.html For the demographics of essential employees during the coronavirus pandemic, see https://apnews.com/029ea874dc964697358016d3628429fa.
3. See https://abcnews.go.com/US/lake-ozarks-memorial-day-partygoer-tests-positive-covid/story?id=70968298 and https://www.advocate.com/health/2020/7/06/fire-island-parties-packed-gay-revelers-spark-outrage-and-worry.
4. https://www.leftvoice.org/From-Farce-to-Tragedy-Zizek-Endorses-Trump?fbclid=IwAR2kpvt0bZbkWytTF9MDUZFPnqQAGGRIV9wJJqdAPBQwq9yW1lSNEjZHswE.

References

Ahmed, Sara (2019), *What's the Use? On the Uses of Use*, Durham: Duke University Press.
Alter, Nora (1998), "Triangulating Performances: Looking after Genre, after Feature," in Ingeborg Majer O'Sickey and Ingeborg von Zadow (eds), *Triangulated Visions: Women in Recent German Cinema*, 11–27, Albany: SUNY Press.
Anzaldúa, Gloria (1987), *Borderlands / La Frontera*, San Francisco: Aunt Lute.
Anzaldúa, Gloria (2015), *Light in the Dark / Luz en lo Oscuro: Rewriting Identity, Spirituality, Reality*, ed. Analouise Keating, Durham: Duke University Press.
Barnes, Djuna (2006), *Nightwood*, New York: New Directions.
Berlant, Lauren (2011), *Cruel Optimism*, Durham: Duke University Press.
Berlant, Lauren, and Lee Edelman (2014), *Sex, or the Unbearable*, Durham: Duke University Press.
The Birds (2000), [Film] Dir Alfred Hitchcock, USA: Universal Home Entertainment.
Borch-Jacobsen (1991), *Lacan: The Absolute Master*, Stanford: Stanford University Press.
Bower, Kathrin (2000), "Outing Hybridity: Polymorphism, Identity, and Desire in Monika Treut's *The Virgin Machine*," *The European Studies Journal* 17 (1): 23–40.
Bowie, Malcolm (1991), *Lacan*, Cambridge: Harvard University Press.
Boys Don't Cry (1999), [Film] Dir Kimberly Peirce, USA: Fox Searchlight.
Brassaï (2001), *The Secret Paris of the 30's*, New York: Thames and Hudson.
Brenkman, John (2002), "Queer Post-Politics," *Narrative* 10 (2): 174–80.
Brown, Wendy (2010), *Walled Subjects, Waning Sovereignty*, New York: Zone Books.
Brown, Wendy (2019), *In the Ruins of Neoliberalism: The Rise of Antidemocratic Politics in the West*, New York: Columbia University Press.
Butler, Judith (1990), *Gender Trouble: Feminism and the Subversion of Identity*, New York: Routledge.
Butler, Judith (1993), *Bodies That Matter: On the Discursive Limits of "Sex,"* New York: Routledge.
Butler, Judith (1994), "Gender as Performance: An Interview with Judith Butler," interview with Peter Osborne and Lynne Segal, *Radical Philosophy* 67: 32–9.
Butler, Judith (1997), *The Psychic Life of Power: Theories in Subjection*, Stanford: Stanford University Press.
Butler, Judith (1998), "How Bodies Come to Matter: An Interview with Judith Butler," interview with Irene Costera Meijer and Baukje Prins, *Signs* 23 (2): 275–86.
Butler, Judith (2000a), "Competing Universalities," in *Contingency, Hegemony, Universality: Contemporary Dialogues on the Left*, 136–81, London: Verso.

Butler, Judith (2000b), "Dynamic Conclusions," in *Contingency, Hegemony, Universality: Contemporary Dialogues on the Left*, 263–80, London: Verso.

Butler, Judith (2000c), "Restaging the Universal: Hegemony and the Limits of Formalism," in *Contingency, Hegemony, Universality: Contemporary Dialogues on the Left*, 11–43, London: Verso.

Butler, Judith (2002), *Antigone's Claim*, New York: Columbia University Press.

Butler, Judith (2004), *Undoing Gender*, New York: Routledge.

Butler, Judith, Ernesto Laclau, and Slavoj Žižek (2000), "Introduction," in *Contingency, Hegemony, Universality: Contemporary Dialogues on the Left*, 1–4, London: Verso.

Campbell, Jan (2000), *Arguing with the Phallus: Feminist, Queer and Postcolonial Theory: A Psychoanalytic Contribution*, London: Zed Books.

Carlson, Shanna (2010), "Transgender Subjectivity and the Logic of Sexual Difference," *Differences* 21 (2): 46–72.

Carlson, Shanna (2014), "Psychoanalytic," *TSQ: Transgender Studies Quarterly* 1 (1-2): 170.

Caserio, Robert (2006), "The Anti-Social Thesis in Queer Theory," *PMLA* 121 (3): 819–21.

Caughie, Pamela (2013), "The Temporality of Modernist Life Writing in the Era of Transsexualism: Virginia Woolf's *Orlando* and Einar Wegener's *Man Into Woman*," *Modern Fiction Studies* 59 (3): 501–25.

Cavanagh, Sheila (2015), "Transsexuality and Lacanian Psychoanalysis," *CNPC 1: The Freudian Legacy Today*: 104–24. https://cnpcrcpc.files.wordpress.com/2015/12/6-cavanagh-transsexuality-and-lacanian-psychoanalysis.pdf (accessed August 10, 2021).

Cavanagh, Sheila (2016), "Transsexuality as Sinthome: Bracha L. Ettinger and the Other (Feminine) Sexual Difference," *Studies in Gender and Sexuality* 17 (1): 27–44.

Cavanagh, Sheila (2017), "Transpsychoanalytics," *TSQ: Transgender Studies Quarterly* 3 (4): 326–57.

Cavanagh, Sheila (2018), "Transgender Embodiment: A Lacanian Approach," *Psychoanalytic Review* 105 (3): 303–27.

Cheng, Vincent (1995), *Joyce, Race, and Empire*, Cambridge, UK: Cambridge University Press.

Chiesa, Lorenzo (2007), *Subjectivity and Otherness: A Philosophical Reading of Lacan*, Cambridge, MA: The MIT Press.

Chiesa, Lorenzo (2016), *The Not-Two: Logic and God in Lacan*, Cambridge: The MIT Press.

Cixous, Hélène (1972), *The Exile of James Joyce*, trans. A. J Sally, Purcell, NY: David Lewis.

Cixous, Hélène (1991), "The Laugh of the Medusa," in Robyn Warhol, and Diana Price Herndl (eds), *Feminisms: An Anthology of Literary Theory and Criticism*, 334–49, New Brunswick: Rutgers University Press.

Coffman, Chris (2006), *Insane Passions: Lesbianism and Psychosis in Literature and Film*, Middleton: Wesleyan University Press.

Coffman, Chris (2018), *Gertrude Stein's Transmasculinity*, Edinburgh: Edinburgh University Press.

Cohler, Deborah (2008), "Teaching Transnationally: Queer Studies and Imperialist Legacies in Monique Truong's *The Book of Salt*," *Radical Teacher* 82: 25–30.

Congregation for Catholic Education (2019), *Male and Female He Created Them: Towards a Path of Dialogue on the Question of Gender Theory in Education*, Vatican City: Vatican Press. Available online: https://www.newwaysministry.org/wp-content/uploads/2019/06/Male-and-Female-Document-June-10-2019.pdf?fbclid=IwAR2srbdxtNrPdGbvQKWuVsaf3h6ZL0GYGDaqsICRGW9sdT4-toAv4R9Zk0k.

Copjec, Joan (1994), *Read My Desire: Lacan against the Historicists*, Cambridge: The MIT Press.

Copjec, Joan (2010), "The Fable of the Stork and Other False Sexual Theories," *differences* 21 (1): 63–73.

Crawford, Lucas Cassidy (2013), "Transgender without Organs? Mobilizing a Geoaffective Theory of Gender Modification," in Susan Stryker, and Aren Z. Aizura (eds), *The Transgender Studies Reader 2*, 473–82, New York: Routledge.

Cromwell, Jason (1999), *Transmen and FTMs: Identities, Bodies, Genders, and Sexualities*, Urbana and Chicago: University of Illinois Press.

de Lauretis, Teresa (2008), Freud's Drive: Psychoanalysis, Literature and Film, New York: Palgrave.

de Lauretis, Teresa (2011), "Queer Texts, Bad Habits, and the Issue of a Future," *GLQ* 17 (2–3): 243–63.

de la Torre, Shanna (2018), *Sex for Structuralists: The Non-Oedipal Logics of Femininity and Psychosis,* Cham: Palgrave.

de Man, Paul (1983), "The Rhetoric of Temporality," in *Blindness and Insight: Essays in the Rhetoric of Contemporary Criticism*, Second Edition, 187–228, Minneapolis: University of Minnesota Press.

Dean, Jodi (2006), *Žižek's Politics*, New York: Routledge.

Dean, Tim (2000a), *Beyond Sexuality*, Chicago: University of Chicago Press.

Dean, Tim (2000b), "Homosexuality and the Problem of Otherness," in Tim Dean, and Christopher Lane (eds), *Homosexuality and Psychoanalysis*, 120–43, Chicago: University of Chicago Press, 2000.

Dean, Tim (2006), "The Antisocial Homosexual," *PMLA* 121 (3): 826–8.

Dean, Tim (2008), "An Impossible Embrace: Queerness, Futurity, and the Death Drive," in James J. Bono, Tim Dean, and Ewa Plonowska Ziarek (eds), *A Time for the Humanities: Futurity and the Limits of Autonomy*, 193–222, New York: Fordham University Press.

Dingledine, Don (2009), "'You Make Such an Exquisite Corpse': Surrealist Collaboration and the Transcendence of Gender in *Hedwig and the Angry Inch*," in Kanta Kochlar-Lindgren, Davis Schneiderman, and Tom Denlinger (eds), *The Exquisite Corpse: Chance and Collaboration in Surrealism's Parlor Game*, 257–77, Lincoln: University of Nebraska Press.

Dinshaw, Carolyn, Roderick A. Lee Edelman, Carla Freccero Ferguson, Elizabeth Freeman, Jack Halberstam, Annamarie Jagose, Christopher Nealon, and Nguyen Tan Hoang (2007), "Theorizing Queer Temporalities: A Roundtable Discussion," *GLQ: A Journal of Lesbian and Gay Studies* 13 (2-3): 177-95.

Edelman, Lee (2004), *No Future: Queer Theory and the Death Drive*, Durham: Duke University Press.

Edelman, Lee (2006), "Antagonism, Negativity, and the Subject of Queer Theory," *PMLA* 121 (3): 821-3.

Elliot, Patricia, and Katrina Roen (1998), "Transgenderism and the Question of Embodiment: Promising Queer Politics?", *GLQ: A Journal of Lesbian and Gay Studies* 4 (2): 231-61.

Eng, David L., Jack Halberstam, and José Esteban Muñoz, "What's Queer about Queer Studies Now?," *Social Text* 84-85 (2005): 1-17.

Enke, Finn (2012), "The Education of Little Cis: Cisgender and the Discipline of Opposing Bodies," in Finn Enke (ed), *Transfeminist Perspectives in and beyond Transgender and Gender Studies*, 60-77, Philadelphia: Temple University Press.

Espinoza, Joshua Jennifer (2018), "Things Haunt." Available online: https://poets.org/poem/things-haunt (accessed August 10, 2021).

Ettinger, Bracha (2001), "Matrixial Gaze and Screen: Other Than Phallic and Beyond the Late Lacan," in Laura Doyle (ed), *Bodies of Resistance: New Phenomenologies of Politics, Agency, and Culture*, 103-43, Evanston: Northwestern University Press.

Ettinger, Bracha (2006a), *The Matrixial Borderspace*, Minneapolis: University of Minnesota Press.

Ettinger, Bracha (2006b), "Matrixial Trans-subjectivity," *Theory, Culture & Society* 23 (2-3): 218-22.

Evans, Dylan (1996), *An Introductory Dictionary of Lacanian Psychoanalysis*, New York: Routledge.

Fausto-Sterling, Anne (2000), *Sexing the Body: Gender Politics and the Construction of Sexuality*, New York: Basic Books.

Fink, Bruce (1995), *The Lacanian Subject*, Princeton: Princeton University Press.

Foucault, Michel (1970), *The Order of Things: An Archaeology of the Human Sciences*, New York: Vintage.

Foucault, Michel (1977), "What Is an Author?", in *Language, Counter-memory, Practice*, 113-38, Ithaca: Cornell University Press.

Freccero, Carla (2011), "Queer Times," in Janet Halley, and Andrew Parker (eds), *After Sex? On Writing since Queer Theory*, 17-26, Durham: Duke University Press.

Freeman, Elizabeth (2010), *Time Binds: Queer Temporalities, Queer Histories*, Durham and London: Duke University Press.

Freud, Sigmund (1961), *The Ego and the Id*, trans. James Strachey, 1-66, London: The Hogarth Press.

Freud, Sigmund (1962), *Three Essays on the Theory of Sexuality*, New York: Basic Books.

Gemunden, Gerd (1998), "The Queer Utopia of Monika Treut," in *Framed Visions: Popular Culture, Americanization, and the Contemporary German and Austrian Imagination*, by Gerd Gemunden, 177–94, Ann Arbor: University of Michigan Press.

Gherovici, Patricia (2010), *Please Select Your Gender: From the Invention of Hysteria to the Democratizing of Transgenderism*, New York: Routledge.

Gherovici, Patricia (2012), "The Transsexual Body Written: Writing as Sinthome," in Santanu Biswas (ed), *The Literary Lacan: From Literature to Lituraterre and Beyond*, 259–90, London and New York: Seagull Books.

Gherovici, Patricia (2014), "The Art of the Symptom: Body, Writing, and Sex Change," in Laura Marcus, and Ankhi Mukherjee (eds), *A Concise Companion to Psychoanalysis*, 250–70, Hoboken: John Wiley & Sons.

Gherovici, Patricia (2017), *Transgender Psychoanalysis: A Lacanian Perspective on Sexual Difference*, New York: Routledge.

Gherovici, Patricia (2019a), "Matters of Life and Sex: Trans-ing Psychoanalysis," *Public Seminar*, 25 June 2019. https://publicseminar.org/essays/matters-of-life-and-sex/ (accessed August 10, 2021).

Gherovici, Patricia (2019b), "Transpsychoanalysis," *philoSOPHIA* 9 (1): 144–8.

Gordon, Peter E. (2018), "The Authoritarian Personality Revisited: Reading Adorno in the Age of Trump," in *Authoritarianism: Three Inquiries in Critical Theory*, 45–84, Chicago: University of Chicago Press.

Gossett, Che (2016), "Žižek's Trans/gender Trouble," *Los Angeles Review of Books*, September 13. Available online: https://lareviewofbooks.org/article/zizeks-transgender-trouble/ (accessed August 10, 2021).

Gozlan, Oren (2015), *Transsexuality and the Art of Transitioning: A Lacanian Approach*, New York: Routledge.

Haggerty, George (2006), *Queer Gothic*, Urbana and Illinois: University of Illinois Press.

Halberstam, Jack (2005), *In a Queer Time and Place: Transgender Bodies, Subcultural Lives*, New York: New York University Press.

Halberstam, Jack (2006), "The Politics of Negativity in Recent Queer Theory," *PMLA* 121 (3): 823–5.

Halberstam, Jack (2011a), *The Queer Art of Failure*, Durham: Duke University Press.

Halberstam, Jack (2011b), "Riots and Occupations: The Fall of the US and the Rise of the Politics of Refusal," 19 October. Available online: https://bullybloggers.wordpress.com/2011/10/19/riots-and-occupations-the-fall-of-the-us-and-the-rise-of-the-politics-of-refusal/ (accessed August 10, 2021).

Halley, Janet, and Andrew Parker (2011), "Introduction," in Janet Halley, and Andrew Parker (eds), *After Sex? On Writing Since Queer Theory*, 1–14, Durham: Duke University Press.

Harari, Roberto (2002), *How James Joyce Made His Name: A Reading of the Final Lacan*, trans. Luke Thurston, New York: Other Press.

Hart, Lynda (1994), *Fatal Women: Lesbian Sexuality and the Mark of Aggression*, Princeton: Princeton University Press.

Hart, Lynda (1998), *Between the Body and the Flesh: Performing Sadomasochism*, New York: Columbia University Press.

Hedwig and the Angry Inch (2001), [Film] Dir John Cameron Mitchell, USA: Killer Films.

Herring, Scott (2010), *Another Country: Queer Anti-Urbanism*, New York: New York University Press.

Hoens, Dominiek, and Ed Pluth (2002), "The *sinthome*: A New Way of Writing an Old Problem?" in Luke Thurston (ed), *Re-Inventing the Symptom: Essays on the Final Lacan*, 1–18, New York: The Other Press.

How to Survive a Plague (2012), [Film] Dir David France, USA: Public Square Films / Ninety Thousand Words.

In & Out (1997), [Film] Dir. Frank Oz, USA: Paramount Pictures.

Irigaray, Luce (1985a), *This Sex Which Is Not One*, trans. Catherine Porter, Ithaca: Cornell University Press.

Irigaray, Luce (1985b), *Speculum of the Other Woman*, trans. Gillian G. Gill, Ithaca: Cornell University Press.

Jacob, Hale, C. (1998), "Tracing a Ghostly Memory in My Throat: Reflections on FtM Feminist Voice and Agency," in Tom Digby (ed), *Men Doing Feminism*, 99–129, New York: Routledge.

Johnston, Adrian (2008), *Žižek's Ontology: A Transcendental Materialist Theory of Subjectivity*, Evanston: Northwestern University Press.

Joyce, James (1977), *A Portrait of the Artist as a Young Man*, ed. G. Chester Anderson, New York: Penguin.

Kay, Sarah (2003), *Žižek: A Critical Introduction*, Cambridge, UK: Polity.

Keating, Analouise (2015), "Editor's Introduction: Re-envisioning Coyolxauhqui, Decolonizing Reality" in Gloria Anzaldúa (ed), *Light in the Dark / Luz en lo Oscuro*, xi–xxxvii, Durham: Duke University Press.

Kessler, Suzanne (1998), *Lessons from the Intersexed*, New Brunswick: Rutgers University Press.

Klotz, Marcia (1998), "The Queer and Unqueer Spaces of Monika Treut's Films," in Ingeborg Majer O'Sickey and Ingeborg von Zadow (eds), *Triangulated Visions: Women in Recent German Cinema*, 65–80, Albany: State University of New York Press.

Knight, Julia (1995), "The Meaning of Treut?" in Tamsin Wilton (ed), *Immortal, Invisible: Lesbians and the Moving Image*, 34–51, London: Routledge.

Krieger, Nick (2011), *Nina Here Nor There*, Boston: Beacon.

Kristeva, Julia (1977), *Polylogue*, Paris: Seuil.

Kristeva, Julia (1980), *Desire in Language: A Semiotic Approach to Literature and Art*, New York: Columbia University Press.

Kristeva, Julia (1982), *Powers of Horror: An Essay on Abjection*, New York: Columbia University Press.

Kristeva, Julia (1984), *Revolution in Poetic Language*, New York: Columbia University Press.

Kuzniar, Alice (2000), "Lesbians Abroad: The Queer Nationhood of Monika Treut et al," in *The Queer German Cinema*, by Alice Kuzniar, 157–73, Stanford: Stanford University Press.

Lacan, Jacques (1977), *The Four Fundamental Concepts of Psycho-Analysis (Seminar XI.)*, trans. Alan Sheridan, New York: Norton.

Lacan, Jacques (1993), *The Seminar of Jacques Lacan, Book III: The Psychoses*, trans. Russell Grigg, New York: Norton.

Lacan, Jacques (1998), *The Seminar of Jacques Lacan, Book XX: Encore. On Feminine Sexuality, the Limits of Love and Knowledge, 1972-1973*, trans. Bruce Fink, New York: Norton.

Lacan, Jacques (2006a), "The Direction of the Treatment and the Principles of Its Power," in *Écrits: The First Complete Edition in English*, trans. Bruce Fink, 489–542, New York: Norton.

Lacan, Jacques (2006b), "The Freudian Thing, or the Meaning of the Return to Freud in Psychoanalysis," in *Écrits: The First Complete Edition in English*, trans. Bruce Fink, 334–63, New York: Norton.

Lacan, Jacques (2006c), "The Function and Field of Speech and Language in Psychoanalysis," in *Écrits: The First Complete Edition in English*, trans. Bruce Fink, 237–68, New York: Norton.

Lacan, Jacques (2006d), "The Instance of the Letter in the Unconscious, or Reason since Freud," in *Écrits: The First Complete Edition in English*, trans. Bruce Fink, 412–41, New York: Norton.

Lacan, Jacques (2006e), "The Mirror Stage as Formative of the *I* Function as Revealed in Psychoanalytic Experience," in *Écrits: The First Complete Edition in English*, trans. Bruce Fink, 75–81, New York: Norton.

Lacan, Jacques (2006f), "Presentation on Psychical Causality," in *Écrits: The First Complete Edition in English*, trans. Bruce Fink, 123–58, New York: Norton.

Lacan, Jacques (2006g), "The Signification of the Phallus," in *Écrits: The First Complete Edition in English*, trans. Bruce Fink, 575–84, New York: Norton.

Lacan, Jacques (2006h), "The Subversion of the Subject and the Dialectic of Desire in the Freudian Unconscious," in *Écrits: The First Complete Edition in English*, trans. Bruce Fink, 671–702, New York: Norton.

Lacan, Jacques (2016), *The Sinthome: The Seminar of Jacques Lacan, Book XXIII*, trans. A. R. Price, Malden, MA: Polity.

Laclau, Ernesto (2000), "Identity and Hegemony: The Role of Universality in the Constitution of Political Logics," in *Contingency, Hegemony, Universality: Contemporary Dialogues on the Left*, 44–89, London: Verso.

Lavery, Grace (2019a), "The King's Two Anuses: Trans Feminism and Free Speech," *Differences* 30 (3): 118–51.

Lavery, Grace (2019b), "Bat Out of Hell: On Susan Stryker," https://grace.substack.com/p/bat-out-of-hell (accessed November 19, 2019).

Lavery, Grace (2020), "Trans Realism, Psychoanalytic Practice, and the Rhetoric of Technique," *Critical Inquiry* 46 (2020): 719–44.

Lawlor, Andrea (2017), *Paul Takes the Form of a Mortal Girl: A Novel*, Chicago: Rescue Press.

MacCannell, Juliet Flower (2008), "The Real Imaginary," *S: Journal of the Jan van Eyck Circle for Lacanian Ideology Critique* 1: 46–57.

Marcus, Sharon (2005), "Queer Theory for Everyone: A Review Essay," *Signs* 31 (1): 191–218.

Marini, Marcelle (1992), *Jacques Lacan: The French Context*, trans. Anne Tomiche, New Brunswick: Rutgers University Press.

Millot, Catherine (1990), *Horsexe*, New York: Autonomedia.

Moncayo, Raoul (2016), *Lalangue, Sinthome, Jouissance, and Nomination: A Reading Companion and Commentary on Lacan's Seminar XXIII on the Sinthome*, New York: Routledge.

Morel, Geneviève (2000), *Ambiguités sexuelles*, Paris: Anthropos.

Muñoz, José Esteban (2006), "Thinking beyond Antirelationality and Antiutopianism in Queer Critique," *PMLA* 121 (3): 825–6.

Muñoz, José Esteban (2013), "'The White to Be Angry': Vaginal Davis's Terrorist Drag," in Susan Stryker, and Aren Z. Aizura (eds), *The Transgender Studies Reader 2*, 79–90, New York: Routledge.

Nealon, Christopher (2001), *Foundlings: Lesbian and Gay Historical Emotion before Stonewall*, Durham: Duke University Press.

Nichols, Ben (2020), *Same Old: Queer Theory, Literature and the Politics of Sameness*, Manchester: Manchester University Press.

Nolan, Emer (1995), *James Joyce and Nationalism*, New York: Routledge, 1995.

North By Northwest (2000), [Film] Dir. Alfred Hitchcock, USA: Turner Home Entertainment.

Pellegrini, Ann, and Avgi Saketopoulou (2019), "On taking sides: they/them pronouns, gender and the psychoanalyst," *Psychoanalysis Today*. Available online: https://www.psychoanalysis.today/en-GB/PT-Articles/Pellegrini167541/On-taking-sides-they-them-pronouns,-gender-and-the.aspx (accessed August 10, 2021).

Penney, James (2014), *After Queer Theory: The Limits of Sexual Politics*, New York: Pluto Press.

Pluth, Ed (2007), *Signifiers and Acts: Freedom in Lacan's Theory of the Subject*, Albany: SUNY Press.

Pollock, Griselda (2006), "Femininity: Aporia or Sexual Difference?," in *The Matrixial Borderspace*, by Bracha Ettinger, 1–37, Minneapolis: University of Minnesota Press.

Prosser, Jay (1998), *Second Skins: The Body Narratives of Transsexuality*, New York: Columbia University Press.
Ragland, Ellie (2004), *The Logic of Sexuation: From Aristotle to Lacan*, Albany: State University of New York Press.
Ragland, Ellie (2015), *Jacques Lacan and the Logic of Sexuation: Topology and Language in Psychoanalysis*, New York: Routledge.
Rajchman, John (1991), *Truth and Eros: Foucault, Lacan, and the Question of Ethics*, New York: Routledge.
Reimann, Andrea (2003), "New German Cinema's Boundaries Opened: Postmodern Authorship and Nationality in Monika Treut's Films of the 1980's," in Barbara Kosta and Helga Kraft (eds), *Writing against Boundaries: Nationality, Ethnicity, and Gender in the German-Speaking Context*, 177–96, Amsterdam: Rodopi.
Restuccia, Frances (2002), "Queer Love," in Kelly Oliver, and Steve Edwin (eds), *Between the Psyche and the Social: Psychoanalytic Social Theory*, 83–95, New York: Rowman & Littlefield.
Restuccia, Frances (2006), *Amourous Acts: Lacanian Ethics in Modernism, Film, and Queer Theory*, Stanford: Stanford University Press.
Riley, Snorton, C. (2017), *Black on Both Sides: A Racial History of Trans Identity*, Minneapolis: Minnesota.
Rohy, Valerie (2000), *Impossible Women: Lesbian Figures and American Literature*, Ithaca: Cornell University Press.
Roof, Judith (2016), *What Gender Is, What Gender Does*, Minneapolis: University of Minnesota Press.
Rose, Jacqueline (1993), *Why War? Psychoanalysis, Politics, and the Return to Melanie Klein*, Cambridge, MA: Blackwell.
Roudinesco, Elisabeth (1990), *Jacques Lacan & Co.: A History of Psychoanalysis in France, 1925-1985*, trans. Jeffrey Mehlman, Chicago: The University of Chicago Press.
Roudinesco, Elisabeth (1997), *Jacques Lacan*, trans. Barbara Bray, New York: Columbia University Press.
Rubin, Gayle (1976), "The Traffic in Women: Notes on the 'Political Economy' of Sex," in Rayna Rapp Reiter (ed), *Toward an Anthropology of Women*, 157–210, New York: Monthly Review Press.
Ruti, Mari (2008a), "The Fall of Fantasies: A Lacanian Reading of Lack," *Journal of the American Psychoanalytic Association* 56 (2): 483–508.
Ruti, Mari (2008b), "Why There Is Always a Future in the Future," *Angelaki* 13 (1): 113–14.
Ruti, Mari (2010), "Life beyond Fantasy: The Rewriting of Destiny in Lacanian Theory," *Culture, Theory, and Critique* 51 (1): 1–14.
Ruti, Mari (2017), *The Ethics of Opting Out: Queer Theory's Defiant Subjects*, New York: Columbia University Press.
Salamon, Gayle (2010), *Assuming A Body: Transgender and Rhetorics of Materiality*, New York: Columbia University Press.

Salamon, Gayle (2016), "The Meontology of Masculinity: Notes on Castration Elation," *Parallax* 22 (3): 312–22.

Salamon, Gayle (2018), *The Life and Death of Latisha King: A Critical Phenomenology of Transphobia*, New York: New York University Press.

Samuels, Robert (2016), *Psychoanalyzing the Left and Right after Donald Trump*, London: Palgrave.

Sedgwick, Eve Kosofsky (1993), *Tendencies*, Durham: Duke University Press.

Sedgwick, Eve Kosofsky (2003), *Touching Feeling: Affect, Pedagogy, Performativity*, Durham: Duke University Press.

Seshadri-Crooks, Kalpana (2000), *Desiring Whiteness: A Lacanian Analysis of Race*, New York: Routledge.

Shepherdson, Charles (2000), "The *Role* of Gender and the *Imperative* of Sex," in *Vital Signs: Nature, Culture, Psychoanalysis*, by Charles Shepherdson, 85–114, New York: Routledge.

Shepherdson, Charles (2008), "The Intimate Alterity of the Real," in *Lacan and the Limits of Language*, by Charles Shepherdson, 1–49, New York: Fordham University Press.

Silverman, Kaja (1992), "The Lacanian Phallus," *differences* 4 (1): 84–115.

Silverman, Kaja (1996), *The Threshold of the Visible World*, New York: Routledge.

Simon, Sunka (1998), "Out of Hollywood: Monika Treut's *Virgin Machine* and Percy Adlon's *Bagdad Café*," in *Queering the Canon: Defying Sights in German Literature and Culture*, Christoph Lorey and John L. Plews (eds), 383–402, Columbia: Camden House.

Snediker, Michael (2009), *Queer Optimism: Lyric Personhood and Other Felicitous Persuasions*, Minneapolis: University of Minnesota Press.

Solanas, Valerie (1996), *SCUM Manifesto*, San Francisco: AK Press.

Stavrakakis, Yannis (1999), *Lacan and the Political*, London and New York: Routledge.

Straayer, Chris (1993), "Lesbian Narratives and Queer Characters in Monika Treut's *Virgin Machine*," *Journal of Film and Video* 45 (2-3): 24–39.

Stryker, Susan (1994), "My Word to Victor Frankenstein above the Village of Chamounix: Performing Transgender Rage," *GLQ: A Journal of Lesbian and Gay Studies* 1: 237–54.

Stryker, Susan (1998), "The Transgender Issue: An Introduction," *GLQ: A Journal of Lesbian and Gay Studies* 4 (2): 145–8.

Stryker, Susan (2004), "Thinking Sex / Thinking Gender," *GLQ: A Journal of Lesbian and Gay Studies* 10 (2): 211–5.

Stryker, Susan (2016), Untitled remarks at the Opening Session of the Trans* Studies Conference at the University of Arizona, Tucson, September 8.

Stryker, Susan, Paisley Currah, and Lisa Jean Moore (2008), "Introduction: Trans-, Trans, or Transgender," *WSQ: Women's Studies Quarterly* 26 (3–4): 11–22.

Svich, Caridad (2019), *Mitchell and Trask's Hedwig and the Angry Inch*, New York: Routledge.

Treichler, Paula (1999), *How to Have Theory in an Epidemic: Cultural Chronicles of AIDS*, Durham: Duke University Press.
Vaccaro, Jeanne (2013), "Felt Matters," in Susan Stryker, and Aren Z. Aizura (eds), *The Transgender Studies Reader 2*, 91–100, New York: Routledge.
Vaccaro, Jeanne (2015), "Feelings and Franctals: Woolly Ecologies of Transgender Matter," *GLQ: A Journal of Lesbian and Gay Studies*, 21 (2–3): 273–93.
Verhaeghe, Paul (2001), *Beyond Gender: From Subject to Drive*, New York: The Other Press.
Verhaeghe, Paul (2002), "Lacan's Answer to the Classical Mind/Body Deadlock: Retracing Freud's *Beyond*," in Suzanne Barnard (ed), *Reading Seminar XX: Lacan's Major Work on Love, Knowledge, and Feminine Sexuality*, 109–39, Albany: SUNY Press.
Verhaeghe, Paul, and Frédéric Declercq (2002), "Lacan's Analytic Goal: *Le sinthome* or the Feminine Way," in Luke Thurston (ed), *Re-inventing the Symptom: Essays on the Final Lacan*, 59–82, New York: The Other Press.
Viego, Antonio (2007), *Dead Subjects: Toward a Politics of Loss in Latino Studies*, Durham: Duke University Press.
The Virgin Machine (1988), [Film] Dir Monika Treut, Germany: Hyena Films / NDR.
We Were Here (2011), [Film] Dir David Weissman, USA.
Weil, Abraham B (2017), "Psychoanalysis and Trans*versality," *TSQ: Transgender Studies Quarterly* 4 (3–4): 639–46.
Weiner, Joshua J., and Damon Young (2011), "Queer Bonds," Introduction to *GLQ: A Journal of Lesbian and Gay Studies* 17 (2–3): 223–41.
Whittle, Stephen (2006), "Foreward," in Susan Stryker, and Stephen Whittle (eds), *The Transgender Studies Reader*, xi–xvi, New York and London: Routledge.
Woolf, Virginia (2006), *Orlando*, 1928, Annotated Edition, New York: Harcourt.
Žižek, Slavoj (1989), *The Sublime Object of Ideology*, London and New York: Verso.
Žižek, Slavoj (1992), *Enjoy Your Symptom! Jacques Lacan in Hollywood and Out*, London and New York: Routledge.
Žižek, Slavoj (1993d), *Tarrying with the Negative*, Durham: Duke University Press.
Žižek, Slavoj (1994a), "Is There a Cause of the Subject?", in Joan Copjec (ed), *Supposing the Subject*, 84–105, New York and London: Verso.
Žižek, Slavoj (1994b), *The Metastases of Enjoyment: Six Essays on Women and Causality*, London and New York: Verso.
Žižek, Slavoj (1996), *The Indivisible Remainder: An Essay on Schelling and Related Matters*, London and New York: Verso.
Žižek, Slavoj (1999), *The Ticklish Subject: The Absent Center of Political Ontology*, New York: Verso.
Žižek, Slavoj (2000a), "Class Struggle or Postmodernism? Yes, Please!", in *Contingency, Hegemony, Universality: Contemporary Dialogues on the Left*, 90–135, London: Verso.
Žižek, Slavoj (2000b), "Da Capo senza Fine," in *Contingency, Hegemony, Universality: Contemporary Dialogues on the Left*, 213–62, London: Verso.

Žižek, Slavoj (2000c), "Holding the Place," in *Contingency, Hegemony, Universality: Contemporary Dialogues on the Left*, 308–29, London: Verso.
Žižek, Slavoj (2008), *Violence: Six Sideways Reflections*, New York: Picador.
Žižek, Slavoj (2016a), "A Reply to My Critics," *The Philosophical Salon*, 5 August. Available online: http://thephilosophicalsalon.com/a-reply-to-my-critics/ (accessed August 10, 2021).
Žižek, Slavoj (2016b), "Reply to My Critics, Part Two," *The Philosophical Salon*, 14 August. Available online: http://thephilosophicalsalon.com/reply-to-my-critics-part-two/ (accessed August 10, 2021).
Žižek, Slavoj (2016c), "The Sexual Is Political," *The Philosophical Salon*, 1 August. Available online: http://thephilosophicalsalon.com/the-sexual-is-political/ (accessed August 10, 2021).
Žižek, Slavoj (2019a), *Sex and the Failed Absolute*, London: Bloomsbury Academic.
Žižek, Slavoj (2019b), "Transgender Dogma Is Naïve and Incompatible with Freud," *Spectator Life*, 30 May 2019. https://spectatorworld.com/book-and-art/transgender-dogma-naive-freud/ (accessed May 30, 2019).
Zupančič, Alenka (2017), *What Is Sex?*, Cambridge, MA: MIT Press.

Index

ACT UP 199, 205, 224
Ahmed, Sara 5–6, 25, 99
 What's the Use? 4
AIDS 189, 213, 217, 224
allegory 61, 67, 72–3
antinomy 3, 12–13, 21, 26, 31–2, 37–9, 41,
 43, 52, 62, 78, 84, 99, 107, 114, 116,
 119–23, 129, 132, 139, 142, 146,
 159, 161, 164, 222
anti-social 17, 58–9
anti-social thesis in queer theory 56–7, 74,
 82, 114, 190, 204
Anzaldúa, Gloria 22, 117, 172, 175–8, 184,
 186, 208, 225
 Borderlands/La Frontera 20–1, 94, 116,
  147, 167–9, 171
 conocimiento 173
 Light in the Dark/Luz en lo Oscuro 21,
  173
 mestiza 20, 117, 167–8, 171–2, 176–7,
  179
 nepantla 172–8
 nepantlera 173–4, 176–8
 new consciousness 117, 167, 169,
  171–2, 186, 208, 225
 psychoanalytic theory of 168–71,
  177–8
authoritarian 22, 213–17, 220, 222
authoritarianism 22, 32, 215

Badiou, Alain 32
Barnes, Djuna, *Nightwood* 188
BDSM 44, 201–2
Berlant, Lauren 12, 73–4, 90, 189, 213
 elastic theory of fantasy 91
 Sex, or the Unbearable 73, 89–90, 189
Bersani, Leo 14, 33, 57, 74, 200
beside 8–9, 17, 27, 77, 91, 125–6, 133, 136,
 141, 145, 147
beyond
 in Anzaldúa 167–72, 178–9
 authoritarian patriarchy 222–3

binary gender 134, 141, 144, 159, 186
border divisions 167–9
dialectical synthesis 169–71, 178
Edelman's theoretical framework 55–6,
 62, 67, 69, 73, 76–8, 82–4, 87–9, 93
fantasy 167–71
in *Hedwig and the Angry Inch*
 (Mitchell) 159–61, 163–5
heterosexual fantasy 8–9, 11–15, 17,
 20–1
identity markers 177
in *In & Out* (Oz) 50–2
Lacan's theoretical framework 8, 21, 56,
 62, 76–8, 83–4, 115, 121–2, 125–6,
 128, 133, 137, 140, 142–3, 146, 156
in *Orlando* (Woolf) 115
in *Paul Takes the Form of a Mortal
 Girl* (Lawlor) 178–82, 193–4, 196,
 198–9, 201–2, 204, 206, 208
political divides 223
sexual difference and romantic love
 151–2, 156, 159–61, 163–5
in *The Virgin Machine* (Treut) 20–1, 94,
 116, 147, 151, 179
xenophobic nationalism 222
Žižek's theoretical framework 25–7,
 32, 34, 43
The Birds (Hitchcock) 59–60, 69, 71–3
bisexuality 144
Black Lives Matter 215
body 16, 33, 63–4, 100, 102, 105, 112–14,
 120, 126, 128–36, 140, 142–5,
 158–63, 176–9, 181, 192–5, 201,
 204–5, 207
borderlands 167, 171, 174
Borderlands/La Frontera (Anzaldúa) 20–1,
 94, 116, 147, 167–9, 171
borders 20, 29, 159, 167, 219
borderspace 120–3, 127–8, 140–1, 145
Borromean knot 78, 104
Boys Don't Cry (Peirce) 113
Brassaï 156

Brown, Wendy 215, 218–20, 222–3
  In the Ruins of Neoliberalism: The Rise of Antidemocratic Politics in the West 214
  Walled States, Waning Sovereignty 220
Butler, Judith 11, 14, 25–6, 28–31, 33, 35–7, 41–2, 45, 47, 49, 51, 58–9, 63, 65–6, 72, 77, 81, 84, 99–100, 108, 116, 124, 133
  Antigone's Claim 81
  Bodies That Matter: On the Discursive Limits of "Sex" 25, 28–9, 37
  Gender Trouble: Feminism and the Subversion of Identity 9, 28, 151
  Undoing Gender 36

Campbell, Jan 170, 177–8
  Arguing with the Phallus: Feminist, Queer and Postcolonial Theory: A Psychoanalytic Contribution 13
capitalism 214, 217, 221
care 15, 19, 94, 117, 183, 187, 208–10, 224
Carlson, Shanna 2, 5, 21, 98, 101–2, 109, 117, 119, 133
  "Transgender Subjectivity and the Logic of Sexual Difference" 109
  transpsychoanalysis 106, 116
Caserio, Robert 56–7, 190, 204
castration 8, 30, 32, 36, 40, 45, 100–1, 107, 111, 121–3, 125, 138–9, 153, 175
Catholicism 1–2
Caughie, Pamela 115
Cavanagh, Sheila 2, 5, 16, 21, 65, 98, 105, 117, 207, 224
  on Ettinger 120–8, 132–6, 140–3, 145–7
  gender embodiment 119–21, 127, 132, 135–6, 139–40, 142, 145
  on the *sinthôme* 125–8, 133–46
  transfeminist theory of embodiment 119–47
  transpsychoanalysis 105, 120
Chiesa, Lorenzo 55, 76–7, 79, 82, 86, 88, 93
  The Not-Two: Logic and God in Lacan 79
  Subjectivity and Otherness: A Philosophical Reading of Lacan 227
Christianity 2, 51, 187, 220

cisgender 10, 134, 140–1
cissexism 93, 124
Cixous, Hélène 68, 86, 89, 120, 124, 142–5, 177
  The Laugh of the Medusa 86, 142–3
class 15, 39, 50, 91, 99, 101, 103, 106, 116, 121, 125–6, 128, 131–2, 136, 141, 144–5, 155, 170, 176–7, 187, 191, 200, 221
colonization 143
conocimiento 173
consciousness 20, 74, 117, 157, 167–72, 177–9, 186, 188, 190, 199, 208, 225
Copjec, Joan 5, 7, 11–12, 26–7, 31, 52, 62, 65–7, 101, 121
  Read My Desire 26
Covid-19 22, 213, 215, 217–18, 221
Crawford, Lucas Cassidy 146
crisis 81, 167, 173, 177
Currah, Paisley 145

Dean, Jodi 39, 45
Dean, Tim 5, 7, 13–14, 20, 30, 32–3, 57–9, 73–5, 131, 139, 204
  Beyond Sexuality 12, 67
Declercq, Frédéric 85, 106
decolonization 143
defenses 3, 12, 44, 108, 132, 219–20
de Lauretis, Teresa 89
  Freud's Drive: Psychoanalysis, Literature and Film 58, 91–2
de Man, Paul 42, 69, 72–3, 87
  "The Rhetoric of Temporality" 61
desire 5–8, 17–18, 20–2, 26, 36, 40, 43–4, 50–2, 56–7, 60–5, 67–9, 77, 83–5, 87–8, 90–1, 99–102, 104, 106, 109, 111–14, 116, 121–4, 126–31, 141, 144, 146
  and gender 151–60, 164, 167, 169–71, 175, 177, 180–1, 183, 185, 191, 193, 195, 197–201, 204, 206, 217, 220
  Lacanian theory 11, 29–32, 36–7, 39–40, 46, 48, 52, 66, 79–80, 84–5, 101, 105, 138, 142
dialectic 6, 42, 61, 63, 65, 72–3, 109, 131, 168–70, 172, 174–5, 178
drive 13, 18, 20, 56, 58, 60–1, 67–8, 70–1, 74, 76, 80–1, 86, 89–92, 123, 132,

143, 189, 201–2, 204–5, 208, 213, 216–19, 222, 224
DSM 215

Edelman, Lee
  analysis of *North by Northwest* 59–62, 68–9, 72
  analysis of *The Birds* 69, 72–3
  anti-social thesis in queer theory 56–7, 74, 82, 114, 190, 204
  futurity 20, 55, 57, 60–2, 66–7, 70–1, 73, 80–2, 93
  negativity 56–8, 60–1, 73–5, 80, 89–93
  nihilism 57, 87
  No Future 2, 13–14, 20, 34–5, 55–95, 169, 214
  queer theory 55–6, 62, 67, 69, 73, 76–8, 82–4, 87–9, 93
  reproductive futurism 2, 13, 20, 34–5, 55–62, 64, 68–75, 81–2, 87, 89, 92
  Sex, or the Unbearable 73, 89–90, 189
  sinthomosexual 55–6, 58–62, 66–74, 80–2, 86–8, 91–3, 144
  view on Real 55–6, 58–60, 62, 65–9, 71, 73, 75, 77–87, 91, 93
ego 27, 74, 78, 85, 133–4, 137, 140, 168, 219
ego psychology 9, 23, 105, 168, 171
embodiment
  Cavanagh's theory 121, 131, 134–5
  Cixous' theory 144–5
  diverse trajectories 146
  Gherovici's theory 121–3, 125, 127–8, 132–3, 136–7, 139–40, 143, 146
  Gozlan's theory 129–30
  Lacan's presentation 119–20, 128–9, 131–3, 142
  Lawlor's *Paul* 178, 185, 192–4, 197, 207
  Millot's pathologization 128–9
  Salamon's theory 119–20, 128, 139–40, 144, 146
  Shepherdson's theory 128, 138
  sinthôme and 126–8, 135–7, 139–41, 178, 224
  Stryker 110–17
Enke, Finn 10
Espinoza, Joshua Jennifer, "Things Haunt" (poem) 147
ethics 14, 110, 120
ethnicity 9–10, 12–13, 17, 22, 26, 34, 39, 52, 55, 59, 77, 91, 101, 106, 121, 125–6, 128, 131–2, 136, 141, 144–5, 167, 169–70, 178–81, 186, 188, 206–8, 210, 221
ethnic studies 221
Ettinger, Bracha 8, 21, 120
  on Lacan's account of the *sinthôme* 125–8, 135–6, 140–1
  matrixial borderspace 121–5, 132–6, 140–2, 147
  matrixial *sinthôme* 126, 133, 135–6, 140–1
  metramorphosis 122–5, 127

fantastic, the 115, 181, 184
fantasy
  beyond 167–71
  Edelman 55–60, 62, 66–70, 72–94
  Freud, Anna 14, 34
  Freud, Sigmund 74, 133–4
  Hart, Lynda 14–16, 20, 34, 86, 112–14, 181
  Lacan 4, 8–9, 11–22, 25–8, 31, 33–5, 46–7, 52, 55, 57, 72, 76–7, 79, 84–6, 88, 169, 176, 178
  Pluth 35, 77, 84–6, 88, 90–1, 143, 145, 175, 208
  Restuccia 14–16, 20, 33
  Ruti 11–12, 16, 27, 35, 74–5, 77, 103, 105–6, 116
  Stavrakakis 18, 50, 77, 80, 82, 86, 112, 223
feminine
  Brown's analysis 220
  Carlson's assessment 101–2, 107, 109, 111
  Gherovici's identification 137
  Lacan's articulation 120–2, 124–7, 129, 132, 140–2, 146, 155
  Žižek's view 33, 38–44, 52, 108
figurative language 69, 89, 100
Fink, Bruce 11, 27
  on "presymbolic real" (R1) and 42
foreclosure 29–30, 48
Foucault, Michel 8, 92, 200
foundlings 182
France, David 14
  How to Survive a Plague 224
Freccero, Carla 6, 18
  After Sex? 4

Freeman, Elizabeth 9, 19, 94, 115, 179-80
  Time Binds 18
Freud, Anna 14, 34, 219
Freud, Sigmund 74, 133-4, 180, 214
fundamental fantasy 3, 11-16, 19-20, 27, 33-4, 47-8, 52, 76-80, 83-4, 88, 90, 92, 98, 100, 103, 105-6, 108, 112, 114-16, 146, 167, 170, 175, 178, 181, 189, 203, 209, 218
future 12, 17-18, 20, 22, 34, 50-1, 73-5, 145-7, 157-8, 173, 192, 208, 210, 224-5
futurity 55, 57, 61-2, 66, 70-1, 73, 80, 82, 93

gaze 112, 134, 153, 156-7, 174-5, 192, 198
gender. *See also* feminine; genderqueer; masculine; non-binary; transgender
  embodiment 9, 21, 32-3, 44, 95, 98, 106, 112, 114-17, 119-21, 127, 132, 135-6, 139-40, 142, 145, 160, 221, 224
  identity 26, 104, 127, 132-5, 139, 159, 161, 207
gender binary 9-10, 16, 21, 100, 105-6, 117, 133, 136, 138, 140, 146
genderqueer 9-10, 16, 21, 121, 133-41, 158-9, 161-2, 210
gender reassignment 127, 135-6, 139, 146, 158, 161
gender studies 17, 32, 221
genre 6, 89, 94-5, 114-15, 139, 147, 167, 178
Gherovici, Patricia 2, 5, 10, 13, 16, 21, 65, 98, 104-5, 114-15, 117, 159, 207
  gender embodiment 119-21, 125, 127-9, 132-3, 136-7, 139-40, 143, 146
  Please Select Your Gender: From the Invention of Hysteria to the Democratizing of Transgenderism 121, 127
  sinthôme 224
  Transgender Psychoanalysis 137
  transpsychoanalysis 105, 120, 132
Gossett, Che 97-8
Gozlan, Oren 2, 5, 13, 16, 21, 98, 105, 117, 119-20, 127, 129-30, 132, 139-40, 146, 207, 224
  transpsychoanalysis 105, 120, 132
  Transsexuality and the Art of

  Transitioning 121
Guattari, Félix 145

Haggerty, George 86
  Queer Gothic 34
Halberstam, Jack 4, 57, 59, 161-2, 169, 186-8, 200, 204
  The Queer Art of Failure 25
  *Trans** 9
Hale, Jacob, "Tracing a Ghostly Memory in My Throat: Reflections on FtM Feminist Voice and Agency" 147
Halley, Janet 9
  After Sex? On Writing Since Queer Theory 4
Halperin, David 14, 33
Harari, Roberto 75-6, 87, 103, 127
Hart, Lynda 15-16, 20, 86, 112-14
  Between the Body and the Flesh 14, 34
  the drive 20, 86, 114
  Fatal Women: Lesbian Sexuality and the Mark of Aggression 34
  the Real (Lacan) 16, 20, 34, 86, 114-15
  sadomasochism 14-15
Hayek, Friedrich 214
Hedwig and the Angry Inch (Mitchell) 20-1, 94, 116, 147, 151, 158, 179, 181
Herring, Scott 164, 167, 179
heteronormativity 2, 11, 64, 71, 73, 109-10, 151-2, 155-6, 180-1, 186, 199, 205-7, 210
heterosexism 31, 37, 43
heterosexuality 12-13, 37, 153-4
heterotopia 92
Hitchcock, Alfred
  The Birds 59-60, 69, 71-3
  North by Northwest 59-62, 68-9, 72
HIV 203-4, 210
Hoens, Dominiek 81, 87, 103
homonormativity 180, 188, 210
homophobia 17, 34, 51, 83, 220
How to Survive a Plague (France) 224

identity
  gender 26, 104, 127, 132-5, 139, 159, 161, 207
  national 155, 159, 184
  sexual 2, 9-10, 13, 16, 31, 98, 157, 180, 183

identity politics 177
imaginary 7, 11, 16–17, 25, 27–8, 30, 32, 35, 48, 55–6, 58, 60, 67, 69, 72, 74–5, 77–82, 84–5, 91–3, 102–6, 111–13, 119, 122, 125, 127–8, 131, 133–8, 140, 142, 144, 168, 170, 173, 175, 178, 189, 204, 207, 217, 219, 222–3
In & Out (Oz) 19–20, 50–2
inversion 30, 181, 207
Irigaray, Luce 122, 170, 177, 191
  An Ethics of Sexual Difference 120, 139

Johnston, Adrian 26
jouissance 7, 20, 34, 55–6, 58, 60–2, 67–9, 71, 73, 75, 82, 85, 87, 89, 101, 103, 121–4, 126, 129, 131, 139, 200
Joyce, James 76, 78–9, 83, 85–8, 103, 105, 147
  Portrait of the Artist as a Young Man 188
  Ulysses 143

King, Latisha 146
Krieger, Nick 140
  Nina Here Nor There 139
Kristeva, Julia 69, 86, 219
  pre-Oedipal 122
  Revolution in Poetic Language 68
Künstlerroman 104, 188

Lacan, Jacques
  anti-essentialism 7
  dialectics 174–6
  drive 58, 67–8, 76, 86–7, 91, 114, 124, 131, 145, 175
  Edelman on 55–95
  on embodiment 119–20, 128–9, 131–3, 142
  fantasy 4, 8, 11–22, 25–8, 31, 34, 46–7, 52, 55, 57, 72, 76–7, 79
  feminine position 120–2, 124–7, 129, 132, 140–2, 146, 155
  "The Freudian Thing, or the Meaning of the Return to Freud in Psychoanalysis" 111, 119
  fundamental fantasy 11
  id-ego relation 219
  imaginary 55–6, 58, 60, 67, 69, 72, 74–5, 77–82, 84–5, 91–3

"The Instance of the Letter in the Unconscious, or Reason Since Freud" 93, 107, 120
jouissance 55–6, 58, 60–2, 67–9, 71, 73, 75, 82, 85, 87, 89
masculine position 64–5, 84
"The Mirror Stage as Formative of the I Function as Revealed in Psychoanalytic Experience" 216, 219
Name of the Father 11, 29–32, 36–7, 39–40, 46, 48, 52, 66, 79–80, 84–5, 101, 104, 138, 142
objet a 32–3, 68, 91, 100, 129, 131, 174
other 120, 122
Other 62–5, 68, 77, 79–80, 83–6, 88, 92–4
psyche 11, 27–8, 64–5, 91, 131, 133, 168, 171, 194, 197, 222
psychical positioning 7
psychoanalytic theory 3–5, 16, 168–9
psychosis 29, 48, 78–9, 104–5, 119, 125, 133, 135, 138, 142
and queer theory 2–3, 14, 17, 169–71
Real 101–2, 105–8, 112–15, 123, 125, 131, 137, 142
rereading of Freud 8
Seminar III 11, 29–30, 32, 35, 48, 79, 84, 88, 104, 138, 145, 147
Seminar XI 11, 33, 35–6, 63, 76–7, 83, 85–6
Seminar XX 2, 6–7, 40, 64, 77, 83–4, 97, 107, 113–14, 116, 119–21, 125, 129, 131
Seminar XXIII 68, 76, 78, 83, 85–6, 103–4
sexual difference, presentation of 2, 9, 13, 15, 119–47, 158–9, 178
sexuation 3, 6–8, 12–13, 26, 38, 97, 101, 107, 111, 113, 115–16, 119–20, 122–3, 127, 129, 131–4, 141, 155
"The Signification of the Phallus" 41, 84, 169
sinthôme 125–8, 159
subjectivity 52, 64, 66, 75–9, 82, 84–5
symbolic 55–60, 62, 64–75, 77–93
theory of aggressivity 216
use of terms 6
Žižek on 25–52
lack 32–3, 36, 52, 63–7, 83, 85, 88, 91,

100–1, 105–6, 131–3, 140, 143, 168–70, 180, 209
Laclau, Ernesto 28, 31–2, 42–3, 80
Laplanche, Jean 91
Lavery, Grace 16, 79, 112, 115, 119, 143
Lawlor, Andrea 179–210
  on embodiment 178, 185, 192–4, 197, 207
  Paul Takes the Form of a Mortal Girl: A Novel 20–2, 94, 117, 147, 167, 179–210, 213
Light in the Dark/Luz en lo Oscuro (Anzaldúa) 20–1, 116, 147, 167–9, 172–3, 178
look 97, 156, 161–3, 175, 192, 197. *See also* gaze

MacCannell, Juliet Flower 85–6
MAGA 215, 223
masculine 3, 6–8, 10, 13, 31–3, 38–44, 52, 64–5, 84, 101–2, 107–8, 111, 119–24, 129–30, 132, 137, 139, 142, 146, 155, 158, 161, 197, 220
master signifier 31–2, 36, 40, 48, 52, 77, 79–80, 84–5, 104, 138, 144–5
matrix 27, 31, 121–2, 124, 127, 133, 136, 140–1, 147
matrixial 120–7, 133–6, 140–2, 145
memoir 105, 114–15, 139–40
mestiza 20, 117, 167–8, 171–2, 177, 179
mestizo 176
metramorphosis 122–5, 127
metronormativity 164–5, 167, 179–80, 190, 207
Millot, Catherine 3, 16, 103–5, 138, 140
  Horsexe 2, 13, 119, 127–8, 135
Mitchell, John Cameron 151, 158–60, 164, 185
  Hedwig and the Angry Inch 20–1, 94, 116, 147, 151, 158, 179, 181
mixing 162, 168, 171, 181, 183, 186
Möbius strip 59
Moncayo, Paul 80, 128, 137–9
Moore, Lisa Jean 145
Muñoz, José Esteban 4, 57, 59, 146
myth 27, 66, 159, 167, 172–5, 181, 184–5, 209, 214, 220

Name of the Father (Lacan) 11, 29–32, 36–7, 39–40, 46, 48, 52, 66, 79–80, 84–5, 101, 104, 138, 142
narcissism 105, 144
narcissistic 105, 144, 219, 219
nationality 9–10, 12, 17, 21, 26, 34, 39, 52, 55, 59, 77, 91, 101, 106, 121, 125–6, 128, 131–2, 136, 141, 144–5, 155, 157, 178
Nealon, Christopher 179, 181–2, 187, 207
neoliberalism 214–15, 223
nepantla 172–8
nepantlera 173–4, 176–8
Nichols, Ben, *Same Old: Queer Theory, Literature and the Politics of Sameness* 4, 37, 57–8
Nietzsche, Friedrich 32, 214
Nina Here Nor There (Krieger) 139
non-binary 9–10, 16, 21, 106–7, 117, 120–1, 124, 133–41, 164, 185
North by Northwest (Hitchcock) 59–62, 68–9, 72

objet a 32–3, 68, 91, 100, 129, 131, 174
Oedipality 6, 68–9, 100–1, 122–3, 134, 152–3
Oedipus 85, 132
Oedipus complex 46, 83, 104, 132
Orlando (Woolf) 115–16, 185–6
other 99–100, 102, 105–6, 113, 117, 120, 122, 133, 136, 138, 140, 144
Other 7, 12, 15, 18–19, 27, 30, 46, 50, 62–5, 68, 77, 79–80, 83–6, 88, 92–4, 106–7, 113–14, 126–9, 131–2, 134, 137, 142, 144, 170–1, 209, 223
Oz, Frank 20, 50
  In & Out (film) 19–20, 50–2

pandemic 22, 213, 215–18, 221, 224
paranoia 219
Parker, Andrew, *After Sex? On Writing Since Queer Theory* 4
paternal law 30–1, 36, 39, 46, 51–2, 85
patriarchal 11, 14, 32, 34, 51, 60, 79, 138, 143, 152, 177, 187, 214, 216, 220
patriarchy 22, 50–1, 59, 124, 138, 142, 213–25
Paul Takes the Form of a Mortal Girl: A Novel (Lawlor) 20–2, 94, 117, 147, 167, 179–210, 213
Peirce, Kimberly, *Boys Don't Cry* 113

Pellegrini, Ann 3, 135–6
Penney, James 5–6, 16, 26, 28, 30–1, 170, 221–2
  After Queer Theory 3, 12, 15, 57, 220
phallic signifier 12, 32, 37, 65, 127, 140
phallogocentric 28, 36–7, 52, 120, 123, 142, 145, 190
phallogocentrism 33, 122, 141–4
phallus 8, 12–13, 21, 32, 36–7, 40–1, 63, 65–6, 84, 101, 104, 120–1, 123–7, 132, 136, 138, 141–5, 169
phenomenology 113
Pluth, Ed 35, 49, 77, 81, 84–8, 90–1, 93, 106, 143, 145–6, 175, 208
  Signifiers and acts 84, 86
point de capiton 11, 27–8, 35–7, 40, 45–6, 48–9, 52, 80–2
Pope, The 1
Portrait of the Artist as a Young Man (Joyce) 188
Prosser, Jay 106, 113–14, 140, 144
  Second Skins 16, 102, 139
psychosis 8, 29–30, 48, 78–9, 104–5, 119, 125, 133, 135–6, 138, 140, 142

queer
  genderqueer 9–10, 16, 21, 121, 133–41, 158–9, 161–2, 210
  genders 9, 16, 26, 39, 55, 65, 94, 100–1, 121, 124, 130–1, 133, 138, 141, 144, 146, 158–9, 161, 178–81, 186, 192, 194–5, 197–9, 222
  people 25, 99, 135–8, 140–1, 182, 208
  sexualities 3, 9, 16, 32, 117
  subjects 15, 22, 121, 133, 135–6, 140, 167
  temporalities 18–19
  and trans theory 5, 7–8, 13, 15, 17, 19, 51, 79, 94, 99, 104, 124
queer theory. *See also specific theorists*
  in *After Queer Theory* 3, 12, 15, 220
  in *After Sex?* 4
  anti-social thesis 56–7, 74, 82, 114, 190, 204
  in *Gender Trouble* 9
  in *No Future* 55–95
  in *Paul Takes the Form of a Mortal Girl: A Novel* 20–2, 94, 117, 147, 167, 179–210, 213
  in *Queer Optimism* 17
  in *Same Old: Queer Theory, Literature and the Politics of Sameness* 4
quilting point 27

race 9–10, 12–13, 22, 26, 34, 39, 52, 55, 59, 77, 91, 94, 101, 106, 117, 121, 125–6, 128, 131–2, 136, 141, 144–5, 147, 155, 170–1, 176–7, 188, 207, 221, 225
racial difference 170
Ragland, Ellie 6–8, 102–4, 113–14, 116, 131, 170
Real 2, 5–6, 11–14, 16, 20
  Anzaldúa on 173
  Carlson on 6, 101–2, 109, 133
  Cavanagh on 128, 133–5, 141
  Dean on 30, 32–3, 45
  Edelman's view 55–6, 58–60, 62, 65–9, 71, 73, 75, 77–87, 91, 93
  Gherovici on 16, 105, 115
  Gozlan on 16, 130
  Haggerty on 34, 86
  Hart on 86, 112–14
  jouissance of 200
  in Lacanian psychoanalysis 101–2, 105–8, 112–15, 123, 125, 131, 137, 142
  Lawlor on 201–2, 205, 207
  Millot on 2, 16, 105, 127
  Pluth on 86, 175
  Restuccia on 14, 16, 33
  Rohy on 34, 86
  Ruti 106
  Salamon on 102, 106, 108, 113, 140
  Shepherdson on 27, 65–6, 138
  Žižek on 25–52
relationality 12, 91, 123, 126, 133, 139–41, 147, 205
reproduction 14–15, 58, 62–7, 70, 151–2, 154, 187
reproductive futurism 2, 13–14, 20, 34–5, 55–62, 64, 68–71, 73–5, 81–2, 87, 89, 92, 209
  Edelman on 55–6, 62, 69, 73, 82, 87, 89
  The Virgin Machine 151–8, 179
Restuccia, Frances 15–16, 20, 33
  Amorous Acts 14
Rohy, Valerie 86

Impossible Women 34
Roof, Judith 7–8, 99–100, 107–9, 132, 192
   What Gender Is, What Gender Does 3, 42
Rose, Jacqueline 213–14, 216, 218–19, 223
Ruti, Mari 5, 11–12, 17–18, 27, 32, 35, 58–9, 68, 73–5, 77, 86–7, 100–1, 103, 105–6, 116, 142–3, 168–9

sadomasochism 15
Saketopoulou, Avgi 3, 135–6
Salamon, Gayle 2, 5, 12, 16, 21, 51, 65, 93, 98, 102, 105–6, 113–14, 119–20, 128, 139–40, 144, 146, 178, 194
   transpsychoanalysis 105–6, 120
Şalcı Bacı 108
Samuels, Robert 214–15, 217–19, 222–3
scarring 139, 160
scar tissue 127
scene 50–1, 60–2, 69–71, 73, 88–92, 94, 132, 139, 151–64, 181, 185, 189–93, 197, 199–203, 207–8, 210, 224
Sedgwick, Eve Kosofsky 8, 17–18, 27, 91, 124–6, 133, 136, 141
Seshadri-Crooks, Kalpana 170
sex-biological 1, 3, 8, 41, 91. *See also* sexuality
sex-cultural 4, 6, 14, 18–20, 25, 41–2, 59, 81, 137, 168, 171–2, 184, 194, 205, 216, 221
sexual difference
   Cavanagh on 65, 119–21, 127–8, 131, 134, 140–1
   Ettinger on 121–6
   hetero 1–20, 55–93, 151–65, 167–210
   Lacanian 2–22, 55–93
sexuality 2, 6–7, 9, 12–13, 16–17, 21, 26, 34, 36–7, 40–3, 51–2, 55, 57, 60, 63–4, 66–7, 77, 91, 110, 125, 130–1, 141, 143, 147, 152, 154–5, 158, 161, 163, 167–9, 176–81, 184, 186, 188, 206–8, 210, 221. *See also* heteronormativity
sexuation 3, 6–8, 12–13, 26, 38, 97, 101, 107, 111, 113, 115–16, 119–20, 122–3, 127, 129, 131–4, 141, 155
Shepherdson, Charles 27, 65–6, 128, 138
shock 173, 177, 193
Silverman, Kaja 36, 40, 100–1

sinthôme 17, 20–1, 56, 58, 68, 75–82, 84–7, 93–4, 103–6, 108, 111–12, 114, 125–8, 133–46, 162–3, 176, 178–9, 205–8, 213, 224
*sintho*mestiza 176
*sintho*mestizx 117, 179, 182, 202, 206, 225
*sintho*mosexual 20, 34, 55–6, 58–61, 66–74, 80–2, 86–8, 91–3, 124, 144, 202, 217–18, 224–5
Snediker, Michael, *Queer Optimism* 17, 35
Snorton, Riley 146
social 3–4, 6–8, 14, 16–19, 25–6, 28, 30–1, 34–5, 39–41, 48, 56–9, 73–5, 80–2, 101, 106, 109, 111, 114, 116, 124, 128, 132, 168–9, 190, 204, 206, 214–19, 221–4
sociality 29, 74, 80, 82, 86, 223
Solanas, Valerie, *SCUM Manifesto* 92
Stavrakakis, Yannis 18–19, 50, 77, 80, 82, 86, 112, 223
Stryker, Susan 110–17, 119, 145
   "The Transgender Issue, An Introduction" 111, 119
subjective position 3, 205
subjectivity 10–12, 20–1, 25–6, 29–30, 47, 52, 64, 66, 75–9, 82, 84–5, 98, 101, 105–12, 114–16, 122–3, 125–7, 129–30, 132–3, 135, 137, 139–42, 145–7, 168–70, 181, 188, 205–6, 222
surrealism 159
symbolic 6–8, 11, 14–17, 20, 25–38, 40–50, 55–60, 62, 64–75, 77–93, 102–8, 111–14, 119, 123–5, 127, 130–1, 133–40, 142–5, 170, 173, 175, 178, 202, 207, 213, 219, 222–4

temporality 18, 61–2, 73, 115, 152, 157, 187
Thatcher, Margaret 213–14, 216
"Things Haunt" (Espinoza) 147
trans
   asterisk use 9
   Carlson on 2, 5, 21, 98, 101–2, 109, 117, 119, 133
   Caughie on 115
   Cavanagh on 119–21, 124, 127–9, 133–6, 138–47
   Currah on 145

Dean, Tim on 5, 7, 13, 30, 33, 139, 204
embodiment theory 119–21, 124, 126–9, 133–4, 136, 138–47
Enke on 10
Ettingerian *sinthôme* 125–8, 135–6, 140–1
fictional narratives 151, 161, 172, 198
genre 6, 89, 94–5, 114–15, 139, 147, 167, 178
Gherovici on 2, 5, 10, 13, 16, 21, 65, 98, 104–5, 114–15, 117, 159, 207
Gozlan on 2, 5, 13, 16, 21, 98, 105, 117, 119–20, 127, 129–30, 132, 139–40, 146
Lacanian *sinthôme* 94
literature 10, 14–15, 19, 73, 94, 119, 181, 186
memoir 114–15, 139–40
Millot on 3, 16, 103–5, 138, 140
Moore on 145
politics 15, 18–22, 27, 31, 34–5, 50–2, 56–8, 72, 74–5, 77, 80–1, 83, 86–94, 154, 170, 177, 187, 197, 214, 216, 220, 222–3
Salamon on 2, 5, 12, 16, 21, 51, 65, 93, 98, 102, 105–6, 113–14, 119–20, 128, 139–40, 144, 146, 178, 194
Shepherdson on 27, 65–6, 128, 138
Stone on 115
Stryker on 110–17, 119, 145
theorists 2
transgender 1–3, 9–10, 13, 15, 17, 21, 31–3, 44, 79, 94, 97–100, 102, 104–12, 114–17, 119–21, 127, 130, 132–3, 135, 137, 139–43, 146, 158, 161–2, 177, 185, 207
transnational 154–5, 157
Žižek on 97–9, 101–5, 108–9, 111–15, 117
trans-affirmative psychoanalysis 4–5, 10, 12–13, 16–17, 21, 25, 94
Carlson on 101–2, 109, 117, 119, 133
Cavanagh on 105, 117, 119–20
Gherovici on 13, 117, 119–21
Gozlan on 105, 117, 119–20
Lacan's theory of embodiment 128
reworkings of Lacan 119–21, 142–3
Salamon on 102, 119–20, 139–40, 144
sinthôme's creativity 133, 135, 139, 144
transgender

Anzaldúa on 177
Carlson on 102, 107, 109, 116
Cavanagh's theory of 121, 135, 140–2
"cisgender" distinction 10
Cixous on 142–3
Crawford on 146
economic hardships 15
embodiment theory 132, 135
genre 6, 89, 94–5, 114–15, 139, 147, 167, 178
Gherovici's theory of 137
Gozlan's theory of 130
Hale on 147
Lacanian transgender theory 17, 32, 79, 94, 106, 114–15, 120
literature 10, 14–15, 19, 73, 94, 119, 181, 186
memoir 114–15, 139–40
Millot's view on 3, 16, 103–5, 138, 140
novel modes 127, 185, 207
pathologization of 3, 10, 13, 33, 79, 103, 105, 119, 121, 128
politics 15, 18–22, 27, 31, 34–5, 50–2, 56–8, 72, 74–5, 77, 80–1, 83, 86–94, 154, 170, 177, 187, 197, 214, 216, 220, 222–3
psychoanalysis 133
Salamon's theory of 51, 93, 102, 105–6, 113–14, 119–20, 128, 139–40, 144, 146
sinthôme and 139
Stryker 112, 119
umbrella term 9–10
Žižek's view 31, 44, 97–100, 104–5, 108–11, 117
transitive 136, 140–1, 145
transitivity 126
Cavanagh on 139–41
concept 145
Ettinger's matrix 147
and relationality 139–41
transpsychoanalysis 105–6, 115–16, 120, 132, 142, 145
Carlson on 116
Cavanagh on 120
Gherovici on 105, 120, 132
Gozlan on 105, 120, 132
Lacan's theory of embodiment 128
reworkings of Lacan 119–21, 142–3
Salamon on 105–6, 120

sinthôme's creativity 133, 135, 139, 144
transsubjectivity
   Carlson on 119, 133
   Cavanagh on 126, 130, 133, 146–7
   Enke on 10
   Espinoza's view 147
   Gherovici on 105
   Gozlan's on 130
   Hale on 147
   Lacan's account 102, 111, 115, 133, 146
   Salamon on 102
   and the *sinthôme* 126–8
   Stone on 115
   Stryker on 111–12
trauma 7, 37–8, 43, 48, 126, 130, 158, 161, 173, 213
traumatic 14, 38, 49, 123–5, 130, 159, 175
traversal
   of authoritarian patriarchy 213–25
   Berlant on 12, 73–4, 90, 189, 213
   in *Borderlands/La Frontera* 20–1, 94, 116, 147, 167–9, 171
   of borders 20, 29, 159, 167, 219
   Edelman on 55–6, 62, 67, 69, 73, 76–8, 82–4, 87–9, 93
   of fantasy 8–9, 11–15, 17, 20–1, 55–95, 213–25
   of the fantasy of (hetero)sexual difference 55–95, 167–210
   of the fundamental fantasy 76–80, 83–4, 88, 90, 92
   Hart on 15–16, 20, 86, 112–14
   In *Hedwig and the Angry Inch* 20–1, 94, 116, 147, 151, 158, 179, 181
   Lacanian psychoanalysis 3–5, 16, 168–9
   in *Paul Takes the Form of a Mortal Girl: A Novel* 20–2, 94, 117, 147, 167, 179–210, 213
   Restuccia on 14–16, 20, 33
   Ruti on 58–9, 68, 73–5, 77, 86–7
   in *The Virgin Machine* 20–1, 94, 116, 147, 151, 179
traversing
   of authoritarian patriarchy 213–25
   Berlant on 12, 73–4, 90, 189, 213
   in *Borderlands/La Frontera* 20–1, 94, 116, 147, 167–9, 171
   of borders 20, 29, 159, 167, 219

   Edelman on 55–6, 58–60, 62, 65–9, 71, 73, 75, 77–87, 91, 93
   of fantasy 8–9, 11–15, 17, 20–1, 55–95, 213–25
   of the fantasy of (hetero)sexual difference 55–95, 167–210
   of the fundamental fantasy 76–80, 83–4, 88, 90, 92
   Hart on 15–16, 20, 86, 112–14
   In *Hedwig and the Angry Inch* 20–1, 94, 116, 147, 151, 158, 179, 181
   Lacanian psychoanalysis 3–5, 16, 168–9
   in *Paul Takes the Form of a Mortal Girl: A Novel* 20–2, 94, 117, 147, 167, 179–210, 213
   Restuccia on 14–16, 20, 33
   Ruti on 58–9, 68, 73–5, 77, 86–7
   in *The Virgin Machine* 20–1, 94, 116, 147, 151, 153–7, 179
Treut, Monika 152, 154–7
   The Virgin Machine 20–1, 94, 116, 147, 151, 179
Trump, Donald 214–20, 222–3
   Covid-19 pandemic 22, 213

Ulysses (Joyce) 143–4
unconscious 7, 11, 13, 27, 78, 85, 93–4, 98, 104–5, 107, 113, 120, 122–4, 129–30, 143, 157, 175, 218

Vaccaro, Jeanne 127, 146
Vatican, The 1–3, 9, 12
Verhaeghe, Paul 85, 106, 131–3
Viego, Antonio 168–9, 171, 176
The Virgin Machine (Treut) 20–1, 94, 116, 147, 151, 153–7, 179

Weil, Abraham L. 145
Weissmann, David 224
We Were Here (Weissmann) 224
Whittle, Stephen 102–3
wholeness 163, 167–70, 175
womb 120–2, 124, 127, 152
Woolf, Virginia 14, 186
   Orlando 115–16, 185–6

xenophobia 17, 218, 221–2

Žižek, Slavoj

antagonism 97–117
on the beyond 25–7, 32, 34, 43
on Butler, Judith 99–101, 108, 116
on class struggle 39, 99, 103
Contingency, Hegemony, Universality Contemporary Dialogues on the Left 28–9, 37, 39, 46, 100
on fantasy 97–8, 100–1, 103, 105–6, 108–17
on fantasy's traversal 105–6, 108, 112–13, 115, 117
on gender 97, 99–103, 105–12
Indivisible Remainder, The 38–9, 108
"Is There a Cause of the Subject?" 80
Metastases of Enjoyment, The 40
on multiculturalism 97
queer theory 25–52, 56–7, 62, 65–6, 80
the Real 80–1

"A Reply to My Critics" 98, 108–10
Sex and the Failed Absolute 26, 41, 109
on sexual difference 92–111
"The Sexual Is Political" 97–9, 108–10
on sexuation 26, 38, 97, 101, 107, 111
the *sinthôme* 93–4, 103–6, 108, 111–12, 114
Sublime Object of Ideology, The 30, 35–6, 40, 45, 49, 80, 82
symbolic 102–8, 111–14
Tarrying with the Negative 38
Ticklish Subject: The Absent Center of Political Ontology 35–7, 40
transgender 31, 44, 97–100, 104–5, 108–11, 117
"Transgender Dogma Is Naïve and Incompatible with Freud" 2, 98
Violence: Six Sideways Reflections 32

Printed in the USA
CPSIA information can be obtained
at www.ICGtesting.com
LVHW050411300723
753749LV00005B/153